INDIAN VOICES OF THE GREAT WAR

Leisure & Community Services

Please return this item by the last date stamped below, to the library from which it was borrowed.

Renewals
Any item may be renewed twice by telephone or post, provided it is not required by another customer. Please quote the barcode number.

Overdue Charges
Please see library notices for the current rate of charges levied on overdue items. Please note that the overdue charges are made on junior books borrowed on adult tickets.

Postage
Postage on overdue notices is payable.

Renewals
01159 293388

www.bromley.gov.uk/libraries

Also by David Omissi

THE SEPOY AND THE RAJ: The Indian Army, 1860–1940

Indian Voices of the Great War

Soldiers' Letters, 1914–18

Selected and Introduced by

David Omissi
Department of History and Centre for Indian Studies
University of Hull

First published in Great Britain 1999 by
MACMILLAN PRESS LTD
Houndmills, Basingstoke, Hampshire RG21 6XS and London
Companies and representatives throughout the world

A catalogue record for this book is available from the British Library.

ISBN 0–333–75144–2 hardcover
ISBN 0–333–75145–0 paperback

First published in the United States of America 1999 by
ST. MARTIN'S PRESS, INC.,
Scholarly and Reference Division,
175 Fifth Avenue, New York, N.Y. 10010

ISBN 0–312–22061–8

Library of Congress Cataloging-in-Publication Data
Indian voices of the Great War : soldiers' letters, 1914–18 / selected
and introduced by David Omissi.
p.   cm.
Includes bibliographical references and index.
ISBN 0–312–22061–8 (cloth)
1. World War, 1914–1918—Campaigns—France.   2. Soldiers—India–
–Correspondence.   3. World War, 1914–1918—Personal narratives,
Indian.   4. India. Army—Biography.   5. India. Army—History–
–World War, 1914–1918.   I. Omissi, David E., 1960–   .
D549.I53I53   1999
940.4'8154—dc21   98–42208
                                                                CIP

This book is printed on paper suitable for recycling and made from fully managed and
sustained forest sources.

10   9   8   7   6   5   4   3   2   1
08   07   06   05   04   03   02   01   00   99

Printed and bound in Great Britain by
Antony Rowe Ltd, Chippenham, Wiltshire

For
the Indian dead
1914–1918

Toute rien se tourne en declin,
tout chiet, tout meurt, tout vet a fin ...
se par clerc nen est mis en livre;
ne peut par el durer ne vivre ...

(Maistre Wace, b. Jersey, c. 1110)

Contents

List of Maps and Plates

Glossary of Indian and Military Terms

Afridi	A Pathan people inhabiting the NWFP; a member of that people
anna	One sixteenth of a rupee
atta	Wheaten flour or meal
babu	A high-caste Hindu, especially of Bengal, with a superficial education in English
badmash	A 'bad character' or rascal. From Persian *bad*, 'evil' and Arabic *ma'ash*, 'means of livelihood'
Bahadur	A great or distinguished person; the official title of a member of the Order of British India. From Hindi 'hero' or 'champion'
bazar	An Eastern market-place or permanent market, consisting of rows of shops or stalls, where all kinds of merchandise are offered for sale
bhalwa	A substance used by *dhobis* to mark and identify washing; employed by malingerers to produce swellings and inflammation
Brahmin	A Hindu of the first, or priestly, *varna*, noted for their aloof manner and fastidious preparation of food
brigade	A body of soldiers, composed of regiments, and forming part of a division
chapatti	A small cake of unleavened bread, flattened with the hand, and baked on a griddle
charas	Cannabis resin; hashish
charpoy	The common light Indian bedstead
chenna	A type of cottage cheese
company	A unit of infantry, composed of platoons, and forming one eighth of a battalion or regiment
crore	A hundred *lakhs*, or ten million (normally written 100,00,000 in figures)
dacoit	A robber, working as part of an armed band, whence dacoity
dafadar	An Indian cavalry NCO, corresponding to a sergeant
dal	Split pulses
Deccan	Southern, or peninsular, India
dhobi	An Indian washerman
dhoti	A loin-cloth
division	A body of soldiers, composed of brigades, and forming part of a corps
Diwali	The Hindu festival of light

Dogra	A high-caste soldier from Kangra, a Himalayan province
durbar	The court or public audience of an Indian ruler. From Persian and Urdu *darbar*, 'court'
Fauji Akhbar	The official newspaper of the Indian Army
ghadr	Revolt or revolution, whence *Ghadrite*
Ghazi	A warrior champion of Islam, especially against infidels; a title of honour. From Arabic past participle of *ghaza*, 'to fight'
ghi	Clarified butter
Granth	The Sikh scriptures
Gurmukhi	The alphabet used to write the Sikh scriptures; the Punjabi language, written in this script. From Sanskrit *guru*, 'teacher' and *mukha*, 'mouth'
Guru	A spiritual leader or head of a religious sect
Haji	A Muslim who has undertaken a pilgrimage to Mecca
halal	To slaughter according to Muslim law, by cutting the throat of the still-conscious animal; lawful food. From Arabic *halal*, 'lawful'
havildar	An Indian infantry NCO, corresponding to a sergeant
Hindustan	The plain of the Ganges, excluding Bengal and Bihar; sometimes all of India
Holi	An important Hindu festival, held at the approach of the spring equinox, in honour of Krishna and the milkmaids, and observed by sprinkling coloured powder or water on one another
hookah	A pipe with a mouthpiece attached to a long, flexible tube, and in which the smoke is drawn through water contained in a vessel
Id	The Muslim festival marking the end of Ramazan
ilakadar	A minor Indian official
izzat	Honour, standing, reputation or prestige
Jat	A member of a major North Indian cultivating caste-cluster, of proverbial stupidity
jemadar	An Indian junior officer, of infantry or cavalry
Ka'aba	The sacred edifice at Mecca, which contains the 'black stone' venerated by Muslims
kafir	An unbeliever in Islam. From Arabic *kafir*, 'infidel'
kankar	A coarse limestone, burned to lime or used for constructing roads
Karbala	The site of a battle in Iraq in October 680 in which Husayn ibn Ali, the grandson of the Prophet, was killed. The anniversary of the battle is commemorated by followers of Shi'ia Islam
Khalsa	The community of baptized Sikhs
kirpan	The ceremonial dagger, worn by Sikhs as a mark of their religion
Kshatriya	A member of the second, or warrior, *varna*
kukri	The war knife of Gurkhas and Garhwalis
lakh	One hundred thousand (normally written 1,00,000 in figures)

lumberdar	The registered head man of an Indian village, responsible for collecting community revenues. From English 'number' and Urdu *dar*, 'head'
Mahabharata	An ancient Hindu epic. In Sanskrit 'the great history of the Bharata dynasty'
mahant	A religious superior; the guardian of a Sikh shrine or temple
Mahsuds	A Pathan people of the NWFP
maidan	An open space in or near a town; a parade ground
malik	A tribal chief or village headman. From Arabic past participle of *malaka*, 'to possess' or 'to rule'
maund	A denomination of weight, varying greatly according to locality
Memsahib	A term of respect, used of a European woman in, or connected with, India; the wife of a Sahib
moulvi	A Muslim learned man, or teacher of Arabic
naik	An Indian infantry NCO, corresponding to a corporal
pagri	A turban
Pathan	A member of a mainly Pashtu-speaking people of the North-West Frontier and Afghanistan
pice	The plural of pie
pie	The smallest Anglo-Indian coin, worth one twelfth of an anna
Pir	A Muslim holy man, with inherited religious charisma
purdah	Seclusion, especially of Muslim women. From Persian *pardah*, 'veil' or 'curtain'
Rajput	A Kshatriya of the major North Indian warrior caste-cluster, noted for their bellicosity and aversion to handling the plough
Ramazan	The ninth (lunar) month of the Muslim year, rigorously observed as a fast from sunrise to sunset
Ram Ram	A popular Hindu greeting, invoking Rama, the seventh incarnation of Vishnu, and one of the most worshipped Hindu deities
regiment	The basic unit of the Indian Army, normally composed of four squadrons of cavalry or eight companies (one battalion) of infantry. On arrival in France, Indian Army regiments had an average strength of some 12 British officers and 750 Indian officers and men
ressaidar	An Indian cavalry officer, under the Risaldar
risala	A troop or regiment of Indian horse
risaldar	The senior Indian officer of a cavalry squadron; the head of a *risala*
risaldar-major	The senior Indian officer of a cavalry regiment
Sahib	A respectful title used by Indians in addressing Europeans; a gentleman; used especially in the Indian Army to denote a British officer
salaam	A Muslim greeting. From Arabic 'peace'

salt	Pay or duty. In Indian Army parlance, to 'eat salt' was to receive pay from the Government, and to remain 'true to one's salt' was to do one's duty
seer	A denomination of weight or capacity, equal in British India to a kilogram or litre
sepoy	An Indian infantryman, drilled under European (especially British) discipline. From Persian *sipahi*, 'soldier' or 'horseman'
silladar	Originally, a cavalry trooper who enlisted bringing his own horse, equipment and weapons; later, one who paid a deposit on enlistment to cover part or all of their cost, or whose pay was docked for that reason. From Urdu *silahdar*, 'armour-bearer' or 'squire'
sirdar	A military chief; an Indian officer
Sirkar	The state or government. From Persian *sar*, 'head' and *kar*, 'agent'
sowar	An Indian cavalry trooper or private. From Urdu *sawar*, 'horseman'
squadron	A unit of cavalry, composed of troops, and forming one quarter of a regiment
subedar	The chief Indian officer of an infantry company, ranking immediately superior to a jemadar
subedar-major	The senior Indian officer of an infantry regiment
sweeper	An Indian of the lowest caste, especially a Hindu who cleans away defiling matter
syce	A groom or horsekeeper
talwar	An Indian cavalry sabre
tehsildar	The chief official of a *tehsil*, a minor administrative district. From Persian *tahsil*, 'collection' and *dar*, 'head'
timuru	A kind of fruit used to produce boils and swellings
tola	The weight of a rupee, fixed in British India as 180 grains; a coin of this weight
Untouchable	An Indian, especially a Hindu, without caste, contact with whom is regarded by caste Hindus as defiling
Urdu	The language of the Muslim conquerors of Hindustan, derived from Hindi, but written in the Arabic script, and with a large number of Persian and Arabic loanwords. The nearest to a lingua franca for the army of British India. From *zaban-i-urdu*, 'the language of the (royal) camp'
varna	One of the four great castes (Brahmins, Kshatriyas, Vaishas and Shudras) into which all Indian society, except Untouchables, is ideally divided. From Sanskrit 'colour' or 'class'
Vishnu	One of the principal Hindu deities, holding the second place in the great triad. From Sanskrit 'all-pervader' or 'worker'
Wazir	A Pathan people of the NWFP; a member of this people
woordi-major	The Indian adjutant of a cavalry regiment
zaildar	A minor Indian official
zamindar	An Indian landlord

Chronology

1914

4 August
Germans invade Belgium. Britain declares war on Germany.

End August
Indian Corps of two infantry and two cavalry divisions sets sail for France.

26 September
Two brigades of Lahore Division arrive Marseilles.

1 October
Indian Soldiers' Fund formally inaugurated to assist Indian troops in France.

21 October
Lahore Division arrives Flanders. Fed piecemeal into defence of Ypres (Belgium).

29 October
Meerut Division reaches St Omer.

October–November
Most of Indian Corps assembled in Givenchy-Neuve Chapelle sector (France) where they remain for nearly fourteen months.

2 November
Russia declares war on Turkey. British and French soon follow suit.

3 November
Censorship of Indian soldiers' mail established at Rouen (later moved to Boulogne)

12 November
Lord Roberts visits Indian Corps in France, dying three days later.

22 November
Poona Brigade captures Basra (Mesopotamia).

November
Sirhind Brigade arrives in France from Egypt.

November–December
Indian Corps involved in heavy fighting near Givenchy and Festubert (France).

1915

January
Mutiny of 130th Baluchis at Rangoon (Burma). Three Pathan companies refuse to embark, fearing they are being sent to fight the Turks.

20 January
Lady Hardinge Hospital for Indian troops opened at Brockenhurst Park, near Southampton.

15 February
Mutiny of 5th Light Infantry at Singapore. Half the battalion run amok, shooting their officers, fearing (wrongly) that they were to be sent against the Turks.

March–August
Scarcity, high prices and plague in Punjab.

10–12 March
Battle of Neuve Chapelle. Indian Corps and British IV Corps attack, suffering nearly 13,000 losses, but capturing the village and gaining some ground.

18 March
Failure of Allied naval assault on Dardanelles (Turkey).

22 April
Germans attack at Ypres using chlorine gas on a large scale for the first time.

25 April
Lahore Division arrives Ouderdom to take part in defence of Ypres.
Allied troops land on Gallipoli peninsula (Turkey).

1 May
Elements Sirhind Brigade (Lahore Division) refuse orders to attack.

5 May
Lahore Division rejoins Indian Corps in front of Neuve Chapelle.

9–22 May
Indian Corps attacks in Festubert sector. No significant gains.

24 May
Italy joins the entente.

Early September
Sir James Willcocks relieved of command of the Indian Corps. Replaced by Sir Charles Anderson.

25 September
British Empire forces attack at Loos (France) using gas for the first time. Indian Corps attacks Mauquissart sector, with little success.

29 September
British-Indian forces capture Kut-al-Amara (Mesopotamia).

31 October
Lahore and Meerut Divisions receive orders to leave France for Mesopotamia.

22 November
British-Indian forces checked by Turks at Ctesiphon, sixteen miles from Baghdad.
Retreat to Kut begins.

Early December
Turks invest British-Indian force at Kut. Beginning of five-month siege.

December
Lahore and Meerut Divisions transferred to Mesopotamia, via Egypt. Immediately
(January 1915) thrown into efforts to relieve Kut.

19 December
Germans attack at Ypres, using phosgene gas for the first time.

1916

January
Allies evacuate Gallipoli.

21 February
Beginning of German assault on Verdun (France)

23 February
Mutiny of 15th Lancers at Basra (Mesopotamia). Muslim sowars refuse to march
against the Turks near the Holy Places of Islam.

2 March
Lady Hardinge Hospital closed, after Indian infantry sent to Mesopotamia.

29 April
General Townshend surrenders to Turks at Kut, with 2,600 British and 10,500 Indian
troops. Only 8,300 of the prisoners survive the war.

31 May
Naval battle of Jutland.

Early June
Husayn, Sharif of Mecca (guardian of Holy Places of Islam) raises Arab revolt against
Ottoman Turks.

4 June
Beginning of broad-front Russian offensive under Brusilov in Galicia. Achieves
great success against Austria-Hungary, capturing 450,000 prisoners by end
September.

5 June
Death of Lord Kitchener when HMS *Hampshire* is sunk on voyage to Russia.

1 July
Beginning of Allied offensive in Somme sector (France). British Army suffers 57,000 casualties on first day. Indian cavalry in reserve for most of the battle (which continues until 18 November).

27 August
Romania declares war on Austria-Hungary.

6 December
Fall of Bucharest to Central Powers.

1917

February
British-Indian forces recapture Kut.

11 March
British-Indian forces capture Baghdad (Mesopotamia).

14 March
Germans retreat to prepared positions of Hindenburg Line (France) scorching the earth as they withdraw. Indian cavalry occupy some of the abandoned ground.

5 April
US Congress votes in favour of war with Germany.

9–15 April
British Empire forces capture Vimy Ridge (France). Indian Cavalry see action.

7 June
British Empire forces begin offensive from Ypres salient. They advance five miles (to Passchendele) by November.

20 August
Edwin Montagu announces in Commons that HMG's policy is 'the progressive realization of responsible government in India as an integral part of the British Empire'.

10 November
Edwin Montagu arrives Bombay. He tours India until April 1918, collecting material for his report.

Late November
Indian Cavalry Corps concentrated for mounted action, to exploit hoped-for breakthrough at Cambrai (France). It does not come.

9 December
Capture of Jerusalem. General Allenby makes his formal entry on foot two days later.

1918

March
Indian cavalry withdrawn from France to replace British units in Allenby's planned offensive against the Turks in Palestine.
End April
Indian cavalry available for offensive action in Palestine.

September
Battle of Megiddo (Palestine). Heavy Turkish defeat. Indian cavalry take prominent part in pursuit.

31 October
Armistice with Turkey.

3 November
Armistice with Austria-Hungary.

11 November
Armistice with Germany.

Acknowledgements

When I began this project, I lightly assumed it would be a brisk, decisive affair of a few weeks – over by Christmas, even. As weeks became months, then several summers passed, I realized despondently that I had embarked on a struggle of attrition. Many people sustained me when morale seemed close to collapse. None of them bear any responsibility for the failings of the final text.

The Centre for Indian Studies at the University of Hull was a lively environment in which to work on matters South Asian. I learned much in particular from Bob Currie, Daniel Mariau, Subrata Mitra, Bikhu Parekh, Douglas Reid, Neena Samota, Indrani Sen and (especially) Thérèse O'Toole.

I also learned a lot from research seminars elsewhere. My embryonic ideas got the usual treatment at the University of Wales, Aberystwyth (History Seminar), at the University of Cambridge (South Asian Studies Seminar), at Coventry University (Punjab Studies Group), at the Institute of Historical Research (Imperial and Military History Seminars) and at the University of Oxford (South Asian History Seminar). For the discussions, I am grateful to all the participants, and especially the seminar organizers – Brian Bond, Judith Brown, Raj Chandavarkar, Gordon Johnson, Andrew Porter, Ian Talbot and Ina-Maria Zweiniger-Bargielovska among them.

When I was an undergraduate, I never really believed university tutors who claimed to learn a lot from their students. I now realize that they do. I have gained a great deal from discussions with many of my students of Indian and Imperial History, as well as greatly enjoying their company. Without them, of course, I would have finished the book in half the time.

Several people read and commented on parts of the typescript, and made editorial suggestions. They include Rodney Ambler, Tracy Borman, David French, Rob French, Theo Hoppen, Clare Horrocks, David Mitchell, Nicholas Owen, Leslie Price and Andrew Thompson. Others who have offered various forms of encouragement over the years include Clive Dewey, John MacKenzie and Douglas Peers.

I am grateful to Her Majesty's Stationery Office for permission to reproduce Crown Copyright material held by the India Office Library in London. I am also grateful to the staff of the India Office for the polite efficiency with which my requests for books, documents and photographs were always met. Similar thanks are due to the National Army Museum and to the Imperial War Museum (especially to Philip Dutton for tracking down photographs). Colin Gray, Sandra Gregory and Charlie Smith alerted me to some of the material.

I am very grateful to Annabelle Buckley at Macmillan for taking an interest in this project; she has been an excellent commissioning editor throughout.

No historian of the Indian Army could long remain indifferent to logistics. Decisive in this regard was a generous grant from the University of Hull Research

Support Fund. My Head of Department, John Bernasconi, made sure I got microfilm readers and study leave when it mattered. My colleages in the History Department at Hull have been unfailingly supportive and helpful; especial thanks are due to Kevin Hall, John Palmer and Kevin Watson for mending broken computers, and for saving work that I thought I had lost.

Consulting documents and checking details required frequent trips to London. I always looked forward to these, not least because of the generous hospitality of Andy, June, Lotty, Lucy, Natalie, Paul, Rebecca, Tom, and (above all) my brother Guido.

Abbreviations

ADC	Aide-de-Camp
AG	Adjutant-General
C-in-C	Commander-in-Chief
CIH	Central India Horse
CO	Commanding Officer
CP	Central Provinces
DAG	Deputy Adjutant-General
FPO	Field Post Office
HE	His Excellency
HH	His Highness
HMG	His Majesty's Government
HQ	Headquarters
IEF	Indian Expeditionary Force
IMS	Indian Medical Service
IOL	India Office Library and Records
IOM	Indian Order of Merit
IWM	Imperial War Museum
L/MIL	Military Department and Records, India Office
NCO	Non-Commissioned Officer
NWFP	North-West Frontier Province
OBI	Order of British India
OC	Officer Commanding
RFA	Royal Field Artillery
RHA	Royal Horse Artillery
UP	United Provinces (now Uttar Pradesh)
VCO	Viceroy's Commissioned Officer
YMCA	Young Men's Christian Association

Indian Army Ranks
and Organization

The Indian Army had its own system of ranks and organization, different in some respects from that of a European force.

Indian infantry privates were known as sepoys, and cavalry troopers as sowars. (For the Persian derivations of these words, see the glossary.) The non-commissioned ranks were roughly similar to those in the British or other European armies. For example, the infantry ranks of naik, havildar and havildar-major (lance dafadar, dafadar and kot dafadar or, later, dafadar-major in the cavalry) corresponded to those of corporal, sergeant and sergeant-major in the British Army.

There was no European equivalent, however, of the Indian officers. They held the commission of the Viceroy (but not of the King) and hence were known as VCOs, or Viceroy's Commissioned Officers. They had the right of command over Indian troops, but not over British; and they were subordinate to all officers who held the King's Commission (who were almost invariably British until well after the war).

The most junior of the Indian officers was the jemadar. Next came the subedar (or risaldar in the cavalry). Cavalry regiments had the additional rank of ressaidar between the jemadar and risaldar.

In general, VCOs were intended to serve as the link between the British officers and the Indian NCOs and men. Their precise tasks varied. They might include commanding a cavalry troop or infantry platoon, or being second-in-command of a squadron or company. Indian officers also carried out staff duties. The British quartermaster, for instance, might be assisted by a jemadar-quartermaster; the adjutant by a jemadar-adjutant (who, in the cavalry, was known as the woordi-major, or 'uniform major').

By far the most important VCO was the subedar-major, who was the senior Indian officer of an infantry regiment. Normally a man of long service, and great experience, it was his task to advise the CO on all matters concerning the religion and customs of the men under his command. (His equivalent in the cavalry was the risaldar-major.)

Indian infantry regiments normally consisted of a single battalion, divided into eight companies, grouped in pairs to form double companies. (The Garhwal and Gurkha regiments differed in having two battalions each.) Cavalry regiments were divided into four squadrons, each of several troops. A double company (or cavalry squadron) was normally under the command of a British captain, assisted by a lieutenant. The remaining British officers – a lieutenant-colonel, normally assisted by a major, a quartermaster and an adjutant – formed the nucleus of the regimental headquarters.

Most Indian battalions arrived in France slightly below establishment, with some 750 Indian officers and men, and normally eleven or twelve British officers. (British battalions were considerably stronger.) After a few months, however, fighting strength could fall to half this, and often less, while awaiting reinforcements. The battalions of the Sirhind Brigade, for example, averaged only 300 men after the Second Battle of Ypres in April 1915.

Regiments were normally either of 'class' or 'class-company' type. The men of class regiments were all of the same caste and religion. In class-company units, on the other hand, each company, or group of companies (squadrons in the cavalry) was of men from different backgrounds. Thus, for example, the 47th Sikhs, a class regiment, had eight companies of Sikhs, all from the Punjab. The 57th Rifles, as a class-company unit, had two companies each of Sikhs and Muslims from the Punjab, two of Dogras from Kangra and two of Pathans from the NWFP. (Full details of the composition of the regiments engaged in France can be found in Appendix II.)

Editorial Note

This book aims to give voice to the Indian soldiers who served in France during the Great War of 1914–18. I have therefore kept editorial intrusions to the minimum consistent with clarity.

In selecting just over 650 letters from a collection of many thousand, I have tried, above all, to be fully representative of the surviving material. I have, however, departed from this principle in three main instances, usually flagged in the notes at the end of each letter: (1) where many similar letters survive from a brief period, I have included only one or two examples to avoid tedious repetition; (2) I have included several unusual letters of particular human or historical interest, or of striking beauty; (3) I have tried to focus on the experience of combat soldiers, rather than that of rear-echelon elements such as supply and transport agents, or vets.

To aid clarity, I have adopted a standard layout for the letter-heads. I have used the short titles of the regiments preferred by the censor. (Full regimental details can be found in Appendices I and II.) Regimental numbers after men's names usually indicate their 'home' regiment, which was not necessarily the one with which they were serving (although the latter is often also stated).

Spellings of proper names have sometimes become garbled in transmission, not least because the censors, in their draft reports, pencilled through the correspondents' names, leaving many of them barely legible. Where it has been possible to identify individuals, I have, if necessary, corrected the spelling of their name (taking the *Indian Army List* as my authority). Numbers in brackets after officers' names indicate their approximate age. Medical officers' dates of birth are given in the *Indian Army List*; ages of infantry and cavalry officers are based on their known number of completed years' service, assuming an average age of eighteen on enlistment. Most of the NCOs and men, of course, would have been much younger than the officers, especially in wartime. Where Indian place-names can be securely identified, I have used the standard modern spellings of *The Imperial Gazetteer of India*. I have tried to supply missing information about dates, units, original language and caste, where there is enough evidence to speculate.

The censors often indicated whether a letter was passed, withheld, or modified through deletions. Where this has not been done I have not attempted to guess at an answer. But where letters are known to have been withheld, I have sometimes suggested a reason in a note, if the censor did not provide one himself.

In general, I have reproduced the wording of the letters exactly as it appears in the original typescript, with a few, minor, exceptions. The translators tended to under-punctuate (perhaps reflecting their familiarity with the originals). I have therefore repunctuated many of the letters in accordance with accepted modern English usage. I have broken a few of the longer letters into paragraphs, where these appear consistent with the writer's train of thought. I have also silently corrected obvious slips of spelling or grammar, and typographical mistakes. (Letters originally written in English, however, I have left exactly as they were.) Square brackets indicate both my own interpolations and those of the censors. All are minor, and I have not distinguished between them.

At an early stage in this project, I had to decide whether to arrange the material chronologically or thematically. My first inclination (and that of publishers I spoke to) was to organize the letters into thematic chapters. This would have had the advantage of grouping related letters together, and thereby giving a rapid indication of the range of soldiers' responses to Europe and to the war. After some thought, I abandoned this idea. Many of the letters range widely in subject matter in a very brief compass. A thematic arrangement would have meant cutting already short excerpts into several separate documents, often of no more than a sentence or two. Furthermore, the development of soldiers' attitudes over time – itself one of the main themes of the collection – is best shown by presenting the letters in the approximate order in which they were written. I have therefore arranged my selection chronologically, and have tried to suggest comparisons and contrasts by means of cross-references in the notes and the index.

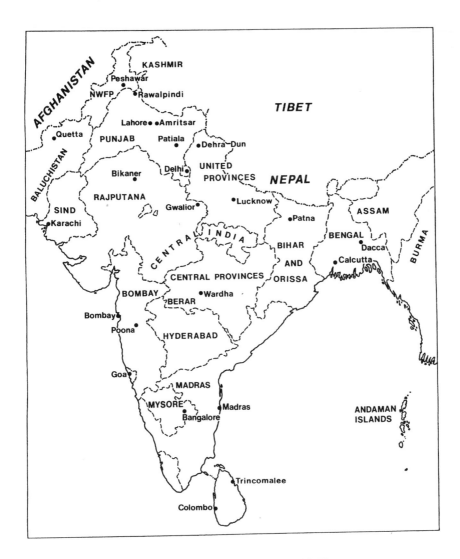

India at the time of the First World War

The Western Front, 1915

Colonial Punjab

Introduction*

At the end of the Great War, a British General, Sir James Willcocks, wrote a laudatory account of what his troops had achieved. He had little need to justify telling his story. For the first year of the war, he had commanded the Indian Corps in France, whose soldiers had fought and died in most of the great battles on the Western Front. The British public, still flushed with victory, retained a keen appetite for stories of how the war had been won.

But Willcocks prefaced his account with an especial plea. The soldiers of Britain and the white Dominions, he thought, would easily find chroniclers willing to tell their tale. India was less fortunate. India's soldiers, he suggested, 'will furnish no writers to thrill the generations to come; they will just pass with the great masses of India, content that they have done their duty and been faithful to their salt'. His book, he hoped, would fill the silence left by the sepoys, victorious but voiceless.

His claim, if not entirely false, was less than completely true. As he well knew, the sepoys had been far from silent witnesses to the war they had helped to win. The Indian troops under his command had written and received hundreds of thousands of letters, many of which recorded their reactions to the great war in which they were so bewilderingly engulfed.

This book gives substance to the belief that Indian soldiers did indeed provide writers to 'thrill the generations to come'. It is a collection of letters to and from Indian soldiers serving in France, or recovering from wounds in England, between 1914 and 1918.

I

In 1914, the Indian Army was a colonial force of some 155,000 officers and men. The Indian Army, the 75,000-strong British garrison of India, the Imperial Service Troops supplied by the Indian Princes, and the Indian high command were collectively known as the 'Army in India', which numbered around 236,000 in all.

The Indian Army was, in peacetime, an all-volunteer force, taking in 15–20,000 recruits a year. Its ranks were filled mainly with illiterate peasants. Some of these men had been driven from the land, but most were willing labour migrants looking to make the most of the economic opportunities created by the colonial encounter. Pay for a sepoy was a modest Rs.11 a month (although increased during the war), but a hard-pressed peasant family, with few other sources of income, would value the remittances sent home by a relative serving in the ranks. Some men, primarily

* The document numbers of relevant letters appear in brackets throughout

1

high-caste Rajputs, were attracted to the Army by the martial self-image of their community; others, such as Mazbhi Sikhs, were landless Untouchables. But soldiering in later colonial India was not generally the occupation of the very poorest; the majority of the sepoys were from the middle peasantry. Soldiers in peacetime would normally serve only with one regiment, to which they could develop a very strong emotional attachment (317). Most men served for five to seven years, before returning to their village.

The Indian Army, however, was 'Indian' only in a nominal sense. By 1914, the vast majority of Indian troops were drawn from the north and north-west of the subcontinent – the provinces of Punjab, the North-West Frontier and UP, and the independent kingdom of Nepal. This regional bias was the result of the 'martial races' theory which had influenced British recruiting strategy since the 1880s. A mixture of indigenous notions of caste and imported Social Darwinism, the martial-races idea had at its core the belief that some Indians were inherently more warlike than others. Very few troops were recruited from southern and eastern India, because of a growing British conviction that southern and eastern Indians had become effete through 'racial degeneracy'. Urban India was not tapped for recruits, for the same reasons. The Western-educated were also excluded from the ranks, for fear of their politically subversive potential. Many of the Indian troops who served in France were Punjabi Muslims and Sikhs, reflecting the ethnic biases of the wider Indian Army; in 1912 just over half of all combatants were from the Punjab.

The Indian Army had three main functions: the defence of the North-West Frontier of India; the maintenance of internal security against threats to the colonial order; and the provision of a Field Force to fight an Afghan or Russian invasion, or to be sent overseas for imperial purposes. Approximately one-third of the Army was assigned to each of these three tasks. The immediately disposable elements of the Field Force normally consisted of two divisions and one cavalry brigade, with their attached British units.

When war threatened in the summer of 1914, Field Force units were put on standby to serve in Europe. When the Germans invaded France in August, the Lahore and Meerut infantry divisions were dispatched quickly from Karachi and Bombay. They arrived at Marseilles in late September and early October 1914, detraining at Orleans before marching to the front. (Other, smaller, Expeditionary Forces were sent to Basra, Egypt and East Africa.)

The Indian troops arrived in France trained and equipped only for a colonial war. Little money had been spent on Field Army support units: there was no mechanical transport, and the artillery – all British – could be made up only by denuding other divisions. The sepoys had to exchange their rifles for the newer (but unfamiliar) pattern carried by the British Army. There were shortages of medical supplies and signalling apparatus. The Germans had trench mortars, searchlights and hand grenades; the Indians had none of these (although they improvised grenades from jam tins). It was even some months before all Indian units had their full complement of warm clothes.

As they arrived, these underequipped troops were fed piecemeal into the front line in an attempt to stem the German rush between Ypres and La Bassée. The 129th Baluchis were the first Indian unit to see action, near Wytschaete in Belgium, in late October (see Plate 2). Decorations were liberally bestowed in these fierce little actions, including the first Victoria Cross to be received by an Indian. But honours alone could not sustain the sepoys' morale, which went into steep decline with the onset of colder weather. The Indian troops were withdrawn for rest after heavy losses.

During the winter of 1914–15, the Indian Corps was built up to two infantry and two cavalry divisions, with an establishment of some 16,000 British and 28,500 Indian troops (see Appendix I for a full order of battle.) In the spring, the Corps was moved to the Neuve Chapelle-Givenchy sector of the front, where it remained for almost a year, apart from the detachment of the Lahore Division for a few days in April 1915 during the Second Battle of Ypres (71).

For most of 1915, the Indian Corps held a front of approximately seven miles. The ground was boggy, cut with ditches, drains and canals, and crossed here and there with bridges. Movement off-road was very difficult and visibility was poor, with morning mists lingering on to midday for months on end. The landscape was almost completely flat, dotted with farmhouses and clumps of trees. The only high ground was the Aubers Ridge, held by the Germans a few hundred yards beyond the Indian front line, an elevation which the Indian soldiers could see but were destined never to reach. Most of the sepoys to die in Europe – some 7,700 – fell in these few square miles.

For the Indians, the war was one of ambuscades – raids and counter-raids, patrols and surprise attacks – punctuated with larger-scale attacks on the German lines. The first of these offensives was at Neuve Chapelle in March 1915 (45). The sepoys' morale was boosted by an apparent success, tempered by very heavy losses – much higher than the Indian Army was used to in the bloody but brisk fighting on the North-West Frontier. A second major attack was made at the Battle of Festubert in early May (88); and a third at the Battle of Loos in late September.

The morale of the troops began to fail again as their second winter in France approached. Despite a year of fighting, and heavy losses, no end to the war was in sight. Casualties had been especially severe among British officers. Some units had lost nearly all their original officers within a couple of days' fighting, and it proved difficult to find men who could speak Indian languages to replace them. All the Indian Army officers who had been on leave in Britain at the outbreak of war had been commandeered to train the British battalions of the 'New Armies', and those currently in post were unknown to their men, inexperienced, and often commanded little confidence.

At the end of 1915, the two infantry divisions were withdrawn in the belief that their morale would not survive another winter of trench warfare in France. They were sent to join Expeditionary Force 'D' in Mesopotamia, where the Imperial war effort was deteriorating badly. In early 1916, the Indian troops were thrown into the failed attempts to relieve General Townshend's mixed British and Indian force besieged by the Turks at Kut-al-Amara, on the Tigris, downstream from Baghdad. From then on, Mesopotamia became the focus of the main Indian war effort in 1917–18; Indian troops were prominent in the capture of Baghdad in 1917, and in the destruction of the Ottoman Empire in the region.

The two Indian cavalry divisions stayed on in France until the spring of 1918. They numbered 13–14,000 men in total, including the British units attached to each brigade. There was little need or opportunity for mounted troops on the Western Front, and they were mainly kept in reserve. The cavalry saw some action on the Somme in 1916 and, the following year, during German withdrawal to the Hindenburg Line, and at Cambrai. Their impact on the fighting was, however, minimal.

In early 1918, the cavalry were also transferred to the Middle East, where they took part in General Allenby's offensive against the Turks in Palestine, helping to win a great success at the Battle of Megiddo in September.

By the time of the Armistice, India had provided over 1.27 million men, including 827,000 combatants, contributing roughly one man in ten to the war effort of the British Empire. The wartime Indian Army reached a highest strength of 573,000 combatants, with a maximum of 273,000 serving outside the subcontinent at any one time (mostly in Mesopotamia). Of the 947,000 Imperial war dead, some 49,000 were sepoys.

II

This collection of letters exists, and has survived, because it was censored. As well as offering opportunities to the historian, the process by which the evidence was created poses certain problems. When reading the letters, we are not simply eavesdropping on the innermost thoughts of the soldiers or looking invisibly over their shoulders as they write. Layers of filtration come between the thoughts of the sepoys and the surviving evidence. There were two main stages of mediation: the process of writing and the process of censorship. Both stages were complex and created distortions. We must first understand what sort of lens we are looking through before we can understand the distortions in the picture we are seeing.

How were the letters written? It is clear that some men wrote (196) or addressed (265) their own letters, but the vast majority of letters were probably written by scribes on behalf of their senders, since most Indian Army soldiers were illiterate. In the Punjab at this time no more than 5 per cent of the population could read; among rural military communities, however, literacy would have been very much less, since the British deliberately recruited from the least educated elements of the rural population, who were thus least affected by 'dangerous' Western political ideas. Indeed, some of the letters contain explicit references to the 'writer's' own illiteracy (187, 265), while others refer to scribes (307, 345). Furthermore, many of the letters were sent to or from soldiers' womenfolk, and, given that virtually all rural Indian women were illiterate at this time, these letters were clearly written on behalf of their female senders, or read aloud to their recipients. There are several references to third parties reading letters to women (561) or writing them for women (233).

There is frustratingly little evidence as to who the scribes might have been. In France, and perhaps England, they were presumably literate Indian soldiers, because there were few others who could have written the necessary Indian languages. Perhaps some scribes were the very Indian officers who were themselves involved in the censorship. At one point, the Head Censor refers to the work of the YMCA in writing letters for troops in rest camps; but he does not reveal how the YMCA acquired Urdu or other Indian languages. In India, peasants would have had access to village scribes, perhaps on payment of a fee; there is one reference to a local school in which scribes could be found (452).

The existence of scribes provides, in one sense, the main opportunity of the collection, in that it is thanks to the scribes that we can read the recorded thoughts of the illiterate (who, for obvious reasons, are normally marginal to the written historical record). But the intercession of scribes also affects the inscription. At a fairly basic level, scribes would have had a repertoire of formulaic phrases, some of which they might have suggested to a letter-sender; and a few of the more elegant expressions may have owed more to scribe than to sepoy. More significantly, the involvement of scribes (and of letter-readers) makes the letters a slightly more public record than a simple correspondence between two literates. This semi-public arena might have constrained what men were willing to say. Clearly there were things that men would not like read out to a group of their peers, particularly in an army which placed a high institutional value on conformity. The letters therefore might overemphasize the socially acceptable. That said, some letters flag their privacy with instructions that they are to be read to one person only and not aloud to a group (195).

The second layer of filtration was the process of censorship, which happened at two levels. In the first place, the letters were censored within the regiment. British officers (perhaps a double-company commander) read their men's letters, or asked a trustworthy Indian officer to read them aloud. This was done in order to remove information of military value to the enemy, such as mentions of place-names near the front line (331). There was nothing especially sinister or colonial about this practice; it was (and remains) the usual procedure in most armies, including the British Army. The troops were fully aware of this regimental censorship (117, 217, 394) and did not appear to have resented it (173, 375).

In the case of the Indian Army, the regimental censorship appears to have been very erratic; some regiments were very strict (173, 188) while others were more lax. In general, however, the regimental censorship became more sketchy as the war went on. As officer casualties mounted, there were fewer potential censors with the necessary command of Indian languages. British officers became too busy to censor many letters, often composed in poor hands and in many dialects. In March

1915, the Head Censor commented that the regimental censorship was in many cases a mere formality; the regimental censor was affixing a stamp to letters he had clearly not read.

The letters themselves support the notion that the regimental censorship was sketchy. The troops were able to transmit plenty of military information; they wrote, for example, about the siege of Kut, and the surrender of the Indian troops there in 1916. They also mentioned French villages by name (499). (Generally, however, Indian troops did not speculate about impending moves as much as the British soldiers did, for reasons which are not clear.) Furthermore, monolingual British officers depended on Indian officers to read and translate the letters, and such Indian officers could, and did, subvert the regimental censorship (67).

Nevertheless, the regimental censorship, however lax, must have affected what the troops were prepared to say. The very threat of censorship, one might assume, would have made the soldiers reluctant to talk about matters which they did not want to reveal to their officers. In particular, expressions of dissent or feelings of animosity towards the officers themselves were likely to be under-represented.

But one should not leap to conclusions. Knowing that their officers might read their letters, the troops had every incentive to say positive things about those in authority over them; in general, however, they did not. They frequently mentioned their officers collectively, in fairly anodyne terms; but, to the surprise of the Head Censor, there were relatively few mentions of individual officers by name. Individual officers do get favourable mentions, especially when a particularly well-liked man has been killed (107, 620). But the troops were also prepared to complain about individual British or Indian officers, whom they did sometimes name (299, 398). These possibly risky complaints suggest that the letters contain other elements of frankness.

The second layer of censorship (and the one that has created this collection) was set up at the Indian Base Post Office, located first at Rouen then moved to Boulogne in December 1914. (A fuller account of its workings appears in Appendix IV.) The original purpose of this censorship was to prevent seditious literature reaching the troops, so it was at first confined to 'inward' mails to the men in France. The censorship was later extended to the 'outward' mails from the wounded in hospital in England, then, in January 1915, to letters from unwounded troops at the front in France.

The first Head Censor was Second Lieutenant E. B. Howell, a member of the Indian Civil Service who had been attached to an Indian cavalry regiment as an interpreter. Under him, he had a team of censors, mainly oriental scholars and old India 'hands'. Originally numbering four, the team was later expanded to eight, then reduced to five at the end of 1915 when the number of Indian troops in France was reduced. Two Indian postal clerks also helped to read the letters. Most letters were written in Urdu, the chief lingua franca of the Indian Army; the others were written mainly in Gurmukhi, Hindi, Mahratti, Garhwali, Gurkhali or Bengali.

The censors read some of the letters, then sent a brief report on their contents to the Secretary of State for India, the India Office, the War Office, the Foreign Office, Buckingham Palace, and to the commanders of the Indian divisions (among others). The first report was completed in December 1914, and the last in June 1918. Originally, the reports were sent every week, but from June 1917 they were sent fortnightly, because 'interesting' letters – as defined by the censors – were becoming fewer. To each report the censors normally appended in the region of 100 translated extracts from the letters, and it is from this budget of extracts that the current selection is taken. The criteria for inclusion in the budget were not explicitly stated, but the censors appear to have aimed at being representative. The letters of British troops with the Indian Corps were also monitored, but were not included in the extracts sent by the censor.

The censors had plenty of work. In March 1915, the Indian soldiers in France and England were writing 10–20,000 letters a week, except when actually fighting or on the march, when there was little for the censors to do. Clearly the censors could not read all the letters; deciphering and translating a single letter could take up to two hours even for the best-qualified censors.

In general, the censorship of letters from France and England was much more effective than that of letters from India. The Boulogne censors read no more than 3 per cent of letters from Egypt and India, and hence could give only an impression of their contents. Elsewhere, there were 'some efforts' at censorship in Bombay, and a 'thorough' censorship in Hong Kong. A censorship in Egypt, on the same lines as that in France, was set up in France in June 1915. Special attention was given to letters from the Indian diaspora, who were seen as more politicized than the Indian soldiers and their families.

The general policy of the Boulogne censorship was to read as much as possible, but to delay and interfere with mails as little as possible. Some letters, however, were suppressed. Indeed, the original motive for extending the censorship to 'outward' mails was to suppress despondent letters home from the Indian wounded.

Suppressed letters were reproduced in the budget of extracts more often than letters which were passed, so we can see what the Boulogne censors found objectionable. The letters which were suppressed usually fell into one of several categories: incitements to crime (287), and even murder (542); accounts of sex with white women, which were seen as damaging to white prestige (170, 192); particularly distressing letters from men who had been badly disabled by wounds (138); letters which were flagrantly dishonest, mentioned drugs (177) or included slighting references to whites (156); and accounts from prisoners of war of receiving good treatment from the Germans, which might have encouraged desertion. In each case, either the offending passage was deleted or the entire letter was destroyed.

The policy of minimal interference accorded with the primary purpose of the Boulogne censorship, which was not to suppress letters, but to monitor their contents. The main task of the censors was to supply information about the morale of the soldiers to those responsible for their well-being. Orientalist assumptions also discouraged the British from intercepting letters. The Head Censor assumed (perhaps rightly) that 'orientals' were much more likely to be inflamed by rumours than by mails; the tales told by badly wounded men returning to India were likely to be more alarming and convincing than anything they might say in a letter. Furthermore, letters which contained deletions were, the censors believed, in most cases more likely to excite the fearful imagination of their recipients than letters which had not been tampered with. The total quantity of letters suppressed was accordingly very small; only two or three letters in every hundred thousand were held back. The suppression of letters by the Head Censor is, therefore, emphatically not a major distortion in the collection.

As far as advertising their activities was concerned, the policy of the Boulogne censors differed between literates and illiterates. Where the sender was a 'literate' (such as a sub-assistant surgeon) the censors generally flagged their activities in the belief that such men, if they 'sinned' at all, were likely to do so 'by commission'. The censors therefore wanted to frighten potentially subversive literates, so that they would not voice dissent in future. On the other hand, the censors believed that 'illiterates' (including most sepoys) did not generally harbour subversive thoughts; the censors tried to conceal their activities from soldiers to avoid frightening them.

Nevertheless, the sepoys did seem gradually to become aware of the Boulogne censorship, despite efforts to conceal its workings from them. In the winter of 1914–15, wounded men in hospitals did not seem to realize that their mail was being censored, partly because they did not see it being done. By about April 1915, however, the soldiers at the front seem to have become aware of the Boulogne censorship, although exactly how is not known.

In general, the soldiers appear to have overestimated the impact of the Boulogne censorship. For various reasons, many of the soldiers' letters went astray: it was difficult to keep hospital lists up to date, as men moved from their unit to hospital and back to their unit again; and many men shared the same names, which made for confusion in postal deliveries. Some men, however, wrongly attributed the non-delivery of their letters to the censorship rather than to simple failures in the postal arrangements (93).

There is some evidence that the troops mildly resented the fact that their mail might be read by someone other than their own officers (434). Perhaps because of this, some men made attempts to evade the censorship. One way of doing this was to use the French civilian post, even though this was expressly forbidden to the troops (455). Other men referred to invisible inks, made from fruit or vegetable juices, which were used to disguise the content of a letter (245, 408). More frequently, soldiers developed simple codes which were intended to deceive the censor, the frequency of such codes increasing in the spring of 1915 as men became more aware of the censorship. Examples of codes included the images of 'black pepper' and 'white pepper' for Indian and British troops respectively (43, 60); 'fruit' for white women (183); 'tentpegging' for a cavalry charge (411); 'tribal feud' for news of the war (28); and 'wedding' for an impending battle (343). Several soldiers also used veiled writing to imply that they intended to desert (536) or that others had already done so (129).

None of these codes was particularly elaborate or sophisticated; most were easily deciphered by the censor. Their existence provides an important clue as to what the troops were trying to hide (which, in general, was exactly that which was most likely to be suppressed).

III

Given these layers of filtration and censorship, can we take the letters at anything like face value? In December 1914, the Head Censor certainly thought that he could: 'the letters are quite unstudied', he remarked, 'and the sentiments almost beyond suspicion genuine'. This, however, was very early in the war (and before the troops had worked out the full extent of the censorship). The censor later came round to the view that it was difficult to feel the genuine pulse of the soldiers; they were unlikely to unburden themselves, knowing that their letters could be read. He then suggested that the stories circulated by the returning wounded were 'of more effect than fifty letters'.

Both these positions are probably too extreme. As the preceding section has suggested, there are problems in reading these sources: the historian must always be alert to the impact of scribal intervention, censorship and self-censorship. Certainly the uncensored record of the troops might have been different; but, equally, most soldiers had no other means of communicating with their families. The sheer quantity of letters (roughly one per man per fortnight) shows the personal importance of the postal service to the troops. Nor does the internal evidence of the letters suggest that they were composed primarily with the censors' reaction in mind: soldiers were too obviously distressed when letters went astray (335) or when mail ships were sunk (225) for this to be true. Letters from their families clearly mattered to the troops (597), who sometimes expressed unfeigned and spontaneous joy at receiving them (632). Obviously mendacious letters were very rare; heart-wrenchingly genuine ones all too frequent (181).

The historian can be too sceptical as well as too credulous. The crucial issue is, surely, less what we *cannot* learn from these letters, than what we *can* learn from them. What do they reveal about the experiences and mentalities of Indian peasant-soldiers?

Most obviously, the letters speak of the war. Although the soldiers were told not to write about the war (370), plenty of them clearly did, and most took no trouble to disguise their meaning.

In the few weeks after their arrival in France (and before the censorship was fully working) the soldiers' letters were full of hope and good cheer. The censor believed that the soldiers wanted to show their loyalty to the King and to prove themselves equal to white men. The sepoys apparently expected that the war in France would be like a frontier campaign except on a bigger scale.

The first combats in Belgium came as a great shock. Losses were very heavy – much higher than the Indian Army had been used to in colonial campaigns. In a few days' fighting around Ypres in late October 1914, for example, the 57th Rifles lost six out of eleven British officers and 290 out of 750 other ranks. The Mahsuds seemed to be the only troops who really thrived on the battlefield; their letters often contained the phrase 'we are fighting with great zest'. Others were less than exhilarated: the many vivid accounts of battle (19) were mixed with sighs of resignation (10) and despair. Winter brought new trials in the form of severe cold and wet; by late November 1914 the whole battleground was deep in snow. Morale had reached breaking point by February 1915: the Indian regiments had suffered an epidemic of self-inflicted wounds (12) and many letters prayed for a speedy return to India, or urged relatives at home not to enlist (22, 59, 63, 73, 78).

The bad news seems to have hit recruiting; the number of men enlisting in India dipped sharply in the spring of 1915 (although this may have had something to do with the need to bring in the spring harvests). Furthermore, the new recruits were not yet trained; in the meantime, the Indian Corps had to replace its losses with men from the depots and reservists recalled to the colours. The latter were men who had already served for between eighteen and twenty-five years; although experienced, many were unfit and did not want to fight overseas.

In March, the Indian Corps played a prominent part in the offensive battle of Neuve Chapelle (45). Although the attack by 30,000 men achieved some success, the losses – some 12,500 – were nerve-shattering (32). The return of spring weather promised an improvement, but morale remained fragile. Some men mentioned malingering (75), or wrote in war-weary (123) or hopeless (82, 84) terms. In the late summer of 1915, this persistent note of despair became more intense (114). The Indian Corps took another round of heavy losses at the Battle of Loos in September (151, 154); but the prospect of victory, and with it a return to India, seemed no closer. Some men sought substances to produce inflammation in order to escape front-line service (147), and the censor also noted a growing tendency for the men to break into poetry when they were especially disturbed (146). Rather than risk another morale-battering winter in France, the General Staff pulled the Indian infantry out of the line and sent them to the Middle East.

For the cavalrymen left in France, surviving a second winter on the Western Front seemed to produce some adjustment to the war. Of course there were still some war-weary (372, 551, 571) or despairing (270, 474, 484, 501, 626) letters, or those urging relatives not to come to France (413, 500, 569). Self-inflicted wounds did not disappear (223, 224, 403), nor did malingering (241). Some men became paralysed with grief (227); others went crazy, and ran amok with their rifles (297).

But, judging from their letters, the troops seemed in the end to become accustomed to the war. Morale did not plummet again as it had done in 1915. In the following spring, the Head Censor commented that it was becoming more and more difficult to find 'interesting' letters – by which he meant those showing signs of depression, desertion, incipient mutiny, self-inflicted wounds, malingering or political dissent. Gloomy letters, he noted, were 'few and far between' from 1916 onwards.

This appearance, however, might reflect the record more than the reality. There seems to have been more external pressure on the men in the latter part of the war not to write despairingly (471). Some particularly cheerful letters do have the air of having been composed for domestic consumption (327), perhaps to reassure anxious relatives. Also, as the war progressed, soldiers might have felt less desire to pen vivid descriptions of their experiences and suffering; their wartime world in France had diverged so greatly from the civilian world they had left behind, perhaps never to see again, that there remained little point in trying to communicate what had become, by then, essentially incommunicable.

None the less, the record may reflect some real adjustment to the war (323). Admittedly, from 1916 almost all the surviving letters were written by cavalrymen – who saw much less action and suffered far fewer casualties than the infantry. The troops themselves were aware that cavalry service was a relatively 'cushy number' (369). Even so, the cavalry were generally exhilarated when they did get the chance to fight; letters written after seeing action on the Somme in 1916 show some satisfaction at having driven the Germans back (356, 363, 415, 447). This confident tone was sustained after the Battle of Cambrai in November the following year (623, 630). The men remained willing to do their bit and were hopeful of ultimate victory (393, 497), but this growing psychological acceptance of the war was often tinged with a sense that personal survival was no longer possible, and several men wrote as if they were quietly resigned to death (226, 351, 458, 529, 557, 595, 618).

These reactions to the war were, in many ways, much like those of British soldiers, who went through a similar cycle of exhilaration, despair and resignation.

However, the Indian troops used very different imagery to convey their experiences. The purpose of imagery is to make accessible the strange by comparing it to the familiar; and the sepoys often compared the unprecedented fighting to the rural labour which their families were used to. The German Army, for example, was 'harder to crush than well-soaked grain in the mill' (123). Classical religious themes also surfaced in battlefield descriptions: Muslims sometimes compared the fighting to Karbala (56), while Hindus preferred the image of the Mahabharata (23, 41).

Indian soldiers' motives for fighting were also distinctive. The Indian Army, it has often been suggested, was a 'mercenary' force; and certainly the material rewards of military service featured prominently in soldiers' letters. Some men hoped for promotion (272) and saw the war as an especially honourable opportunity to obtain it (191). Many men made positive remarks about their good rations (527), pay rises (463) and pensions (308), plentiful clothing (479), and the other material benefits of military service (476, 547, 588, 628), including the excellent postal service (309). Men even praised the attention paid to the wounded (51), and the burial arrangements in England (215).

Even more important than 'mercenary' motives, however, were the 'traditional' concerns of shame and honour. Judging from their letters, Indian soldiers fought, above all, to gain or preserve *izzat* – their honour, standing, reputation or prestige (491, 600). Men expressed the desire to place their 'names on the tongues of the entire world' (306). They could gain *izzat* by winning medals; several men recorded their delight upon receiving decorations (238, 511) – especially of the Victoria Cross (29, 651-2). A soldier's *izzat* operated posthumously as well as during his lifetime. It was considered glorious or honourable to die in battle (305, 493, 552) or to 'become a martyr' (199). Men who died in this way could be remembered 'for a thousand years' (87). Clearly there was an element of the conventional to these expressions, some of which appear to have been written partly to reassure families (178, 401). One soldier even voiced some embarrassment at receiving exhortations to distinction (174), although he was hardly typical. But, despite these caveats, the discourse about *izzat* revealed a widely shared value system to which soldiers were expected at least to aspire.

The quest for *izzat* was driven by negative as well as positive impulses. For men to risk death in battle, they must either value something more than their life or fear something more than death. Most Indian soldiers, it seemed, had an intense fear of shame – the openly voiced contempt of the peers and kin whose good opinion they valued. The troops themselves often expressed indignation or contempt for those who ran away or deserted, or who otherwise failed in their duty (532). It was 'better to die, than to fail in one's duty', remarked one old soldier, from the safety of the Punjab (322). In soldiers' eyes, shame could involve an excruciating loss of masculinity; unsurprisingly perhaps, given the highly gendered nature of military service. To be a coward was to be 'like a woman', or even a 'sodomite': it is hard to say which was more demeaning. The range of acceptable military behaviour was tightly constrained by the types of masculinity available to the soldiers.

Shame and honour operate through identity, whether individual or collective; and soldiers' comments about honour suggest the forms of identity that they held most dear. Soldiers, it seemed, defined themselves primarily in terms of religion, caste (133) and clan. The purpose of fighting was to raise the status of one's caste (528, 635) or clan (282), while medals brought credit to the clan (467). Rajput caste-cluster identity, in particular, asserted itself in relation to martial activity (111, 234); on several occasions, Rajputs reminded each other that it was their duty to fight and die on the battlefield (256, 533, 581, 647), and Rajput women seem to have shared these values (576). Soldiers' concerns about *izzat* clung to these very 'traditional' sources of identity, which (because of deliberate British recruiting policy) often overlapped with the military primary groups of platoon, company and regiment. The reputation of the regiment clearly mattered to the troops (466, 496). Shame, like honour, attached itself to the micro-identities of regiment (175), tribe (325) and caste (473). The Head Censor found the 'absence of any wider basis of indignation' – such as 'India' – especially noteworthy.

The letters also reveal the centrality of religious practice to Indian soldiers. Admittedly, it is difficult to disentangle consciously expressed religious belief from scribal formulae and the stock phraseology embedded in everyday language. Nevertheless, religion clearly permeated almost every aspect of the sepoys' lives. The British were sensitive to this, as the soldiers themselves recognized; one man virtually ordered the censors not to tamper with his letter, because it discussed a 'matter of religion' (353).

For the most part, the soldiers' consciously stated religious beliefs were fairly orthodox: several Hindus, for example, suggested that death in battle would release them from the cycle of death and rebirth, rewarding them with immediate Paradise (17, 25, 118, 198, 624). But the soldiers were not learned men, and expressions of religious orthodoxy co-existed with superstitions of a more popular nature (57, 97, 391, 456).

Wartime conditions, however, did tend to erode some religious orthodoxies. In general, the sepoys were allowed scrupulous observance of their religious customs; the British had no desire to provoke another mutiny like that of 1857 by tampering with what the soldiers held sacred. During the war, the Indian authorities made sure that Indian soldiers received culturally appropriate food (98), but the soldiers themselves seem to have become less fastidious as the war went on. Some Sikhs were unwilling to exchange their turbans for steel helmets (339); but other daily observances were neglected. Several letters, slightly defensive in tone, mentioned the erosion of caste or religious distinctions. Hindus ate and drank 'polluted' things (251), took food and tea from the hands of Europeans, shared food with Muslims, or went openly to cafés in Suez. The YMCA encouraged caste Hindus to treat sweepers as equals. The vast majority of Muslims were prepared to eat with the French (490), with only a few deploring the effect of prolonged residence in Europe on their religious purity (104, 454, 488, 582), while some even believed that the war would lead to the spread of Islam (275).

With wartime conditions making daily religious observance more difficult, the major ritual occasions of the religious calendar became all the more important. Soldiers who had abandoned everyday food taboos might remain very strict about observing the Guru's birthday, Ramazan, or the Id (554). Muslim troops disapproved of the frivolous way in which the Egyptians celebrated the Id (383); or expressed disappointment at having to spend the Id away from home (378). British officers, sensitive to the men's religious needs, made great efforts to accommodate these ceremonies and received warm praise for doing so (113).

Soldiers also became especially concerned about the availability of religious artefacts, including *kirpans*, Granths and Qu'rans (158, 176) – clinging, perhaps, to shards of normality otherwise buried under layers of trauma and bereavement. Certainly, the letters which acknowledged receipt of such items sometimes expressed heartfelt gratitude (254).

Partly with the supply of cherished religious artefacts in mind, the British set up a charitable fund for Indian soldiers in October 1914. Under the chairmanship of Sir John Hewitt, a former Lieutenant-Governor of UP, the fund was managed by the Indian Soldiers' Committee of the Order of St John of Jerusalem. Lord Curzon lent his London residence as a headquarters. Besides supplying religious artefacts, and helping to pay for hospital ships, the fund gave money, clothing and other comforts to Indian soldiers in France and Mesopotamia. A hospital, named after the late Lady Hardinge of Penshurst, the wife of a former Viceroy, was established at Brockenhurst near Southampton.

The soldiers mostly appreciated this charitable work, but it was not without potential problems. For example, the YMCA gave notepaper to wounded soldiers who wished to write home. But this paper was headed with YMCA devices, which the censor worried might start inflammatory rumours in India that the troops were being converted to Christianity. From February 1915, the headed paper was accordingly replaced after the censor had drawn attention to this danger. (The incident is a neat example of the censorship working exactly as planned – alerting the authorities to potential problems of morale, which could then be dealt with promptly.)

In general, however, the censors were surprised by the excellent spirit of the troops, who suffered so much and complained so little; nor did the British discover any systematic attempts to tamper with the loyalty of the men. Nevertheless, there were plenty of minor grumbles (211). Pay and family allowances were a frequent source of irritation (189, 237, 288, 320), especially for men cross-posted to new regiments, whose pay sometimes went missing. Promotion was another fertile source of dispute (370, 482, 633); again, cross-posted men could lose out on advancement, either in their 'home' regiment or in their new one (190, 252, 321). The behaviour of Indian officers occasionally caused friction (419), especially where they oversaw promotion to non-commissioned rank (266, 420, 645). Some men used drugs, such as cannabis and opium, which the authorities frowned upon (137, 431); while men from the Pathan borderlands were wont to bring their tribal feuds into the ranks (180, 201) – sometimes with murderous intent (430, 460, 464).

But the most important grievance in the first year of the war concerned the treatment of the lightly wounded, who were sent back to the trenches once they had recovered. The sepoys felt very strongly that such men had already 'done their bit', and had earned, through their wounds, the right to return to India. Many letters, from all classes of troops, voiced this grievance openly (45–9, 52). But, even when protesting, the wounded still expressed gratitude for the efforts made to secure their comfort in hospitals (44, 63). Nor did they regard the authorities as inflexible: some men asked British officers to intervene on behalf of individuals (9), while others petitioned the King for a change in policy (68, 128). These protests, noted by the censor, seem to have worked, for the policy of returning the wounded to the fray was later moderated to the satisfaction of the troops (88).

Apart from the issue of the returning wounded, major discipline problems during the war were very few. The most serious incidents involved three Muslim units, who mutinied rather than fight against their Turkish co-religionists. At

Rangoon, in January 1915, the 130th Baluchis peacefully refused to embark for Mesopotamia (20, 40). The following month, a similar if more serious episode took place at Singapore involving the 5th Light Infantry, who this time opened fire on their officers. The mutiny of the 15th Lancers, a year later, aroused particular interest among sepoy letter-writers (276, 397). Most of the regiment were imprisoned (407) after they refused to march from Basra against the Turks. Soldiers wrote quite openly about the mutiny, the Head Censor making no attempt to interfere, partly because the tone of the letters was, as he put it, 'excellent' – meaning that other soldiers generally disapproved of the Lancers' dereliction of duty (259, 313, 315), even though there was some sympathy for their plight (340), and general relief when most of them were eventually freed (550, 590).

These three mutinies were the most visible symptoms of a wider problem – the unpopularity among Indian Muslims of the war against Turkey, the home of the Khalifa (the spiritual head of Islam). Muslim troops wrote fairly freely about the religious issues raised by the war. Although sometimes praising the bravery of the Turkish Army (132), most Muslim sepoys decided, after some debate, to fight the Turks if need be (1, 291). Pathans, however, were a notable exception. Once Turkey had entered the war, Pathan units experienced many desertions (179). The British eventually stopped recruiting transfrontier Pathans because of worries about their loyalty: enlistments were minimal after May 1915 and had ceased altogether by the end of the year (274). Pathans deserted in such large numbers not just because of their religious scruples; they also had a workable exit option, in that their territory was not formally administered by the British, and punishment was therefore unlikely.

In June 1916, the revolt of Husayn, Sharif of Mecca, the guardian of the holiest shrines of Islam, was another issue which tested Muslim opinion. In general, old-fashioned 'orthodox' Muslims (represented in the Indian Army) were broadly sympathetic to the revolt, while the less traditional, Pan-Islamic elements (better represented in the Muslim League) were more hostile (346). The troops were well aware of the revolt, and corresponded about it (349). There was little evidence of Pan-Islamism in letters to the troops from civilians in India, and very few attempts to subvert the troops using Pan-Islamic language (279). There was even some relief at the capture of Baghdad from the Turks in 1917 (507), if only because Shi'ite Muslim soldiers could then pray at shrines that were especially sacred to them.

Homesickness was a more widespread and serious problem; unsurprisingly, given the vast cultural gulf between France and India. Wishful rumours periodically circulated that the troops were going home – that leave to India would be opened (410), that the men would not have to winter in France again (380), or that all the troops would be sent back to India (38, 64, 65, 376, 450). In the summer of 1917, three years into the war, rumours spread that the troops would be able to disengage, several men apparently not realizing that they had enlisted for three years or for the duration of the war. Many relatives wrote letters lamenting the long separation (381), imploring soldiers to return on leave (563, 601, 612) or for marriage (556), and sometimes petitioning officers on behalf of their menfolk (599). In general, the soldiers wrote sensible, patient replies, explaining that their return on leave would be impossible (278, 328, 418, 521, 526, 531, 622, 642), or that it would be shameful to return without first obtaining victory (289, 416). But the prayers for victory contained in many letters were also prayers for the safe return of soldiers to India (153, 248, 437, 478, 519, 605, 615, 640, 646).

Leave to India was eventually opened at the end of 1916, but only for those who had been in France for more than two years (441, 443). Men were permitted to stay three months from the date of their disembarkation in India (435); roughly one man in twenty was eligible.

As the war progressed, the growing pressure to find recruits put another strain on the Indian military system. By the autumn of 1916, it had become official policy that Indian units should relieve British divisions in secondary theatres, thus allowing the British Army to concentrate on the Western Front. To do this, the Indian Army had to be expanded.

Several measures were tried in order to procure the necessary men. An enlistment bounty of Rs.50 was introduced in June 1917 to encourage recruits (609), but this failed to have much impact. More drastic steps were taken. The height and weight requirements were lowered, to make more men eligible for military service. Communities with little or no previous association with the Army were tapped for recruits, new districts being opened up to the recruiting officer (250). This policy, combined with that of transferring men between regiments (120), disrupted the traditional composition of Army units, many of which had for a long time been linked to particular castes and districts. Most soldiers resented this disruption (371, 653), either because they feared that their own caste might lose out (362, 440), or because they might end up with unsympathetic (296, 366) or unfamiliar (258) officers.

From the autumn of 1916, various forms of coercion were also used to secure recruits (444). The Government of India discussed conscription, but preferred to employ informal methods of compulsion, especially in the Punjab. For example, Indian officials were told to produce a given quota of men on pain of losing their posts if they failed (625, 631). Some men were simply kidnapped, or their womenfolk held hostage until the men enlisted. After the war, the authoritarian Governor of the Punjab, Michael O'Dwyer, was even accused of using 'terrorist methods' to find recruits. He fought and won a libel case over the phrase, but there remained no doubt that forcible recruitment was widely resented.

The soldiers wrote so extensively about the war partly because they were immediately embroiled in it, and partly because, for most of them, it was easily the most traumatic event thus far in their lives. But their letters illuminate things other than the war. Most obviously, the letters provide raw material for a look at the later colonial Punjab 'from below' – that is, with the experiences and values of subordinate groups at the foreground of the historian's concerns. The letters open a window onto the attitudes of the Punjabi middle peasantry, who made up most of the Army.

I do not propose here to examine the complex arguments which surround the question 'Is a "history from below" really possible?' Suffice it to note that attempts to approach history 'from below' are – especially in the colonial context – normally hampered by the problem of finding sources generated by the 'subaltern' or subordinate classes themselves. Historians typically have to recover the experience and values of marginal groups by making inferences drawn from their recorded actions, or by deconstructing texts written by and for the colonial elite. The significance of the soldiers' letters therefore lies partly in the simple fact of their existence: they allow us to read (admittedly at several removes) the words of the illiterate, and to hear the voices of those who were (at least from the point of view of historical records) normally voiceless.

The vast majority of the letters to or from the Indian Expeditionary Force in France contained nothing but personal or family references (99, 185). As the Head Censor remarked, most of the letters were, 'from a censorial or political point of view, quite colourless'. But this lack of 'colour' is, of course, precisely what makes the letters of such potential interest to historians of India, since personal and family references produced by the peasantry themselves are otherwise largely absent from much of the documentary record.

The letters hint at the affective life of peasant marriages and family relationships. Pathans discussed buying and selling wives, apparently with more feeling for their own *izzat* than for the women concerned (182, 219). One Rajput woman wrote to her husband, for years, in touchingly devoted if distinctly subordinate terms (206, 487). But conjugal reproaches, on both sides, became more typical as the war dragged on. Wives began to resent their husbands' continued absence (244, 429). Family allowances were a frequent cause of dispute between soldiers and their people at home (386, 390, 502). For their part, men feared losing *izzat* as their marriages back home collapsed, perhaps because of adultery (354). 'All the women are rampant', remarked one correspondent in India, perhaps with distressing accuracy (302). Some Muslim troops specifically instructed writers to say nothing about women (336, 644) because the censor should not know what happens 'behind the purdah' (475). But many men still discussed personal matters with some frankness.

Many letters from India talked about prevailing agricultural conditions, and the fortune of the season's crops. Soldiers worried about the material well-being of the families they had left behind; unsurprisingly enough, when they were hearing about drought (214, 231, 243), high prices (149) and raids by dacoits (14, 228). Plague and scarcity afflicted the Punjab in the spring and summer of 1915 (39, 42, 53, 55, 124), which clearly worried the troops (56). Punjabi soldiers certainly seemed anxious for more information (112). These letters are a pointed reminder that the Indian Army was mainly an organization of peasants in uniform, and that peasant concerns and mentalities were far from abandoned on enlistment.

Prominent in the sepoys' experience during the war, was an encounter, sometimes culturally unsettling, with Europe and with Europeans. Many soldiers had very positive reactions to the French with whom they were billeted. They admired their beauty (207, 359) and generosity (451), and tried to learn the language. One man praised his French host's willingness to prepare food according to the rules of Islam (449). Several soldiers exhorted Indian civilians to follow the example of bereaved French men (470) and women (79, 485), who faced loss with great stoicism. Sepoys seem to have developed especially warm feelings towards the French women who acted as surrogate mothers to them (24, 212, 294).

France itself attracted admiring comments, for the beauty of its countryside (85) and for the richness of its agriculture (121, 255). Sepoys who went on leave came back astonished at the wealth of European cities (293), especially Paris (260, 374). In general, soldiers explained Europe's great wealth and apparent social harmony in terms of extensive popular education (205, 358, 592), and especially the education of Western women. The encounter seems to have given the cause of female education in India a boost; after seeing the example of European women, several sepoys urged that their own womenfolk be sent to school (448, 654).

The encounter with Europe gave sepoys some practical insight into European mores. But soldiers' perceptions were often clouded by occidentalism – the tendency to essentialize the West as much more 'Western' and much less 'traditional' than it really was (355). This tendency was particularly marked in their perceptions of European gender roles (311). The sepoys imagined Western marriages as conforming to an occidental ideal type: entirely unarranged, companionate, harmonious and non-violent (334, 656). Or, alternatively, they regarded Western women as 'shameless' because they mingled so freely with men (184, 247).

Any sexual association between Indian men and white women, however, touched very raw British nerve endings. Inter-racial sex was a particularly fraught area of colonial consciousness, which for decades had been fed by fantasies of lascivious sepoys raping, then dismembering, white women during the 1857 mutiny. Even consensual sexual relations between sepoys and white women would, it was thought, damage the *izzat* of European women, and would be, in the delicate words of the Head Censor, 'most detrimental to the prestige and spirit of European rule in India'. The British at first attempted to keep the Indian wounded in England on a very tight rein, to prevent them socializing with white women; but the rules were later relaxed because of the resentment they caused. The scruples were not all on one side: some Muslim soldiers wrote home assuring their families that they would not 'pollute' themselves by having sex with Christian women (172, 200). But most soldiers were prepared to seek sexual comfort where they could (171). Some asked for love potions (269); many received what the Head Censor called 'violently amatory' letters from French women.

Love affairs were one thing, marriage was another. Even when the military rules were relaxed to permit marriages between sepoys and Frenchwomen, soldiers remained wary of offending their families by marrying Christians (424). The example of Mahomed Khan, a trooper in the 6th Cavalry, is instructive. His marriage to a Frenchwoman in April 1917 surprised and upset his comrades (492) and family (568), who feared for his religion. He was reduced to claiming that he had married only on the express orders of the King (535).

The encounter with Europe encouraged sepoys to draw comparisons with India in which India seems to have come off rather badly (15, 135, 209, 462, 505). Sepoys came to regard India as backward (58), remarking, for example, on the unreliability of Indian newspapers compared with those in Europe (80). Above all, the sepoys became ashamed of India's relative poverty. They variously attributed this to excessive spending on ritual occasions (572, 655), to arranged marriages, to child marriage (283) or, most often, to poor education (273). The 'India' that they wrote about, however, was very much a geographical expression, and one that was not central to a sepoy's main sense of self. Even in Europe, the sepoys left little evidence that they imagined themselves to be primarily 'Indians'. Letters remarking that their actions would bring fame to 'the whole of Hindustan' (316) or to 'mother India' (26) were very rare.

Other silences were equally deafening. Prominent people never mentioned in the letters read like a political *Who's Who* of the First World War: Woodrow Wilson, Lloyd George, Herbert Asquith, Lenin, Trotsky and Gandhi are among the many who failed to make an impression. However, the soldiers were not ill-informed; they followed the military course of the war, if at a slightly garbled distance. Their letters mention the entry of Italy into the war (70), the Brusilov offensive in Galicia (333, 365), the Battle of Jutland (326), the siege and surrender of Kut-al-Amara (298, 304), the death of Edith Cavell (292), the introduction of conscription in Britain (236), and the cruise of the German ship *Emden* in the Bay of Bengal (2). But the soldiers never discussed war aims or international politics, except in cases which, for Muslims, had an obviously 'Islamic' angle, such as the revolt of the Sharif of Mecca, or the entry of Turkey into the war.

Nor were the troops aware of, or interested in, Indian 'high' politics. The only Indian politician ever mentioned was Maulana Azad, and then only once, and in a more 'Muslim' than political context (603). There were a couple of references to the Muslim League (453, 619), and one to Edwin Montagu's trip to India in 1917, but the writer of this letter (from India to France) seems to have been too well-educated to have been a soldier (616). Two men voiced a hope for self-government after the war, but neither were soldiers: one was a labourer (637) and the other was, again, clearly an educated man (388). The only letter which could in any way be described as subversively 'nationalist' was written by a storekeeper (148). Clearly, the soldiers had an incentive not to talk about 'politics' in a context in which almost any form of political activity was seen as seditious. But even when soldiers *were* overtly expressing dissent, they did not do so in 'nationalist' terms. Nationalism was simply not the sort of political language they would have used, for its vocabulary was not then culturally accessible to the Punjabi peasantry.

The sepoys also had surprisingly little sense of their place within Allied or Imperial political and military structures. Although they wrote a great deal about France, they never mentioned the French Army. Nor did they talk much about their British comrades (356, 400; possibly 361), a near-silence which seems all the more remarkable when it is remembered that British and Indians were brigaded together, and fought together on the battlefield. The troops of the white dominions, and Africans serving in France, were equally disregarded. On the basis of this evidence, it would have been difficult for the sepoys to have developed a coherent anti-colonial mentality, if only because they seemed to have had little coherent awareness of being part of the wider British Empire.

The sepoys' attitudes to their British officers are difficult to fathom, mainly for lack of evidence. As already observed, the soldiers did mention British officers, but normally in anodyne and general terms. Only very few British officers were ever mentioned by name (162, 220, 238, 319), and then, typically, when there was a problem (106, 299, 440, 570). This reticence perhaps owed something to the very high casualty rate among British officers, which meant that the Indian soldiers were often serving under men that they did not know. It certainly suggests that the bond between British officers and Indian men was not as close as the former often liked to assume. Lord Kitchener provided one exception to this general picture of indifference, his death at sea in June 1916 being the occasion for several laments (330, 332). As a former Commander-in-Chief of the Indian Army, he might have been an important figurehead.

More than any loyalty to their British officers, the soldiers were motivated by an abstract sense of duty to the Sirkar, or government. Some letters seem to overstate this sense of obligation, perhaps having been written with their impact on the recipient (or the censor) more than usually in mind (650). Nevertheless, the Sirkar was typically seen as the father of the people, to whom the soldiers had filial obligations (564). As the soldiers saw it, their central duty – to fight in wartime – derived mainly from their receipt of material goods from the government (7, 573, 585). Soldiers often expressed this relationship in terms of having 'eaten the salt' of the Sirkar (125). The performance of duty, in return for 'salt', was part of a system of deepening reciprocity. Once they had performed the essential duty of military service, soldiers felt that their families should then be exempt from other duties, such as providing war contributions (538, 639), or that the Sirkar should reward them in other ways (69, 465); for example, by providing civil appointments (555). The duty of finding recruits was also thought to deserve a reward (319). Soldiers' families occasionally expressed a more generalized sense of the value of the British Raj (515), but this feeling was typically confined to those with some education (284).

More significant still in the sepoys' mental universe was the person of the King-Emperor, who is mentioned in the letters far more than any other individual. Indian soldiers had a very clear sense of personal duty to the King (3, 634) and suggested that, in performing this duty, they could almost become his near relatives (290). These expressions of loyalty to the King were, of course, partly self-interested:

there was no harm in trying to impress the censor (141) or in obtaining helpful publicity (134). Recurring phrases also might have owed something to the formulaic writing of scribes; but it is surely significant that soldiers chose one 'royal' formula rather than other, equally acceptable, 'Indian' or 'nationalist' ones. The mention of the King is simply too frequent and too heartfelt to be reducible to calculated self-interest or scribal formulae. Soldiers greatly enjoyed meeting the King (126, 286), or receiving letters from him (514). They admired his ability to recognize people who had attended him during the 1911 Delhi Durbar; they gave thanks for the justice of his reign (610), and believed they could earn religious merit by serving him (3, 25). Expressions of devotion reached their greatest heights when the King-Emperor presented medals in person (130, 164). These comments about the King suggest that, in one important respect at least, the peasant-soldiers were (or had become) the very people that their colonial masters wished them to be.

The British did what they could to take advantage of this sense of loyalty to the monarch. One tactic was to set aside Brighton Pavilion, a former royal residence, as a hospital for Indian soldiers. The site was deliberately chosen for its royal connections (see Plate 4), and the soldiers seem to have appreciated the gesture (63). Another device was to ensure that every Indian soldier received a picture of the King as a New Year's present in January 1917, along with improvements in pay and allowances. Again, this went down very well (472, 483).

It should be stressed, however, that the soldiers' loyalty to the King was directed very much at his person, in direct relation to the troops themselves; most soldiers either did not know, or did not seem to care, that George V was British, and was also King of Great Britain, and Head of State for the rest of the Empire.

Indian soldiers were also surprisingly venomous about the King's enemies. Although they had great respect for the fighting power of the German Army (18, 52), the Indians otherwise held the Germans in contempt. Some sepoys suggested that the German cause was unjust (578), and that the Germans were tyrants (426) or even 'savages' (136). Others drew attention to German atrocities (213), such as the first use of poison gas (76). Indian soldiers were especially outraged by the destruction of fruit groves and farmland by the Germans in the spring of 1917, during the German Army's withdrawal to the Hindenburg Line. Many sepoys, themselves from cultivating communities, lamented the devastation (522, 534, 545). Even allowing for a certain reticence caused by an awareness of the censorship, the letters show minimal evidence of pro-German sympathies (598). From the internal evidence of the letters, however, it is difficult to say whether the sepoys' views derived from propaganda or from the circumstances of the battlefield.

IV

What scholars will make of these letters remains to be seen. But, scholarship aside, the soldiers' words have a value beyond their helpfulness to the historian of later colonial India. The Head Censor, a man simply doing his (rather intrusive) job, hinted at their worth. 'The Indian correspondence constitutes a document of some psychological interest', he remarked. 'If the publication of selections should ever be permitted, a very entertaining book would result.'

Entertaining? Perhaps. Certainly eloquent, at times. Some letters possess qualities more usually associated with 'literature'. They are sharply observed, sometimes through apposite and arresting images. 'As a man climbs a plum tree and shakes down the plums [so that] they fall and lie in heaps, so are men here fallen', writes one man to his mother (100) – evoking the unpleasant sensation, shared by the wanderer through the autumnal orchard and the soldier on the corpse-strewn battlefield, of treading on organic matter in decay. A homesick and wounded Dogra, his courage leaking away, compares himself to 'a man who, once burnt, is afraid of a glow-worm' (88). A Pathan yearns for his exiled soldier-brother: 'when the rain of his presence falls on me again, the dust of separation which is settled on my heart will be swept away' (314).

But the letters are not just 'literature'. They derive some of their emotional power from the fact that we know that they are 'real' eyewitness accounts: they say what was lived and felt in ways which literature can only simulate.

And part of what the soldiers lived and felt was the closeness of death, in the very intimate form it took on the Western Front in the Great War. For the soldiers, death was all around, not only on the battlefield, but pushed unavoidably to the centre of their concerns; and many letters are steeped in an awareness of immanent mortality. Some men even seemed to sense that their letters might become their memorial. As a wounded Sikh wrote to his brother: 'I must finish my letter ... In a few days I shall go back to the war ... If I live, I will write again' (10).

1914–15

A Muslim officer to his brother (Central India)

France   December 1914

What better occasion can I find than this to prove the loyalty of my family to the British Government? Turkey, it is true, is a Muslim power, but what has it to do with us? Turkey is nothing at all to us.[1] The men of France are beyond measure good and honourable and kind. By God, my brother, they are gentlemen to the backbone! Their manners and morals are in absolute accord with our ideas. In war they are as one with us and with the English. Our noble King knows the quality and the worth of his subjects and his Rajas alike. I give you the truth of the matter. The flag of victory will be in the hands of our British Government. Be not at all distressed. Without death there is no victory, but I am alive and very well, and I tell you truly that I will return alive to India.

1. The entry of Turkey into the war confronted Muslim soldiers (who made up some 30 per cent of the Indian Army) with a difficult choice: doing their duty to the King-Emperor might involve fighting against the Ottoman Empire, the home of the Khalifa, the spiritual head of Islam. Most soldiers decided to fight on (this writer's response, presumably written to reassure his family, is fairly typical) but there were some discipline problems. By 1915, for example, the rate of desertion among Pathans (particularly those from Afghanistan) reached alarming proportions. See No. 274. There were also three mutinies in Muslim units – the 130th Baluchis at Rangoon, the 5th Light Infantry at Singapore and the 15th Lancers at Basra. See Nos. 20, 21, 40, 259 and 276, but contrast No. 275.

2

A Garrison Gunner (Sikh) to a relative (France)

China   3rd December 1914

The English have suffered severely. Nothing is put into the news, but we know a good deal from day to day. The German ship *Emden* has sunk forty English ships near this land, and is sinking all the seventy English ships of war. She has not been much damaged although she gets little help.[1] The English have eight kings helping them, the Germans three. We hear that our king has been taken prisoner. Germany said that if she were paid a *lakh* of rupees by five o'clock on the first of the month, she would release the king. The money was paid, but Germany refuses to let him go. I have written only a little, but there is much more for you to think of.

1. The German light cruiser *Emden,* known as 'The Swan of the East' was built at Danzig in 1908. Between September and November 1914, she sank fifteen Allied merchantmen and captured eight more, mainly in the Bay of Bengal and the Indian Ocean. She was herself sunk, by the Australian cruiser *Sydney*, off the Cocos Keeling Islands on 9th November 1914.

3

An unknown writer to a Jemadar (34th Sikh Pioneers, France)

Gobind Garh   [Urdu]
Punjab   [early January 1915?]

I was distressed to hear that you had been wounded. But God will have pity. Keep your thoughts fixed on the Almighty and show your loyalty to the Government and to King George V. It is every man's duty to fulfil his obligations towards God, by rendering the dues of loyalty to his King. If in rendering the dues of loyalty he must yield his life, let him be ready to make even that sacrifice. It is acceptable in the sight of God, that a man pay the due of loyalty to his King. God grant you life and happiness. Those heroes who have added lustre to the service of their country and King, let them offer this prayer before God, that victory may be the portion of their King, and let them show the whole world how brave the people of India can be. The final prayer of this humble one before God Almighty is this – that God may make bright the heroes of Hindustan in the eyes of the world and with his healing hand may soften the sufferings of the wounded and restore them to health, so that they may go back to the field of battle and render the dues of loyalty to their King of peace, the King of kings, George V, and secure the victory for him.[1]

1. See Nos. 7, 198 and 483 for other examples of the many prayers for the King's victory.

4

Subedar-Major [Sardar Bahadur Gugan] (6th Jats, 50) to a friend (India)

[Hindi]
Brighton Hospital   [early January 1915?]

We are in England. It is a very fine country. The inhabitants are very amiable and are very kind to us, so much so that our own people could not be as much so. The food, the clothes and the buildings are very fine. Everything is such as one would not see even in a dream. One should regard it as fairyland. The heart cannot be satiated with seeing the sights, for there is no other place like this in the world. It is as if one were in the next world. It cannot be described. A motor car comes to take us out. The King and Queen talked with us for a long time. I have never been so happy in my life as I am here.

5

A Pathan to a friend in the 57th Rifles (France)

40th Rifles   [Urdu]
Hong Kong   13th January 1915

Return this letter signed and with your thumb impression on it, on the very letter itself. Of the dead say 'so and so sends you greeting' and of the wounded say 'greetings from so and so'.[1]

1. Many letters contain similar instructions for encoding messages. See Nos. 28, 43, 60, 73, 151, 154, 183 and 195, among others. The censor easily deciphered most of them.

6

A Garhwali to his father

[39th Garhwal Rifles?]   [Garhwali]
France   14th January 1915

It is very hard to endure the bombs, father. It will be difficult for anyone to survive and come back safe and sound from the war. The son who is very lucky will see his father and mother, otherwise who can do this? There is no confidence of survival. The bullets and cannon-balls come down like snow. The mud is up to a man's middle. The distance between us and the enemy is fifty paces. Since I have been here the enemy has remained in his trenches and we in ours. Neither side has advanced at all. The Germans are very cunning. The numbers that have fallen cannot be counted.

7

A wounded Sikh to his brother (Amritsar District, Punjab)

England

[Gurmukhi]
15th January 1915

Brother, I fell ill with pneumonia and have come away from the war. In this country it rains a great deal: always day and night it rains. So pneumonia is very rife. Now I am quite well and there is no occasion for any kind of anxiety ... If any of us is wounded, or is otherwise ill, Government or someone else always treats him very kindly. Our Government takes great care of us, and we too will be loyal and fight. You must give the Government all the help it requires. Now look, you my brother, our father the King-Emperor of India needs us and any of us who refuses to help him in his need should be counted among the most polluted sinners. It is our first duty to show our loyal gratitude to Government.

8

A Parsi to a lady friend (India)

A hospital ship

[Gujerati]
16th January 1915

I am not in a position to write adequately about the people and the country here. What beautiful cities, pleasant gardens, rivers, streams, houses, shops, roads, carriages, cows, horses, fowls and ducks! Whatever one sees is different from our country. What manners, what conduct, what discipline, etiquette and energy! The war has absorbed everyone's attention and filled all minds. They are greatly impressed by the Indian troops and by the men from India. They show extraordinary affection and even the women and children express unbounded delight. When we first reached England, the people came to the steamer and joyfully mingled with us. When we used to go out for walks at Avonmouth the people used to rush out of their houses to '*salaam*' us. We played with the children and kissed them. Many women, young and old, tried to shake our hands. Whatever has been written in the Indian press about our welcome is quite accurate. There is no difference made in our treatment here. Once having come here our people will never want to return. These people have a beautiful colour, and it is impossible to describe the beauty of the children (whom personally I love the best). I wish only that I had such a child. After looking at the two pictures of their children which I enclose, can you not see that it becomes difficult for us to return?

9

A father, whose son has been wounded, to a British officer

India

[Urdu]
14th January 1915

My son has given full proof of his loyalty. He went six or seven times into action. Now he has been wounded. I trust that your honour of your kindness will have him sent back to the depot, so that he may be well-rubbed with oil and make his appearance in the mosque. When he is well, he can be set to train the recruits or sent on recruiting duty, if he is able to walk. I make this request at the insistence of his mother who has been ill and helpless since we heard of his wound.

10

A wounded Sikh to his brother (Punjab)

Milton Hospital
England

[Urdu]
18th January 1915

I am well and pray ever for your welfare. My dear brother, this is a very fine country. They have an excellent way of doing things, and there is such beauty in the country. There is no doubt about it. Very many people come to see us, and one cannot tell the lord from the beggar. All are alike and they do everything with great intelligence and skill. They use dogs to drive their animals (that is cattle) and to extract butter from milk.[1] They grind wheat and do everything by machinery, and thresh the straw – all by machinery. And they plough with horses. As for the shopkeepers, they are very honest and make no difference in their prices. Whether it be a child or a grown man, they ask they same price of everyone. There is no theft or dishonesty. The shops remain open all day long and never a penny is stolen. And if a man commits theft they inflict a very severe punishment on him. They fix him alive and upright to a stake and fasten his hands with nails, and there he dies.[2] So nobody commits theft. And the buildings (that is the houses) are very, very fine indeed. Each house has at least seven storeys and the workmanship that they put into them is beyond description. You many look at it all day and still not satisfy the desire of your heart to see. And they are very rich and full of intelligence. Even the children speak well. And they deal with one another in very brotherly fashion. And there is no doubt of their cleanliness: they are very clean. And they eat with wonderful skill and daintiness. The boys and girls go to school from their earliest years to be educated, and there are many Indians here who are here for their education.

My dear brother, I have received a letter from home and after reading over the earlier letter my heart was filled with such happiness to describe makes the earth hard and the heavens high [sic]. My dear brother, when I read the letter and heard all about the village I was quite overjoyed ...

My dear brother, I must finish my letter. For here I am as a king, but the war is still going on. Hundreds and thousands are engaged and it goes on day after day ... There can be no confidence of life or of seeing again the dear children or of seeing you once more. For in a few days I shall go back to the war. When shall come the day when I shall see again my dear children? When shall I see you? Well, my brother, do not be anxious. We shall see what will come of it. My love to the dear children and greetings to all my friends. If I live I will write again.

1. The ingenious inhabitants of rural Flanders obtained much of their butter from dog-powered churns. See No. 255.
2. This is a garbled, if touching, reference to the wayside Calvaries that were a common sight in Northern France.

11

A wounded Sikh to his father

Brighton Hospital

[Gurmukhi]
18th January 1915

Tell my mother not to go wandering madly because her son, my brother, is dead. To be born and to die is God's order. Some day we must die, sooner or later, and if I die here, who will remember me? It is a fine thing to die far from home. A saint said this, and, as he was a good man, it must be true.

12

A wounded Sikh to his brother (Amritsar District, Punjab)

New Milton Hospital   [Gurmukhi]
England   21st January 1915

I pray the Guru that I may return to my home. I do not know for certain, but I expect so. For I was hit on my trigger finger and the third part of it is cut off.[1] So I hope that I shall return neither to the battle nor to the trench. I have twice escaped the bullet and am ready to do loyal service again. I am certain that I shall not die until I am again in my country. Since none of us fear death, the Guru has hardened our hearts to stone. Not one of us who went into battle took any thought of his home or his brothers. Every one of us repeated the name of the Guru. It is good for a man to die in battle in this way. He goes to Heaven. So all of us at that time kept in our hearts a prayer to the Guru. For those who die thus, Heaven is completely fulfilled. Those who die in their villages, they die among their children and brothers. For them Heaven is incomplete.[2] At this time, none of us cherish any earthly love. We shall all come home and then we shall enjoy such love. Whom God preserves, He preserves in this manner, even as the Guru preserved the cat. The cat has had kittens in the potter's kiln. The potter comes and lights the kiln. Then the poor cat comes and sits beside the burning kiln. The potter says in his heart 'why does this cat sit here?' He does not know that the cat has kittens there. The kiln is red hot. Then the potter sees the kittens still alive. He is astonished. The pots are still unbaked. The potter marvels at the power of God. Thus, if the Guru's will be to preserve me, he will preserve me. The battle is beginning and men are dying like maggots. No one can count them – not in thousands but in hundreds and thousands of thousands. No one can count them.

1. This injury may well have been self-inflicted, like many wounds to the hand. See Greenhut, 'Imperial Reserve: The Indian Corps on the Western Front, 1914–15', pp. 57–8.
2. He means that those who die in battle will go straight to Heaven, ending the cycle of death and rebirth, while those who die at home will be reborn. See Nos. 17, 118 and 198 for similar comments.

13

A wounded Punjabi Rajput to a relative (India)

England

[Urdu]
29th January 1915

Do not think that this is war. This is not war. It is the ending of the world. This is just such a war as was related in the Mahabharata about our forefathers.[1]

1. Hindu soldiers often drew this parallel when attempting to convey the scale of the fighting which they had witnessed. See Nos. 23 and 41. Muslims usually chose the image of Karbala. See No. 56.

14

A Khatri Sikh to a friend (France, regiment unstated)

[Punjab]
India

[Gurmukhi]
30th January 1915

Here in the Punjab dacoities have become very common. The people in their sin do not remember that the Government which protects us is fighting an enemy. They are getting up a mutiny [*ghadr*] and what trouble is brought upon the Government! We pity their ignorance. The Lord will give them sense. In one week there were fifteen dacoities. When will God give peace? The Government has made many arrests and in the investigations it was discovered that the dacoits were men who had been turned back from America.[1]

1. The discrimination and racial prejudice endured by Sikh emigrants to Canada was becoming a sensitive political issue immediately before the war. In May 1914, the Japanese steamer *Komagata Maru* arrived in Vancouver with 376 emigrants. They were refused entry, and in July the ship left for India. On arrival in Calcutta, the passengers refused to be shipped straight to the Punjab; eighteen of them were killed when the police opened fire. Some of them later joined with other returning emigrants to carry out a series of robberies, associated with the revolutionary Ghadrite movement.

15

A Sub-Assistant Surgeon (Hindu) to a friend (Peshawar District, NWFP)

A hospital ship   [Hindi and Urdu; some English]
England   [late January or early February 1915?]

I have received only one letter from you for which I have already thanked you. Why only one? You ought to write to me every week or at least every fortnight.

Today I am sending you a bundle of newspapers as samples by packet post. You will see from them how up-to-date the papers of this country are. For example, the events of this evening are printed during the night and tomorrow morning will be in the hands of the people in every corner of the country. The papers have an enormous circulation. You may rely on almost everything being reported in different papers ... Even the working classes read the papers and keep themselves informed of the state of affairs in their country and the events of the war. *The Times* is the best of all the newspapers. It has raised a subscription of a million [pounds] (that is a *crore* and a half of rupees) for its relief fund. This paper devotes its efforts to the advancement of patriotism and the service of the nation and not to squabbling with its fellows. The papers here do not quail-fight as do the papers of the Punjab.[1]

Further, in the papers, pictures of the scenes of events appear with the news. The mind is amazed when one sees their cleverness. Whenever a ship sinks, a printed picture of it appears in the papers.

Besides the newspapers, proclamations and the attractions of theatre-folk excite the people. They arouse the women and stir up the children all for the profit of the nation and give a stimulus to recruiting.

When one considers this country and these people in comparison with our own country and our own people one cannot but be distressed.[2] Our country is very poor and feeble and its lot is very depressed. Our people copy the faults of the British nation and leave its good qualities alone. We shall never advance ourselves merely by wearing trousers and hats and smoking cigarettes and drinking wine. In fact they have a real moral superiority. They are energetic. We are poor and hunger for ease. They limit their leisure, do their work justly and do it well. They do not follow their own inclinations, but obey their superior officers and masters. They avoid idle chatter. Their delight is cleanliness. Even a sweeper will not remain in a bare house. He will adorn it with some green plants and flowers and will take pains to improve his condition. Never under any circumstances do they tell lies. As for shopkeepers, everything has a fixed price. You may take it or leave it as you please. They do not marry until they have reached maturity. For a lad of sixteen to marry and beget children is looked upon with disapproval. You will never find a case of a boy leaving school and going to college who is already the father of children. Our boys are spoilt by our evil customs.

There is a carpenter who works on our ship, who gets seven shillings a day. He is over thirty. When I asked him, he told me that he was not yet married. I asked him 'why not?' and he answered that his old mother was still alive. So long as she lived, he would not marry, for two women could not live in one house, and he would not leave his mother. Therefore he could not marry. The children are very pretty and well-mannered. They meet a foreigner in a very pleasant fashion. Here in front of every house and every shop are fixed great big glass panes – as it were doors of glass. I could not help thinking as I walked along the other day that if these were in our country the children would soon put more stones through them. Here little, little children smaller than my Madan come boldly up to strangers and put out their hands to shake. The children are very clean. You never see any of them eating or easing himself in the public streets.

If a woman is walking alone and does not wish to speak to anyone, no matter whether she be respectable or not, it is a breach of good manners to talk to her first. You must wait till you are invited. This is very different from India where a lady cannot venture unescorted into any street.

1. See Nos. 80 and 240 for similar remarks about the quality of British newspapers.
2. For another unfavourable comparison of India to Europe see No. 135.

16

A Pathan (regiment unstated) to a Dafedar (19th Lancers, France)

Colombo   [Urdu and Pashtu]
[Ceylon]   4th February 1915

[Urdu] Such a time as this comes upon brave young men. In the bravery of youth you must not lose your spirit. Whatever is fated of God, that comes to pass.

[Pashtu] These words that I have written above I have written only for this purpose: that if any great folk open the letter, they may be pleased. So far as possible, look after your life and your brother's life. This is not such a war [as warrants you taking unnecessary risks] and to preserve your life is your duty. This is my prayer – that God may bring you both home in safety.[1]

1. The writer of this letter is clearly aware of the censorship, and wants to evade it. He assumes the censor can understand Urdu (the main language of communication in the Indian Army) and therefore adds his real message in Pashtu. 'Not such a war' means 'not a religious war'.

17

A Gurkha to Jemadar Budhiman Gurung (1/1st Gurkhas, France)

2/1st Gurkhas
Chitral   [Gurkhali]
[NWFP]   7th February 1915

Brother, this is the opportunity to show your worth. To give help to your family
and render aid to Government, fight well, kill your enemy and do not let him attain
his object. If you die, you will make a name up to seven forefathers and will go
straight to Paradise. You will become as famous as the sun. Bravo! Bravo!

18

A South Indian Muslim to a friend (India)

                                                      [Urdu]
A hospital ship   9th February 1915

The war is a calamity on three worlds and has caused me to cross the seas and
live here. The cold is so great that it cannot be described. Snow falls day and night
and covers the ground to a depth of two feet. We have not seen the sun for four
months. Thus we are sacrificed. I have neither sleep by night nor ease by day. In
the world there could never have been such a war before, nor will there be again.
It is sad that God who has so much power and who sent the flood should have
brought such a day to pass. He has given them [the Germans] such a spirit that it
cannot be described. He has made them fowls of the air, dragons of the earth and
poisonous crocodiles of the sea. And he has given them such skill that, when we
encounter their deceitful bayonets, they set light to some substance which causes
a suffocating vapour, and then they attack. How can I describe this? The like will
never happen in the world again that seven powers shall be confronted by ten. We
have often heard before that in war they fired cannon from seven or eight miles
and attacked from the same distance, but in this modern war they fight from 100
or 150 yards and not more. If war has become like stone throwing, why should
there not be another flood? If God enables me to see my people again, I shall look
upon it as a new life.

19

A wounded Garhwali to his elder brother (India)

[Hindi]
England   12th February 1915

The King's people are powerful. But victory has not yet been obtained. This is because the English people are not so numerous as the others. The English have two million men, the Germans five million two hundred thousand, and the Russians five million four hundred thousand. All the kings are powerful, especially the Russian and German Emperors. Twelve kings are fighting, but as yet no victory has been achieved.

The fighting is of five kinds. First, there are the aeroplanes which move about dropping bombs and causing great havoc. They are like the great bird of Vishnu[1] in the sky. Next is the battle of the cannon which is earth-splitting. Then there is the fighting on the sea, of which the fashion is this: that the ships remain concealed in the parts of the sea and then, watching their opportunity, the English fire at the Germans and the Germans at the English. The Germans have caused about four thousand men to be drowned in the sea and have made great destruction. In the fighting with rifles the bullets fall fast like hail.

My dear brother, great damage has [been] caused to India. Nearly two hundred thousand men have been killed. About four thousand have lost arms or legs and many have lost their sight. In India, three quarters of the population will be women and only one quarter men. Here the state of things is such that all the world over there will be two women for each man. This you must think over till you understand it.[2] All the kings have been ruined. Here an extraordinary amount of rain falls and the mens' feet become frost-bitten from the snow. Six months have passed since I saw the sun, because there is constant rain and clouds.

1. Each of the major Hindu deities is traditionally associated with a steed. That of Vishnu was Garuda, a mythical eagle.
2. In other words, there is a deeper meaning.

Plate 1. Recruit at Gorakhpur Recruiting Depot.

Plate 2. Battle of Messines, October 1914. Muslim sepoys of the 129th Baluchis line an improvised trench on the outskirts of Wytschaete.

Plate 3. Indian stretcher bearers bringing in one of their wounded officers, near Ginchy, 14 September 1916.

Plate 4. 'Our hospital is in the place where the King used to have his throne' (Letter No. 63). Convalescent Indian soldiers in Brighton Pavilion.

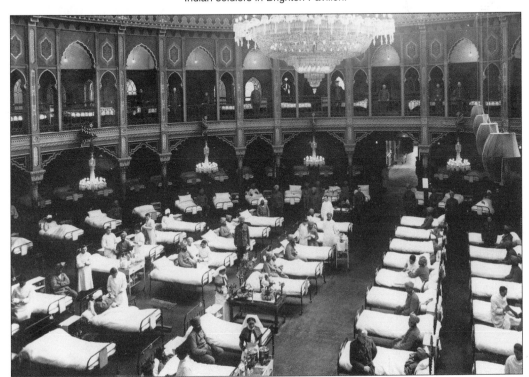

Plate 5. Wounded Gurkha, *c.*1915.

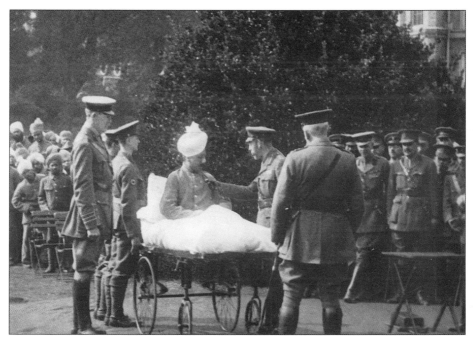

Plate 6. 'By the great, great, great kindness of God, the King with his royal hand has given me the decoration of the Victoria Cross .... The desire of my heart is accomplished.' (Letter No.130). George V awarding a medal to a badly-wounded Indian soldier, Brighton Pavilion.

Plate 7. Indian officers visit the Royal Mews, and examine the King-Emperor's state coach.

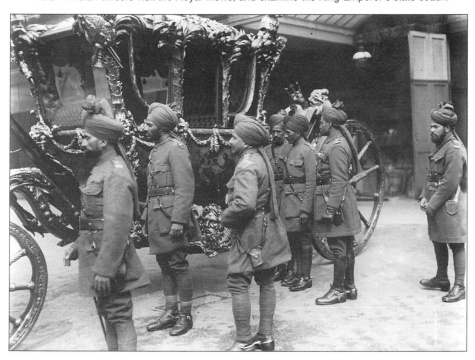

Plates 8 and 9. 'What I saw in the course of the advance I shall never forget.' (Letter No. 356) The 20th Deccan Horse in Carnoy Valley, near Mametz, hours before their attack on 14 July 1916.

Plate 10. Slaughtering goats according to religious custom. The area on the right was reserved for Hindus (and Sikhs), that on the left for Muslims. Curious British troops look on.

Plate 11. Indian barber at work, Indian Cavalry Camp, near Querrieu, 29 July 1916.

Plates 12 and 13. Men of 9th Hodson's Horse near Vraignes, April 1917.

20

A non-Afridi Pathan to a friend (129th Rifles, France)

Peshawar [Urdu]
[NWFP] 13th February 1915

If there is any excitement in your direction, write to Karachi and tell me of it. This is my most earnest injunction. As for the 130th Baluchis, the regiment of which two companies have gone from Rangoon to the Andamans, one jemadar and one havildar have been shot.[1] There is great excitement about this in Peshawar. Amongst the Afridi people there is a hope that their object with regard to them may be effected. That hope is this: that they may come back and be released, because the Lord Sahib of Peshawar [the Chief Commissioner for the NWFP] has assented to this. Be not anxious or distressed or troubled. For God will bring everything to rights.

1. In January 1915, three Pathan companies of the 130th Baluchis refused to embark at Rangoon when they learned that they were destined for Mesopotamia. The men had religious scruples against fighting the Turks near the Holy Places of Islam. See Nos. 21 and 40. For examples of similar problems, see Nos. 259, 274 and 276.

21

An Afridi Pathan to a friend (129th Rifles, France)

Kohat [Urdu]
[NWFP] 14th February 1915

[Five names] have taken an oath with me. We are very anxious. The 130th refused to go to the war.[1] Subedar-Major Sultan Mir [38] has been court-martialled, and all the Afridi sepoys have been put in custody. Ninety sepoys are in custody. But our *maliks* have gone to Peshawar to make a representation.

1. See Nos. 20 and 40.

22

A wounded Sikh to a brother (India)

A hospital [Gurmukhi]
England 14th February 1915

Stay in the village and carry on the work as headman. Do not go anywhere else. Think over what I say and you will understand what I mean when I say 'stay in the village'.[1]

1. He is urging his brother not to enlist.

23

A wounded Garhwali to his guru (India)

England

[Hindi]

17th February 1915

I have been wounded by a bullet in the head. The wound is slight, however. A little bit of the bone was broken above, but I am glad because my life is safe. I am fit to fight again, but what can I do? It does not rest with me. The reason is this. The Government has only a few men. Therefore they send wounded men a second time to fight.[1] Of the British troops, about three *lakhs* have been killed and about two *lakhs* wounded. Some five or six thousand men have had their hands or feet cut off. In India there remain one third men and two thirds women. Now that the fighting has begun it will go on for three years. What can be done? Great fear is on me, but a higher power must decide. Twelve kings are fighting, eight on the side of the English and four for the Germans. How much can I write about the war? It would be like writing another Mahabharata.[2] I am greatly distressed in mind.

1. Returning the wounded to the front, once they had recovered, would become a major grievance. See Nos. 24 and 68.
2. See No. 13.

24

A Sikh to his father (Punjab)

A hospital
England

[Gurmukhi]
20th February 1915

My father and mother, brothers and sisters, you call those your sons and daughters who give you money. Those who do not, you refuse to look upon and you even drag them before the law courts. Here the ladies tend us, who have been wounded, as a mother tends her child. They pour milk into our mouths, and our own parents, brothers and sisters, were we ill, would only give us water in a pot. There you see the brotherhood of religion, and here you see the brotherhood of the English, who are kind to us without any further motive. The ladies even carry off our *excreta*,[1] so kind are they; and whatsoever we have a liking for, they put it into our mouths. They wash our bed clothes every week and massage our backs when they ache from lying in bed.

They put us in motor cars and take us through the city. When, at four o'clock, we go out from the hospital, the ladies of the city give us fruit. They say 'we have never seen such men. Only have we heard of them that they are the Sikhs of India who once fought against England. Now do we see them with our own eyes as we see our sons.' They cheer us for routing the Germans. Their kings say 'brothers, what manner of men are the Indians?' The Government gives us envelopes every week.

This is a devils' war. When will it end? If I recover, I shall not remain a soldier, but serve my parents who have food enough and to spare. [Military] service is great weariness. I shall browse on the grass at home and keep myself alive. I am wounded. [Only] the man who has lost a leg or an arm returns to India.[2] My ankle is broken. I was hit twice. My life is safe, but my leg is useless.

1. In India, this ritually polluting task is performed by low-caste sweepers or Untouchables, hence the man's astonished comment.
2. In other words, the lightly wounded are returned to the trenches once they have recovered. See Nos. 68 and 129.

25

A wounded Garhwali Subedar to a friend (India)

[Hindi]
England   21st February 1915

England is a superb country with an excellent climate. Think it a great honour that we have an opportunity of showing our loyalty to our great Emperor by the sacrifice of our bodies and by the favour that is accorded to us of being present on the field of battle. Have no anxiety about my illness. If my desire is fulfilled, what is to be gained by anxiety? It is a noble fate for us to be allowed to sacrifice our bodies for our King. If our ancestors help us and God shows us favour, if we die on the battlefield in the service of our King, this is equal to entering heaven.[1] And if I am not to die, then what does it matter whether I fall sick or am wounded by bullet or sword on the field of battle? Having shown my loyalty and caused my great Emperor to be victorious I will return to my own country. In either case it is a good fate. There is no need for anxiety. If I am to die for the sake of the great Emperor, then what could be more glorious? Although I am in hospital, yet my spirit yearns for the battlefield. My prayer is that the great God will quickly make me well and give me an opportunity of showing my loyalty.

1. See Nos. 12, 17, 118 and 198 for similar comments.

26

A Tamil woman to her husband (France, regiment unspecified)

Southern India

[Urdu]
21st February 1915

I have been starving for lack of food. Money has become scarce and foodstuffs are very dear. I did not receive the present you promised to send while at Bombay. As yet I have had no remittance. The Lance Naik did not send me Rs.7.8.0. Show a brave spirit in the midst of this war of machines. Fight with all your might and come away, rifle in hand, victorious over the barbarous Germans. You will not only add glory to the name of mother India, but will also induce peace of mind, prosperity, and long life to our gracious King George V, the Emperor of India, and his subjects.

27

Mountain Gunner Kesar Singh (Sikh) to
Sepoy Dharm Singh (107th Pioneers, France)

Rawalpindi
Punjab

[Gurmukhi]
11th March 1915

The harvest is good, but grain is very dear. There is great unrest in our villages. Letters are coming from outside and the people are very frightened ... We shall perhaps go to Kohat in the hot weather, because the black [Indian?] batteries have all gone to Europe, and there is unrest among the people there [in Kohat].

28

Shahab Khan (Pathan) to his brother Abdulla Khan
(112th Infantry, Chakdara, Swat, NWFP)

Meerut Division Signalling Company
France

[Urdu]
15th March 1915

I read your letter with close attention. I read it about five times, and grasped its purport completely. Now it is enjoined upon you, that you also scan this letter with equal attention.[1] I have received a letter from your village, my brother. In it was written as follows: that your co-tenants Jallal Khan, Ahmad Din, and Rahim

Bakhsh had a quarrel and came to blows with your brothers Amir Khan, Rahmat Khan, Faqir Muhammad, Barakat Ali, and Sawar Khan.[2] First, Jallal Khan and Ahmad Din beat Barakat Ali and Sawar Khan very severely.[3] Afterwards this became known to Amir Khan, Faqir Muhammad, and Rahmat Khan. The both sides had a fine fight. Later on Rahim Bakhsh came up.[4] Where the struggle of Amir Khan together with Faqir Muhammad took place, there the struggle is still going on.[5] Perhaps you will understand this. Amir Khan and Faqir Muhammad made several appeals. All were dismissed. It was written in the letter, that all your brothers acting together had employed a very great lawyer. I hope, please God, that when the case is brought on, it will be decided. Your co-tenant Jallal Khan is a man of great valour.[6] He kept giving them all a great deal of trouble. It is expected [or hoped] that, by the grace of God, [all] will be well. I am ever making this prayer before the throne of God: 'Oh Lord of Mercy, may the case be to my brothers.' For the rest, God alone knows. As it will be, so shall we see. This too was written that Ahmad Din, Rahim Bakhsh said to Jallal Khan, 'let us make peace together'. But Jallal Khan would not agree. The appeal which has now been made and the lawyer who has now been engaged will, I hope [or expect] by the grace of God be successful. If I live, when I come back to India I will rehearse to you the whole story from beginning to end, like the book of the *Arabian Nights*.

1. He asks him to take care because the letter contains a coded history of the war. His efforts were redundant, however. Generalized information of this nature would not normally be prevented from reaching its intended recipient. Furthermore, the censor deciphered most of the letter (of which this is merely an extract). For codes in general, see note to No. 5.
2. Each of the participants in the 'village feud' represents one of the warring powers. Jallal Khan is Germany; Ahmad Din is Austria; Rahim Bakhsh is Turkey (Roum); Amir Khan is Britain (Angers); Rahmat Khan is Russia; Faqir Muhammad is France; Barakat Ali is Belgium; and Sarwar Khan is Serbia.
3. 'Germany and Austria defeated Belgium and Serbia'.
4. 'Then Turkey joined the war'.
5. 'Fighting continues on the Western Front'.
6. 'The German troops fight very bravely'.

29

Bigya Singh (Garhwali) to a friend (Garhwal District, UP?)

[39th Garhwal Rifles]   [Garhwali]
France   15th March 1915

And our regiment has exhibited great bravery. The fame of the Garhwalis is now higher than the skies. One of the Garhwalis, a havildar, has won the honour of the

Victoria Cross and, having made the reputation of his family for three generations, has arrived in Lansdowne.[1]

1. He is probably referring to Naik Darwan Sing Negi of the 1st Battalion, who won the award for an action at Festubert on 23rd November 1914. Although wounded twice in the head and once in the arm, and streaming blood, he bombed his way along a German trench, helping to capture over a hundred men. His return to Lansdowne, the regimental centre, on the border of the Garhwal district, was probably for the purpose of recruiting. Rifleman Gobar Sing Negi, of the 2nd Battalion, the Garhwal Regiment, was awarded a posthumous VC for a similar action at Neuve Chapelle on 10th March 1915. Mason, *A Matter of Honour*, pp. 418–20; Willcocks, *With the Indians*, pp. 132, 210–11. For a British soldier's view of the Garhwalis, see No. 167.

30

A Bengali to Sub-Assistant Surgeon 3rd Class Dinesh Chandra Sen (129th Indian Field Ambulance, British Expeditionary Force A, 24)

12 Basaburi Lane
Tanti Bazar   [English]
Dacca   16th March 1915

It may easily be presumed that the bravery and heroism of the British soldiers will ultimately be crowned with complete success and glory. But there is no knowing how long the war will last. Be that as it may, we are all praying to God for a speedy termination of the war and [the] triumphant victory of the British arms.

31

Senior Assistant Surgeon J. N. Godbole to a friend (Poona, Bombay)

No. 8 Indian General Hospital   [Marathi and English]
Bournemouth   18th March 1915

The people here are of a very amiable disposition. They talk pleasantly, treat us kindly, and are pleased to see us. We do not hear the words 'damn' and 'bloody' at all frequently, as in India. But this only applies to those who have not seen India. Those who have, gnash their teeth at us; some laugh and some make fun; but there are not many who do this. The people here are charming. It is impossible to say why they become so bad on reaching India.

I have written to you from Brighton to tell you how the wounded are treated. But the good treatment is only to be seen where British and not Anglo-Indian officers are in charge. As soon as the latter have control, confusion reigns. As a result of such treatment, men in the hospital prefer to go to the front. Such are the methods of our Anglo-Indian officials.

The war news is good. It appears to me that the war will be over soon.

32

*Amir Khan (Punjabi Muslim) to his brother Lance Naik Khan Zaman
(84th Rifles, Rawalpindi District, Punjab)*

129th [Baluchis]   [Urdu]
France   18th March 1915

[After giving a list of the killed and wounded in his company, the writer continues.] For the rest, all is well. Do not be anxious. I am not wounded and I hope that all will be well. There is no other hardship. So good are the arrangements that rations of every kind of thing to eat are brought right up to the trenches. We get plenty of cigarettes. The enemy is weakening. In the fighting of the 10th March, up to the 12th, according to my estimate, 5,525 Germans were taken prisoners of war, and 25 guns and machine guns.[1] This is true. I saw some German prisoners on the road with my own eyes and counted them. One party alone had taken 38. The enemy is growing weaker – our wounded [sic] – for this reason that in the defeat of the 12th March the enemy collected his guns from every quarter and made a great hailstorm upon our trench. But our new army is collected in great numbers. Wherever he shows strength, our guns at once knock him flat. Please God, I speak with certainty, our King – God bless him – is going to win and will win soon. I have heard that you have become a Lance Naik. Now study hard, and take pains, and do good service, and put anger far from you.

[On a separate scrap of paper] God knows whether the land of France is stained with sin or whether the Day of Judgement has begun in France. For guns and of rifles [sic] there is now a deluge, bodies upon bodies, and blood flowing. God preserve us, what has come to pass! From dawn to dark and from dark to dawn it goes on like the hail that fell at Swarra[?] camp. But especially our guns have filled the German trenches with dead and made them brim with blood. God grant us grace, for grace is needed. Oh God, we repent! Oh God, we repent![2]

1. Between 10th and 13th March 1915, the Indian Corps and the British IV Corps (under Sir Henry Rawlinson) attacked German positions around the heavily fortified village of Neuve Chapelle. More than 12,500 men were killed or wounded; little ground was gained. See Nos. 36, 41 and 45.
2. This letter was probably written in the trenches under fire, or soon after. The censor described it as 'a curious psychological study, showing traces both of the nerve-shattering experience through which the writer has passed and of the exhilaration induced by success'.

33

Asim Khan (Pathan) to his brother (59th Rifles)

Brighton Hospital

[Urdu]
19th March 1915

I am exceedingly displeased with you that you have left your parents and enlisted. I am very much annoyed at this. But if you have become a soldier, get out of it as best you can. For this is a time of war and the conditions are not known.[1]

1. According to the censor, this was 'a very typical letter. It is in no way disloyal or inspired by anti-British feeling, but simply by a desire to save one in whom the writer is interested from hardship.'

34

Sepoy Zarif Khan (Afridi, 58th Rifles, now in hospital) to Havildar Bedullah Khan (58th Rifles, France)

England

[Urdu]
19th March 1915

I am praying every day and night from the throne of God for your welfare and [for] that of all the people of Islam. On the 18th March I started for India. Night and day I pray to God, saying 'oh God, keep all my friends in safety, and lead them home again soon, and bring us together. Grant Paradise to all who are dead and forgive their sins.'[1]

1. The censor commented that 'this extract exactly reflects the mental attitude of the average devout Muslim, and repays close attention'.

35

L. R. to a friend (India)

Rouen Camp
[France]

[Hindi]
22nd March 1915

As for beauty, I believe France is the home of beauty. Here everything is beautiful. The hills are covered with beautiful pastures from top to bottom all over the country. The soil is rich for fruits. The woods, even, are good. Every village, even a small one, is built beautifully into beautiful roads everywhere. Everywhere there is cleanliness.

The dresses are very fine, both of men and women. The Indians can hardly make distinctions in dresses of rich and poor, of a Lord and a farmer. Every business is exceedingly clean and neat. The features of the people are very beautiful. Their colour is reddish white. The inhabitants are honest and very polite.

The morals are also good as regards civilization, but as regards spirituality I am very sorry. They are all and all for sensual enjoyments. It seems to me that 'eat, drink and be merry' is the motto of their life. They have a Catholic religion which is almost reduced to nothing but etiquettes. And owing to this weakness they are very weak in spiritual morality, and at best I come to the conclusion that with the loss of spirituality they will lose their national strength as our India did. The present bad condition of India is due to the loss of spirituality. In India also the religion is nothing but etiquettes.

36

Rifleman Amar Singh Rawat (Garhwal Rifles) to a friend (India)

Kitchener's Indian Hospital [Garhwali]
Brighton 26th March 1915

I have been wounded in the head, but hope to get better soon. My fate now is very lucky [in] that I am alive while all my brethren have been killed. All those who have been wounded are saved and the rest are killed. Such a scene has been enacted as when the leaves fall off a tree and not a space is left bare on the ground, so here the earth is covered with dead men and there is no place to put one's foot. Up to now the war has been as follows – the Germans kept on firing from their trenches and we from ours. But on the 9th and 10th March we attacked the Germans.[1] So many men were killed and wounded that they could not be counted, and of the Germans the number of casualties is beyond calculation. When we reached their trenches we used the bayonet and the *kukri*, and blood was shed so freely that we could not recognize each other's faces; the whole ground was covered with blood. There were heaps of mens' heads, and some soldiers were without legs, others had been cut in two, some without hands and others without eyes. The scene was indescribable. If I survive I will tell you all. As regards those men who have been killed it is well, but if I get killed it does not matter, when so many of my brethren have been slain it would not matter about me, but my great scene has been enacted. I have heard that the Pandevs and the Kauris had a great war, but their battle could not have been so great as this one. I think the Germans have been shaken and that the war will end soon, because the whole world is being destroyed, no men are being left, some hundreds of thousands, nay millions; the whole world is being finished. Both sides are now taking a little breathing space. At first in Belgium the Germans thus treated the inhabitants – they cut off the hands and feet of little children and let them go; and also in the case of women they cut off one hand or one foot or blinded one eye. The whole Kingdom of Belgium has been destroyed, and half of France. But up to now we have escaped and we have stopped the Germans, and on both sides fortified trenches have been constructed. We have been constantly fighting for six months, but we have not even seen the sun; day and night the rain has fallen; and the country is so cold that I cannot describe it. The produce of the country is nothing; beyond wheat they have no crops. Wheat is now being sown. There is plenty of fruit and flowers; the rest I will describe later on. In the time of calamity these four things are tried – faith, fortitude, friend and wife.[2]

1. At the Battle of Neuve Chapelle. See Nos. 32, 41 and 45.
2. The same man writes again, with a similar tone, on 1st April 1915. See No. 41.

37

Rahman Ali (Hindustani Muslim) to M. Pargan Singh (6th Jats, France)

Peshawar   [Urdu]
[NWFP]   29th March 1915

From this war lasting so long, great uneasiness is caused in the whole of India. There is no one who has not some friends or relatives engaged in this campaign. When the telegrams announcing the casualties arrive, in all the districts, near and far, great grief and trouble is caused, because each one is connected with the other by the chain of friendship or relationship. May God soon end this war! In the whole of India there is no fresh news worthy of mention, except the high price of grain, which is a needle in the hearts of high and low.[1] During this week in the neighbourhood of Thall there was a severe conflict between the English forces and the Pathans on the [North-West] Frontier. In this the enemy lost about 500, but our forces had no loss.

1. For rising food prices see Nos. 39, 42 and 124. There was scarcity and plague in Punjab in March and April 1915.

38

Jiwan Jiwan (Jat) to Jemadar Bhani Singh (6th Jats, France)

Indian Convalescent Home

[Hindi]
30th March 1915

I have heard that the Indian troops will go back to India in April. Tell me the real news about this – whether it is true or false.

39

Jemadar Khan Muhammad (Punjabi Muslim, 31) to
Lance Naik Sher Khan (84th Punjabis)

102nd Grenadiers
Muscat

[Urdu]
March 1915

In our country [the Punjab] there is great scarcity. The price of maize is 4 *chauhas*,[1] and wheat at 3 *chauhas* per rupee cannot be had. In this calamity there is also the misfortune of separation from you. O young men, be careful and do not get confused: even if you die, show some bravery! One day we all have to die.

1. A *chauha* is presumably a measure of weight or volume.

40

Bahadur Sher to Lance Naik Badshah Mir (129th Baluchis)

127th Baluchis
Karachi

[Urdu]
March 1915

Sher Khan has got two years' imprisonment, and the remaining five men who deserted with Wazir Naik received five years, and other men also of number two Company have been caught. Some of them have got five years' and Wazir seven years' imprisonment. All is well in the Regiment. Allah Mir Jemadar has been court-martialled and dismissed. He has gone to his country. And all the Afridis of the 3rd Baluchis [130th] who refused [to do duty] have received fifteen years', and the Mohmands have got twelve years' imprisonment. All these are of the 3rd Baluchis [130th] who have been imprisoned.[1] Sultan Mir Subedar-Major has been dismissed and has gone to his country. Said Amir Subedar and Turab Gul both have been dismissed, and have gone to their homes.

1. See Nos. 20 and 21 for other references to this mutiny.

41

Rifleman Amar Singh Rawat (Garhwal Rifles) to
Dayaram Jhapaliyal (Garhwal District, UP)

Kitchener's Indian Hospital   [Garhwali]
[Brighton]   1st April 1915

The condition of affairs in the war is like leaves falling off a tree, and no empty space remains on the ground. So it is here: the earth is full of dead men and not a vacant spot is left. As many of the men get wounded they live – the rest are killed. One has to stay on top of the corpses and even sleep on them, because not an empty place remains anywhere. Such is the scene that goes on here. You have heard that the war between the Kauris and Pandevs[1] was a great conflict, but it was not so great a fight as this one. When we attacked the German trenches[2] we used the bayonet and the *kukri*, and the bullets flew about more thickly than drops of rain. The Germans lost a lot and we also had many casualties. Consider this true: there was not an empty spot on the ground. In some places men had lost their eyes, in others men [were] without legs, but what could one do? As is in one's fate, so it will happen. Such is the scene and one was powerless. Now I have not any sure confidence that I will see you people again; there is nothing but hopelessness.[3]

1. He is referring to the central conflict of the Mahabharata.
2. At Neuve Chapelle between 10th and 13th March 1915. See Nos. 32 and 45.
3. For a similar message from the same man, see No. 36.

42

Muhammad Khan to Jemadar [Malik] Mihr Khan (15th Lancers, France, 22?)

Lahore Cantonment   [Urdu]
[Punjab]   1st April 1915

In the district of Jhelum and in Rawalpindi the plague is bad, but in Campbellpur things are all right. Here in the country the price of wheat is 9 *seers* and *chenna* 12 *seers* [per rupee] and in Lahore six and a half *seers* wheat, *chenna* five and a half *seers atta* [sic].[1] In the depot with regard to reservists, those who are above twenty years' service are sent before a committee. Of the remainder above fifteen years and below twenty are considered fit for the depot, and those under fifteen are held fit for active service, when orders are received to send a party. Formerly recruiting was carried on as much as possible, but since the 15th of February it has been entirely stopped. I don't know why. We hear that the war in Egypt is going on as usual. As regards that in France, you yourself know.

1. The average price of grain in the Jhelum and Rawalpindi districts was 12–15 *seers* per rupee for wheat and 15–18 *seers* for *chenna*; and in Lahore 13–15 *seers* per rupee for wheat, 11–13 for *atta* and 15–18 for *chenna*. He is therefore describing near-famine conditions. See Nos. 37 and 39.

43

Bugler Mausa Ram (Jat, 107th Pioneers) to Naik Dabi Shahai Jat
(121st Pioneers, Jhansi District, UP)

Kitchener's Indian Hospital [Hindi]
Brighton 2nd April 1915

And my dear brother you have written, that you have become a naik so I am very pleased, and you have written that you will become a havildar and I am very pleased. I have received your card dated 24th February 1915 and mastered its contents. The state of affairs here is as follows: the black pepper is finished. Now the red pepper is being used, but, occasionally, the black pepper proves useful.[1] The black pepper is very pungent, and the red pepper is not so strong.[2] This is a secret, but you are a wise man. Consider it with your understanding. There is no necessity for me to write more. And to write more is without advantage because you can understand it so much. And, brother, somebody once said 'a pearl is not famous for friendship; it is found in a lake and gets strung on a necklace'. Brother, understand if you can, life does not remain. Brother, here the fighting is difficult and will not become easy. And the black pepper which I have with me is very pungent; but what can I do – only a little remains. In the foreign country nowadays black pepper seems to be stopped; at this time red pepper is a little pungent, but compared to red [black?] pepper it seems like insipid green vegetables. Enough, enough, what shall I write? The country of England is worth seeing. One gets everything for eating and drinking ...

In twenty days or so I will rejoin the regiment, but I don't know for certain: the future is in the hands of God. If I stay a long time, then it will only be for two months. But even so I must go back to the firing line. What is that but to die? How long can one conceal one's life or save it? A brave man can only live a short time. Why should there be any ridicule in that?

1. This is a favourite coded message. 'Black pepper' means Indian troops, and 'red pepper' British troops. See No. 60, and note to No. 5.
2. 'The Indian troops fight more fiercely than the British troops'.

44

Gulab Singh (Dogra, 57th Rifles) to Bhur Singh (25th Cavalry, Bannu, NWFP)

A hospital   [Urdu]
England   3rd April 1915

Do not be anxious for us. Whatever may be approved of God, that will happen.
Do not take any thought of us, but take thought for yourself and for our home. You
yourself are wise ... I hear regularly from the trenches. They are full of water, but
this affair is not of the world at all.[1] Well, it is fate. So it was written. Many men
have had their feet cut off, for they had been burnt by the frost ... The fighting is
as before ... We have heard that fighting has begun on the part of the Amir of Kabul
against India. Is it true or not? Write and tell me. The wounded go back to the trenches.
Some men come here who have been wounded twice over ... Jemadar Rabet
[Jagat?] Singh had a very insignificant wound, but, so I hear, he has gone to India
... My wound has not got well, but do not be anxious, it soon will. There is no trouble
here. The arrangements for our food are excellent ... The Gora Log [British soldiers]
are most attentive to our wants. It is a very good arrangement ... When I have had
my 'committee' I will tell you where I was ordered... Do not be anxious. It will be
as God wills. But great oppression has been exercised and still continues. However
[to fight] is the work of Rajputs.[2]

1.   'It is beyond all earthly precedent'.
2.   A typically Rajput statement. See Nos. 111, 234 and 256.

45

A Sikh sepoy (59th Rifles) to his brother (India)

A hospital   [Gurmukhi]
England   5th April 1915

In Europe our bodies are suffering great hardships, but God has saved my life. The
Guru can preserve us in flames of fire. He will preserve us in this world of trouble.
Then we shall return to the Punjab – if not, who knows where our future lies, here
or elsewhere. This is the will of God Almighty. What is written in our destiny must
be. When you write, let me know if the wounded arrive in India. What do you think
of the war in India? Is there fighting in Waziristan [NWFP] or not? We have heard
that the fort beyond Peshawar has been taken by the people of Tirah and that the
Waziris have occupied the country beyond Bannu. Write and tell the truth.

Now hear what happened to us. On the 9th March, the General told the Lahore and Meerut Divisions that they were to make a grand attack and glorify the name of the Punjab throughout Europe. The attack came off on the 10th at seven o'clock in the morning.[1] We fix bayonets and look towards the enemy. The enemy trenches are two yards off [sic]. They have been well built. In front is barbed wire and we are not expected to attack here. With a shout to our Guru we hurl ourselves forward. The enemy's bullets scorch our heroes, while machine guns and cannons spread their shot upon us. We leap the wire entanglements and overwhelm the enemy, killing some and capturing the rest. On the 10th we captured 1,050 Germans and took four lines of trenches defending the city of La Bassée. Here from the beginning the enemy have been very strong. On the 10th and 12th we took two miles of enemy positions. Next day at five o'clock the Germans attacked in eight lines. There was fine fighting on the battlefield. Eight lines of the enemy were destroyed. We also suffered great loss in killed and wounded. On that day no one took thought of his friend, and the slightly wounded man made his way back himself. If severely wounded, a man lay out in the battlefield. When the sun set in the evening, the rain began to fall. The wounded were picked up and sent back. The enemy attacked fiercely but were beaten back with great loss. We did not give up our trenches but pressed the enemy hard. They could not recapture their lost lines. From the 10th to the 25th the Germans lost 70,613 men.

In the hospital is rumoured that the remnants of five or six regiments will be returned to India. Only the strong man sees the battle and he will never during his life forget its taste. Those who returned to India wounded early in the war have not seen the real battle. Some lucky men have returned to India without having known the taste of battle. They returned smiling to their country. Now only the lame and halt with one leg and broken bones are sent home. No sound man can return.[2] You will say 'you have not told me about the battle'. Well, I can't describe it – so many are killed and wounded. Please write and say if any more regiments are coming here. Here in England, two pounds of flour cost one rupee [sixteen pence]. Everything is dear.

The German arrangements for the war are very good. They have many machine guns. Their little bomb guns [mortars?] throw bombs to a distance of 500 yards, and they spray vitriol acid [gas?] which burns our clothes and dries up our bodies. At night they send up star shells, and also make light with electricity [searchlights]. The war is a great sight at night. Here cannons are firing, there machine guns; here there are bright lights, there bombs hurl through the air. Bullets fly day and night incessantly drinking the blood of heroes.

1. The start of the battle of Neuve Chapelle. See Nos. 32, 36 and 41.
2. A reference to the unpopular policy of returning lightly wounded men to the trenches, once they had recovered. See No. 68 for a petition to the King.

46

Jemadar Rajaram Jadhow (Maratha, 107th Pioneers, wounded, 31) to
Kashaba Jadhav [Jadhow?] (107th Pioneers, France)

New Milton [Hospital]   [Marathi]
England   6th April 1915

I have tried hard to rejoin you [in France] but without result, because it is not possible
to overcome the Doctor's objections. They say that as long as my foot is not all
right, I cannot be allowed to rejoin: that my foot would only reswell, leading to
an amputation. I am therefore helpless. It is God's will that we should be thus parted.
Such is the Divine will, but all may yet come out right. I am unable to write much
as my countenance is downcast. I am not what I was. I am in great debt to you. I
am your servant, but God would not let me do my duty by you and help you. I am
not afraid of dying, but I cannot speak ... I hear that the weak are sent back [to the
front] and should it be your wish, and if you can so arrange it, I ask you to make
the effort [to let me rejoin you].[1]

1. Of a similar letter, the censor remarked, 'the sentiment expressed [the desire to return
    to the front] is sufficiently rare to merit being placed on record'.

47

Sepoy Baghal Singh (Sikh) to his brother (2nd Lancers, France)

New Milton Hospital   [Gurmukhi]
England   6th April 1915

I am not one of those who are to return to India. Only those go to India who have
but one arm or one leg.[1] This is the fact. Germany has made us a fine lot of
specimens. It makes one cry, and even laugh, to see them.

1. See Nos. 24 and 68.

48

Sepoy Gurdit Singh (Sikh) to his father (Amritsar District, Punjab)

Brighton Hospital

[Gurmukhi]
6th April 1915

Here it is said that men are being forced to enlist by order in India, and they also say that plague is very rife. Write me some news of our country ... So long as the war goes on, no sound man can return to India – only those who have lost a limb can return. In my heart I feel that I shall have to go back to the war.

49

*Ragbir Singh (Dogra, 59th Rifles) to Gajander Singh
(Dhada Village, Kangra District, Punjab)*

Indian Military Depot
Milford-on-Sea

[Hindi]
8th April 1915

I have been wounded twice, and now this is the third time that I am being sent to the trenches. The English say it is all right. How can it be all right! As long as one is unhurt, so long they will not let one off. If Parmeshwar[1] allows I will escape, but the butcher does not let the goat escape.

1. *Parama Isvava,* 'the highest lord' or 'God'.

50

A Pathan to his brother Harzat Shah (129th Baluchis)

Brighton Hospital

[Urdu]
12th April 1915

I have heard that you have come to the war. I am very angry with you. It was more than enough that I should be there, and it is a pity that you too have to come. If I was in my regiment then we could meet, but now I cannot come. Wake up! Work so as to spare your life, and do not do anything foolish. Do exactly as I did. I have saved my life, and also have become a 'Bahadur'. Now I am getting a havildari, but I have fulfilled my purpose, and I have no need of a havildari. I hope to go to India. I hope that by God's mercy I have succeeded in magnifying the name of the whole Khatak clan. Do your best to save your life and do not act like an idiot. I am 'sick', but do not be anxious. I am quite well. Tell Shiraz Khan to keep the brotherhood well-united and save their lives. Keep your lives well sheltered.

51

Dafadar Muhammad Husain (36th Jacob's Horse) to
Dafadar Ray Muhammad Khan (37th Lancers)

[England]

[Urdu]
13th April 1915

I am in the English hospital. The English doctors pay great attention to the Indian sick. We get very good food, beds, etc., and I cannot sufficiently praise the building: it is a very splendid building.[1] Old pensioned officers and their wives come to the hospital and enquire after our health, and give fruits and sweetmeats to the sick, and we also get fruit and sweetmeats from the state. May God make our King victorious; it is proper for you to pray so, too. The state of the Indian troops in the battlefield is very prosperous; they get excellent food, and you should not believe what liars say; the Germans are but 'guests of a few days', for on all four sides the English and French and Russians have enclosed them, and they are very hard up for rations. How can hungry men fight? ... England is a very fine country. The King and Queen themselves came to visit the sick in hospital, and asked everyone if he had any sort of inconvenience. Every soldier blessed them and said that they were well served in every way and prayed for their Majesties' long lives.

1. He is presumably referring to Brighton Pavilion. See No. 63.

52

Giyan Singh (Sikh) to his brother (India)

Indian Artillery Depot
Milford-on-Sea

[Gurmukhi]
15th April 1915

The German is very strong. His ships sail the clouds and drop shells from the sky; his mines dig up the earth, and his hidden craft strike below the sea. Bombs and blinding acid are thrown from his trenches which are only 100 or 50 yards from ours. He has countless machine guns which kill the whole firing line when in attack. When he attacks we kill his men. The dead lie in heaps. England is full of wounded. No man can return to the Punjab whole. Only the broken-limbed can go back. The regiments that came first are finished – here and there a man remains. Reinforcements have twice and three times brought them up to strength, but straightaway they were used up. The German is very strong.

53

Firoz Khan (Muslim) to Mir Khan (129th Baluchis)

Rawalpindi [Urdu]
[Punjab] 16th April 1915

Here the plague is very violent, and everyone is in danger of his life; in my parts the plague has caused great distress and Abdullah Khan's mother has died of it. The rats are falling down dead in every house, and our village Kirpa has become entirely devastated. Provisions of all kinds are very scarce. The sickness has spread all through the Nimar Bazar, and in your house, and indeed in all the houses throughout the quarter, rats are falling dead; all the houses have been abandoned, and the people have taken refuge in a large house that has been repaired outside the town.

54

Havildar Ghufran Khan (Afridi) to a friend (India)

129th [Baluchis] [Urdu?]
France [mid-April 1915?]

Our people have many lice in their clothes, and they bite terribly. They are worse than a rifle bullet. But there are no mosquitoes or other creatures which bite mankind, and no snakes or scorpions at all.

55

Maulavi Chiragh-i-Alam (Punjabi Muslim) to Naik Ghulam Haider (69th Punjabis)

Jhelum [Urdu]
Punjab 23rd April 1915

I am always praying that the merciful God may preserve you and all good Muslims from all calamities of earth and heaven. And everything is well in this country;

they have cut the autumn crops but the current price of grain is still dear; and in the districts of Sialkot, Waziribad and Gujrat, and the southern part of Jhelum, an epidemic is raging; nay, in that part, many villages have been utterly devastated by the plague; but, by God's mercy, there is as yet good health in our part, and there is no complaint of sickness in the neighbourhood of Jhelum ... Further, if there is any proposal for conciliation or peace, just write in your letter 'there is some proposal as regards that matter', and if there is no proposal, then write 'there is no proposal as regards that matter' and I shall understand what you mean.

56

Allah Ditta (Punjabi Muslim) to his father (Punjab)

129th [Baluchis]   [Urdu]
France   23rd April 1915

I cannot write about the fighting because it is very grievous. But it is not [ordinary] fighting, it is Karbala.[1] This fighting is the task of those Kings. No one else can achieve it. Here the people are being butchered as a butcher slaughters goats. The man who will return to his own country will be a man of very exceptional fate. In every letter that we receive, there is mention of the plague and we are very anxious. Please send us news every week.

1. Karbala in Iraq was the site of a battle in October 680 in which an army sent by the Umayyad Caliph Yazid I defeated and killed Husayn ibn Ali, the grandson of the Prophet. The anniversary of the battle (on 10th Muharram) is an annual holy day of public mourning among Shi'ite Muslims, the followers of Husayn. The tomb of Husayn is one of the holiest sites of Shi'ism. Several Muslim soldiers use the analogy of Karbala to convey the intensity of the fighting on the Western Front. Compare No. 13.

57

Naik Nizam-ud-Din (Punjabi Muslim, 129th Baluchis) to a friend (Punjab)

[Kitchener's Indian Hospital]   [Urdu]
Brighton Pavilion   26th April 1915

Bagh Ali is here with me in this hospital. He is quite well and happy. Send word to his home. A few days ago he lost his *tawiz* [amulet] and now he has begun to be possessed and subject to seizure at intervals.

58

Sub-Assistant Surgeon Naragen Moreshiver Pundit (Maratha) to D. M. Pundit
(Sangola, Sholapur District, Bombay)

Bournemouth

[Marathi]
27th April 1915

[After seeing parts of London, including Madame Tussaud's, he writes] the arts
and ways of the English people are a credit to them. It is because they possess such
merits and are so industrious that England is the home of such wealth and riches.
It will take at least five hundred years for India to attain to such conditions – we
must at least try. Looking to the deeds of our ancestors will not lead to any
improvements.

59

Naubat Khan (Yusufzai Pathan) to his brother, Sowar Amin Khan (37th Lancers,
Jullundur, Punjab)

107th Pioneers
France

[Urdu]
April 1915

I have heard that Mihr Najab Khan has arrived, but I have not seen him. Do your
utmost not to come with any party of troops to the war. Make some arrangement,
because this is not a war. The righteous God has sent down a calamity: it is the
destruction of the Indians by a Flood. But I hope by the grace of the pure God and
by the prayers of the Saints and Prophets to return safe and sound to my native
country.

60

Sepoy Mansa Ram (Jat, 107th Pioneers) to Guard Rameshwar or
Divisankar (G.I.P. Railway, Station Seepri, Jhansi, UP)

Kitchener's Indian Hospital
Brighton

[Hindi]
April 1915

I have heard that plague is bad in India, so let me know the true facts ... I have no
trouble of any kind in this hospital, and get everything in the way of food and drink.
Don't you be anxious about me, because it is fitting for anyone who has eaten the

salt[1] of the great Government to die. So it is very necessary and proper for you to be loyal to the Government for that is the reason why it employs you. The black pepper which has come from India has all been finished, so now the red pepper is being used.[2] But the red pepper is little used and the black more. You understand everything so I need not write any further.

1. 'Eating salt' was a common term for 'receiving pay'. The expression harked back to times when salt was used as currency.
2. 'Black pepper' and 'red pepper' here mean Indian and British troops respectively. This code was frequently used, but did not deceive the censor. See No. 43.

61

Mian Ludar Singh (Dogra) to Mian Ghanbiya Ram Galsingh (Haib Village, Palompun Tehsil, Kangra District, UP)

Lady Hardinge Hospital[1]   [Hindi]
Brockenhurst   April 1915

What Pramatma[2] had to do has been done, so whatever sins and wickedness I committed in a former life, so in accordance with that I have been brought into this country and suffered endless troubles and hardships: these are all the fruit of one's actions, but this does not matter if my life is to be saved.

1. Opened on 20th January 1915, Lady Hardinge Hospital was paid for by donations from the Indian Soldiers' Fund.
2. *Parama Atman*, 'the highest soul' or 'God'.

62

*Havildar Bhura Singh (Dogra) to Subedar Hamira
(44th Merwara Infantry, Egypt, 43)*

Lady Hardinge Hospital   [Hindi]
[Brockenhurst]   [c. April 1915]

In the hospital there is great bustle and excitement as it is going to be moved forward, and when I next write to you I will have joined my section. I hope that I will kill ten Germans before I die. After that it is God's will.

63

Isar Singh (Sikh, 59th Rifles) to a friend (50th Punjabis, India)

Indian General Hospital   [Gurmukhi]
Brighton   1st May 1915

The battle is being carried on very bitterly. In the Lahore Division only 300 men
are left. Some are dead, some wounded. The division is finished. Think of it – in
taking fifty yards of a German trench 50,000 men are killed. When we attack they
direct a terrific fire on us – thousands of men die daily. It looks as if not a single
man can remain alive on either side – then (when none is left) there will be peace.
When the Germans attack they are killed in the same way. For us men it is a bad
state of affairs here. Only those return from the battlefield who are slightly
wounded. No one else is carried off. Even Sahibs are not lifted away. The
battleground resounds with cries. So far as is in your power do not come here. If
you come, get yourself written down ill of something in Marseilles, and say you
are weak. You will do better to get the Doctor to write down that sickness you have
in the head. Sick men do not come to the war. Here things are in a very bad way.
In France the news is that dogs churn milk in machines and look after the cattle.[1]
A man who keeps a dog has to pay five rupees a month to the King.

   Do not be anxious about me. We are very well looked after. White soldiers are
always besides our beds – day and night. We get very good food four times a day.
We also get milk. Our hospital is in the place where the King used to have his throne.[2]
Every man is washed once in hot water. The King has given a strict order that no
trouble be given to any black man in hospital. Men in hospital are tended like flowers,
and the King and Queen sometimes come to visit them.

1. See No. 10.
2. Brighton Pavilion, a former royal residence, was turned into a hospital for Indian
    troops. See Plate 4.

64

*Gopal Bahiravo Methe (Maratha) to Clerk K. B. Methe (Kolhapur State,
Bombay)*

                                                           [Marathi]
Brighton Hospital   3rd May 1915

The feeding and clothing arrangements are very good and you need not be anxious
about me. May our *Badsha* [King] soon be victorious, because those who fight for

the cause of truth must succeed. Thus, loving the truth, the British Government have given Belgium complete assistance. In one or two months' time we shall be victorious, and I shall, I think, then return in three or four months' time to my home. We should pray God that he may garland our King with victory, and you should also pray for this result.

65

A Sikh sepoy to Gurun Ditta Mal (Depot, 47th Sikhs, Fatehgarh, Farrukhabad District, UP)

[Probably 47th Sikhs]　　　　　　　　　　　　　　　　[Gurmukhi]
[France]　　　　　　　　　　　　　　　　　　　　　12th May 1915

Here there is no news of our return to India. On the 9th, the big General gave out that we should be sent back within two months at the latest, but since then not a word has been said about this, and it appears that he has changed his mind. We must eat our food where we find it, and if it is our fate we shall meet again ... You will be hearing about this country from the wounded who have gone back from England. Some of them tell fine tales about the number of water-drawing machines [women]. I long to see England. When the war is over perhaps the regiment will go there. There are crowds of 'machines' here also, and the sight of them delights us, but we are ashamed to touch them lest we lose caste. The men and women of the place treat us very lovingly.

66

Muhammad Faizul Hasan (Punjabi Muslim, 30th Lancers) to Dafadar Nur Ahmed (30th Lancers, Ambala, Punjab)

　　　　　　　　　　　　　　　　　　　　　　　　[Urdu]
Brighton Hospital　　　　　　　　　　　　　　　19th May 1915

And here they are planning an attack by the cavalry, but, thanks be to God, the ground here is altogether bad, and it is continually raining. The horses cannot by any means move without roads; if the horses are sent below the roads, they sink in up to their knees. In this manner the precious God has preserved us. Thanks be to God, and to the prayers of you elders, all the cavalry are still well. If these sahibs had had the choice, then the matter would have been decided long ago, but thanks be to God, every one must do as he wills, and we are ten to twelve miles from the firing line, housed comfortably in French villages. God is omnipotent. In fact this is the result of the prayers of you elders; if God wills it, then provided we live, we shall know it. And the fighting is in just the same state; it is still but the first day of it, and there is no news of peace; we shall see when the prayers of us sinners will be heard.

67

Havildar Abdul Rahman (Punjabi Muslim) to Naik Rajwali Khan
(31st Punjabis, Fort Sandeman, Zhob District, Baluchistan)

59th Rifles [Urdu]
[France] 20th May 1915

For God's sake don't come, don't come, don't come to this war in Europe. Write and tell me if your regiment or any part of it comes and whether you are coming with it or not. I am in a state of great anxiety; and tell my brother Muhammad Yakub Khan for God's sake not to enlist. If you have any relatives, my advice is don't let them enlist. It is unnecessary to write any more. I write so much to you as I am Pay Havildar and read the letters to the double company commander.[1] Otherwise there is a strict order against writing on this subject. Cannons, machine guns, rifles and bombs are going day and night, just like the rains in the month of Sawan [July–August]. Those who have escaped so far are like the few grains left uncooked in a pot. That is the case with us. In my company there are only ten men [left]. In the regiment there are 200. In every regiment there are only 200 or 280.

1.   A British officer, normally a captain or lieutenant. For other references to the censorship, see Nos. 217 and 239.

68

To the King

[Roman Urdu][1]
Milford-on-Sea 24th May 1915

[Envelope] England. The Emperor. Let no one except the King open this. From the Indian sick in hospital, Barton.

   [Contents] To the Emperor of India, England, from the sick whose petition is this: that no British Officer nor Indian Doctor cares for us. They deal hardly with the sick ... Let the King – God bless him – understand more than the little that is written. Your Majesty's order was that a man who had been wounded once should be allowed to return to India; or that if he had recovered he should not be made to serve again. The heart of India is broken because they inflict suffering on the sick. Blessed King, what can I say? There is nothing worth describing. We do not get new clothes. In the morning only ... tea, at ten o'clock a *chapatti* and a spoonful of *dal*. In twenty-four hours, five cigarettes. In the evening the *chapattis* are half baked and there is no meat. No sick man gets well fed. The Indians have given their lives for eleven rupees.[2] Any man who comes here wounded is returned thrice and four times to the trenches.[3] Only that man goes to India who has lost an arm or a leg or an eye.

1. Urdu written in the Roman, rather than the Arabic, script. This letter was very badly written, and parts were illegible and impossible to translate.
2. The monthly pay of a sepoy until the middle of the war.
3. This is the central grievance, and one that was very widely shared. See Nos. 47, 48, 49, 52, 88 and 129. The complaint about hospital conditions is less typical: there are plenty of letters expressing the opposite view.

69

Sayid Ghulam Abbas (Muslim spiritual guide) to
Jemadar Muzaffar Khan (59th Scinde Rifles, at the front)

Makhad   [Urdu]
Punjab   25th May 1915

Furthermore, this present war has raised the question of a sort of perception and comparison of the characteristics of each race, and of their good and bad reputation, as evinced by the way in which they have carried out their duties; but the native papers contain no traces of this problem. For this reason, I am writing to you in a special manner, my sincere friend, to suggest that two or three of your native officers should meet together and make a representation to some of your English officers – whether captains, or majors, or if a colonel then very much better – and ask them to say what is their opinion concerning our race, and the work we have done, and our loyalty. When they have expressed their opinion, you should then say 'will your honours kindly represent our loyal behaviour to our spiritual chief, showing with what self-sacrifice we Muslims have devoted our lives in carrying our our duties? He will be very pleased with us, on hearing this, and will give us his blessing.' Then they will either write a letter of thanks and send it to me, or you will get them to write it and send it by post to me so that we may be able to present the letter to high military officers on behalf of the whole of the Muslims showing the facts of our state: there will be great advantage in this to all the followers of our spiritual guides, and more especially to the whole body of Muslims. And do you consider it your duty to get this letter written, and if any officers should ask you the reason of this letter being written then you should say that at the time of our departure, our spiritual chief directed us to serve the Government with loyalty. Now, when your letter will go to the chief, then he and all our co-religionists will rejoice.

70

Subedar Muhammad Agia [Azim Khan] (Punjabi Muslim, 57th Rifles, 29) to Subedar-Major Firoz Khan (56th Rifles, Force F, Egypt, 39)

[Kitchener's] Indian Hospital   [Urdu?]
Brighton   28th May 1915

I am telling you the trouble. What can I say of the war? It is a manifestation of divine wrath. There is no counting the number of lives lost. We have to deal with a terrible and powerful enemy, who is completely equipped with every sort of contrivance. Out of the 84th Regiment,[1] which arrived in full strength, only about ten men are left. In my regiment, the 57th, absolutely none are left, with the exception of Jemadar Iman Ali [42] (now appointed subedar) and one newly joined lieutenant. Not a single British or native officer of the old regiment is left, and not a sepoy. It is just like the grinding of corn in a mill. The enemy is one completely equipped with all contrivances ... There remains to be seen what effect the joining of Italy will have on the war.[2] It is possible that the war may end soon, as Italy has an army of three millions.

1. This regiment was not in France. Presumably he means the 89th Punjabis, who were brigaded with the 57th Rifles.
2. By the Pact of London, signed on 26th April 1915, Italy agreed to join the Allies within a month, in return for territorial gains at Austrian expense.

71

Havildar Abdul Rahman (Punjabi Muslim) to Raja Sajawal Khan Lumberdar (Dalwal Village, Jhelum District, Punjab)

59th Rifles   [Urdu]
[France]   May 1915

For six months I have not taken off my boots for one second, nor taken off my uniform, nor have I had one good night's rest. This fighting goes on day and night all the same. The Kings of England, and Belgium, France, Russia [and] Australia are on the one side. On the other are the Emperors of Germany and Austria. But the Emperor of Germany is the greatest and most powerful of all. The line of battle in France is 300 miles long. On the Russian side it is perhaps 400 miles long. The Germans have the most numerous cannons and machine guns and shells. I cannot find words to describe the skill of the Germans. On the 26th April we marched from France into Belgium. In Flanders there is a city called Ypres. There was a great battle there.[1] There was a great army of the French, the English and the Belgians. They attacked the Germans. This attack they repulsed by lightning, fire and smoke, blasting some to pieces and blinding others [with gas?]. Others were killed by cannon and machine gun fire. My friend, the Germans have got the most perfect contrivances. Our Sirkar's army retreated to save its life. About half the army was destroyed. This is what happens whenever there is any fighting. Then we come back to France. The Germans captured the city of Ypres.[2] At night they send up flashlights which show up men two miles away. Now our Sirkar is preparing contrivances similar to those of the Germans. Let us hope that we will defeat them, but we can only do so when all the Kings on the face of the earth will join us against the Germans.

1. In the last week of April 1915, the Germans attacked the Allies in Belgium at the Second Battle of Ypres. In their desperation to break the line, the Germans used poison gas extensively for the first time (in defiance of the Hague Convention, to which Germany was a signatory). The gas attack came as a complete surprise, throwing the troops of a French Colonial Division into panic. The Lahore Division marched north to take part in the defence of the city. On 26th and 27th April the Allies counterattacked, the 59th Rifles losing 62 men. Total Lahore Division losses in the few days of fighting were 3,889 out of 15,980.
2. Here our correspondent errs. The Allies successfully defended the city until the Armistice, although at a cost of around 500,000 casualties.

72

Jodh Singh (Dogra) to a subedar of the 38th Dogras (Malakand Cantonment, NWFP)

Kitchener's Indian Hospital   [Hindi]
Brighton   May 1915

You have written and said that I do not tell you much [but] the condition here is the same as before: to write a little is useless and to tell lies is not good. In India one can travel by trains very cheaply, but here one can do the same in motor cars ... Our people used to boast a lot [about bravery] but to show it in reality is difficult. I regret that I have got wounded so soon. I have seen several men who are in the forefront at eating time, but at the hour of fighting are in the background.

73

Lance Naik Ram Carup Singh (Rajput, 9th Bhopal Infantry) to
Lance Naik Dobi Singh (16th Rajputs, Calcutta)

Indian Military Depot [Hindi]
Milford-on-Sea May 1915

You wrote and asked about the feeding arrangements. In regard to this, I let you
know a few things. Every man gets *atta, dal* and vegetables. There is no weighing
(as much as he wants, it is brought) and of other things four annas worth of *ghi*,
and fruit of every kind; three ounces of sugar, and of cigarettes as many as he likes;
eight ounces of wheat and as much clothes as he may wish; wine two ounces. But
don't you think that, simply because it is to be had, Ram Carup Singh eats or drinks
these things. Not at all – it is just as one feels inclined. Of the 13th Rajputs there
are four ward orderlies. They get letters. Their regiment is in Africa. What fresh
news am I to write? You know that it is seven months since I was in Bhopal ... Do
your work for Government with zeal but at your ease. You wrote about going to
the fair of the ship fort [to the war]. Don't you go but stay and do your work for
Government. What sense is this, that one should count the leaves of the pipal tree[1]
in the month of Phagun? [February–March] You have not become mad that you
should leave your work and shake the pipal tree.[2] Give my salutations to the
Subedar. Please do me the favour of letting me know what is the condition of the
market for black pepper.[3] That which I brought with me has all been finished and
some more has been sent.[4] On the 27th April there was a great calamity.[5] You probably
know that there is lots of red pepper but they want black. The leaves of the tree are
falling. Think about this.

1. The *pipal (ficus religiosa)* is a large, shade-giving fig-tree, regarded as sacred, under
   which Guatama attained the enlightenment which constituted him 'the Buddha'. Also
   known as the bo-tree or bodhi, meaning 'tree of perfect knowledge', its long, thin leaves
   resemble swordblades. The sentence means, roughly, 'there is no point coming to the
   front to see how many troops are engaged'.
2. 'Unless you are mad, you will not take up the sword yourself'.
3. 'Tell me how recruiting is going in India'.
4. 'All the original Indian contingent are dead or wounded, and reinforcements have been
   sent'.
5. He is probably referring to the attack of the Lahore Division, north of Ypres, on
   26th–27th April 1915. It may well have been this action in which he was wounded. See
   No. 71.

74

Major Hira Singh (Punjabi Muslim) to Rustam Singh and
Didan Singh (41st Dogras)

Poona State Cavalry   [Urdu]
Kashmir   May 1915

O dear friends, you know that for three or four generations we have been eating the salt of the British Government, so that, if we fulfil the obligations of this salt, what shame is there in that? It is for this very occasion, indeed, that the Government have been giving us pay and pension. Did you do any hard labour for Government, or perform any obligation while you were in cantonments? These parades and exercises only kept you busy for a couple of hours, and it was good for the health of the troops. Now, indeed, is the opportunity of showing your worth to Government. If you betray any cowardice, weakness or disloyalty, you will be for ever dishonoured and disgraced. The man who fears on the battlefield, or displays any pusillanimity, is sure to be killed. *Dulce et decorum est pro patria mori.*[1] Imagine that the dust of your ancestors has been carried by the wind over to France, England and these other places. Would that I were also with my cavalry and could enjoy these sights, and fulfil the obligations of loyalty to the Government! I am very unfortunate that I left the service of Government and entered into the [service of Poona] State. O friends, I will be delighted if any one of you ... displays great bravery, and makes a name for himself amongst his countrymen and before the Government. God has afforded you a splendid opportunity to display your loyalty. You must know that our ancestors have for a long time been sitting at home, and enjoying a pension from the Government, and have not even heard the mention of war. Instead of them, you have now the chance of doing justice to your bravery. Finally, I exhort you to show your loyalty and devotion, and to do your utmost to earn name and fame. Think not the war a toil! After troubles comes rest! Without pain there is no gain! He who labours hard is sure to find rest! You will obtain honours amongst your countrymen and reward from Government. Think now that it is *our* ancestors and *our* fathers who are looking after you, and have provided nourishment for you from diverse lands and countries. Never regret for a moment your loyalty and devotion to Government, or you will be sorry for it afterwards. Look at those who have displayed their loyalty to Government – how they have been rewarded with lands and honours! O friends, at this time forget all your connections and think only of your duty and loyalty to Government: this will earn you glory and renown!

1. 'It is a sweet and seemly thing to die for one's country'.

75

Mohammad Gaki Khan (UP Muslim) to Sowar Mohammad Rafi Khan
(30th Lancers, France?)

[Urdu?]
[UP?]   6th June 1915

I went and saw Khalka Pershad today and asked him about that matter [malingering].
He said that he had no experience of his own, but that he knew so much, that the
smoke of the *bhalwa* plant is used for this purpose. The plant is ground down and
then thrown on burning coals. The smoke is then allowed to play upon that part
of the body on which it is desired to cause an inflammation, but the rest of the body
must be carefully protected by clothes so that the smoke should not touch any other
part. That part which the smoke touches by the grace of God becomes inflamed.
Its effect lasts three days. If it is desired that the inflammation should last longer,
the operation should be repeated every third day. I have learnt from several other
people that the smoke has this effect. I made enquiries of Kalka Pershad about some
other method, but he said he knew of no other. He added that the smoke should
be applied for ten minutes. He added that there is another method which will succeed
in deceiving the doctors – that is, to pretend to suffer from sciatica.[1] He said the
doctors would believe you but I do not think so myself. However, I leave it to you.
Also I learnt from other people that if you want to make your eyes sore, you should
do as follows: grind the seed of the *rand* plant and apply it to the eyes as one does
surma.[2] Then lie down for a while with closed eyes. The eyes will at once become
reddened. But you must apply the stuff two or three times a day. By the grace of
God no harm will be done to the eyes. Another prescription for the eyes is as follows:
apply the wax from your ears with a blunt-pointed needle to your eyes. The eyes
become reddened. A method for bringing about fever is as follows: mix some *safrida*
[white lead] in curds and drink it. Fever will set in at once. You must choose for
yourself from among all these methods and use what suits the opportunity. The
first and most important thing is to try and have yourself sent to hospital as soon
as possible. Do not think of a pension or anything else ... Lalla Hajjan also told
me a method of causing injury to the foot. First, make a cut in your foot with a
knife, and then put a piece of copper in the wound.

1. A form of neuralgia characterized by intense pain along the course of the sciatica nerve,
    from the back of the thigh to the calf.
2. A black dye, derived from antimony, and used for darkening the eyes.

76

Jaginal Singh (Rajput, 4th Rajputs) to
Pensioned Risaldar-Major Jaswant Singh (Hissar, Punjab)

[Hindi]
Bournemouth Hospital   7th June 1915

Since I have been in hospital in this country, I have not received a letter from your hand; I don't know what sort of mismanagement exists. And I see the 9th Bhopal Regiment is going to India,[1] that is to say, the Suez Canal; there is nothing but ease there; the warmth and the cold, in fact everything, is like our own country. Even the water is just like that of my own village, and the fighting there is nothing – the Turks are not able to fight against our Government soldiers. Further, here I am in this place, and I don't know where I shall have to go. Everything is difficult for one of our Rajput caste; all arrangements are made for Jats, Sikhs, Muslims and Gurkhas, and it should be the same for our caste. And look at this German show; they are now using poisonous shells and asphyxiating gas: what is to be done? When things are done with such malevolence, our British Government must follow their example. The proverb 'against blackguards one must be a blackguard' is quite apt here. Don't be anxious, I shall soon meet you.

1. The departure of this regiment (for Egypt) prompted many false rumours that the Indian troops would soon return to their own country.

77

Nur Mast Khan (Afridi Pathan) to Havildar Zargar Khan (57th Wilde's Rifles, France)

55th Rifles
Thal
[Kohat District]   [Urdu]
[NWFP]   8th June 1915

There has been a great fight between the Malik Din Khel and the Qambar Khel. The Misri Khel have killed one man, the son of Qutb-ud-Din. There has been no rain in our country [the NWFP] and the people are in great distress. Nothing else has happened worth writing to you. One of our lance naiks has deserted from Thal and taken ten men with him. We are not allowed to go more than half an hour's distance from the camps and are in great distress. But what can we do? ... A line has been fixed for us and a line has been fixed in Miramshah [in Waziristan, NWFP]. We are very much afraid because many Afridis have deserted and people say that the Regiment is going to Jullundur [in Punjab], and we are much annoyed at this. Here we are receiving rations at Government expense, and there is no fighting.

78

Naik Main Ram (Jat) to Sepoy Dani Ram (102nd King Edward's Own Grenadiers, Muscat)

Kitchener's Indian Hospital   [Hindi]
Brighton   9th June 1915

You should know that you should not on any account come out to the war. What more shall I write? In this you should understand the whole matter: here it is like fire – there is no word suitable to express it – and you are an old soldier and are intelligent. If a man wishes to remain [away] he can do so in any case – there are many subterfuges for a man, and you should endeavour in every manner to protect your life. God is the dispenser. Do not tell this matter to anyone, and, my brother, you will see that it is necessary for a man to save his life by all means ... There are a hundred things you can say – [that you are] weak, [or have] a pain in the chest, or asthma – there are fifty excuses. And here [at the front] they slash with their knives until there is nothing of you left: you have no time to eat either by day or by night. [Only] that man comes here whose luck is bad and who has no resting place either in earth or heaven ... What more can I write: beyond this, the matter is in your [own] hands.

79

Sub-Assistant Surgeon T. H. Gupta to Sub-Assistant Surgeon Gunpat Ram (Burma)

Kitchener's Indian Hospital   [Bengali?]
Brighton   9th June 1915

The women here are of great spirit. You will not see a woman or girl crying because of the loss of a near relative in the war. I have had several opportunities of talking to widows who have lost their husbands in the war; but, strange to say, I never heard a word of lamentation from their lips. Always they spoke with pride that 'my husband or my brother has been killed in the war' ... Even in this terrible time, one can hear the sound of music in the houses. From this you can form the idea how greatly favoured by fate this nation is.

80

Subedar Muhammad Azim Khan (Punjabi Muslim, 57th Wilde's Rifles, 29) to his
father Captain Kurban Ali Khan, Khan Bahadur (Rawalpindi District, Punjab)

Kitchener's Indian Hospital   [Urdu]
Brighton   10th June 1915

I now expect to return to the front at any moment, as I am quite recovered. If I
return I shall be the only one of the original native officers left. In fact the 57th
Regiment exists no longer. There are not thirty men left of the original number.[1]
There is only one British officer left with the Regiment – a lieutenant who has lately
come from India. So that until I actually see you again I do not consider myself
alive. Do not concern yourself too much about me. I do not think of myself at all
now. Fighting is now to me nothing more than an ordinary game. I am never put
out. Everything is in the hands of God. As He has kept me in safety so far, so I
hope He will continue to do so. The fighting is going on with great violence, more
violently than previously. My regiment has been in trenches at Neuve Chapelle
for one and a half months. Believe me, there is no doubt [that] this war will last
another two years. That power will win which has the longest purse. As our Sirkar
is the richest of all, we hope it will win. The news one sees in the papers is not at
all true. I see one thing in the Indian newspapers and another in the papers here.
The English newspapers are much more reliable and truthful than the Indian.[2] Much
light can be gained on the true state of affairs from the newspapers here. It is a
great pity that you do not learn the real state of affairs. I will fight to the end for
my King, and will have no hesitation in sacrificing my life.

1. By this stage, his comment would not be much of an exaggeration.
2. For a similar comment see Nos. 15 and 240.

81

A Pathan sepoy to Ghulamdin (Peshawar, NWFP)

General Hospital for Indian Troops   [Urdu?]
Brighton   11th June 1915

I have been sent to hospital from the trenches suffering from frost bite in my feet.
I am now quite recovered. As to what you said in your letter that Subedar-Major
Mala Khan was reported as missing in the newspapers, the fact is that on the 21st
December [1914] the Germans made an attack upon us.[1] Of the 129th Regiment,
180 sepoys and Subedar-Major Mala Khan were taken prisoners. Letters are

received from the prisoners. All this is true, because the post carries letters between our side and the Germans. Do not [?] tell the brother of the Subedar-Major, because the latter is quite comfortable and the brother will be concerned about him.

1. Allied attacks in the Festubert area had achieved only partial success, with heavy losses, by 19th December 1914. The German counter-attack at Givenchy from 20th December fell on the Indian Corps. He could be referring to this action.

82

Ratna Singh Bisht (Garhwali) to Jot Singh Bisht (Garhwal District, UP)

Brighton Hospital

[Garhwali]
21st June 1915

On the 12th May, I was wounded, and came into the Brighton Hospital. I was struck by bullets in both legs – in the left thigh, and the right knee. I am easier now but cannot yet walk. I shall get all right, for God protected the bone. The fight is still raging, and the number of killed is beyond counting. Mothers' good sons do not turn their back to the enemy in battle. Reverence is paid to seven generations of those whose fathers were engaged in war. Such a war has never been before, and never will be again. For a year has passed, and the war is still going on. Hundreds of thousands of corpses are strewn on the ground; the line of battle is 900 miles long; but in England *lakhs* of armies are collecting, so don't have any anxiety. The Hindustani soldiers who will come here will have a second birth [meaning 'will die']. So I have no hope of returning. May the true Narayan [Vishnu] have mercy on us.

83

Sepoy Lal Chand (Jat) to Fath Singh Zamindar (Rohtak District, Punjab)

Kitchener's Indian Hospital
Brighton

[Urdu and Hindi]
25th June 1915

And brother, what can I write? No such state of affairs has happened before, nor will happen again. This is not a war that will allow us to return [home] but what can we do? We must serve the state and cannot help ourselves. This is the business of the military caste; if they are killed, it is no matter.[1] But we unfortunate ones should not have the task of fighting in the field of battle.

1. He is probably referring to Rajputs, the main warrior caste-cluster of North India, and the traditional enemies of the cultivating Jats.

84

Prabhu Dayal (Dogra) to Subiya Ram (Kohima, Naga Hills District, Assam)

Kitcheners Indian Hospital   [Hindi]
Brighton   25th June 1915

What more can I write? There are orders against writing. Oh, my elder brother, by your favour I am well, and my life has been spared hitherto; but I am not certain for the future and have no hope of life.

85

An Afridi Pathan to his brother (55th Rifles, India)

57th Rifles   [Urdu and Pashtu]
France   27th June 1915

[Urdu] Do not be anxious. Death is from God. Do not think that all who have gone to the war will die. No, have hope that we shall come back to our own country. No doubt, in the end, we must die. But such a sight no man has seen as we have seen. If I were to spend Rs.40,000 I should not get such a sight for it. There is no country like the country of France. It is a most beautiful country and the women of this country are women like the good fairies. [Pashtu] Oh happy paper, how I envy your lot. We shall be here but you will go and see [India].

86

*Havildar Fazl Mehdi (Punjabi Muslim) to Subedar Muhammad Nawaz Khan
(28th Punjabis, attached 57th Rifles, France, 34)*

28th Punjabis   [Urdu]
Colombo   28th June 1915

I went home to get recruits. Everything is very quiet at home. Everyone's thoughts are always with their soldier sons across the sea, and they are in ceaseless anxiety. May the God of mercy soon grant peace and health in all the world. I had got eleven recruits and was to produce them at Jhelum at 6am on the 25th June at the Recruiting Officer's bungalow. On the 24th I had them all collected, when at 4pm there came a telegram addressed to Ghakkar of Khilaspur to say that Sahibzada, the son of Shakir of Khilaspur, had been killed in action. When they heard this the heart of the recruits was shaken. But they said nothing at the time. At 4.30pm it began to rain and a dust storm came on. I went off to bring my kit indoors and all the recruits ran away. When I came back, there was not one. I hunted high and low for them, but I could not find them. By seven o'clock I had only found two – one a man of Jamir Ghal, and one belonging to Dhok Juma. These I took with me, and one was passed [fit] and the other not. [Letter passed]

87

Mohammad Ali Bey (Deccani Muslim) to Lance Dafadar Ranjit Singh (Depot, 20th Deccan Horse, Neemuch, Mindasok, Gwalior, Central India)

20th Deccan Horse   [Urdu?]
France   [June 1915?]

My friend, tell everyone at the Depot that this is the time to show one's loyalty to the Sirkar, to earn a name for oneself. To die in the battlefield is glory. For a thousand years one's name will be remembered. The British Army is now pressing the Germans very hard. It is our destiny to conquer. As for those who are frightened of the fighting and trouble, it were better for them to die. We have all got to die some day. Why should one trouble oneself and be a coward. Government is now testing men of all nationalities, and is watching what men are making pretexts. It is the duty of everyone now to sacrifice one's life and property for the Government and to show one's courage. Let the man at the Depot know what I have written. If you people do not show your loyalty to the Sirkar at this juncture, the Sirkar will not overlook it, and there will be no prosperity for your children. My friend, you should try and get your relatives and friends to enlist and to take part in the war. What are the Germans in the face of the Indian troops? They do nothing but run away in front of us. Our artillery fire has upset all the plans of the Germans. Perhaps the Germans are now thinking of making peace, but Britain and France wish to crush the Germans utterly and set their flags flying over Berlin. It is the desire of everyone to take vengeance on the Germans for the loss of our comrades and to drink their blood ... Judged impartially the Germans are not the equals of the Indian troops.

88

Luddar Singh (Dogra, 41st Dogras) to Ragubir Singh (Kangra District, Punjab)

Barton Hospital   [Hindi]
[England]   1st July 1915

My brother, Salig Ram, was wounded on the 13th June, but he was not badly hurt. You should not be at all anxious on his account, because it is very fortunate for a man to be wounded here. For whoever is wounded escapes; but at first they used to act with great injustice and want of faith. After a man had been three times wounded, and had gone to hospital and recovered, he was passed as fit for duty by a medical board, and having joined was sent back to the trenches. Now I hear that the men who are wounded and are sent back to hospital will not be sent again to the trenches, and that the wounded are brought before a board and sent to Marseilles. Afterwards I heard – and this order has been promulgated – that the wounded would not be sent back during the war.[1]

My brother, my heart was day and night fixed on home when your card arrived, and I was like a man who, once burnt, is afraid of a glow-worm.

My brother, on the 9th of May, there was an attack by the whole of the English and the French, and the whole line of the Indians (but as you may not understand what 'the whole line' or the 'attack' means, you should ask someone who belongs to the Army). So, my friend, when my regiment went up to the trenches for the attack, it had a strength of 850 men. When the attack began, in the course of one hour 411 men were wounded, and 80 were killed, and 341 [sic] remained unhurt.[2] On the 13th again there was a small attack, and severe losses ...

These losses that I have written of were in my own regiment alone ... The destruction that occurred in the other brigades, God alone knows. I cannot write it, for over the whole earth, and the ground between the trenches, bodies were lying on bodies like stones in heaps (which no words can be found to describe or relate). This is nothing but the anger of the Almighty and it is His will. When a man dies in this world, I and you think it a great event. But here in this war, corpses are piled one upon another so that they cannot be counted.

1. See Nos. 68, 128 and associated documents.
2. On the afternoon of 9th May, the first day of the Battle of Festubert, the Bareilly Brigade attacked strong German positions in front of the Aubers Ridge. They made little headway, and suffered heavily. The 41st Dogras lost 401 men out of 645 engaged. See Merewether and Smith, *The Indian Corps in France*, pp. 361–2.

89

Bakhsh Muhammad (Punjabi Muslim) to Subedar Raja Khan
(22nd Punjabis, Mesopotamia, 39)

A hospital   [Urdu]
England   1st July 1915

I did not write to you because I was ashamed. I was on duty one night. I had had a few words with the Lance Naik of the guard. At midnight, while I was standing sentry, the Lance Naik went to where all the company was sleeping. After that, I was relieved at 2pm [sic: ?am] and was asleep when a naik came and called me saying 'you are under arrest'. I asked why, and he said the Lance Naik of my guard had put me under arrest. When [the] Lance Naik came up, there chanced to be a stick lying on the ground. I took it up and gave him something for his pains with it. I reflected then that it would be difficult to get off. Well, the Lance Naik first reported to the Indian officers that I did not stand sentry when on guard. Later they consulted together and made out that I was asleep on guard and that I had struck the Lance Naik. This is what he told the Sahib. Well, by the grace of God, I got off with a year's imprisonment. But I shall die of the shame of this. It is difficult for me to live, but all things are in the power of God.

90

Maksud Khan (Punjabi Muslim) to Jemadar Ghulam Baboo Khan (Punjab)

Kitchener's Indian Hospital [Urdu]
Brighton 2nd July 1915

I was wounded on the night of the 28th April. We were on patrol with the General Sahib, ten troopers and Jemadar Fateh Sher Khan. On the evening of the 28th April we were ordered to retire some distance as shells were falling heavily. I could not describe how the shells rained. We then went back. But our good luck deserted us. We tethered our horses at another spot. It was then night. Shells were falling all round there also ... I had lain down and so had the others, but none of us could sleep.

I was about ten yards behind the horses. A shell burst about 200 yards from us, and another about 100 yards above our heads. I cannot say which of the two shells struck me. All I knew was the sound of blood pouring from my side. My left leg had become paralysed. I sat up and began to pray to God that I should not be maimed, and if I was to be disabled it were better to lose my life. After praying, calling on the name of God I stood up. My leg was paralysed. The sentry asked me, 'why have you got up and then sat down again. Is everything all right?' I replied 'all is well, but I have been wounded slightly'. The sentry came up to me. I placed my hand on his shoulder and began to walk. Then my wound was examined with the light of matches and they wondered I was able to walk. By the grace of God and the efficacy of your prayers I did not suffer pain. Now only a slight wound remains and there is no occasion for anxiety.

91

Shahzada Khan (Khattak, 57th Rifles, now wounded) to his uncle Hashmat Khan (Peshawar District, NWFP)

The Pavilion Hospital   [Urdu]
Brighton   6th July 1915

You say that you have only received pay for two months. If you have not yet got the rest, let me know. For I am sure that the government would never devour any man's right. [Letter passed]

92

Mubarak Khan to Jahandad Khan (Punjabi Muslim, 9th Hodson's Horse, France)

Saidpur
Rawalpindi [District]   [Urdu]
[Punjab]   7th July 1915

In this part of the country all is well. There is no sickness of any sort, and we have had good rains ... I am always praying to God that he will let us meet again. Do your work well, so that no one can cast aspersions on your good name. Have no anxiety, for misfortunes always come to us.

93

Subedar Muhammad Azim Khan (Punjabi Muslim, 57th Rifles, 29) to his brother Mohammad Azim (Rawalpindi District, Punjab)

Kitchener's Indian Hospital   [Urdu?]
Brighton   9th July 1915

Letters arrive from India in fifteen or twenty days. It appears that all the letters I write do not reach you. The man who does the dishonest act of stopping my letters will never succeed in attaining his purposes. The result of the war, whether it be victory or defeat, will not be influenced by the tearing up of letters – especially by the tearing up of letters of men who entrusted their lives and fortunes and comfort and their country and their home to that nation whose blood is being shed upon the battlefield. Now my letters do not reach their destination. Allah metes out justice for every act, and you may be sure that that side will conquer which has justice with it. The side that is fighting for right will be victorious.[1]

1. Of this excerpt, the censor commented, 'no letters of this writer have been stopped by the censorship. It is possible that his letters to his brother, who is in the Forest Department in an out-of-the-way mountain district, have been delayed in transmission.'

94

Sowar Sohan Singh (Dogra, 9th Hodson's Horse) to Jodh Singh (Bitaspur, Punjab)

Kitchener's Indian Hospital [Urdu]
Brighton 10th July 1915

The state of things here is indescribable. There is a conflagration all round, and you must imagine it to be like a dry forest in a high wind in the hot weather, with abundance of dry grass and straw. No one can extinguish it but God himself – man can do nothing. What more can I write? You must carefully consider what I say. Here thousands of lives have been sacrificed. Scratch the ground to a depth of one finger, and nothing but corpses will be visible. They say that God is the great and everlasting soul of the universe, and it is only a year since all these souls were seated amongst their friends and relations and enjoying all the delights of life, and now the whole of them are lying hidden under the ground.

95

Subedar Mir Dast (Pathan, 55th Coke's Rifles, attached 57th Rifles, 38) to
Subedar [?] Khan (57th Rifles, Kohat, NWFP)

The Pavilion Hospital [Urdu]
Brighton 12th July 1915

I am in England. I have been twice wounded, once in the left hand, of which two fingers are powerless. The other injury is from gas – that is *dhua* [smoke]. I suppose you know about that. It gives me great pain and will go on doing so ... The men who came from our regiment have done very well and will do so again. I want your congratulations. I have got the Victoria Cross. The Victoria Cross is a very fine thing, but this gas gives me no rest. It has done for me.[1]

1. The 57th (Wilde's) Rifles were in the line until Christmas, then they rested and reorganized. They were back in the trenches in February, but did not see heavy fighting again until April, when they were sent, as part of the Lahore Division, to repair the breach

in the line that had resulted from the German suprise gas attack on the Ypres salient (described in No. 71). Ordered to counter-attack, the regiment was met by heavy machine gun and artillery fire. Three British officers were killed, and four wounded; six Indian officers also became casualties. A cloud of poison gas then rolled towards the regiment. The men had no gas masks, so resorted to dipping their turban-ends in chloride of lime and holding them over their mouths. Mir Dast rallied all the men he could, and held the line until ordered to retire. While falling back he helped to bring in eight wounded officers, although himself wounded and gassed. He was the fourth Indian to win the Victoria Cross. See Nos. 128 and 130. See Mason, *A Matter of Honour*, pp. 416–17; Merewether and Smith, *The Indian Corps*, pp. 313–14. His brother, also a soldier, deserted. See No. 165.

96

Mir Zada Khan (Mahsud, 127th Baluchis) to
Azim-ud-Din Khan (127th Baluchis, Karachi)

A hospital   [Urdu]
England   12th July 1915

Our people lie at a distance of twenty, thirty, fifty or a hundred yards from the Germans and we throw stones at one another. It is a fine sight to see and a fine game, the game which we are playing with the Germans. It is a great disgrace that in India the sepoys are deserting from their regiments. This is not well. The Government has shown great confidence in them. They are its servants and they have eaten its salt. It is not well to return dishonesty for this.

97

Havildar Muhammad Said (Punjabi Muslim) to
Nur Alam Khan (Hazara District, NWFP)

                                                                       [Urdu?]
The General Hospital for Indian Troops   14th July 1915

I have heard that not only in the villages, but all over the country, soothsayers are practising their art, and giving out that so-and-so is lying wounded in such-and-such a jungle and is eating leaves, and that so-and-so is dead. A sepoy named Najaf Khan died here and his death was notified to his people by the Sirkar. Now a letter from his father has been received here saying that a soothsayer had told him his son was living and lying wounded in a jungle. There were three other wounded sepoys with him. There was only one unwounded sepoy with them. He plucked leaves from the trees and gave them to his companions to eat and lived on them himself. My object in writing this is to tell you that the official information is correct, and true information is given by the Sirkar. That poor man's son is dead. The soothsayers cheat him and get money out of him. They deceive people by practising their arts and pretending to tell things that have happened thousands of miles away. Take care not to fall a victim to them yourself.

98

Bir Singh (Sikh, 55th Rifles) to Gunga Singh (55th Rifles, Kohat, NWFP)

A hospital   [Gurmukhi]
England   17th July 1915

They take great care of us here such as no one else would take except a man's mother, not even his wife. If a man falls sick at home and remains ill for a month the whole household grows weary of his illness, but these people do not grow weary. The arrangements for our food are very good, because men have been selected from the regiments to look after it and every man is served by his caste-fellows. First we suffered because the trenches were ill made, but now they are very strong and there are no losses in the trenches and no hardship. Much rain falls and if you dig down a little way in the ground you come upon water. It is very cold but we have plenty of clothing and get good rations. Our regiment has got the better of all the other regiments. They agreed to eat biscuits and European bread, but our regiment refused. So now we get *atta*, and the other regiments get biscuits – and bad [ones] at that. People told us there was no *atta* in this country, and we should have to eat biscuits; but, where there are inhabitants, there *atta* must be obtainable. Besides, there are plenty of mills.

99

Fath Khan (Punjabi Muslim) to Makhan Khan (52nd Sikhs, Bannu, NWFP)

A hospital   [Urdu]
[England?]   19th July 1915

A letter came from my home. When I had read it, I had scarce life or reason in me. I can scarcely tell you about it. My brother, Khan Muhammad Khan, Jahan Khan and Begam Nur – all these people had died. I showed the letter to my CO, but nothing could be done.

100

Santa Singh (Sikh) to his mother (India)

The hospital   [Gurmukhi]
Barton   20th July 1915

Many sons of mothers, brothers of sisters, and brothers of mothers have been lying dead for a whole year on the field of battle. A year has passed and there they lie. He who sees them for the first time says that there is no place left empty. All the ground is covered with corpses. So many corpses are there, and all have perished in forty seconds. As a man climbs a plum tree and shakes down the plums [so that] they fall and lie in heaps, so are men here fallen ... They too are the children of mothers.

101

Sowar Dawak Ram (Jat) to Dafadar Gordhan Singh (16th Cavalry, Persia)

16th Cavalry, attached 29th Cavalry   [Urdu]
[France]   22th July 1915

And what you say in your letter, that you are doing business with the sword, is quite true – but what can I do here? I get no opportunity of fighting with the sword, although I came here for that very purpose. And, my brother, what are you troubling yourself about? You are engaged in fighting against an enemy whom I look upon as an army of cobblers and sweepers [men of low caste]. See this: it is real fighting where I am, but what sort of fighting is it where you are? The war there is exactly as if a lot of cobblers were fighting amongst themselves. Now just you wait a bit while I tell you what is the real meaning of war. You talk as if you were a very great hero, but what are you in comparison with us? We have come from India like lions, and are still as lions. As yet we have had no opportunity [to fight with the sword] but we hope most surely to get the opportunity.[1]

1. The cavalry did get the opportunity to charge on horseback, but had to wait a long time for it. See No. 356.

102

Shah Baz Khan (Afridi) to Mir Badshah (A hospital, Boulogne)

40th Pathans [Urdu]
France 22nd July 1915

By the grace of God we are now resting. But we do not like it, because we are worried so much. We prefer being in the trenches.

103

Khan Muhammad (40th Pathans) to Sher Jang (40th Pathans, a hospital, France)

A hospital [Urdu]
England 26th July 1915

As yet I have not been before the medical board, to decide whither I am to go. When I know, I will write. But I expect that I shall remain here another month or six weeks. Your complaint, that of having had the trench fall on you – is a very good one. But do not straighten your back. Wherever you go, do not straighten your back. Then, please God, something good will come of it. But do not straighten your back. I wish to impress this upon you as strongly as I can ... Do not straighten your back. Your position is a very good one.

104

Badshah Khan (Afridi) to Torai Khan (57th Rifles, France)

Meerut Stationary Hospital [Urdu]
[France?] 26th July 1915

I am praying for you and beseeching the welfare of all Muslims. I have seen some who did not even keep the fast. The Punjabis do not keep it at all. They are dishonest rogues. When they are in the trenches they call upon the name of God, [but] when they are at rest, then it is 'bonsoir madame'.

105

Dhunjibhoy Chinoy (Parsi) to H. R. Mistry
(Purshotum Morarjie's House, Grant Road, Bombay)

Kitchener's Indian Hospital   [Gujerati]
Brighton   [c. mid-July 1915]

Brother, there is plenty to eat here and it is a land of fairies; but the supervision
over us is very strict, and we are not allowed to go anywhere, and are hard pressed,
and we do not like it. At first the *salas*[1] allowed us more freedom and we acted
according to our pleasure and stayed out – sometimes all night. We were even placed
outside in billets; but some men abused the privilege,[2] and it was entirely stopped.
We had plenty to eat wherever we went and the people were greatly pleased, not
ever having seen natives[3] before, and they thought we had come to save them. Some
became diseased[4] and some were flogged. If God releases us from this soon it will
be well ... I feel afraid to write openly as perhaps the censor may open the letter.

1. A term of abuse, probably being here applied to whites.
2. Probably a veiled reference to sex with white women, as is the remark about staying
    out all night.
3. This word was originally written in English.
4. A sexually transmitted disease is probably implied.

106

Havildar Karim Ullah Khan (Pathan, 58th Rifles) to
Ghazan Khan (58th Rifles, France)

Kitchener's Indian Hospital   [Urdu]
Brighton   30th July 1915

Here I am very well and happy. My arm is quite well. But I do not want at all to
leave you in Europe. For when I go home, everyone will say 'how did you leave
Ghazan Khan and Khuda Dad Khan?' And my sister when she sees me will be beside
herself and will suspect that there is some other reason. My brother Abdullah Khan
and she will give me no peace. Moreover, my heart is not at all willing that I should
come away, leaving my friend in the flames. If it is to be India, then by God's order
it shall be India for all of us of the brotherhood. If we are to die, then let us all die
together. I have been before the medical board and have been ordered to return to
the *firing line*[1] – that is, to the *front*.

The facts are as follows: there is a wounded sepoy of the 129th [Baluchis] here
and a hospital babu named Kali Charan, in block J, the place where I was. The

sepoy told the babu that he wanted some milk. The babu replied, 'after placing your backside at the disposal of the Germans, you have come here to drink milk, have you?' There was a stick lying by my bed. It was about 10am. I called upon God and His Prophet[2] and, taking up the stick, I gave the babu what for. His right forearm was broken and two of his teeth. A report was made about it. Forthwith, doctors, majors, lieutenants and all the lot of them came charging on to me.

I was put before the Chief Doctor [and?] the Colonel of No. 3 Division, with the babu. The babu was all wounded. The Colonel Sahib asked me what it was all about. The sepoy and I replied, telling him what the babu had said. The Colonel Sahib said 'I expect your havildari will be broken.' I made representation, saying 'Huzur, have we been fighting the Germans, or getting ****** by them? I should like to write a petition to General Wil Kak Sahib Bahadur.'[3] The Colonel asked me what sort of court martial I should prefer. I said 'military officers, please'. All the Indian officers who are here, about twenty of them, went to the Colonel on my behalf. Meantime, the OC of the 19th came here, from the Suez Canal. When he heard that a havildar was to be court-martialled he went and spoke to the Doctor-General, and said that it was a great shame and he would send a telegram to London.

So the enquiry was resumed. The babu was formerly in the first class. He has been reduced to the single stripe – that is, he has been broken. The OC of the 19th, Sahib Bahadur, gave me Rs.10, and the order now is that I, a havildar, am in a room with three Indian officers and no black babu is allowed to come into it. The Major Sahib comes there and talks a lot with us. I said of my own accord that I wanted to go back to the *front*. The order has been given, and I shall shortly come, but first of all I shall go and see London. [Letter passed]

1. Italicized words are in English in the original.
2. The religious expression suggests that the writer objected in particular to the use of offensive language by a Hindu to a Muslim soldier.
3. A respectful, and very rare, reference to General James Willcocks, the C-in-C Indian Corps in France.

107

Lance Naik Jadhbir Thapa (Gurkha) to Baboo Sham Singh Thapa (F Section, No. 11 Indian Field Hospital, 6th Indian Division, Basra, Mesopotamia)

[Gurkhali]
France   July 1915

I am very sorry to say that those officers and men who came from India first are nearly all gone. The battalion is now composed of Assam and Burma Military Police and 2/6th Gurkha Reserve. We are now out of the trenches for a rest which we have all earned. I am very sorry to inform you that one of our officers named Lieutenant [Arthur] Carter [4th Gurkha Rifles] was killed accidentally two or three days ago [20th July 1915] when he was instructing the bomb party, as the bomb burst in his hand. Nothing fresh. With love, and praying for a speedy victory of our kind Government.

108

Ram Kirshan Thapa to Naik Kishan Sing Kanwar (1/4th Gurkha Rifles, France)

Kitchener's Indian Hospital   [Gurkhali]
Brighton   July 1915

You wrote and told me not to try to come to India. What you wrote is right. But, according to my understanding, I have not tried to go there. What I said about going to France is because this hospital is a very bad place. All the natives of India, by practising deception, have made the doctors in charge displeased with them. If they are slightly wounded in the hand, they pretend that they cannot move their hands at all. The Gurkhas are all disgusted with the natives of India. Here for every work they seek out Gurkhas. But still this place is a very large prison. I cannot put on my belt; nor can I double; I am troubled with coughing and sneezing; but I tell the Sahibs here that I am all right. Because I say that, from this hospital I have no chance of going direct to India: perhaps I will go to France. [Letter passed]

109

Itirza to Havildar Thuia (Rajput, 38th Dogras, France)

Hoshiarpur District   [Urdu]
[Punjab]   July 1915

In every village the war is the leading topic and chief affair, and you will not meet many men. Wherever you go you will find two or three men engaged in recruiting duty. The rains have begun and crops have been sown.

110

Jemadar Gujar Singh (Dogra) to Subedar Kapur Singh (38th Dogras, Malakand, NWFP, 39)

Kitchener's Indian Hospital   [Hindi]
Brighton   July 1915

What Charat Singh wrote is all false. No one did any great work. I have heard that the 39th Garhwalis were retiring and Charat Singh was amongst them. God knows that when Charat Singh came to the 41st [Dogras] and heard that an attack was to take place on the 9th May ... he reported sick[1] ... But when the Indian officer was wounded in the attack he rejoined so as to try and get the vacancy. These people accomplish their end in this way. You do not know them. But I have heard from the sepoys that Udini Singh did very good work. He was carrying a box of ammunition and when he got to the big trench Charat Singh relieved him of the box, took it to the British officer, and told him that he had brought it. For this reason he was given the jemadari. Do you consider this bravery? This I have heard from some Garhwali sepoys who were doing duty in the 41st. So I let you know that our sepoys behaved well but it is a pity that we did not have any of our own officers. [Letter passed]

1. The 41st Dogras were part of the attack by the Meerut Division on 9th May. See No. 88.

111

Gulab Singh (Rajput, 16th Rajputs) to Kalu Singh (3rd Cavalry, France)

Brockenhurst [Urdu]
England 2nd August 1915

I am quite sure and confidently expect that you will go on doing your duty in the same spirit as you write. God will make you famous. Have no fear. God is master of all. I expect that you will fasten on the medal of victory and will shortly return to your native village. This is the first occasion on which our quivering arm is showing to a tyrannous enemy on the fields of Europe the jewel of the real Rajput blood.[1] Our benign government is grateful, heart and soul, for the way in which we are fulfilling our duty. The time is at hand that our reputation will be exalted. It is a good opportunity to obey the behest of our superiors and to pray to God, from whom alone comes justice. We can do nothing. We must cleave to our duties, and on our so doing our claims as men depend.

1. Typically Rajput sentiments. See Nos. 234 and 256.

112

Muhammad Khan (Punjabi Muslim) to Nawab Khan (India)

129th Baluchis [Urdu]
France 4th August 1915

Sajawal Khan has written to me from Cawnpore Cantonment [UP]. He said that he could not get any leave to go home. He said that the wheat harvest had been utterly ruined. Please write and tell me whether this is true or not. Anyhow, Sajawal Khan said that he had sent Rs.25 home from Rawalpindi [in Punjab], and he was going to send Rs.10 more. Other men here get letters from our country, and they tell me that there is terrible scarcity there. Please write and tell me whether this is true or not.

113

Havildar Ghufran Khan (Afridi, 129th Baluchis) to Subedar Zaman Khan
(Depot, 129th Baluchis, Karachi, 43)

Pavilion Hospital   [Urdu]
Brighton   4th August 1915

The arrangements here to enable our people to keep Ramazan are excellent. Colonel Southey [?] Sahib – perhaps you know him – has made excellent arrangements and takes great trouble for us Muslims. His arrangements for our food during the fast are very good, and he has put us all together in one place, because during the fast it is not easy to live with Sikhs and Dogras. I cannot describe how good his arrangements are. I have heard from the regiment. They are still behind, resting, but I do not know how long it will last. I saw the Adjutant, [Lieutenant Griffith-] Griffin Sahib, here. His wound has healed and he said he had been passed as fit by the doctors and was going back to the regiment. He had a bullet wound in his foot. [Letter passed]

114

Buta Singh (Sikh) to Harnam Singh (23rd Pioneers, Aden)

[Kitchener's Indian Hospital?]   [Gurmukhi]
Brighton   5th August 1915

I have to tell you that all of us who were suffering from piles have returned to India. If you are still unwell, why do you not return? Your excuse is a good one. If you come any further you will probably lose your life. We were 200 strong when we arrived. Now there are forty of us. No! Make any excuse you can, and return home, so that one of us can be saved. We know from letters that the wives of men still alive have taken other husbands. People of the Punjab have lost all hope. [Letter withheld]

115

Sepoy Abdul Ghani (Punjabi Muslim) to his brother
Nur Dad (Jhelum District, Punjab)

125th Napier's Rifles   [Urdu]
[France]   5th August 1915

The whole day passes in expectation, and the whole night in consternation, but your letter never comes. My friend, to us travellers the time passes as it did at Karbala when our high priest [Husayn, the younger son of Ali] fought and met his death as a martyr at the hand of the infidels.[1] Then our warriors used to meet in the morning, and march off, saying to one another 'farewell: go, and God be with thee'. So they died the deaths of martyrs. In like manner the time passes with us, who with our brothers and relatives, have men in thousands, and remain congregated together, and seated writing until the lives quit the bodies of those whose time has come. And at such a time you do not send a letter. Well, the grief of this will accompany me to the grave; second, I regret [?] that my mother and sisters will not be with me at my last moments; and third, that as yet I have seen nothing of the world. Well, praise be to God: His will is mine.

See our prophets who gave their sons in the way of God. When the Almighty by way of trial ordered Abraham (on whom be peace!) to sacrifice his son Ishmael [sic] he was pleased and said 'Amen; for thou O God gavest him to me, and he is thy property.' And when Abraham took his son, his beloved son, into the wilderness to sacrifice him, he said to him 'my son! I am about to sacrifice you in the name of God.' Then Ishmael also was pleased and said 'Oh my father! bind my hand and my feet with cords; that way, when you slay my body, neither my hands nor my feet shall be in your way; for my will is His will.'[2]

My brother, you should give thanks to God, and remember me, your poor brother, for my time is come to be sacrificed. At some time the knife of death will descend. Pray that God may be gracious both in this world and the next, for His mercy is necessary. [Letter passed]

1. See No. 56.
2. Wilfred Owen used a similar image in his war poem, *The Parable of the Old Man and the Young*.

116

Murarao Shinde to Havildar Krishna Shinde
(Maratha, with the 107th Pioneers)

Tandurwadi
Satara [District]   [Marathi]
[Bombay]   5th August 1915

What we all have to say to you is this – that you should serve the Government loyally and well. God will reward you, and you will increase the reputation of our people. The Marathas are as a mountain and cannot be moved. Do not show your back to the enemy, for your religious teaching forbids this.

117

Teja Singh (Sikh) to Dafadar Bhagat Singh (13th Lancers,
Risalpur, Peshawar District, NWFP)

                                                             [Urdu]
France   6th August 1915

To the person who examines this letter. Please cut out what is unnecessary and do not destroy the letter.[1] [Letter passed]

1. Several soldiers directly address the censor. See for example Nos. 314, 353 and 375.

118

Sonu Gaekwar (Maratha, 107th Pioneers) to Shankerao Gaekwar
(Poona District, Bombay)

Kitchener's Indian Hospital   [Marathi]
Brighton   12th August 1915

You must not be in the least bit anxious. This material universe is merely an illusion, because just in the same way as you weep so do my father, brother and sister. But this is a useless proceeding on your part, because at such a time as this, even if my life should be lost, it should cause you all intense joy. First, for many days I have eaten the salt of the Government. Second, such an opportunity to die is never likely to recur. Such a death is a true liberation from future birth.[1] Not only is this so for me alone; but it is the same for all heroes. Everyone knows this, but you should take it into your careful consideration and tell others.

1. He means, if he dies in battle in the service of his King, he is liberated from the cycle of death and rebirth, and goes directly to Heaven. See Nos. 12, 17, 62 and 198.

119

To Sowar Amir Ali Khan (Khattak Pathan, 36th Jacob's Horse, France)
from his mother.

Kohat   [Urdu]
[NWFP]   13th August 1915

I must inform you that in the first instance there was much foot and mouth disease here, through which your father got into debt, and all our jewellery was pawned ... And although indeed there was an abundance of grain this year, we had to sell a portion of the grain to pay for the redemption of the jewellery, and now the cattle disease has begun again. Much millet and Indian corn was sown, but God knows whether a famine is not coming. Grain is growing dearer daily, and wheat is five rupees eight annas a *maund*, and barley three rupees eight annas. If you had sent money to your father, why should he have to sell the grain? Therefore consider and bethink you whether you cannot send your father half what you have in the Government treasury, and settle a monthly payment on him. Without fail send money to your revered parent. I implore you urgently to do so. If you should return home in safety, you should bring the money yourself. Therefore if you come home, it is well. Your father is ashamed to write himself: he says 'when he is in such a situation of danger how can I ask him for money?' I beg you urgently to send without fail half the money you have in hand, and a further allowance of ten rupees a month. Do not fail.

120

Khan Muhammad (Punjabi Muslim, 40th Pathans) to Waria [Waris?] Khan[1]
(69th Punjabis, France)

Pavilion Hospital   [Urdu]
Brighton   16th August 1915

In our regiment [the 40th] the following drafts have arrived: from the 18th, the 113th, the 33rd and the 17th; and I have heard that a draft from the 74th has come to the 69th.[2] [Letter passed]

1. This could be a letter to Waris Khan, killed in the attack of 25th September. See No. 181 for a lament.
2. His comments reveal how difficult it was to maintain the traditional ethnic composition of regiments, and their *esprit de corps,* in the face of heavy losses.

121

Saif Ali (Punjabi Muslim) to Kasim Din (19th Punjabis, Seistan, Persia)

40th Pathans or 129th Baluchis   [Urdu]
France   17th August 1915

The country is very fine, well watered and fertile. The fields are very large, all gardens full of fruit trees. Every man's land yields him thousands of *maunds* of wheat. The chief products are wheat, potatoes, beans and every kind of grain except the noble millet. All the year round it rains three times a week. There is no need to water the land. For three months there is snow; for the rest, the climate is good and delightful. If one were to plant a garden anywhere, it would grow. Even vegetables need no watering, because every week at least three or four good showers fall. The fruits are pears, apricots, grapes and fruits of many kinds. Even the dogs refuse them at this season. Several regiments could eat from one tree. The people are very well mannered and well-to-do. The value of each house may be set down as several *lakhs* or *crores* of rupees. Each house is a sample of paradise. The people far surpass the Egyptians. The wits are set wool-gathering by rosy cheeks and dainty ringlets. Wherever you look you see the same. One is tempted to exclaim 'O merciful God, that hast made all this from a little dirty semen! Praise be to God!' [Letter passed]

122

Jemadar Muhammad Khan (Punjabi Muslim) to
Jemadar-Adjutant Abdulla Khan (129th Baluchis, France, 33)

Zossen   [Urdu]
Germany   17th August 1915[1]

A letter came from you once before, which I answered. So now I am writing to you a second time. I am now all well by the Grace of God. I am a German prisoner. I hope you will send me an answer quickly on receipt of this, though I know that you have not much leisure.

1. This letter reached London on 2nd September 1915, was forwarded to India by mistake, and thence was returned. The intended recipient probably did not read it until the end of October 1915.

123

Santa Singh (Sikh) to his uncle (India)

A hospital [Gurmukhi]
Brighton 18th August 1915

As tired bullocks and bull buffaloes lie down in the month of Bhadon[1] so lies the weary world. Our hearts are breaking, for a year has passed while we have stood to arms without a rest ... Germany fights the world with ghastly might, harder to crush than well-soaked grain in the mill. For even wetted grain can be ground in time ... We have bound ourselves under the flag and we must give our bodies.

1. August–September. In this month, the tanks are full of water, from which it is often difficult to dislodge tired and hot cattle.

124

*Abdul Rahman to Muhammad Nawaz Khan (Punjabi Muslim, 28th Punjabis,
attached 57th Rifles, France)*

Lahore [District] [Urdu]
[Punjab] 20th August 1915

When I went recruiting I got one recruit. I produced seven recruits before the Recruiting Officer, but they were all rejected.[1] I got four recruits here and am continuing my efforts. As God wills, so will it happen, and all is for the best. But no men of our tribe are now to be found. They have all been recruited already. Very few young men are to be seen now, and those the Recruiting Officer will not take ... All is well at home. At first there was a great shortage of rain. The people sowed *bajra*,[2] but the produce was very scanty. On the 16th August the rain began. God showed mercy and the people are sowing. Wheat is selling at six *tolas* and *bajra* and maize at seven *paropis*;[3] *moth*, *mung*, *mash* and *massur* [varieties of lentils] are at three *tolas* ... Everything is very dear.

1. Presumably on medical grounds.
2. A dry grain, used by the rural poor of North India to make *chapattis*.
3. A *paropi* is presumably a measure of weight or volume.

125

Waris Khan (Punjabi Muslim) to Sepoy Hazir Khan (89th Punjabis, France)

82nd Regiment
Nowshera
[Peshawar District]   [Urdu?]
[NWFP]   20th August 1915

Do not be anxious my dear friend. Every man whom God created is bound to die
some day. There is no doubt about it. And my friends, do your work well, and fight
well. Now is your opportunity. We also are looking forward for our opportunity
to come. Both we and you have eaten of the salt of the Sirkar, and it is for us to
show loyalty in return. It is laid down in the law of the Prophet that he who has
eaten of the salt must show loyalty in return. We and you both send up our prayers
that God may grant victory to our King. God will be gracious. It was your great
good fortune my friends, that, having eaten of the salt of the Sirkar, you can now
show your loyalty. He who having eaten of the salt joins the field of battle and
remains there stoutly fighting, acquits himself of his duty. What else should I say?
Do not be annoyed at what I have written. We also are ready. It is only fate which
is delaying us. When shall we get the order to go to the war and show our loyalty
to the Sirkar? We are sore at the delay. [Letter passed]

126

Sub-Assistant Surgeon Abdulla (Punjabi Muslim) to a friend (India)

Kitchener's Indian Hospital   [Urdu]
Brighton   23rd August 1915

Yesterday the Emperor inspected this place and I had a very good sight of him.
There was great excitement. He stayed nearly an hour in the hospital and spoke
very kindly to the patients, asking about their condition. The sight of the Emperor
delighted the hearts of all. [Letter passed]

127

Asmat Khan (Pathan) to his father (Usterzai, Kohat District, NWFP)

40th Pathans   [Urdu]
France   23th August 1915

As for what you wrote telling me to do good work for the Government, I am doing
so. We are five brothers. If one or two are killed in the war, it is no matter.

128

Yusaf Khan (Pathan) to Harif Khan (40th Pathans, France)

Kitchener's Indian Hospital [Urdu]
Brighton 25th August 1915

The King and the King's Memsahib, and the King's daughter came here. They saw all the patients and gave decorations to seven men who had done brave deeds. There was a subedar of the 57th Rifles, named Mir Dast, who also received a decoration.[1] The day before, he received a telegram from the King telling him to write out a paper containing whatever request he had to make, and the King would ask him about it when he came. The request which he made was this: 'I have no son that you might give him a jemadari or a havildari. But this is my request, that when a man has once been wounded, it is not well to take him back again to the trenches.[2] For no good work will be done by his hand, but he will spoil others' also.' [Letter passed]

1. The Victoria Cross. See Nos. 95 and 130.
2. The most important grievance of the sepoys. See especially No. 68 and associated documents.

129

Jemadar Mad Amir (Afridi) to Naik Ghapur (28th Punjabis, Colombo, Ceylon)

57th Rifles [Urdu]
France 25th August 1915

Please tell me anything fresh that may happen in the regiment, and think this over and make an enquiry of Mir Gul. If you do not understand, [let us say] that a letter came from our country [the NWFP] to me and there has been fighting between the Malik Din Khel and the Qambar Khel, and one Samat Ullah Khan of the Malik Din Khel has joined the Qambar Khel. And if you know, then send me an answer; and if you do not know, then again send me an answer ... And Lance Naik Samat Ullah Khan has been guilty of rank treachery and has disgraced the name of the 28th.[1]

1. This coded letter, ostensibly about a tribal feud, in fact tells of the Lance Naik's desertion to the enemy. The 'Malik Din Khel' and the 'Qambar Khel' stand for the British and the Germans, respectively.

130

Subedar Mir Dast, VC (38) to Naik Nur Zada (55th Rifles, Kohat, NWFP)

[Kitchener's Indian Hospital?]

[Urdu]
27th August 1915

By the great, great, great kindness of God, the King with his royal hand has given me the decoration of the Victoria Cross.[1] God has been very gracious, very gracious, very gracious, very gracious, very, very, very, very, very [gracious] to me. Now I do not care. I want the kindness of God. If I go to Egypt, I do not regret it. The desire of my heart is accomplished ... Show great zeal in your duty, and be faithful, and eat the salt of the Government with loyalty. [Letter passed]

1. See Nos. 95 and 128.

131

A Punjabi Muslim soldier to his sister (Rawalpindi District, Punjab)

[Unnamed RFA battery]
France

[Urdu]
31st August 1915

Do not lose heart. I will certainly arrange some means to come [home] ... Your brother will soon come. If this cannot be, for we are here on Government service and have no choice of our own – you are wise and think things out for yourself – take great care of our parents' house, and look after your own house, too.[1] [Letter passed]

1. Of this letter, the censor commented 'if it were not so familiar as to be altogether commonplace, it would be almost incredible that [this] extract ... should on the whole be typical of sepoy sentiment, but so it is. They would like to get out of it if they could, but are prepared to go on enduring, if necessary.'

132

Ghulam Abbas Ali Khan (Punjabi Muslim) to
Risaldar Muhammad Sarwar Khan (Mardan, Peshawar District, NWFP)

Guides Cavalry
Attached Jullundur Brigade Staff
[France]

[Urdu and Punjabi]
31st August 1915

Our party so far are all well and happy. Only three men have been wounded. We are now going on foot into the trenches. There has been no cavalry work at all.

Hereafter, we cannot tell. This [the German] is not such a King as can be defeated quickly. There are three very powerful Kings against him. What can I write about it? You yourself are wise. We used to hear at home that the King of Russia was a great King. But this one has knocked forts out of him and smashed him and taken much of his country. There is a country belonging to the Turks too which they call Dadarnes [the Dardanelles]. There has been fighting there with the Turks, about which I cannot tell you. There France, Italy, England and another four Kings had their armies. The Turk smashed and bashed the whole lot, and the losses were heavy.[1] The Turks are the bravest of all. We are ever praying that the victory may be granted to our King, the King of peace.

1. After the failure of an attempt to force the Dardanelles with warships, Allied troops landed on the Gallipoli peninsula in April 1915. They were unable to make much headway in the face of severe Turkish resistance, and the operation was abandoned at the end of the year.

133

Shiv Ram (Jat) to Shri Dutt (Sheriya Village, Beri, Rohtak District, Punjab)

Indian Military Depot   [Hindi]
Milford-on-Sea   August 1915

And brother, day and night I think of this – that the Divine Being may give victory to the Government, and that our fame may remain in accordance with the work which we have done. There is only one regiment of Jats [in France?], but it has won renown, and there is no doubt that there is a race of Jats. Now the people who talk say that it is a very brave race, and has done very well; and they know that those who have suffered heavy losses have done good work. For the duty is of that nature, and now is the opportunity to take service if one wishes. [Letter passed]

134

Havildar Bohar Khan (Punjabi Muslim) to his uncle
Mohammad Niamat Khan (Hoshiarpur District, Punjab)

Lady Hardinge Hospital   [Urdu?]
[Brockenhurst]   1st September 1915

Since I came to this country I have enjoyed excellent health. There is no cause for anxiety on my account. The climate is very healthy. The people of this country are all of respectable family. They treat the Indians with courtesy and kindliness.

There is no country in the world like England. May God bestow on it honour and glory, and grant victory to our King over the other Kings. I receive letters constantly from Wilayet Khan. By the favour of God he is in good health.

If it can be done, I would like you to write me a letter in flowing style as if you were composing a prayer for the victory of our King. You might say that for India the rule of a King is the best. You might give me also some good advice, and add also that I myself have been giving good advice in the same strain in my letters to Wilayet Khan in East Africa – such as to fight bravely on the field of battle, and that it is the duty of Rajputs to display courage.[1]

Send me a letter of this sort, written in full and flowing style, and be careful to give full particulars of your address. My idea is, on receipt of your letter, to send it to the London press which will print it. The King's office will make a note of the letter, and it will be noticed by the offices of high authority also. Your name will become illustrious. Those who read the letter published in the papers will become favourably disposed towards the Sirkar, and its perusal will comfort them. You must remember that after this war there will be no other opportunities afforded for the display of courage. Please be careful to address this letter to me, <u>not to Wilayet Khan</u>. [Letter passed]

1. No. 174 gives a very different picture of such letters, which were very common.

135

Shah Nawaz (Hindustani Muslim) to *Signaller Daiyad Abdul Shah (Shahpur, Allahabad, UP)*

Indian General Hospital
Base Depot   [Urdu]
Marseilles   1st September 1915

We are all in contentment and ease. Have no anxiety. Only pray that God Almighty will keep us in health. Life and death are in the hands of the Omnipotent One. No one can help himself. And as long as man is engaged in war, any sort of illness, even for a second, is the wrath of God. But all days, good or bad, must pass. What can I write of this part of the world? I have neither the ability nor the leisure. The Creator has shown the perfection of his beneficence in Europe, and we people [Indians] have been created only for the purpose of completing the totality of the world. In truth, it has now become evident that the Indian is not fit to stand in any rank of the world. You may be sure that India will not rise to the pitch of perfection for Europe for another two thousand years. The French nation is highly civilized, and they have great affection for us. Believe me that they honour one of our soldiers to an extent of which we are not – and never could be – worthy. [Letter passed]

136

Colour Havildar Bhola Khan (Punjabi Muslim) to
Lance Naik Chulam Haidar (106th Pioneers, Quetta, Baluchistan)

129th Baluchis [Urdu]
[France] 1st September 1915

The arrangements of the British Government are excellent, and I cannot sufficiently praise them. For everything necessary for comfort is to be had, and all the troops spend their time in ease. Please God, He will of His grace and mercy speedily show us the day on which civilization will triumph, and the race of savages [the Germans] will be extirpated. [Letter passed]

137

Ram Prasad (Brahmin) to Manik Chand
(c/o Sikander Ali, Bamba Debi Bazar, Marwari Water Tank, Bombay)

Kitchener's Indian Hospital [Hindi]
Brighton 2nd September 1915

And send me fourteen or fifteen *tolas* of *charas*, and understand that you must send it so that no one may know. First fill a round tin box full of pickles and then in the middle of that put a smaller round box carefully closed, so that no trace of the pickles can enter. And send a letter to me four days before you send the parcel off. [Letter withheld]

138

*Rajwali Khan (Punjabi Muslim or Pathan) to Ghulam Hussain
(59th Rifles, France)*

Kitchener's Indian Hospital [Urdu]
Brighton 4th September 1915

If only I could see you once, then I should have nothing to regret. If God grants life, then I shall see you again. But it is difficult, for we are plunged in great and grievous calamity. Whenever I write to you, I am filled with anxiety. But nothing can be done. Alas! Alas! What am I to say about myself, that would be fit to write? There is nothing but my corpse left. They have cut off the whole of one leg, and one hand too is useless. What is the use of my going to India thus? I am always in distress on your account. Please write soon ... They have given me a leg, but it is made of wood, and vile. I cannot walk. I shall start for India in a few days. You must write at once ... I am taking nothing but a picture back to India. There is nothing left of me. I have lost a hand and a leg. What am I to do? [Letter withheld]

139

*Adam Khan (Yusufzai Pathan) to Shadi Khan
(Guides Infantry, attached 57th Rifles, France)*

Guides Infantry
Mardan
[Peshawar District] [Urdu]
[NWFP] 4th September 1915

I went home on leave for the Id and reached home on the 15th August 1915. On my way back I rejoined at Rustam where [the regiment had been] on active service. Fighting took place on the 17th, but our regiment had no loss. Ten men – Sikhs and Dogras – were hurt. There was fighting on the 17th, 21st, 26th, 28th and 31st at Rustam. The Ghazis suffered very heavy loss.

140

Lal Baz (Afridi) to his brother (Frontier Constabulary, India)

40th Pathans [Urdu]
France 7th September 1915

Do your duty well. I am not pleased that you have entered the service of the Government, but I am pleased that you are in the militia.[1] I know very well that you will have many hardships to undergo, but you must not take them to heart ... How many of our Aka Khel and Marai Khel have enlisted, and who are with you? How many have enlisted in the 40th? Write me all their names, and say that 'so and so are with me, and so and so in the 40th'. Write home and tell them that I am well and there is no cause for anxiety. You wrote that I was dead, but I am very well. Send this letter home and do not do such a wicked act again. Do not quarrel with anyone and do not waste your money. Ours is a poor country. Do not commit sodomy with your messmates, but remain on good terms with them and spend money on them freely. Do not resort to harlots and do not gamble. My greetings to all the Aka Khel. [Letter passed]

1. Because militiamen were not liable for active service outside India.

141

Abdul Shakur Khan to Sowar Muhammad Shafi
(Punjabi Muslim, 23rd Cavalry, attached 4th Cavalry, France)

Mandalay   [Urdu]
Burma   12th September 1915

Continue thus to write letters [informing us] of your welfare so that we may not be anxious ... The news has already been written and is no doubt already known to you ... Further, in these days there is a very strict *order*[1] of the *Government* Sahib Bahadur that no news of fighting ... should be written at all. Anyone who writes [such things] will receive severe punishment. Think much of this small writing. Keep writing exactly every fortnight, because the letters take exactly a month to come ... [PS] This is my advice to you, not to write anything ~~against~~[2] about the affairs of the Sirkar Emperor of India [but speak only of] your welfare. As far as possible you must show a good disposition towards your Sirkar. [Letter passed]

1. Italicized words were in English in the original.
2. Word deleted, but apparently left legible in the original.

142

Ser Gul (Pathan, 129th Baluchis) to Barber Machu Khan
(57th Rifles, serving at the front)

Indian Hospital   [Urdu]
Rouen   13th September 1915

I have no need of anything, but I have a great longing for a flute to play. What can I do? I have no flute. Can you get me one from somewhere? If you can, please do, and send it to me. Take this much trouble for me. For I have a great desire to play upon the flute, since great dejection is fallen upon me. You must, you simply must, get one from somewhere. I have no need of anything else. But this you must manage as soon as you can. Make a small wooden box, put a little cotton wool in it, and put a flute to play on in the middle of the cotton wool. Then put a little cloth over it. Get Umar Din to write the address in English and it will reach me all right. Pack it so that the flute will not shake about. I shall be very grateful. I have no need of anything else ... You must arrange this as quickly as possible.[1] [Letter passed]

1. Of this letter, the censor commented, 'Indian Soldiers' Fund please note!' It is impossible to discover whether the administrators of the Fund took any action in this case.

143

Sowar Jalal-ud-Din to Dafadar Ghulam Muhammad Khan
(Pathan, 9th Lancers, France)

British Consulate
Shiraz   [Urdu]
Persia   13th September 1915

May God destroy and annihilate the mad German who has upset the whole world – and by God's help, and your valour, annihilated he will be.

144

Pensioned Sergeant of Police Gobind Saha to Jemadar Ganda Singh
(Punjabi Hindu, 6th Cavalry, France, 37)

Rawalpindi District   [Urdu]
[Punjab]   14th September 1915

I am ... always in prayer, especially for your regiment, and my heart longs for a glimpse of the Sahib Bahadurs [the British officers]. I have already mentioned that if any regimental rule will permit, I would like to go and do some service. But the way is long and weary and to arrive without the order of the Government is difficult. If you cannot send for me, write and tell me, so that I may go to Sialkot [in Punjab] and serve the Government there. If anything from this country is wanted for your Sahib Bahadurs, I can send it. Convey my greeting to them all. When I saw the picture of the great and exalted Lord Roberts[1] on your letter from the theatre of war, my heart was overjoyed and I felt a longing, if only I were near at hand, to go and hang a wreath of flowers round his horse's neck. But the distance is great and I have no means to pass. Please, when you have a little time, make a wreath of the best flowers that you can get round the neck of the horse which His Excellency [Roberts] rides, and another round the neck of the Colonel's horse, when he goes forth to ride. Then let me know when you have done so. If you cannot do this, let me know and I will send the two wreaths in a parcel from here. When I saw the picture of the Sahib Bahadur my mind was transported with delight. Every morning I regard it with pride. There is a shortage of rain and the autumn crop is poor. [Letter passed]

1. Frederick Sleigh 'Bobs' Roberts, First Earl Roberts of Kandahar (1832–1914). Commissioned Bengal Artillery, 1851; won a Victoria Cross in the Mutiny; Abyssinia, 1867–68; Afghanistan, 1878–80; C-in-C Madras, 1881–85; Burma, 1886–87; C-in-C India, 1885–93; C-in-C South Africa, 1899–1900; C-in-C British Army, 1901–4. He died in November 1914 while visiting Indian troops in France. The writer appears to be unaware of his death.

145

Hakim Abdul Ghufar Khan to Dafadar Nur Mohammad Khan
(Pathan, 38th CIH, France)

Peshawar   [Urdu or Pashtu?]
[NWFP]   15th September 1915

There was some fighting in Swat in the neighbourhood of the Fort at Chakdarra. The Swatis suffered very heavy loss and ran away. There has been no more fighting in that direction since. There is still some fighting going on against the Mohmands. The Sirkar has, however, cleared the country from Abazai to Shabqadr on the north of the road by destroying with shell fire all the villages in the neighbourhood. All the people have been ruined. The reason why the villages were destroyed was that they had been harbouring the men who had been raiding British territory. The Mohmands had raided the Doaba in the Peshawar District. They looted the houses of all the well-to-do people, and outraged the women. On one night alone they raided nine villages. The whole country is now full of troops and things are quietening down. The unrest is nothing like so great as it has been, one reason being that the Babra Mulla is displeased with the Mohmands because, instead of fighting openly, they are merely making raids against unprotected villages. It is said that he has declared that he will never live among them again, and that he has left them. The Sirkar has dealt with the Mohmands with great vigour and we hope that this time they will be disposed of once and for all. [Letter passed]

146

Sant Singh (Sikh) to his wife

<table>
<tr><td>[France?]</td><td style="text-align:right">[Gurmukhi poetry]
18th September 1915</td></tr>
</table>

We perish in the desert: you wash yourself and lie in bed. We are trapped in a net of woe, while you go free. Our life is a living death. For what great sin are we being punished? Kill us, Oh God, but free us from our pain! We move in agony, but never rest. We are slaves of masters who can show no mercy. The bullets fall on us like rain, but dry are our bodies. So we have spent a full year. We cannot write a word. Lice feed upon our flesh: we cannot wait to pick them out. For days we have not washed our faces. We do not change our clothes. Many sons of mothers lie dead. No one takes any heed. It is God's will that this is so, and what is written is true. God The Omnipotent plays a game, and men die. Death here is dreadful, but of life there is not the briefest hope. [Letter suppressed]

147

'Ram Lal, Dhobi' to Dhobi Siraj-ud-Din (Depot, 40th Pathans,
Fatehgarh, Farrukhabad District, UP)

<table>
<tr><td>40th Pathans
France</td><td style="text-align:right">[Urdu]
19th September 1915</td></tr>
</table>

You must send me about at least one hundred nuts of the *bhalwa*, which is used for marking clothes. I have need of them.[1]

Greetings to all present when this is read and to all friends. Our prayers for them. Ram Ram to all Hindus.

1. Although the letter is signed 'Ram Lal' (a Hindu name) it is clearly from one Muslim to another, and the signature is bogus. He is posing as a *dhobi* in order to obtain *bhalwa* for the purpose of malingering.

148

Storekeeper Ram Jawan Singh (Hindustani Hindu) to M. Jacques Derel
(Avenue Victor Hugo 5, Vernon, Eure, France)

<table>
<tr><td>Kitchener's Indian Hospital
Brighton</td><td style="text-align:right">[English]
26th September 1915</td></tr>
</table>

I believe that you must have got my previous letter to this. When you send a reply to that, please note that you should inform me about the treatment of the French

Republic towards its Algerian subjects or fellow-citizens (whatever you like to call them) now serving on the French soil in the present war. First, how are they kept? Whether they are allowed to go out to the town when off the duty without any guard to look after them, which means a sort of generous trust placed in their characters and good conduct, or [whether] the failings and weaknesses of human beings is taken into consideration beforehand by your Government, or military authorities when so permitting them, which also means a liberal treatment of the matter and not snatching away the rights and privileges of good ones for the faults of the bad where a cool judgement is needed to draw a wise line. Second, what pay [do] they get under the French Republic? Is it what the French soldiers receive or with some difference, and why? What uniform are they given? I think that in the matter of uniform there will be some distinction – not of quality but of distinction as to their nationality – which too in my humble opinion should not be when fighting under the same French flag. [Letter withheld]

149

Lewa Singh (Sikh, 89th Punjabis, apparently away from the regiment) to Naranjan Singh (89th Punjabis, at the front)

[no address given]

[Urdu]
30th September 1915

A letter has come from our village which I enclose. There has been no rain. For this reason the price of grain has become very dear. Wheat is 19 *seers*, grain 25 *seers*, *ghi* one and three-quarter *seers*, maize (for sowing) seven *seers* local weight. Two rupees purchase one bundle of straw. Prices are very high. If you get a letter from home, send it to me. What I told you has come to pass.[1] You must understand this. Give me the latest news of the regiment and tell me who are the new Indian officers, havildars, naiks and lance naiks who have been appointed.[2] [Letter passed]

1. This seems to refer to a recent attack, perhaps that of 25th September. See Nos. 151, 154 and 155.
2. The censor comments, 'this would amount to a statement of the casualties in those ranks'.

150

Man Singh Rawat (Garhwali) to Pertab Singh (Dharampur, Ringwari, Garhwal District, UP)

Indian Military Depot
Milford

[Garhwali]
September 1915

What is your pleasure: shall I get married here or will you be displeased? But if it will make you angry, I will not do it, but [will] endeavour to come back to India.

And if you will send the medicine[1] then I can manage it, otherwise not. So you must send the medicine. A Bengali *babu* told me about this medicine: be sure you send it. Its name is *timuru*. Extract the seeds and pound them fine ... I am busy here from 9.30 to 12.30. After that, I wander about, or go to the seaside, or to the bazar, or go to a house and sing along to an English piano. I return about 7.30 in the evening. If any one wishes to marry, I can get a nice wife for him. Marriage in England is very cheap. If it be necessary I can get thousands of women for marriage for your brothers. This is quite true. [Letter withheld[2]]

1. For the purpose of malingering.
2. Presumably because of the hints about malingering, and the reference to white women.

151

Muhammad Khan (Punjabi Muslim) to Lal Khan (Garrison Artillery, Kohat, NWFP)

A field hospital   [Urdu]
France   2nd October 1915

On the 1st September we marched ... from that place ... and are now in the place where Ali Muhammad is, or perhaps even further on. On the 25th of this [that?] month a very terrible affair came upon us.[1] May God not show the like of it even to our enemies. I am sorry that I cannot tell you about it. But we are forbidden. I was slightly wounded. My wound is trifling, but I am in hospital. I expect that official information will be sent in a few days to my home and you will perhaps hear it. So I am writing to tell you not to be in the least anxious. I am quite well and will rejoin in a few days ... All is well with Mehdi Khan and Jahan Khan ... and the Subedar-Major and Jemadar Akbar Ali and Ghulam Ali. This that I write you must understand. I expect that you will understand these names. [On the back of the letter] Alas, alas; alas, alas; it is God's will.[2] [Letter passed]

1. He is referring to the first day of the battle of Loos, in which the Meerut Division attacked, with little success, in the Mauquissart sector. See Nos. 154 and 155.
2. The lamentation indicates that, far from being 'well', the named men are dead.

152

Sub-Assistant Surgeon Hukam Singh (Sikh?, 34) to his wife (India)

Meerut Casualty Clearing Station   [Gurmukhi]
France   2nd October 1915

What you were told about the war being over in three years' time is very short of the truth. This war will bring us to the end of the world and no one knows how long it will last. The news in the papers is all lies. All is in the hands of the Guru ... There is no one to hear [my complaints]. I am not allowed to write. The hope of returning soon is false. There is no saying what will happen. The Guru has the power, and if pity enters his heart he will put an end to the sufferings of all. [Passage deleted]

153

Dafadar Manir Khan (Punjabi Muslim) to schoolmaster Zaman Ali Khan
(Peshawar, NWFP, India)

Lahore Signalling Company   [Urdu]
France   2nd October 1915

I am in France, and the people of this country are exceedingly well-mannered, and in appearance, habits and clothing they are just like the English. The only difference is in the language. You know well that all the people in Europe live like Christians. There is no other caste but the Christian caste. This brief letter will no doubt have given you all the information you want. Here you can get anything you want. Take for instance fruit. You can get apples, grapes, pears and various other kinds of fruit. They also grow wheat. Europe is not jungle or mountainous regions. When you were studying you no doubt read all about Europe ... May our King and the other Allied sovereigns be victorious. We ought always to be praying for our government, for undoubtedly there is no other sovereign who is as kind-hearted as our King. For this reason, my petition goes up day and night to the Almighty that one day all the Indians, victorious, may reach Bombay, and – with flags in their hands, and beating drums, and singing songs of victory – may go away on leave and meet their parents again. [Letter passed]

154

Jemadar Ghulam Hassan Khan (Punjabi Muslim, 34) to Said Hassan Khan
(Rawalpindi District, Punjab)

33rd Punjabis[1]   [Urdu?]
[France]   4th October 1915

I arrived in France on the 19th September and reached the trenches on the 23rd. Our regiment made a charge and suffered great losses.[2] Havildar Sirdar Khan is missing. There is no trace of him. The Subedar-Major was killed. Many others – about 300 – were killed or wounded. Our regiment has won a good name for itself.

There are many other things I might write about, but have not the time. I am now writing quite close to the trenches. It rains day and night – both sorts of rain.[3] I cannot describe it. If God is merciful to me, I will escape with my life, otherwise not. To describe what is happening is one thing; to see it for yourself is an entirely different matter. Even if I were to write a whole book about it, it would fall short of the reality. The arrangements made by the Sirkar are very good. Even in the trenches we are fully supplied with everything we want – food, matches, tobacco, etc. The cold is what we suffer from most, besides the constant rain and hail of shells. I cannot complain to anyone except to God. Please arrange some code by which I can communicate with you. [Letter withheld[4]]

1. This unit was not in France. Judging from the content of the letter, he was attached to the 69th Punjabis, who lost 348 men out of 663 on 25th September 1915. See No. 181.
2. Presumably on 25th September. See Nos. 151 and 155.
3. Meaning rain from the sky, and the rain of shells he mentions later.
4. The censor probably withheld the letter because of the request to establish a code. The rest of its contents seem unobjectionable.

155

Naik Buland Khan (Punjabi Muslim) to Muhammad Ashraf Khan, son of the late Subedar Gul Muhammad Khan (Peshawar, NWFP, India)

69th Punjabis   [Urdu]
[France?]   5th October 1915

The Subedar [your father] has been killed. We are all very sorry, but his day had come. With him Sepoy Nur Khan was killed and I was wounded, but slightly. The Subedar was killed on the 25th September at 6am.[1] A very sad thing is that both his officers who were with him were also killed. If only one of them had been spared, the Subedar and I and the whole family would have won a great name. Our reputation is good enough as it is, but it would have been greatly enhanced. Fateh Khan has been known in the regiment as 'Khan Bahadur' and the Subedar Gul Muhammad Khan [42] showed himself a pattern of valour. He was also a very strict observer of every practice laid down for the orthodox Muslim and he was besides, God knows, a pattern of loyalty to the Government. He was ever on the look-out for the faint-hearted, and if he heard anywhere of a young man who was troubled in mind he went to him and talked to him in such a way that all his discomfort, exile and his homesickness faded away. [Letter passed]

1. At the beginning of the assault, during the Battle of Loos.

156

Yusuf Khan to Abdullah Jan (Pathan, 40th Pathans, France)

Kitchener's Indian Hospital [Urdu]
Brighton 6th October 1915

The news is that the white men here have refused to enlist, declaring that the German Emperor is their King no less than is the King of England. An Indian black man went off to preach to them. He asked them if they were not ashamed to see us come from India to help the King while they, who were of the same race, were refusing to fight for him.[1] But really, the way these whites are behaving is a scandal. Those who have already enlisted have mutinied. [Letter detained[2]]

1. This may be a garbled reference to the conscription controversy.
2. Presumably because of the slighting reference to whites.

157

Bostan Khan (Punjabi Muslim previously serving with an Ammunition Column at the front) to his father Gulab Khan (Rawalpindi District, Punjab, India)

A hospital [Urdu]
France 10th October 1915

I swear that my thoughts are ever turning homeward. But what can I do? No device is of any avail. I am in the country of France. I can do nothing ... If I live, I will send some money, but alas, I am very far off, and that is how this matter has come about. If I live, I will set it right. Well, as God wishes, so will it be ... It is my constant prayer that God in His mercy may grant me my life to see you and my brothers once again. For to look after my home now is difficult. So be it. This is God's will. Day and night my thoughts are towards my home. Do not write because I shall not get your letters until I get well and rejoin my unit. [Letter passed]

158

Sepoy Ashraf Khan (Pathan) to sepoy Mira Khan (40th Pathans, France)

Kitchener's Indian Hospital [Urdu]
Brighton 10th October 1915

You wrote and said that small copies of the Holy Qu'ran would be supplied to this hospital. My brother, as yet none has been given. I will do my best, but I have

not yet got one myself. What can I do? If they are given out I will send you one.[1]
[Letter passed]

1. There are many requests of this nature from Muslim troops. See No. 176.

159

Jalal-ud-Din Ahmad (Hindustani Muslim) to Haji Saadat Mir Khan (Etmadpur, UP, India)

Rouen   [Urdu]
France   14th October 1915

Today I purchased some pictures in great haste and am sending some of them to
Bashir. I could not find any more pictures of that woman who stands, clad in armour,
with her glance turned up towards heaven, and [who] seems to be a very fine,
handsome, young woman. I am looking for them and have searched many shops.
Four hundred years ago that woman gained some notable victories in war against
the English. However, she was caught and the English burnt her alive.[1] I think this
is why the sale of the picture has been stopped, lest it should affect adversely the
present friendship between the French and the English. The French people, seeing
it, would remember that their blessed, beautiful, brave and peerless maiden had
been burnt alive by the English and would resent it. No doubt here in France is
the extreme of beauty, but the very name of modesty and chastity is unknown.
Therefore, the beauty of India, clad as it is in modesty and chastity, is far better.
In India one may see fine handsome men, such as are never seen here. [Letter passed]

1. He is referring to Joan of Arc, a popular subject for contemporary French postcards.

160

Jumna (Jat) to Havildar Ram Saran (Depot 6th Jats, Jhansi, UP, India)

Kitchener's Indian Hospital   [Hindi]
Brighton   14th October 1915

My foot hurts a little, but I shall get home by the grace of God. The bone is
damaged and I can only walk with a stick. Kanhye is not with me. The regiment
has moved and I cannot find him. No one has any trace of him. What can I do?
All the new men who join the regiment are in a state of anxiety, but what can be
done? You should look out. You wrote to me that I had 'won my fame'. I can assure

you that this is not winning a game at all. You suffer pain for the rest of your life. One man has lost his foot, another his arm, another his eye or some other organ. One man has got a bullet in his mouth and another in his buttocks. Listen, brother Ram Saran, there is nothing to be gained by this. May God keep you out of it. But we must do as God decrees. [Letter passed]

161

Lance Naik Nanak Singh (Punjabi Hindu) to Tara Chand (Gurdaspur, Punjab)

4th Brigade RFA [Urdu]
France 16th October 1915

If I send the money from here, there is no certainty that you will ever get it. If you do, it will be after a very long time. You will get my letters and not the money, and will think me a liar. There is also risk of the money being lost, for Rura Singh and several others sent off money *four* months ago, and nothing has yet been heard of it, and probably they will never get it. [Letter passed]

162

*Rifleman Gokul Singh Rawat (Garhwali) to Subedar Ram Kishan Rawat
(Nadar Syang, Upper Burma)*

[39th Garhwal Rifles?] [Hindi]
[France?] 17th October 1915

Grandfather mine, you were right to say that he who died fighting went straight to Paradise.[1] But we four are the true sons of our Rawat fathers – Bhawain Negi, Nain Singh, Nata Singh, Gokul Singh. If we die, it will be fighting in France or Europe or on the battlefield. As for the men who have in cowardly fashion returned to India, they no doubt are safely in Rupiman slapping their chests and saying 'we are the real Chattris' [warriors]. Just tell them 'you have up to date not done a day's work: you are mere catamites'. This is not a marketplace for cattle and goats as Rupiman is. There is a jemadar, Mokunda by name, son of a Rajput, who has gone back to Lansdowne; his liver has all melted away. Then there is a subedar who came from Chinhel, Bhagat Singh by name, also another jemadar, Dula Singh by name, who came from Lasok. These two men have defecated in their *dhotis* through sheer fright. What sort of officers are these who have taken in their men? These leaders are giving their men a bad name. We are to be congratulated that we have lost our leaders of this stamp and are fighting in the midst of a rain of shells. We have now got no Indian officer at all and no Sahibs are left. Gott Sahib was wounded and went off to England. Tell them to loot the Government Treasury and fill their own pockets. There are many others in Lansdowne who, by spitting and coughing, have got the Doctor Sahib to pass them as unfit for service. [Letter passed]

1. For similar sentiments, see Nos. 12, 17, 118 and 198.

163

A Sikh to Mahant Partab Das (Patiala State, Punjab)

FPO.13   [Gurmukhi]
[France?]   18th October 1915

What you say in your letter about not being disloyal to the Emperor, and it being the religion of Sikhs to die facing the foe – all that you say is true. But if only you yourself could be here and see for yourself! Any shrivelled *charas*-sodden fellow can fire the gun and kill a score of us at our food in the kitchen. Ships sail the sky like kites. Wherever you look, machine guns and cannon begin to shoot, and bombs fly out which kill every man they hit. The earth is mined and filled with powder; when men walk upon it, the powder is lit and up go the men! There is no fighting face to face. Guns massacre regiments sitting ten miles off. Put swords or pikes or staves in our hands, and the enemy over us with like arms, then indeed we should show you how to fight face to face! But if no one faces us, what can we do? No one stands up to fight us. Everyone sits in a burrow underground. They fight in the sky, on the sea in battleships, under the earth in mines. My friend, a man who fights upon the ground can hardly escape. You tell me to fight face to the foe. Die we must – but alas, not facing the foe! My friend, the cannons are such that they throw a shell weighing twelve *maunds* which destroys the earth five hundred paces round about where it falls. We are in France. It is a very cold country ... It is a fair country and the people are like angels. All they lack is wings ... The fighting is along a line of 300 miles. England, France, Italy, Belgium, Russia – these five are on one side; Germany, Turkey, Austria, Hungary, Bulgaria – these five on the other. The battle sways evenly balanced. None can kill the other. When it ends there will be peace. No one knows when this will be. [Letter detained because not franked or signed]

164

Subedar-Major Sundar Singh Bahadur (Sikh, 89th Punjabis, 44)
to Havildar Basant Singh (1st Sappers and Miners, France)

Brighton

[Gurmukhi]
19th October 1915

On the 14th, the Emperor gave me two medals.[1] He decorated me with his own hands in his palace in London. An account of it has been published with a photograph in all the papers. By mistake only one medal was mentioned, but I was given two. The occasion did me very great honour. They treat me with very great respect in London. I am always given a motor car in which I go to see the famous palaces. All this is by the Grace of God, and the favour of the captain of our company, and the [good work] of the company itself. And I was only a poor Jat! My thoughts are now very much towards my company and I pray always to the Guru for its welfare. [Letter passed]

1. One of which was probably the Order of British India, Second Class.

165

Ajrud Din (Afridi) to Havildar Gul Badshah (58th Rifles, France)

Tirah
[NWFP]

[Urdu]
19th October 1915

I have returned home to our country in safety and there are no new events in our country that I have heard of worth writing to you. A Hindu has come from Shilobar [?] of whom I made enquiries about your household. All is well there. Do not be anxious. There is no other news of Tirah, but there is one thing [from outside]. I have heard that an army of the Sultan Badshah [the Sultan of Turkey] and of the Germans has come to Kabul, and I have heard that it numbers eleven *lakhs* of men, and with it Jemadar Mir Dast [the brother of Subedar Mir Dast, VC][1] too has come to Kabul – that is to say [Jemadar] Mir Dast is now in their [the Central Powers'] service. This that I have heard is true. For the rest, please do me one kindness. I have left some things in Khair-ud-Din's bedding roll. It will be very kind of you [to take them out], for [if you do not] I shall suffer great loss – as much as Rs.50 worth of loss. If you do not know Khair-ud-Din's bedding roll, it is tied with a red rope ... Do this that I have written for me, because I think Khair-ud-Din has deserted, and this will cause me very great loss. [Letter passed]

1. See Nos. 95, 128 and 130.

166

Sowar [?] Khan (Punjabi Muslim) to his father (Rawalpindi District, Punjab)

France

[Urdu]
21st October 1915

All the others get letters here. They come every week. But I get none. All the other men's letters say that this year famine has befallen. There has been no rain and there are no crops. You never wrote that there had been no crops, and that famine had befallen, or that you had need of money. If you do not write, how can I know? [Letter passed]

167

From an English sergeant to a friend in London

1/3rd London Regiment[1]
[France?]

[English]
22nd October 1915

We get on fine with them [the Indians]. They are a decent lot, the ones that are with us, but some of the regiments are not up to much – refuse to go over the top in a charge. The ones we have got here are the Garhwalis[2] and Gurkhas. They are the chaps. As long as a white soldier is going to be there, they fight like tigers. [Letter passed]

1.   Brigaded with the 39th Garhwalis in the Meerut Division.
2.   The men of the 39th Garhwalis gained a great reputation in France. Two of their men, Naik Darwan Sing Negi and Sepoy Gobar Sing Negi, won the Victoria Cross, the latter posthumously. See Nos. 29, 36 and 41.

168

Bahadur Khan (Pathan or Punjabi Muslim) to Ghulam Muhammad Khan (69th Punjabis, France)

Pavilion Hospital
Brighton

[Urdu]
23rd October 1915

I am now a little better. I had ten wounds. Now only three are left. I hope these too will soon be well. [Letter passed]

169

Hayat Ali Khan (Punjabi Muslim) to Lance Naik Maulavi Talib Khan
(Goat Slaughterer,[1] 129th Baluchis, Infantry Rail Head, France)

Indian Military Depot   [Urdu]
Milford   23rd October 1915

I expect to stay here some days but do not know for how long. Parties come from all the hospitals to this place of men who are for the lines of communication or the firing line. The arrangements for prayers here are good. But there are two opinions here. Some say that the Qasr [short service] should be read: others that the service should be performed at length. There is always quarrelling about this, as to how the Command of God may be. Please write and tell us about this. We shall do as you decide. And what is the order about Friday prayers? Can we read them or not? We have agreed to act as our Maulavi Sahib shall direct. They read the Friday prayers here. There was formerly a Hafiz Sahib here who used to read them. But he has been transferred ... And some now say that the Friday prayers ought to be read and some say not. There is no sort of obstruction here in the performance of religious duties. The arrangements are very good. Please write quickly. We shall act according to your decision. [Letter passed]

1. Judging from the content of the letter, the Goat Slaughterer was an arbiter of religious correctness; much depended upon the way food was prepared. See Plate 10.

170

Tura Baz Khan (Pathan) to Sepoy Gul Hassan Khan
(40th Pathans, Boulogne Depot, France)

Kitchener's Indian Hospital   [Urdu]
Brighton   23rd October 1915

[He encloses a cigarette card of 'The Duchess of Gordon after Sir Joshua Reynolds'] This is the woman we get. We have recourse to her. I have sent you this [her picture] and if you like it, let me know, and I will send her. We get everything [we want]. If you do not, let me know, and I will try to procure it for you. [Letter withheld[1]]

1. Presumably because of the reference to the availability of white women.

171

Balwant Singh (Sikh) to Pandit Chet Ram (Amritsar, Punjab)

FPO.39   [Gurmukhi cipher]
[France?]   24th October 1915

The ladies are very nice and bestow their favours upon us freely. But contrary to
the custom in our country they do not put their legs over the shoulders when they
go with a man.[1] [Deleted]

1. Compare Nos. 172 and 200.

172

Maula Dad Khan (Punjabi Muslim) to his father (India)

Brigade Office
Sialkot Cavalry Brigade   [Urdu]
France   24th October 1915

Muhammad Khan's letter dated the 27th September reached me on the 22nd
October. When I read it, every hair on my body stood on end. Before that I was
happy, but after I had read it I was very vexed. It is true that I wrote to Allah Lok
Khan for a pair of [women's] shoes. The fact is, father, that a young Frenchman
of my acquaintance asked me to send for something from India. He asked me to
get him some shoes which would fit his wife. I wrote that. Of what do you suspect
me? My father, I swear in the name of God and His Prophet and declare that there
is no [ground for suspicion]. Am I such a wretch and such a blackguard as to leave
my noble wife and child and behave thus? ... There are very strict orders against
such action on the part of our people. I came from home to earn money and
renown, not to put such shame upon you. [Letter passed]

173

Muhammad Adris Khan (Hindustani Muslim) to
Sowar Taj Muhammad Khan (1st Lancers, Peshawar, NWFP)

38th CIH   [Urdu]
France   25th October 1915

You wrote to say that I did not give any news in my letters. It is possible that I did
not give much, but I cannot help it. We are not allowed to write anything, except

that we are well. The mail is inspected and signed by an Indian officer, so that no information from here may be written. If anyone does write [a letter containing news] that letter does not arrive. It is torn up and destroyed in the office.[1] This arrangement is quite right. I am very well. Do not be anxious. I want for nothing. Our noble Government gives everything in plenty. All is well. May God bring us home again. [Letter passed]

1. Clearly, censorship arrangements in this unit were especially strict.

174

*Naik Ibrahim Khan (Yusufzai Pathan) to Sepoy Akbar Khan
(57th Rifles, Hospital No.10, Marseilles, France)*

55th Rifles, attached 57th [Rifles]   [Urdu]
France   29th October 1915

I became a naik on the 25th August 1915, because I did good work; and I hope for further promotion. I did not write to you before because I did not know where you were ... Three or four letters have come from Master Abd-ul-Qaiyum [of the 55th Rifles at Kohat] of which one is enclosed in this letter. This was read out before everybody and in it he says 'distinguish yourself thus and thus'. You write and tell him that one letter of that sort is enough. He must not write more. Everybody laughs at it. I have written thus to him too. Tell him not to write another letter like that. It makes everyone laugh.[1] [Letter passed]

1. Contrast No. 134.

175

*Ressaidar Kabul Singh (Sikh, 41) to Risaldar Sirdar Bahadur Mohinddin Sahib,
ADC to HE the Viceroy (Remount Base Depot, Marseilles)*

31st Lancers, attached 29th Lancers   [Urdu]
France   29th October 1915

Asil Singh Jat and Harbans have done a vile thing. They forcibly violated a French girl, nineteen years of age. It is a matter of great humiliation and regret that the good name of the 31st Lancers should have been sullied in this way. [Letter passed]

176

A Pathan to Sepoy Bahram Khan (40th Pathans, a hospital, Brighton)

40th Pathans   [Urdu]
France   31st October 1915

Please make enquiries very carefully about the matter which I have written below.
By all means get me a Holy Qu'ran of the same pattern as your own, even if it
costs ten rupees, and send it to me. You can send it by the hand of any man who
is coming to the front, or by parcel post ... Make every effort to get me a Holy
Qu'ran. Never mind the price; I will pay it. [Letter passed]

177

Naik Sarju (Brahmin) to Havildar Suchut (Mhow, Indore, Central India)

20th Hospital
Meerut Division   [Hindi]
FPO 15   October 1915

Please send me one *seer* of tobacco and in it enclose five *tolas* of *charas* and two
tolas of opium. If you can do this, it will be a great favour. [Words deleted]

178

Juma Khan (Punjabi Muslim) to Dulu Khan Gahi (India)

40th Pathans   [Urdu]
[France?]   1st November 1915

I tell you that if God wishes to spare me, he can deliver me even from the blazing
fire ... You increase my grief and trouble. I do not like this at all, as thousands of
warriors are present in the field of battle. It is the duty of young men to fight as
lions in the field of battle. It is of no consequence – to die is one's duty. At all times
pray through Saints and good men that we may meet again. My dear friend, wise
men have said that he who rests his head on the pillow of God, is always provided
for. Do you also place the pillow of God under your head? If I live, we shall meet
again, otherwise I leave you under God's protection; but [remember] it is always
man's duty to do acts of bravery, because it was for this very purpose that God
created man.

From letters received by me I learn that it was rumoured in India that I had been killed. My dear friend, at the time of my departure I gave you some advice. You did not act on it. Consequently this trouble came on you. You should know that when any calamity overtakes any of us, the CO himself sends information of the fact. You, however, accepting as true the words of faithless men, undertook this unnecessary expense of performing my funeral rites. In this way one's enemies defeat us.

In future, do not listen to any rumours. Unless you hear definitely (either from Ali Khan or Zaman Ali Khan or from the CO) do not believe any report or rumour concerning me. My dear friend, you must understand that in future, even if you receive any reliable report, you must wait a few days and make all necessary enquiries before acting on it. What an unseemly affair it was after all ... as though someone had come and lied to you ... that a dog had bitten off your ear and you, instead of examining your ear, proceeded to chase the dog! This is the action of a fool. In future, be more careful, and should you hear from a reliable source that I am dead, even then perform as small a funeral ceremony as is reasonably possible. Meanwhile, let me know exactly what you spent on the last occasion. [Letter passed]

179

Ghulam Habib Khan (Afridi) to Havildar Baz Mir
(South Waziristan Militia, India)

57th Rifles   [Urdu]
France   2nd November 1915

There is no news here [except that] our maternal uncle's son Naik Khan Mast has deserted to the Germans – that is, he went into the German trenches. A Kuki Khel too went with Khan Mast. There is no other news worth sending. Subedar Mir Akbar was not on good terms with Khan Mast ... Khan Mast went on the 8th October. [He belonged to the] 27th Regiment. [Letter passed]

180

Muhammad Akbar Khan (Afridi) to his home

Indian Military Depot   [Urdu]
Milford   5th November 1915

Is my parrot still alive or dead? I suppose Khair Dil Khan my enemy was delighted to hear that I had been wounded. Please God, in a month or six weeks I shall be starting for home. I think that he has spent about Rs.300 in that case, which has cost us Rs.200; and when I get home I shall start a case against him, for I shall then have Rs.400 in hand. When I get home I shall certainly spend that Rs.400 on a case, and make him spend even more. [Letter passed]

181

From the mother of Waris Khan (69th Punjabis, killed in the attack of 25th September) to Sultan Khan (Punjabi Muslim, 69th Punjabis, France)

[Punjab?]   [Urdu]
[India]   5th November 1915

All your letters have come thrusting fresh spears of grief into my heart. Till this day I have not regained my senses. The fatal news reached me on the 17th October. I have written one letter before this to Anwar Khan, telling him to inform all the men of Dharabi and Kot Sarang from the grief-stricken mother of Waris Khan that they must ask the CO [of] the 69th Punjabis for the body of my dear, only son (for whose sake alone we seven women live) who fell in France. Let his body quickly be sent home, that his grave may be made here and we may spend the rest of our lives weeping over it ... If Government will not pay for this, I will pay. [Letter passed]

182

Sepoy Baldar (Afridi) to Sepoy Minadar Khan (57th Rifles, France)

Frontier Constabulary
NWFP   [Urdu]
India   10th November 1915

I have married Jabar's wife and paid him Rs.560. I have sold my sister to Yar Baz for Rs.560. My other wife I have sold to my father for Rs.640. Do not be anxious. When you come back, I will find you a wife. [Letter passed]

183

Ahmad Khan to Shamsher Ali Khan (Punjabi Muslim, 34th Poona Horse, France)

Rawalpindi   [Urdu]
India   10th November 1915

I am not surprised that exile, and the bad weather, and many other troubles have disturbed your mind. God is our only refuge. He can protect you – and only He.

Everything else is a pretence and an illusion. There is no doubt that Bulgaria's coming in means a prolongation of the war.[1] May God destroy this enemy – this shameless enemy – who has ruined the peace of the world. We many now hope that the power of the enemy in France will be speedily destroyed. It will be an excellent thing if you go away to Egypt, where at any rate you will not have to face an uncongenial climate. We are very grieved to hear of His Majesty's fall from his horse, but it is a subject for thankfulness that he was not seriously hurt. I am rather afraid that his Indian troops did not get the honour of being reviewed by him. Well, we may hope that he will soon be all right again and gladden your eyes with his presence. What you say about the apples and pears[2] makes my mouth water, but when one thinks that bombs are more plentiful than apples, and shells than pears, and that there are more bullets flying about than grapes, it makes one's hair stand on end. I am sure that, just as our Indians run to pick rare fruit like this, so they face fearlessly the messenger of death. [Letter passed]

1. On 12th October 1915, Bulgaria declared war on Serbia, which was quickly overrun.
2. In this case, as in many others, 'fruit' seem to be a coded reference to white women.

184

Storekeeper D. N. Sircar (Maratha Brahmin) to
Telegraphist S. K. Bapat (Indore, Central India)

Kitchener's Indian Hospital   [English]
Brighton   12th November 1915

This place is very picturesque, and the Indians are liked very much here. The girls of this place are notorious and very fond of accosting Indians and fooling with them. They are ever ready for any purpose, and in truth they are no better than the girls of Adda Bazar of Indore.[1] [Deleted]

1. Contrast No. 200.

185

Mir Aghai (Pathan) to his brother Mir Mast (59th Rifles, France)

58th Rifles   [Urdu]
Jullundur   14th November 1915

You wrote asking who had been left at home, since I enlisted. Your son Shah Zarir is very strong and he is at home. I left all the bullocks in his charge. There is a great dearth in the land. There is no crop, but all else is well. I enlisted because you did not send any money home, and we were very badly off, because you did not send any money. That is why I left Shah Zarir at home and enlisted. Do not be anxious about things at home. My wife and your daughter will look after Shah Zarir very well. If [my wife] does not, she is no wife of mine. Please send some money to Shah Zarir. We have only sown wheat in one field. There was no rain ... Send money to Shah Zarir because there is a great dearth and [if you do not] he will [have to] sell the bullocks. [Letter passed]

186

Sowar Jivan Mal (Jat) to Lance Dafadar Ganda Singh
(28th Cavalry, attached 2nd Lancers, France)

29th [Lancers]   [Urdu]
Persian Gulf   17th November 1915

This country in which are encamped is an extremely bad place ... In the hot weather one water melon costs one anna, and the price has now risen to four annas. All the inhabitants are Muslims and the customs of the country are very evil. There is a great deal of coquetry and their complexion is fair and they are very pretty. They have wicked eyes; at any rate this is true of fifty out of a hundred of them. They do very little cultivation and grapes are very plentiful, but there is little else. There is considerable industry in rugs and carpets and you can also get silk. If I had only gone to France, I could have been with you and seen men of all kinds. We have all got to die some day, but at any rate we should have had a good time there. [Letter passed]

187

Clerk Ghulam Muhammad (Depot 29th Punjabis, Jhansi, UP) to Sowar Mansab
Ali Khan (23rd Cavalry, attached 36th Jacob's Horse, France)

Talagang[1]   [Urdu]
Jhelum District   21st November 1915

It is a pity that the letters which you are good enough to write do not have the correct address written on them, so that an answer might be sent to all of them without delay. All the envelopes which you addressed with your own hand arrived, but I am sorry to say that they are still lying idle beside me unread. I myself do not know

Shastri [Sanskrit or Hindi] and here in Talagang there is no one who can read them. [Letter passed]

1. Although based at the depot in Jhansi, the man was writing from his home.

188

Muhammad Ali Khan (Punjabi Muslim or Pathan) to Sher Ali Khan (82nd Punjabis, Nowshera, Peshawar District, NWFP)

82nd Punjabis, attached 69th Punjabis   [Urdu]
France   24th November 1915

The cold here is intense and it rains every day. The wind is terrible and the water is very cold. A fowl is sold here for seven rupees and a goat for twenty-five. I have heard that a draft from our regiment is coming to join the 69th – two British officers, two jemadars and men of the regiment ... All the Indian troops in France are to leave the country.[1] I do not know where they are to go. You asked me to write to you about affairs in this country. But two or three [Indian] officers have been broken [for doing so] and therefore I cannot write.[2] The Double Company Commander has the letters read out to him before they are closed, and he also has the letters from India read out before they are given to the men. [Letter passed]

1. The Meerut and Lahore Divisions left for the Middle East in December.
2. Compare No. 173.

189

Sowar Mashuq Ali (Hindustani Muslim, 8th Cavalry) to OC 8th Cavalry (Jhansi, UP)

Kitchener's Indian Hospital   [Urdu]
Brighton   24th November 1915

With respect, I beg to represent that I have received a letter from home to the effect that my salary has not been paid since July last – I mean the allotment of Rs.20 a month which I made before leaving for the maintenance of my family. My mother states that she has already made a representation to you about this matter. It is probable that you have acted upon it, because you will doubtless bear in mind that when we, here at the war, receive good news from home, we work cheerfully; but when we receive news that makes us anxious, our hearts are no longer in our work, and we are constantly worried with anxiety. The government have accepted responsibility for the welfare of those men who have gone to the war, to the extent even that they have promised that if a claim is made against any of those men, no action at law can be taken till they return from the war. [Letter passed]

190

Lance Naik Khwaju Gul (Pathan or Punjabi Muslim) to Jemadar Imandar Khan
(127th Baluchis attached 129th Baluchis, Karachi, 30)

Kitchener's Indian Hospital   [Urdu]
Brighton   24th November 1915

You must speak to the Colonel Sahib about me, that my service of seven years with my previous regiment should be credited to me, so that I may have the extra 'time' [service]. I will fight with great bravery. Government itself has ruled that when a man resigns one regiment and takes up service in another his 'time' [service] should count from that date. It is a matter of great regret to me that the Colonel Sahib ordered that I should be given my 'time' [only] after I had served for another three years. Moreover, the Colonel Sahib has deprived me of my right of promotion to naik. When I qualified in drill, the Colonel Sahib said I should be promoted to naik on the ship, and that if I was not promoted then, he would promote me as soon as I landed in France, and all on board ship congratulated me on my promotion. But the promotion order did not issue. You must speak to the Colonel Sahib about this and represent to him that he should not oppress me, but give me my due.

191

Kot Dafadar Said Ahmad Shah (Mian Khel Pathan) to
Sowar Abdur Razzaq Khan (9th Hodson's Horse, France)

Peshawar District   [Urdu]
[NWFP]   30th November 1915

Be attentive to your duty. This is your opportunity for showing your courage, when people from all corners of the world under the dominion of King George V are sacrificing their lives, and when others too are ready to sacrifice theirs.[1] For one who seeks promotion over the heads of others, war is the best opportunity. Promotion thus gained is the reward of courage and devotion. It is not the promotion won by others in peace time by flattering their officers and by putting on their socks and boots. Such conduct is the work of a coward and a slacker. You must be careful to keep out of the ranks of such people. Do not think 'perhaps I may be shot'. No one can escape the fate allotted to him. Are not men dying in their homes? [Letter passed]

1. Contrast No. 174.

192

Umed Sing Bist (Dogra) to Sali Seok (Lohana, Kangra District, Punjab)

1/1st Gurkhas [Hindi and Urdu]
[France] November 1915

If you want any French women there are plenty here, and they are very good looking. If you really want any I can send one to you in a parcel. [Obliterated]

193

Naiz Khan (Punjabi Muslim, 69th Punjabis) to Dhaman Khan (Jhelum District, Punjab, India)

[Urdu]
Brighton November 1915

The regiments that came to this country – British and Indian – have gone to the rear. It is not known where they are going, but by the grace of God they are leaving France. Thanks be to God that he has heard the prayer of these sinners and rescued them from the cold of France. It is not known where they are going, but we hear that there is fighting in the direction of Peshawar. If we were to be taken there it would be a great blessing by comparison. [Letter passed]

194

Clerk Mir Hassan (Pathan) to his father (India)

40th Pathans [Urdu]
France 1st December 1915

Please tell my mother that her prayers are very potent. Except for the abundance of lice there is no hardship. We get warm *paranthas* [*chapattis* fried in oil] and meat twice a day. Ghulam Hassan writes that mother says she will keep all my money safe. Please say to her from me 'what is money? There is such a curse upon wealth, and in the next world it will turn into snakes and scorpions and devour those who have heaped it up. You have my permission to do what you like with it' ... I hope to see you and refresh my dead heart. [Letter passed]

195

Qasim Khan (Punjab Muslim) to his father (Shahpur District, Punjab, India)

36th Jacob's Horse   [Urdu]
France   7th December 1915

Note to the person who reads this letter: it is to be read only to my father and in secret ... I understood what you meant.[1] You are taking all this trouble to prevent people from mocking at me, saying 'he has gone to the war and in his absence [his people] will not let his wife sit at home'. That was what you meant? I am very grateful to you. God prolong your life. But I do not at all like what you say. Now I will tell you – never mind her. Do not think of her any more. Let people say what they like, but give up thinking of her. If she gives you any further trouble about money, tell her to ask for money from her [new] master. I have nothing to do with it. When anyone asks me, I shall count out payment to them in such sort, that they will remember it all their lives ... I shall make a report from here that he [Nur Khan] has dishonoured me, in that, while I was away from here at the war, he enticed away my wife and took her to his own house. His motive for doing so was this – that he might at his ease eat the money which is paid for by the Government to the wives [of men on service]. Then Malik Nur Khan will remain in prison as long as the war lasts, and the Government will set the woman down at home [and keep her there]. That would be quite easy for the poor wanderer to do. But I do not like this either and you might not like it. Why not? Because people would hear of it and laugh ... When you get this letter, if before that you have had a reconciliation, well and good. If not, say nothing to her after you have received this letter. If you have sent anyone to her, I shall be very angry. It seems to me that you think more about her than you do of me. If I were not there, what would you do with her? Now let the reader explain the next sentence carefully. You ought to be thinking of me, not of my wife. When by God's order I come home safe and sound, I shall not lack for wives. [Letter passed]

1. In other words, his father's letter was encoded, to prevent his son's embarrassment if it were read aloud in public.

196

Signaller Nattha Singh [Sikh?] to Dafadar Wazir Singh
(7th Lancers, Force D, Mesopotamia)

30th Lancers   [Gurmukhi]
France   8th December 1915

The cold here is excessive. Here are two stories about it. One day, three or four of us signallers were working at the telegraph and telephone. When the message we were at was finished, a Jat added through the wire 'if this cold continues for another month or two we shall leave the earth with pleasure'. When I think of this story, or hear it told as a joke, I laugh out loud. The second story is that on the 19th of November I began writing a letter and found that the ink was frozen in the inkstand. I broke the ink-pot, took out the ink, melted it over a fire, and wrote the letter to you with the melted ink. [Letter passed]

197

Sepoy Kharka (Dogra, 57th Wilde's Rifles) to Lance Naik Harnam Singh
(57th Wilde's Rifles, Ferozepur, Punjab, India)

Pavilion Hospital   [Hindi]
Brighton   11th December 1915

My medical board is over and I am ordered to the front. Such tyranny has been practised on me that words fail me to describe it. I cannot walk and I can get no justice. Well, no one is to blame, as it is my fate. If my livelihood is at an end, no one can restore it. I shall live as long as I have to live and when the end is due, no treatment can avail. If I were destined to live in India at all, would they not have sent me back there now after I have been thirteen months in hospital? This is my fate. Wherever I go, I get pushed about. Write to my home in Kangra and say that if I never come home again at all, it will not turn day into night there; and if I do turn up, the light will go on as usual. [Letter passed]

198

Pirbhu Dyal (Dogra) to Ji Singh (Kangra District, Punjab, India)

Indian General Hospital   [Hindi]
Brighton   11th December 1915

Do not be worried, my friend, we all have to die sooner or later – it may be now or it may be ten days hence. To run away or try and hide is the work of a coward, for it is the Rajput's duty to fight. I have been born once, of my mother, and in this world I cannot get another birth.[1] I am always praying that my master and King may be victorious, or that death may be my lot. I cannot fight for anyone else, for I have taken up service for my King and whether I am spared to serve him faithfully, or whether I die on the battlefield, I shall go straight to Heaven.[2] We must be true to our salt and he who is faithful will win Paradise for his parents as well as for himself. The faithless man will disgrace his parents. God knows all about the course of this war, but this I do know – that our King will be victorious, for he is fighting this war as a King should. Do not be anxious and worried. I will come back when the King wins the war, and we will destroy the evil Germans who ought to have been strangled at their birth. Now, since we spared them at their birth, they have lived to annoy us. My idea is that we ought to play with them as a cat plays with a mouse. That is the way we are playing with the Germans now. [Letter passed]

1. Only if he dies can he be reborn.
2. The Hindu cycle of death and rebirth will end, and he will go to Paradise.

199

A sepoy of the 47th Sikhs (Sikh) to a friend (India)

A hospital   [Gurmukhi]
Brighton   14th December 1915

Chur Singh has suffered martyrdom in the war. The 47th Sikhs were charging. [The] Sahib said 'Chur Singh, you are not a Sikh of Guru Govind Singh, [you] who sit in fear inside the trench!' Chur Singh was very angry. Chur Singh gave [the] order to his company to charge. He drew his sword and went forward. A bullet came from the enemy and hit him in the mouth. So did our brother Chur Singh become a martyr. No other man was like Jemadar Chur Singh. [Letter passed]

200

Risaldar Anjamuddin Khan (Pathan, 42) to
Muhammad Suraj-ud-Din Khan (Agar-Malwa)

38th CIH   [Urdu]
France   20th December 1915

Do not be disturbed. If anything should happen I will inform you forthwith. God be thanked, we shall not see the trenches again. We are living in comfort in large splendid houses the like of which we have never seen before. Married ladies, and young unmarried women, attend to our wants and tidy our beds, and eat at the same table as we do. They are beautiful as fairies, but for us they are like mothers and sisters. I assure you that by the grace of God my faith will remain unbroken.[1]

1. Meaning he will not have sex with Christian women. Contrast Nos. 170, 171, 183 and 184.

201

Lala Jan (Pathan) to Malik Jan (Kohat District, NWFP, India)

36th Jacob's Horse   [Urdu]
France   21st December 1915

Now I have found out all about that affair of Habib's. Please arrange to send the things for which I asked in my former letter. Since Nasim Khan has enlisted in [another] regiment he cannot be transferred to ours. If Shah Bazi persists in not leaving you alone, pull his trousers down and put him to shame. Never mind what it costs ... If you can somehow get up a case against Shah Bazi, so much the better. [Letter passed]

202

Wahid Baksh (Punjabi Muslim) to Muhammad Khan Ab-Dar
(Sirhind Club, Amballa, Punjab)

Amballa Cavalry Brigade   [Urdu]
France   21st December 1915

It is probable that I shall return very soon. About the war and when it is likely to end I can say nothing at present. As I learn anything, I will let you know. Our cavalry regiment is about to leave France, but where it is going I cannot say. It is very cold and wet here; but we are very comfortable now. The events of the past are gone; they are not repeated now. Do not be troubled in mind. If God is merciful and we are true, we shall meet again; but doubtless the end of the world has come on us. [Letter passed]

203

Lal Khan (Hindustani Muslim) to Jemadar Sikander Khan
(Jhun Jhun, Jaipur, Rajputana, India)

Amballa Cavalry Brigade   [Urdu]
France   22nd December 1915

I know very well that you are very anxious about me, but you should not give way
to anxiety. The time of death is fixed for each man and that time can never be altered.
If a man's time has not come, the guns may rain shot and shell over him day and
night, but he will remain unscathed. On one occasion, two shells fell quite close
to me, but, by the grace of God, I was untouched by even so much as a blast of
air. Truly, whom God protects who can injure? My trust in God is greatly
strengthened. If God spares me, we shall meet again. If not, well, we are given life
only to reach death in the end; but I have a presentiment that I shall return in safety
and with renown. [Letter passed]

204

Abd-ul-Rahman Khan (Isa Khel Pathan) to his brother
(Mianwali District, Punjab, India)

36th Jacob's Horse   [Urdu]
France   27th December 1915

This is a very good country. The water and the climate are good. All the year round,
day and night, rain upon rain is ever beginning and we have no sort of discomfort
except the cold. We get excellent food and clothing and the country is very
prosperous. We get fine houses to sleep in and very good fruit to eat. The people
are very comely. On active service there is no furlough or leave or pension, but
whose salt we have eaten, to him the debt must be paid. While I live, I will remain
in my valour and will exalt the name of my tribe. The men who have gone back
have done ill, for now is the time for service. Pray that our King and the British
Empire may be victorious so that we people in safety and in renown may return
to our dear country. [Letter passed]

205

Dafadar Ramjilal (Jat) to Babaji Harnam Das (Rohtak, Punjab, India)

6th Cavalry   [Hindi]
France   December 1915

What shall I say about this country? It is impossible to find words to describe it adequately, and yet one is forced to say something. This country is beyond praise. If I were to describe everything fully, I cannot say how many days it would take me. It is a very fine country. All the inhabitants pay us great attention. They are all, men and women, educated; and – just bear this in mind – where there are brains, there all the work is carried on with skill and intelligence! We get any amount of milk, and the Government gives us every possible thing that we can want. The man that could not get one coat in India has a dozen here, and he spends money as if it were *kankar*. This is what the Government has done for us, and the arrangements are perfect. The climate is so good that no one has even a headache. Nowadays we Jats are treated with such respect by the Government that it is beyond words. Bravo the Jats! They have fought right well. May God give our Government the victory and then we shall meet again, and I will tell you all about it. [Letter passed]

206

To Dafadar Prayag Singh (Rajput, 2nd Lancers, France) from his wife[1]

Moradabad   [Hindi]
UP   December 1915

My dear, when your letter comes, my heart is made happy. I write to you every week, but sometimes your letters to me are delayed. Why should I be annoyed with you? I am your servant, and you are my all ... Every morning when I wake, I do homage to your picture; and my picture, is it not imprisoned in your heart? Why then are you distressed in mind? Often do I see you in my dreams, but never in a state which would cause me anxiety. Question your heart. Does it not tell you that at all times I am with you in spirit? Who is there in this world, beside yourself, to whom I would give a thought? What does it matter how or where one lives, in a mansion or in a wilderness, so long as the heart is true. I am steadfast in my faith always. There are but two conditions in this life, peace and trouble. When you were with me all was peace; in your absence all is trouble. God alone knows when I shall see and do homage to you again and thus be freed from trouble ... Your letters reach me on Wednesday. When a letter comes, I am happy till the following Tuesday. When a letter does not come I am sunk in despondency for a week, asking myself 'what can it be that has deprived me of a letter from my Lord this week?' And I never fail to write weekly to you. I could not forget you, for you are to me what the broad, deep sea is to the fish ... Why do you praise me so much? I am not worthy of praise. Nor could I become estranged from you, for then I should make a hell of this house. No, no; in no circumstances can I be separated from you. You are my lord and master, you alone can fathom the depths of my heart and understand its desires. For me there is not your equal in this world. Therefore, trust me and believe that no thought of mine is hidden from you. You ask me to write in more detail. The reason why I do not do so is because I do not wish to weary you. Occupy yourself with the duty the performance of which will give satisfaction to God; and now indeed is the time, above all others, when you can work so as to please God ... Today a letter has come from Kheri in which uncle has asked me to lend him all the money I have as Kalmawatti is to be married ... I shall raise no objection because I do not wish anyone to say that I raised any obstacle in the family. Besides, I have no need for money – it is your presence that I desire. You are my joy. What is money to me? ... Do not worry yourself about anything. Do your duty and your work with all your heart. [Letter passed]

1. This apparently loyal and devoted woman was still writing in similar vein in February 1917. See No. 487.

1916

*Dafadar Fath Muhammad Khan (Punjabi Muslim) to
Ram Saran Das (Rohtak District, Punjab, India)*

[6th Cavalry or 19th Lancers]   [Urdu]
France   3rd January 1916

There is nothing here to write about, except that today [sic] is the Great Day, on which the New Year begins. I believe it is celebrated in the same way all over Europe, but I think France must surpass the other countries. Although all the men of the country are busy at the war, if this were not so, I cannot imagine what limit there would be to the revels, when even in wartime such a pitch is reached. In every village there are four or five hotels, and each of these today is an ample realization of the paradise of which we have read in books and heard from Mullahs. I cannot attempt to describe it. In the house where I live, they have had a splendid feast, with singing and dancing afterwards, to which many other French men and women were invited. It was a brilliant assembly, such as I shall never forget. What robes these fairies wore, like the Houries of Paradise! When the party broke up, all expressed regret at our having to leave France and go to some other theatre of war. Everyone praised the excellent behaviour of the Indian troops and prayed for a speedy victory and our return to France, to see our hosts again. This was quite an ordinary party, because it was a feast among these people, to which all relatives were invited. I send you a picture of a girl. When you see it, you will understand what beauty there is in France. [Letter passed; enclosed indecent photograph destroyed][1]

1. See Nos. 105, 171, 183, 184 and 247 for related letters. No. 170 also included a female portrait. Contrast No. 200.

*Acting Lance Dafadar Muhammad Adris Khan (Hindustani Muslim) to
Jemadar Muhammad Umar Faruk Khan (1st Lancers, Peshawar, NWFP, 30)*

34th Poona Horse (attached)   [Urdu]
France   3rd January 1916

As for what you were good enough to write about a quilt, the fact is that we cannot keep any spare kit in addition to the Government outfit. We are only allowed to keep two blankets, and when we march, we put them under the saddle ... As for the quilts and other things which we brought with us from home, we had to leave them all at Marseilles. So I beg to be excused ... Our kinsman Suleman Khan tried to get an exchange from the 30th Lancers to the 34th Poona Horse, and the CO of the 34th Poona Horse had agreed to take him, but Risaldar Mardan Khan did not bring up our kinsman before the OC 30th Lancers. You know the ways of that tribe well enough. Indeed, they have made a great fuss here about your promotion too ... It may be that the Indian Force is going to leave France for some other theatre of war. [Detained]

209

Sowar Natha Singh (Sikh) to Sapuran Singh (Lyallpur District, Punjab)

FPO.19 [Urdu]
France 4th January 1916

The country is exceedingly pleasant. In it India is forgotten. I do not wish the war to end soon. I should like to die in this country, and I have no intention of returning to India. If you want anything, write to me. May the Holy Guru save me from India. I hope you will answer this quickly, telling me you are well. I am in great comfort as I am always away from the squadron. Tell Basant Kaur from me to look carefully after the children, and have them well schooled, fed and clothed. There is no need to think of the cost; she can spend as much as she likes on them. But I have no hope of seeing them again – nor do I wish to see them. For I have found a good opportunity of sacrificing my life, and I hope to repay my debt with loyalty. [Letter passed]

210

Abd-ul-Hakim (Hindustani Muslim) to Akbar Ali Khan
(Depot, 6th Cavalry, Sialkot, Punjab)

Signal Troop
FPO.18 [Urdu]
France 5th January 1916

We are all well. There is a rumour that we are going to some other front. The cavalry brigades have been proved useless here. Here infantry are wanted. Infantry can fight here, but not cavalry. It is thought as impossible for us to get across the trenches and attack the enemy as it is supposed to be for a fly to get out of the spider's web. And the enemy is in the same plight. No doubt the cavalry brigades can show their mettle in other parts – Egypt for example, and elsewhere. We have been nearly a year and a half in France, and are now going away to some other front. After we are gone we shall mostly remember France very kindly.[1] [Letter passed]

1. In fact the Cavalry Corps remained on the Western Front until spring 1918.

211

Abdul Alim Khan (Punjabi Muslim) to
Hafiz Abdul Karim Khan (Farrukhabad, UP)

Signal Troop
Sialkot Cavalry Brigade   [Urdu]
France   5th January 1916

Compared with last year the winter has been very mild. January has begun, yet wearing only a vest and a shirt we feel no cold. We can carry out our morning ablutions thoroughly with cold water. The greatest relief is that, so far, we have not been troubled with lice. Last year was such that you might put on all the clothes you possessed and yet you shivered with cold, and you could not even touch cold water. As for the lice last year, you might completely change your clothes one morning, and yet you would be infested with lice the next morning ... We have become quite acclimatized during the past year and a half. [Letter passed]

212

Sher Bahadur Khan (Punjabi Muslim) to
Raja Gul Nawaz Khan, BA, LLB (Jhelum, Punjab, India)

Secunderabad Cavalry Brigade   [Urdu]
France   9th January 1916

I have seen strange things in France. The French are a sympathetic and gracious people. Some time ago we were established for about three months in a village. The house in which I was billeted was the house of a well-to-do man, but the only occupant was the lady of the house, and she was advanced in years. Her three sons had gone to the war. One had been killed, another had been wounded and was in hospital, and the third was at that time in the trenches. There is no doubt that the lady was much attached to her sons. There are miles of difference between the women of India and the women of this country. During the whole three months, I never once saw this old lady sitting idle, although she belonged to a high family. Indeed, during the whole three months she ministered to me to such an extent that I cannot adequately describe her [kindness]. Of her own free will she washed my clothes, arranged my bed [and] polished my boots – for three months. She used to wash down my bedroom daily with warm water. Every morning she used to prepare and give me a tray with bread, butter, milk and coffee. I was continually wishing to find a way to reimburse her the expense; but however much I pressed her, she declined. When we had to leave that village the old lady wept on my shoulder. Strange that I had never seen her weeping for her dead son and yet she should weep for me. Moreover, at [our] parting she pressed on me a five franc note to meet my expenses en route. [Letter passed]

213

Muhammad Hussein Khan (Punjabi Muslim) to Lumberdar Said Hafiz Khair Muhammad (Jullundur, Punjab, India)

Sialkot [Cavalry] Brigade   [Urdu]
France   10th January 1916

There is no news about my return. It is not the work of days or months; it is becoming the work of years. May God be gracious and protect those of us in the fighting line, because hundreds of thousands of God's servants are being ruthlessly slain. The enemy has commenced such atrocities as to murder without pity defenceless villagers, old men and young children, and to sink hospital ships. God bring him into a proper way of thinking! Owing to a mail steamer having been sunk, our mails to India for a week will not reach their destination. In that mail a Money Order for Muhammad Hussein has been lost. I have applied for a duplicate order. [Letter passed]

214

Hazari to Sowar Ami Chand (Jat, 2nd Lancers, France)

Delhi   [Urdu]
India   10th January 1916

There has been no rain and there is severe scarcity. Prices are very high; grass is very dear.[1] Recruiting is going on with a great rush. Birma has enlisted for the second time and Hukma has been caught. [Letter passed]

1. Of this letter, the censor commented that, 'the reference to drought and high prices ... is typical of very many letters from all parts of the country'. See Nos. 243 and 264.

215

Saddler Ibrahim (Punjabi Muslim) to
Babu Rukan-ad-Din (Sialkot, Punjab, India)

15th Cavalry [Lancers]   [Urdu]
Brighton   10th January 1916

On the 16th December a *syce* belonging to our section died, and the Government made arrangements for his burial. A fine coffin was provided on which his name and age were engraved. The inside was lined with silk cloth and cushions of silk. In our country doubtless only the greatest in the land are furnished with coffins of this sort. He was buried in a Muslim cemetry near London with great honour and dignity. The exalted Government has showered every blessing on us here, which I shall remember all my life, and which will bind me in complete loyalty. Yesterday some Royal princesses came from London to see us. They spoke to each one and treated us kindly as if we had been their children. [Letter passed]

216

Dafadar Sher Muhammad Khan (Punjabi Muslim) to
Muhammad Khan (Khushab, Jhelum District, Punjab)

Meerut Cavalry Brigade   [Urdu]
France   11th January 1916

Well, I can say nothing since (according to you) I am a liar and never tell the truth. Still, the 15th Cavalry [Lancers] has gone away; probably it has gone to Egypt or to Persia.[1] I cannot say for certain ... Our job is a big one; but there is no cause for alarm. If anyone should be alarmed it is we who are bearing the burden and not you. Therefore why do you weep and cry out? You have money; you may also make use of my property, and there are two of you, brothers, so live quietly and contentedly and do not trouble me with distressing letters. [Letter passed]

1. In fact it went to Basra, with the Lahore infantry division to which it was attached. In February 1916, the regiment, composed of Muslims, mutinied when ordered to the front. See Nos. 259 and 276.

217

*Abdul Rahman Khan (Punjabi Muslim) to Sirdar Muhammad Ismail Khan
(Khushab, Jhelum District, India)*

Meerut Cavalry Brigade   [Urdu]
France   11th January 1916

Did you speak to the Colonel about me or not? Here I have no one to speak for
me. Here the practice is for letters to be examined by the Risaldar of each troop
before they are signed and passed by the British officer. If anything is written which
is out of the ordinary the letter is forthwith torn up.[1] [Letter passed]

1. Clearly, censorship practices varied from unit to unit, since plenty of men did write
    messages that were 'out of the ordinary'. But see No. 239 for a similar comment about
    the censorship, although that writer does include an account of a murder in his regiment.

218

Abdul Aziz (Muslim) to Said Ahmad (Muslim, 3rd Skinner's Horse, France)

Rutlam   [Urdu]
Central India   14th January 1916

The newspapers are full of stories about the conclusion of peace, but like the old
blind woman in the fable I shall believe it when I see it. [Letter passed]

219

*Muhammad Ishaq (Hindustani Muslim) to
Hazrat Ahmad Mian (Moradabad, UP, India)*

Marseilles   [Urdu]
France   14th January 1916

My master, they tell me that by the end of January or February at [the] latest we
shall leave this place, but I have no idea where we shall go. I have been here for
one and a half years and you can well understand what I feel. For this reason I beg
of you to consider this – that my family must be very distressed at my long
absence; and that we are helpless. I am reminded with regret that it is told of Caliph
Hazrat Umar, the son of Firokh (may the Mercy of God rest on him) that every

night he used to make a tour of inspection. On one occasion he came near to a house where a woman was reading some beautiful verses. He listened and told one of his attendants to put a mark on the house so that he might be able to recognize it on the morrow and make enquiries. The next day he came to the house and asked the woman what it was that she had been reading the previous night. The woman replied that she was reading odes of love and affection to her husband who was absent at the wars. The Caliph returned home and asked his daughter for how long a time a woman could remain [sexually] continent. The daughter raised her hand and showed three fingers. The Caliph understood that a woman could remain separate from her husband for three months, and he forthwith issued an order that whenever soldiers were sent to the wars they should be returned to their homes every three months.[1] My master, although these days of pure justice no longer remain, and that model of justice has departed this life, his successors among the Faithful still remain. Therefore pray to God for me that my difficulties may be removed and that I may soon return in safety [and] with honour. [Letter passed]

1. For a variant of this story, see No. 349.

220

Nawab Khan to Sowar Nur Muhammad Khan
(Punjabi Muslim, 34th Poona Horse, France)

Attock District [Urdu]
[Punjab] 16th January 1916

We are always praying to God for victory, and that you may safely return home. We pray that Britain and her sworn Allies may be victorious, and that Germany, Austria, Hungary and Bulgaria may be utterly ashamed and broken. It is they who have spread misery throughout the world. We are delighted to hear that the Indian cavalry are having a long rest in France. I saw in the papers that the Indian cavalry has sent a telegram to the Indian infantry wishing them goodbye.[1] Only the Indian cavalry are left in Europe; and they are to stay there until the British Corps, which has been recently enlisted, and is now being trained, is ready to take the field.[2] When they are ready the Indian Cavalry will be sent to another field of operations. We have been reading about the war in the papers. When I was in England in the hospital I met Captain Grimshaw[3] who is a very brave gentleman.

1. The Indian Infantry Corps departed for the Middle East in the winter of 1914–15. For other references to the move, see Nos. 210, 216 and 235.
2. He refers, presumably, to conscription. See No. 236.
3. Captain R. W. W. 'Roly' Grimshaw (1879–1932). Born of an Irish Protestant family, he was commissioned into the Royal Irish Regiment in 1899, and transfered to the 34th

Poona Horse in 1902. He arrived in France with the 34th in October 1914, taking part in the battles of First Ypres and Festubert. He was severely wounded in December 1914, and did not recover sufficiently for further front-line duty. His publications included *Letters on Polo in India*. See chapter on Further Reading for details of his published diary for 1914–15. He is referred to again in No. 570.

221

Shambo (Jat) to Nathu (Hissar District, Punjab)

Meerut Cavalry Brigade   [Hindi]
[France]   18th January 1916

Now listen, brother, and hear what troubles I have to put up with. You cannot understand because you have a bed to sleep on and you get a bellyful [of food] and are able to live with your wife and family. You have the society of your caste fellows and plenty to talk about, and if you get ill in the least you have the whole family to look after you and your every wish is satisfied. You have not to think of dying at all. Look at the state of things where I am. It is bitterly cold and I only get three blankets which are no good as we have to sleep on the ground. I cannot write more than this because I do not want to worry you. If I told you everything you would be full of anxiety. [Letter passed]

222

Inspector of Police Eshar Singh to Jemadar Jai Singh (Sikh, 6th Cavalry, France, 43)

Punjab   [Urdu]
India   19th January 1916

We are all thinking of you, and this is our prayer in the presence of the Almighty – that the Guru may bring you back with victory. You must know that you are very fortunate in that you have got a chance to defend your country and serve the British Government. You will remember that British rule was foretold by our true leader Tegh Bahadur, the ninth Guru.[1] It was established in India only for the protection and help of us Sikhs. It was on the voice of the Guru that the Eternal sent the English here. The blessings which this rule has brought to India are not concealed from you. The rise of the Sikhs is due solely to this power. But for this, the poor Sikhs would have brought their unhappy existence to an end in some crows' pond [sic]. I shall be very pleased to hear of your valorous deeds. You are a brave soldier. Now is the time to display your manhood. Now is the time for loyalty. You are a true Sikh. By the Guru's order you must remember the promise of the Almighty, who said:

> Recognize the hero in him who fights for his faith;
> Though cut to pieces he will not quit his ground.

This war for the Sikhs is a religious war, because the war is directed against the [British] rule which our Guru established. [Letter passed]

1. Guru Tegh Bahadur (1621–1675) was the ninth Guru of the Sikhs, and the youngest son of the seventh Guru, Hargobind (1595–1644). He succeeded to the personal Guruship in 1664, a time of religious persecution under the Mughal Emperor Aurangzeb. After reflection, he courted martyrdom, and was beheaded in Delhi in November 1675.

223

Jalal Khan to Dafadar Mohammad Din Khan
(Deccani Muslim, 20th Deccan Horse, France)

Nimach   [Urdu]
India   21st January 1916

In the end there will be a [medical?] board on the 27th of this month. We shall see – God preserve us. They first discharged me. Then, three days later, the order was cancelled, and I was kept for twenty-two days under arrest in the Quarter-guard.[1] But prayers were made and I was let off. Now I am at home. We shall see – God is master – what comes of the board. Your prayers are needed, and God's grace. Success will come. Great efforts have been made, but the situation is in hand.[2] [Letter passed]

1. For malingering.
2. See No. 224, below, for a comment on this incident, and No. 241 for a similar one.

224

Sharf-ud-Din Khan to Sowar Shams-ud-Din Khan (Deccani Muslim, 20th
Deccan Horse, France)

Nimach   [Urdu]
India   21st January 1916

Jalal Khan [the writer of the above letter] made a great fuss, but no heed was paid, and he went about in a state of blindness. Then the Government discovered that he had blinded himself. So he was kept for five days under arrest in the Istandar, and used to go every day from there to the hospital. His eyes got well and the CO is very angry with him and keeps telling him to return to duty. [Letter passed]

225

Kamyab Khan to Risaldar [Mir] Shamshad Ali (Muslim Rajput or Punjabi Muslim, 3rd Skinner's Horse, France, 29)

Depot, 3rd Skinner's Horse
Bareilly   [Urdu]
[UP]   21st January 1916

I got your letter of 29th December, but the letter before that is at the bottom of the salt sea. The ship with its crew of 450 souls was sunk. Two other ships were also sunk and some Indian ships. When I heard this complaint of the non-receipt of the letter, I boiled over with rage at the thought that, though letters are sent off every mail, there was no letter, but only silence. There is no news from here. The Risaldar Sahib will probably stay on in command, but it depends on his passing the Medical Board. The Doctor Sahib here is very strict. [Letter passed]

226

Signaller Kartar Singh (Sikh) to Kunar Khan (Ludhiana District, Punjab)

[Probably 6th Cavalry]   [Gurmukhi]
France   22nd January 1916

Now listen. We have been fighting for fourteen months, and the fighting has been very fierce. I have been in every fight and have fought with great valour. Our people have exalted the name of our country. When the order comes that the enemy is advancing in this direction, as a tiger advances on his prey [so we stand to] and with fine spirit knock the senses out of him. Our troops have been accounted the stoutest of all the troops. At this time, they are in such heart that they would stay the tiger unarmed. [Every man] fighting with heroic bravery becomes himself a hero. It was my very good fortune to be engaged in this war. We shall never get such another chance to exalt the name of race, country, ancestors, parents, village and brothers, and to prove our loyalty to the Government. I hope we shall renew our Sikh chronicles. Do not be distressed ... Such hardships come upon brave men. What is fated must be endured. I pray to God to give us a chance to meet the foe face to face ... To die in battle is a noble fate. I expect we shall get our chance. It is a fine death to draw two or three breaths only, after being hit. It is not good to die painfully. There will never be such a fierce fight nor such arrangements made. Food and clothing, all is of the best; there is no shortage. Motors convey the rations right up to the trenches. When we go to the trenches we go in such spirits as to the wedding of a younger brother, or like boys to the fair ... We go singing as we march and care nothing that we are going to die. The fighting is strange – on the ground, under the ground, in the sky and in the sea, everywhere. This is rightly called the war of kings. It is the work of men of great intelligence. We have seen many things of which we cannot write. If we return alive, I will tell you all about it.

227

Mir Aslam Khan (Pathan) to Muhammad Azghar Ali Khan
(Jalozai, Peshawar District, NWFP)

19th Lancers   [Urdu]
France   27th January 1916

It is long since any letter came to me from you. What is the reason, when I write to you? For I am at the war, and sometimes we get leisure, and sometimes there comes a day in which there is no leisure at all to write letters. Even on that day do I write to you. If you do not write every week, at least you must write once in every two weeks, and comfort my heart. Tell Granny from me to pray for the soul of my brother Sher Ali Khan. Save our prayers nothing from us can reach him. My mother,[1] when we two brothers came to the war, we were both of us in one place and were always meeting together. If my brother went out on any duty, I used to wander after him until I saw him again, and when I saw him my heart would thrill with joy. And he too would so wander after me. If I were out of his sight for a minute, he too used to stroll moodily about the whole day. And we had great love for each other. But the last day came. He passed away very quickly, and to whom can I now look here? My brother is gone from me; my brother is dead ... Now I am dead ... All the grief that is in the world is now upon me. The world is about to pass away ... When the merciful God made wretched men, why did he not slay them in their childhood? [Letter passed]

1. Although the letter is addressed to a man, its contents are intended for his mother, who is probably illiterate.

228

Mohamed Nur Khan to Nisar Mahomed Khan (Pathan, 38th CIH, France)

Tangi Zai   [Urdu]
NWFP   27th January 1916

You asked me to tell you about the Charsadda raid. This is what happened. I was asleep when the dacoits came, and went out when I heard the guns and went into the bazar. As I arrived, the raiders set the bazar on fire, and then left. Two Mohmands were shot: one died on the spot and the other was left wounded at Nahakki and Mohamed Nur Khan took him prisoner. That day, the Chief Commissioner and the Deputy Commissioner came to Charsadda, and the Chief Commissioner ordered the dacoit to be sent for at once and brought to him within an hour. Directly he arrived, the Chief Commissioner ordered his execution, and he was at once strung up on the nearest tree. Charsadda is utterly ruined. I am not allowed to write any more. [Letter passed]

229

Bir Singh (Sikh) to Jowala Singh (Ambala District, Punjab)

6th Cavalry or 19th Lancers   [Urdu]
France   28th January 1916

You say that the parcel came back from Bombay. What sort of parcel was it? If you wrote 'opium' on it, do not do so again, but put 'sweets' or 'dainties' on it, and send off the opium. Have no fear; parcels are not opened on the way and cannot be lost. So keep on sending the drugs. Let Indar Kaur be the sender. [Letter passed][1]

1. It was very unusual for a letter requesting drugs to be passed.

230

Ressaidar Hushyar Singh (Sikh, 34) to Jemadar Harband Singh
(9th Hodson's Horse, France, 24)

16th Cavalry   [Urdu]
Mesopotamia   30th January 1916

We have got a fine opportunity of fighting. No doubt you are right in thinking that you too are fighting; but you are having a very different time from us, for you have everything you can want while the country here is absolutely uninhabited and desolate.[1] Never mind: when we are winning we are equally indifferent to comfort and inconvenience. [Letter passed]

1. Compare Nos. 261 and 271.

231

Hussain Shah to Syed Mahommed Shah (Punjabi Muslim, 104th Field Ambulance, Mhow Cavalry Brigade, France)

Alamgir [Urdu]
Punjab 31st January 1916

I give your wife the money she actually requires for expenses. The Commanding Officer, Peshawar, has not sent any allowance for four months – from 1st October 1915 to 31st January 1916. Before that, we received the allowance for nine months, and you sent Rs.41. All has been spent ... It is the time of famine and everything is expensive. There is no rain ... Everything – men, mules, camels – are being impressed and sent to Egypt [and] Basra ... When you send money, send it by telegram. It will cost more but we shall be certain to get it. When it is sent by money order the money is kept in deposit [by the Post Office]. [Letter passed]

232

Azmat Khan (Punjabi Muslim) to Kazi Muhammad (Jhelum District, Punjab)

Mhow Cavalry Brigade [Urdu verse]
France 31st January 1916

May God keep my respected friend;
Though there be even *lakhs* of your enemies like Germans,
May the Almighty keep you safe.
Without God's orders death can never come nigh.
God will preserve you travellers – recognize His goodness.
By the force of prayer the enemy will be defeated.
May death seize the King of the Germans (who is no king at all)
And our King, the King of Britain, may he win.
The standard of victory is in our hands and the enemy will be destroyed.
The whole Indian forces will return with glory to India.
Those heroes who have given their lives in battle,
Their souls will ascend to heaven and dwell there.
On that great day the souls will rejoice,
Whose bodies lie mouldering on the battlefield.

[Letter passed]

233

Nur Muhammad on behalf of the wife of Din Muhammad[1] to
Din Muhammad (Hindustani Muslim, 2nd Lancers, France)

2nd Lancers
Saugor   [Urdu]
CP   [c. January 1916]

In six months I [your wife] have received only two months' allowance, which I spent on my maintenance. Now I have had to pawn my jewellery to keep myself alive. The order has now been issued that we are to get only half the usual allowance. How am I to live on Rs.2.8 a month? Why is it that we do not get our allowances regularly and promptly, and why is the allowance now reduced by half? Reflect on this.[2] [Letter passed]

1. For a similar intercession of literate males, see No. 227.
2. The censor commented, 'this letter is a sample of many written on the same subject, namely, difficulties in obtaining family allotments'. See Nos. 231, 258 and 268. But see Nos. 206 and 244 for a contrasting view of the importance of sending money home.

234

Dafadar Ram Prasad Singh to Sowar Thakur Gajendra Natu Singh
(Rajput, 2nd Lancers, France)

Khair   [Hindi?]
Aligarh   [January 1916?]

What you write in your letter pleased me very much and I have shown it to my friends who are delighted too. You say you will stand fast and not be disturbed in mind. Bravo, my boy, this is the duty of brave men and is what a Rajput ought to do.[1] Do your Government work with bravery and earnestness, for our Government is fighting. Fight bravely, with the name of God on your lips and He will protect you. I am always praying night and day that He may give you victory and bring you back with glory and in safety to your native land. The Government now sorely needs your services. Show loyalty, and faith in your King, for loyalty and service have always been a tradition in our family. [Letter passed]

1. Rajputs frequently defined themselves in terms of martial activity. See Nos. 44, 111 and 256.

235

Pokhar Das (Punjabi Hindu) to Lala Chiniot Lal
(Indian Expeditionary Force D, Basra)

Military Accounts   [Urdu and Punjabi verse]
Rouen   1st February 1916

What I have written below is on everyone's lips here:

> When Lahore and Meerut left,[1] rumour fell upon Rouen.
> Rumour will be rife again when the Cavalry Corps depart.
> Weep, weep ye lovers.
> One has dubbed himself 'Prince',
> Another has covered himself with medals,[2]
> And another has felt the slipper applied.
> Weep, weep ye lovers.

This poem is the work of Sirdar Bishan Singh. When he writes more I will send
them to you. [Letter passed]

1. The reference is to the departure for the Middle East of the Lahore and Meerut Infantry
   Divisions. The Cavalry Corps remained in France.
2. A reference to the small charms in common use in Roman Catholic countries, frequently
   given as love tokens.

236

Amir Singh to Sowar Kanh Singh (Sikh, 34th Poona Horse, France)

Forest Department
Muree
[Rawalpindi]   [Gurmukhi]
Punjab   2nd February 1916

If you can possibly manage it, get your name struck off the rolls and come away.
By any means in your power, good or bad, you should save your life. In the end
do as you please. I have written to you frequently about this matter, and I am very
concerned about you ... Write before eating your food[1] and tell me everything about
the war ... No snow whatever has fallen here this year ... It has been ordered in
England, we hear, that all European adults are to be compulsorily recruited.[2] Here

many of our men have enlisted. More cannot be found. Men are very scarce.
[Letter passed]

1. The writer implies 'as soon as possible'.
2. Conscription was introduced in Britain in January 1916. See No. 220.

237

Tal Singh (Sikh) to Jemadar Bhan Singh (19th Lancers, France, 33)

19th Lancers
Sialkot   [Urdu]
Punjab   4th February 1916

For this reason I write to you privately regarding Pay Sowar Hazara Singh. Tell only
the Risaldar-Major Sahib about the matter. Hazara Singh made a mess of his
accounts and appropriated the money. Sirdar Albeil Singh commenced to examine
the accounts, in the ordinary course, and found some apparent errors in them.
Hazara Singh thereupon sent an Urdu petition to the Commanding Officer, in which
all sorts of things prejudicial to the Sirdar Sahib were said. We, however, saved the
situation. I did not show the petition to the Sahib Bahadur [the CO]. I took it to the
Sirdar Sahib's house and showed it to him, and there an English translation was made,
which was given to the CO. Then the Sirdar Sahib commenced a careful examination
of all Hazara Singh's accounts, but Hazara Singh had completely muddled them.
For eight days the accounts were under examination, then the Sirdar Sahib gave
Hazara Singh the opportunity to write out his accounts clearly. For this reason he
[Hazara Singh] could not be court-martialled, but he received this punishment – he
has been removed from the Pay Sowar's billet and sent back to ordinary duty in the
troop and one good conduct badge has been taken away. [He] also [lost] the rough
rider's badge. Being a holder of rank [acting Lance Dafadar] he escaped with a
reprimand. Now the pay work of the squadron is in my hands. [Letter passed]

238

Subedar Dhan Singh Lama (Gurkha, 2/2nd Gurkhas) to
Subedar-Major Gopi Ram Lama (Depot 2/2nd Gurkhas, Dehra Dun, UP)

                                                                        [Hindi]
Milford-on-Sea   6th February 1916

Your son on the 5th February went to London to the King's Durbar at Buckingham
Palace. His gracious Majesty with his own hand decorated me with the [Indian]

Order of Merit [Second Class]. I spent the day wandering about London and in the evening returned to camp. A Colonel Sahib from the depot was with me. I also saw General Macintyre and his Memsahib and had a talk with them. He now commands a division in England. The medal I have received is one that in England commands such respect that I cannot put it into words. When I came out of the Palace, many distinguished Sahibs and Memsahibs shook hands with me. What more can your son say. [Letter passed]

239

Inayat Beg to Haidar Beg (Deccani Muslim, 22nd Cavalry, attached 34th Poona Horse, France)

22nd Cavalry
Bolarum   [Urdu]
Hyderabad   7th February 1916

Do your work intelligently and well, and illuminate the name of your tribe, for without the will of God a single leaf cannot be shaken [by the wind]. We pray incessantly that God will give you victory soon and bring you back in safety and honour ... I have written several letters, but I don't know why they do not reach their destination. I have never written anything so bad in my letters that those who inspect them on the way should tear them up at sight.[1] As regards the regiment, of those people who were implicated in the murder of Ressaidar Kaim Khan the following were acquitted – Alam Khan, Sahib Gul and Naim Shah. But they are to be dismissed the service on 15th February, together with twelve other Afridis. Naimat Khan, Wali Mahomed and Hazrat Gul are to be hanged on 15th February. [Letter passed]

1. See No. 217 for a similar comment.

240

Hazura Singh (Sikh) to Sirdar Harnam Singh (11th Lancers, Delhi, India)

FPO.39   [Urdu]
France   7th February 1916

What you heard, that we were leaving France and going elsewhere, has proved false. All who were to go have gone. If hereafter we receive orders to go, I will let you know. My dear Harnam Singh, people tell me that last year the cold here was intense, but now it is no worse than the Punjab. We had a few days' snow, but it ceased. Sometimes we have hoar-frost and then it is very cold: otherwise the cold is nothing.

We have at present nothing to do. We are better off than in cantonments. Matches are fixed to take place between the regiments, at tug-of-war, wrestling, football and running. We are the winners at football in our division. In the second division the 9th [Hodson's Horse] have won. We are to play them. I will let you know who wins.[1]

I went to pass the machine gun school. There Ressaidar Mehr Singh's squadron was engaged and he used to come and see me every day. He is working better now, but still takes far too much liquor. He sometimes comes to see me in the regiment too. The orders here are that on Sunday any man can go to any other regiment to see his friends, if he likes. I have not heard anything of Sirdar Bachan Singh for some time. If you have any news of him, keep me informed of his welfare.

As for the war – read the papers. What is written in them is quite true.[2] Think now, if the Germans have been unable to do us any harm in a year and a half, what can they do now? Our Government has very boldly set the enemy's teeth on edge, and for some years after this war, he will have some difficulty in recovering his senses. He will never regain the power which he has now. Our Government's intentions are honest. It always helps the weak. [The German] thought to secure in his power all the small kings, but since his teeth have been set on edge, he has sat down in silence.

1. See No. 265 for another reference to inter-regimental games.
2. For other favourable comments on British newspapers, see Nos. 15 and 80.

241

Muhabbat Khan (Pathan) to Mohr Dil Khan
(38th CIH, Agar-Malwa, Central India)

38th CIH   [Urdu]
France   9th February 1916

On the 23rd January, Risaldar Anjam-ud-Din [Anjamuddin Khan, 42] started for India all well. He went on pension, and so we are left alone. Dafadar Pal Singh came to hospital [on the ground] that he had done twenty years' service and earned his pension. [He said that] he could not walk any more. A Court was appointed [to consider] his [case]. Dafadar Pal Singh was sentenced to a year's imprisonment. It was a heavy sentence, as of course he lost his dafadari and his twenty years' service went for nothing.[1] This is the position here, but what can we do? [Letter passed]

1. For the sequel to this incident, see No. 267.

242

Nabidad Khan to Woordi-Major Muhammed Umar Khan
(Deccani Muslim, 29th Lancers, France, 28)

Bolarum [Urdu]
Deccan 10th February 1916

Be careful not to say anything in your letters to Bismullah Khan, Fyaz Khan, Azam Khan and Mohamed Hasain, beyond the mere fact that you are in good health, for these people go shouting whatever they hear all over the bazar. There is a very strict Government order on this subject, and many people have already been punished for transgressing it. Detectives are always on the look-out. [Letter passed]

243

Sitar Khan to Baghi Shah (Pathan, 19th Lancers, France)

Kohat [Urdu]
NWFP 10th February 1916

I have not received pay [family allotment] for a year. I have now petitioned the Deputy Commissioner. The Rs.40 that you sent me have been received. You must indeed make endeavours for money to reach your home, as the need for it is very great. It is famine time, rain did not fall at the proper season, and no crops were sown.[1] At home no one is dead and no one is ill. A truce [in the feud] has been fixed for over a year. Sarwarai, Sadullah and Golabai – these three amongst our enemies have died. [Letter passed].

1. See No. 214.

244

To Sikhandar Sirdar (Punjabi Muslim, Indian Ordnance Depot, France)
from his wife

Rawalpindi [Urdu]
Punjab 11th February 1916

You write about the family. Well, during the day-time I can watch well over them, but who is to watch over them at night? I have no father or brother, and there is no male relative of yours old enough to protect us. Two of your daughters have now grown up, and God alone is their protector. Several families have been dishonoured. The times are bad, and I am all alone with small children. You should not be so inconsiderate. Several of your fellows have returned to their homes, while you remain sitting unconcerned there with your friends. You say 'I sent you money – spend it and be happy'. My reply is that I have no need of money and clothes. I want you. If anything should happen here, it would be disastrous. We have no protector save God. Therefore, leave your idleness, have some sense, and take measures to return. I impress this on you most strongly. We are quite dismayed. Never mind whatever means are required to achieve it, return home. I have received the money: hereafter don't send any money or parcels. There is no need for anything. Jawari Singh, [the] shopkeeper, was assaulted by thieves and robbed on the 9th February. Now he lies in hospital. No one went to his assistance. On this account I am still more disturbed. I shall look out for your return, till I get a reply to this letter.

245

Mahomed Yakub to Mahomed Wazir Khan (Pathan, 18th Lancers, France)

15th Lancers
Sialkot   [Urdu]
Punjab   11th February 1916

I reminded you at the time of starting that if you were unable to obtain oranges you should get onions; they are quite as serviceable[1] ... The news here is that Waziri dacoits are giving trouble. Every day some town or village is raided. [First part censored, rest of letter passed]

1. A reference to liquids, used like ink, but which leave no mark on the paper until it is warmed by fire.

246

Azim-ud-Din Khan to Sowar Abdul Azim Khan (Punjabi Muslim, 20th Deccan Horse)

Depot 20th Deccan Horse
Neemuch
[Gwalior]   [Urdu]
[Central India]   13th February 1916

It is a great pity that you have not got the Victoria Cross. I have quite tired my eyes over the newspapers looking for your name but have not found it. I don't know where you are, whether with the regiment or not. Everybody is getting promotion right and left but you have got nothing. Well, I at any rate have spent 20 rupees in newspapers! [Letter passed]

247

Lance Dafadar Chanda Singh (Sikh) to his wife Pertab Kor
(Lahore District, Punjab)

[France]
[Gurmukhi]
15th February 1916

This [France] is a very fine country. The father and mother invite a visitor to kiss them. If he declines, they are offended. Then all the family, men and women, indulge in indecent talk, and are very much amused. In the presence of the father, one will say to two others 'go and sleep together', and they will all laugh. It is indeed a very free and easy country. Nothing is prohibited, whatever may be done. In the presence of father and brothers one [a man] will catch another [a girl] by the arm and lead her outside. They [the father and brother] will say nothing. They are quite at ease.[1]

1. The censor remarked that this letter 'gives a curious picture of life in a billet which one may hope is hardly typical. The writer is either drawing on his imagination or has fallen by chance into a very loose family ... [The passage] was excised from the letter as being calculated to convey a wrong impression and discredit our Allies in India.'

248

Kaisar-i-Jahan to her brother Khabit Allah (Hindustani Muslim,
8th Cavalry, attached 2nd Lancers, France)

Muttra
[UP]
[Urdu]
16th February 1916

What you wrote to me [was] that you would be ahead of everyone in killing the enemy and would fall yourself in the field of battle and be called 'Bahadur' [brave one]. My brother, do they call those 'brave' who kill the enemy and are killed themselves? Nay, those who are the really brave [are those] who go gently like a tortoise and kill the enemy quietly and take care of themselves and their comrades. Such men do numerous brave acts. Brother mine, I am a poor, useless little thing, but my advice is not to get excited on such an occasion. Whatever you have got to do, do it quietly and carefully. Don't be too eager and don't lag behind. Take care of your own safety and help others, for God looks after those who do this. It is fatal to be too eager, and such a man is a danger to others. We are all praying that God may give victory to our King and bring you back victorious. I have heard that all the soldiers got boxes at Christmas. Don't go and give your box away for I am very keen on seeing it. [Letter passed]

249

Sukh Dyal (Dogra) to Naik Sarjan Singh (41st Dogras, Persia)

Lady Hardinge Hospital   [Hindi]
England   18th February 1916

I have been shot in both feet and in the right arm. I am all right but my feet have withered and I am neither dead nor alive. I can't put my foot to the ground, but it is my fate. I have been invalided to India and am going home ... I am going home and you are going to Persia. Well, play in the rose gardens there and have a good time. Forgive my faults and think of me. We shall meet some day in India and till then I will see you in dreams. [Letter passed]

250

Mohamed Sharif Beg to Mirza Imbarik Beg (Lahore District, India)

34th Poona Horse   [Urdu]
[France?]   20th February 1916

You speak of getting recruits. If you want to do any recruiting, you should get men for the 22nd Cavalry, for in that regiment our family and our caste fellows have always enlisted and the officers know us. If I am spared and can rejoin the 22nd I am sure to get promotion. No one can stop that. Here no one knows us, and in the 34th Horse there are none of my caste fellows. Now is your time for the 22nd, if you can get any recruits. This is the time because anyone who does such service to the British Government, however unimportant he may be ... has a note taken of his name in the Lord Sahib's office. You should if possible go and put your name down at the 22nd office and get recruits in the name of Ressaidar Mayal Beg. You will get your name and that of your caste noticed in the newspapers and you will always get consideration from the British Government. You should recruit anyone you can get without distinction of caste. [Letter passed]

251

M. L. Tilhet (Hindustani Hindu) to Pyari Lal Tilhet (Muzaffarnagar, UP)

Indian Convalescent Home   [Urdu]
New Milton   21st February 1916

Some time ago I received a letter from Lala Hira Lal in which he wrote something about my eating and drinking [prohibited or polluted things]. There is no doubt that I had not practised abstinence [from such things] because I could not continue to remain hungry. Originally I certainly did try to abstain, but since I came here I have ceased to do so – otherwise I could not have existed. In Egypt not only I but numbers of other Hindus – some of whom would, formerly, have rejected their food if only the shadow of a passer-by had fallen on it – have eaten from the hands of sweepers. Had we not done so there would have been no alternative but starvation, which could not be tolerated. We used to go openly to hotels [cafés, restaurants and refreshment rooms in Suez]. Of course, this was not known in India until Gurdial [?] let it out in his letter. Now everyone knows it and I am not alone in having transgressed [caste principle]. I have no compunction. You too, I suppose, know that the youths who come here for education never abstain in any way. Thus I did not introduce any new fashion. Along with me is a Doctor Lieutenant, by caste a Brahmin, who abstains from nothing. Moreover, if anyone tries to abstain, he advises them against doing so.[1] [Letter passed]

1. He invokes the alleged practice of the Brahmin to ameliorate his own transgressions.

252

Jehan Khan (Punjabi Muslim) to Gholam Mahomed Khan
(39th CIH, Goona, Central India)

2nd Lancers   [Urdu]
France   23rd February 1916

Try and do something for me if you can. Here no promotion is given to those who come from India as reinforcements. This is quite correct. Try and see what can be done with the help of your sirdars. In the case of the reinforcements sent to other regiments, promotion is given to them in their own regiments in India. If you cannot arrange it, well, it will be my bad luck. [Letter passed]

253

Kartar Singh (Sikh, 15th Sikhs) to Gurdit Singh (Raswind, Punjab)

Milford-on-Sea

[Gurmukhi]
24th February 1916

And my friend, this is the photo of our King's granddaughter – he who was King of the Sikhs, Ranjit Singh.[1] She has distributed her photo amongst Sikh brethren at the depot [Milford] on the evening of the 23rd February at five o'clock. [Written on the back of a photo of a lady friend, signed Sophia A. Duleep Singh, 1916]

1. Ruler of the Sikh state in Punjab, until his death in 1839. For another reference to him, see No. 308.

254

Mohan Singh (Sikh) to Sirdani Bishan Devi (Lyallpur District, Punjab)

6th Cavalry
France

[Urdu]
25th February 1916

You say that you have heard that the entire Indian Army has left France. This is not so. The infantry have left but the cavalry is still upholding the honour of the Government here.[1] By the Grace of God the cavalry are flourishing like fields of sarson [rape seed] in the spring. At the present time much rain and snow are falling and consequently the cold is very severe. The snow accumulates all day ... Sirdar Buta Singh of Rawalpindi has sent a copy of the Granth. He has conferred a great favour on us, since we can have worship celebrated during our sojourn in a foreign land. [Letter passed]

1. See Nos. 210, 216 and 235.

255

Bakhshish Singh (Sikh) to Sher Singh (Ferozepore District, Punjab)

Sialkot Cavalry Brigade
[France]

[Gurmukhi]
27th February 1916

Here it is very cold at present. It snows much. The little discomfort that we experience is due to cold and rain. Otherwise the country is like heaven. It rains frequently. You are, no doubt, astonished at what I say and wonder how this country can be heaven. Listen to one little thing. Here, no one drinks water. When they desire to drink, either at meals or any other time, they drink the juice of apples. So many apples are produced that the people press the juice and store it in barrels, [from] which they drink throughout the year. They let us have a bottle full for two pice. All the men drink it. There is no prohibition – you may bring as much as you like inside the house. Barrels upon barrels are full of it. Moreover, there are barns full of apples. If I return alive I will tell you all about this country. You shall be staggered at all I shall tell you. It is a real heaven. There is plenty of milk, but only cow's milk. The people, however, drink very little milk. They milk the cows and they then extract the butter at the rate of a *maund* of milk in ten minutes. The skimmed milk they give to cows, calves and pigs. The people are very honest: there is no sign of theft. Goods to the value of *lakhs* of rupees lie in glass houses.[1] No one pays any regard to them. Grain, potatoes and such like things lie in the fields unguarded. In short, the cat plays with pigeons and chickens; and the dog plays with the cat and tends the sheep, churns the butter, and draws a cart and guards it too.[2] When a cow calves, they immediately take away the calf and do not let the cow see it. They rear it on skimmed milk. They milk the cow daily – two or three times daily – without the calf being present. The cows in fact do not know whether they gave birth to a calf or not. It is the golden age. [Letter passed]

1. He implies 'houses that could easily be broken into'.
2. See No. 10.

256

Thakur Pertab Singh to Ram Sarup Singh (Rajput, 2nd Lancers, France)

Bijnor   [Urdu]
UP   28th February 1916

There is no doubt that you have ... difficult and trying work ahead of you. But, brave Rajputs, have no concern, and do your duty towards the Government with energy and wholeheartedness. You have eaten the salt of Government for a very long time. We ought at all times to be thankful towards the country and our Government, under whose protection we have lived and are living in perfect security and freedom:

What! have you forgotten the bravery of our ancestors
Who used to meet the swords [of the enemy] with their breasts!
Their names are honoured throughout the land
Who wore medals in their breasts and embroidered ends to their turbans.

You are Rajputs [whose duty it is] to die on the field of battle, if necessary, and thus to secure paradise. For a Rajput to die on horseback is a matter for pride.[1] You heroes leave a name behind you, so that those who come hereafter may be illuminated through it.

> Who is exempt from death?
> Today is your turn – tomorrow, mine!

[Letter passed]

1. See Nos. 44, 111 and 234 for similar comments.

257

Nand Lal (Jat) to Zemindar Surjan (Rohtak District, Punjab)

2nd Cavalry Division   [Urdu]
France   February 1916

You have written that you would like to get a job in the gold mines where they give you eighteen rupees a month. My idea was to get you to enlist in the cavalry because you are a young man and now is the time to serve your country. You ought to be able to enlist at once and join the expeditionary force here. You can ride and you know the rules; why not come at once and join me here? It would be a capital thing. You are not of the age to work on foot. You are the man for a rider. You ought to make arrangements for your wife and children and join the forces. What use to you is it that I am serving the Government as a *chaukidar* [village watchman]. The cavalry service is the only one worth entering. But I can say nothing more than this. You are your own master. Why not drive buffaloes or be a village *chaukidar* at Rs.4 a month? That is fine pay! Where have your brains gone? [Letter passed]

258

Abdul Majid Khan (Punjabi Muslim) to Haji Alladad Khan
(Nabha State, Punjab)

Sialkot Cavalry Brigade   [Urdu]
France   1st March 1916

You write that you have had no pay for two or three months. I cannot imagine what the reason can be. I wrote to the Munshi [secretary or writer] in the regiment whose duty it is to make the family remittances and I trust it may be all right. I have done my best to increase the family allowance, but without success. I have no Indian officer to whom I can apply as I belong to another regiment and the Sahib says he does not know the custom of my regiment and can do nothing. I have been in the trenches, and so was Mahomed Sadiq, and we were together for a month, and came back to the regiment on 1st March. Men went from every regiment but God was good to all. Now we are thirty miles behind the firing line. It is very cold and the snow is thigh deep. I never think about the chance of being killed, nor do I feel any particular satisfaction at the idea of going on living. There is absolutely no end to this war and no prospect of a decision. If any wise man or ancient says it is going to finish by any particular date, don't believe him. I think it will last ten years and all the signs point to this. Yet God is great and he can, if he will, stop it today. [Letter passed]

259

Ressaidar Khan Alam Khan to Jemadar Sirdar Sultan Khan
(Punjabi Muslim, 18th Lancers, France)

Jullundur   [Urdu]
Punjab   4th March 1916

We expect that you, and all those that are with you, will remain in every respect loyal to our King, and by your bravery will give proof of the fidelity of your race. Some of the 15th Lancers failed in their loyalty, and they have been heavily punished by transportation from their country.[1] A letter was received lately from Jamali, written by Sirbaland Khan, in which it was stated that the 15th Lancers had been released from imprisonment, but no intimation to that effect has reached our regiment yet.[2] Amongst those that received punishment were fifty-seven men who belonged to our regiment.[3] All the Sirdars [Indian officers] reasoned with the men, saying that we have sworn that by land or sea, wherever the Sirkar orders, we will never object to serve. But God clouded the understanding of certain of the men, and they disobeyed so just a Government under whose shadow we dwell in safety, and receive such dignity, and the like of whom has never existed. We hope that you will instil into the minds of all our race that they should uphold their own honour and that of our King, and illuminate it with the splendour of four moons. Well done, brave men! Add to the renown of your race! You will never have so good an opportunity for doing so [as the present].

1. In February 1916, the 15th Lancers were ordered to march from Basra to the front. Most of the regiment refused, owing to their very strong religious objections to fighting the Turks near the Holy Places of Karbala, Najaf and Baghdad. All 429 men involved in

the mutiny were punished, most receiving long sentences of transportation to the Andaman Islands. The news clearly travelled fast. See Nos. 276, 313 and 315.
2. In fact, the men were not released for over a year. See No. 550.
3. Presumably men of the 18th Lancers, seconded to the 15th Lancers.

260

Mahomed Firoz Din (Punjabi Muslim) to Firoz Khan (19th Lancers, Sialkot, Punjab)

Sialkot Cavalry Brigade   [Urdu]
France   7th March 1916

What am I to say to you about England? May God grant victory to our King. If I were to set about writing down the praises of Marseilles, my hand would be wearied with writing. Further, I went to Paris for seven days. What is Paris? It is heaven! [Letter passed]

261

Abdul Rauf Khan to Lance Dafadar Abdul Jabar Khan (Hindustani Muslim, 6th Cavalry, France)

21st Combined Field Ambulance   [Urdu]
Mesopotamia   7th March 1916

You know very well that I am not in India. I am here with Force D. You must know very well where Force D is [Mesopotamia]. Since coming here I have met many men who were formerly in France. From them we have heard all about France. In truth you must be very comfortable there, since the 'public' there are so civilized, and money, too, is plentiful. The particular part of the world where I am is a strange place. The seasons here are quite different from what you experience anywhere else. We have already had experience of the cold and wet. Now the heat is threatening us from afar. It rains very heavily and the entire surface of the land becomes a quagmire in which the slush is knee deep. When I used to march in this slush, I used to remember God! Since I left India I have not seen a metalled road. Except for date trees which one sees here and there along the course of the river, there is not another tree to swear by. We drink river water. Wells cannot be dug here. Except for the barren, naked plain, there is nothing to see.[1] The soil certainly is fertile, but the 'public' here are so thoughtless and careless that they do not make any attempt to till it. The lice infest one's clothes to such an extent that our hope [of release from them] is in God alone. The summer is coming on gradually. It is stated here that the mosquitoes are enormous, and I have been afraid of them from the beginning.

1. For similar negative views of Iraq, see Nos. 230 and 271.

262

Tiram Singh (Rajput) to Jemadar Narain Singh (Jhansi District, UP)

Meerut Cavalry Brigade [Urdu]
France 7th March 1916

When I was leaving Jhansi, certain people said 'look, the sea journey will take twenty days, and thereafter [in] seven days more you will be finished'. Goodness knows from what ancestral source of wisdom they were able thus to fix the date of my death! They ought to have had some hesitation in taking on themselves the functions of the Almighty. Now tell those stupid people that I have been here for eighteen months and am well and strong, and ask them what answer they can make, except one admitting their shame. Some of them, having been invalided, have returned to India. Others have gone with Force D [to the Persian Gulf] where their sins will become manifest. I am still alive and exist in comfort. All of us are well. We, as it were, play the Holi festival, except that instead of throwing balls of red powder at each other, we throw balls of snow. The snow for which in India we pay as much as four annas a *seer* lies deep all over the country and is trodden under foot as a thing of no account. In former days when a man used to visit England for a week or two he used to be regarded by us with as much respect as if he had been a great prophet. Now all that is changed. People of that kind will perhaps not think it worth while even to say that they have been to England. [Letter passed]

263

*Peshawra Singh (Sikh) to Sirdar Mahindar Singh
(19th Lancers, Sialkot District, Punjab)*

19th Lancers [Urdu]
France 9th March 1916

I hear that very few Sikh recruits are being enlisted into the regiment. You and Sirdar Bava Singh are both present there. You should strive to get recruits with all your ability and energy. This is no time for slackness. Consider the way in which the whole country is exerting itself and doing its duty. [Letter passed]

264

Buali Hasan Khan (Punjabi Muslim) to Rahimdad Khan (38th CIH, France)

Jhelum   [Urdu]
[Punjab]   11th March 1916

There is a tremendous amount of recruiting going on in this part of the country. Recruiting parties go from village to village, and the reason is that the famine is driving thousands to enlist.[1] It does not matter what the caste may be – sweepers, oil sellers, dancing girls' attendants – they take them all, even up to forty years of age. Everybody is talking about the war, even women and children. There is nothing else on anyone's lips. [Letter passed]

1. See Nos. 214 and 243 for similar comments.

265

Mir Zaman Khan (Muslim Rajput) to Akwan Raj Lal Khan Sahib
(Jhelum District, Punjab)

38th CIH   [Urdu]
[France]   12th March 1916

We had a wrestling competition on horseback the other day in which the 36th [Jacob's Horse] and the 2nd [Lancers] took part. The 36th won. The members of our football team who won the match the other day all got medals.[1] The General himself presented them. We have received orders to learn Roman Urdu[2] and two Sirdars have been appointed to teach us. I am now able to read and to write my name. Next week I hope to be able to address my envelope to you with my own hand in Roman, and if I learn [for] another two months I shall be able to do good work. [Letter passed]

1. See No. 240.
2. Urdu written in the Roman, rather than the Arabic, script.

266

Quartermaster Dafadar Samander Khan to Malik Sher Zaman Khan
(Dera Ismail Khan, NWFP)

36th Jacob's Horse   [Urdu]
France   14th March 1916

I wrote to you before that without [recommendation] there is no getting on in the army. Risaldar-Major [Muhammad] Nasir Khan and Ressaidar [Muhammad] Wazir Khan have upset all my promotion. It is necessary to have your caste men in great numbers in the regiment or else to have some one to say a word for you. Neither of these conditions exist for me in the regiment, but you might get Ball Sahib to say a word for me, or the Deputy Commissioner of Kohat might recommend me as he has got my file and knows about me. [Letter passed]

267

Nur Mahomed (Pathan) to Kot Dafadar Alladin
(Tarang Zai, Peshawar District, NWFP)

38th CIH   [Urdu]
[France]   14th March 1916

My friend, go on praying as usual. Prayer is no doubt useful but you must realize that as long as God wills our service in this country it is hopeless to expect your prayers for our return to be heard. When God forgives our sins which have brought upon us our present troubles, then – and not till then – will your prayers be heard. The squadron is much as it was when you left. Severity is increasing. Take the case of Pal Singh who was a dafadar of D Squadron for eighteen years and was a great opium eater. He went to hospital and said he was unfit for service and asked for pension. The Doctor Sahib told him that he was all right and that he should go on working. After three or four visits to the hospital he was arrested and a court-martial was held, in which he was reduced to the ranks and sentenced to imprisonment for a year. When the Colonel Sahib (who was on leave at the time) came back he was very angry and got him out of prison, and got him made a dafadar in Marseilles, and allowed him to take his pension and go back to India. This is the state of things here. If you open your mouth at all you are imprisoned. [Letter passed]

268

Bhawal Khan to his son Sowar Sher Baz Khan (Punjabi Muslim,
22nd Cavalry attached 34th Poona Horse, France)

Gadari
Jhelum   [Urdu]
Punjab   14th March 1916

After promising to send money, you have even ceased to write for three weeks. It
is famine time and how are we to manage? For two years you have sent nothing.
Other servants get wages: perhaps you serve gratuitously? If the Sirkar pays you
no wages, I have no hidden treasure here from which to supply the needs of your
family. Your companions have received in wages over Rs.1000 each. Yet you
[apparently] get nothing! If you get no wages, then where is the benefit in service?
It would be preferable to dig or to beg. I am so wearied with writing to you, week
after week, but you have paid no heed. Well done! When I am dead, then come
and lay the money on my grave! Others think about their families and send them
money, but you have no concern for your family.[1]

1. See No. 233 for other references to difficulties in obtaining family allotments.

269

A Jat to P. Balder Ram (Rohtak District, Punjab)

3rd Skinner's Horse   [Hindi]
France   15th March 1916

What I want you to do is to get some of that medicine which attracts one person
to another. Put it in a little box and send it over. The sort of medicine I want is that
which would make a woman come to me directly she put it on.[1] [Letter passed]

1. For another example of such superstitions, see No. 391.

270

Sowar Saiyid Harif (Deccani Muslim) to Mohamed Ibrahim
(Depot Saugor, Central Provinces)

29th Lancers   [Urdu]
France   15th March 1916

I cannot tell you the calamities that we endure. When I wake at the dawn of day
I can see no relief from the misery in store for me. God alone knows it and He

has permitted us to endure it, and He will end it when He thinks fit. I am not in any special appointment such as orderly, but am doing the work of an ordinary sepoy. If you were to write to the Ressaidar Sahib I daresay he would hear you. If you write, ask for me to be made orderly. All the squadrons live separately and are split up in billets in various villages. I am utterly sick of it and can stand no more. [Letter passed]

271

Abdul Najid Khan (Muslim) to Suliman Khan (3rd Skinner's Horse, France)

Rohtak [Urdu]
Punjab 18th March 1916

I had a letter received from my brother Sadikall Khan from Basrah, three days ago. He says he is constantly ill, and that every few days his health changes. He says also that the heat is unbearable and that the country [Mesopotamia] is the very opposite of France; that he is neither fit to fight nor ill enough to return to India; that, except for dates and the heat, nothing is to be found. Where, he asks, is that France, and those courteous people; where those fine open roads; where all those nice things? In short, this country, he says, is the entire opposite of France.[1] [Letter passed]

1. See Nos. 230 and 261 for similiar comments about Mesopotamia (Iraq).

272

Kot Dafadar Abdulla Khan to Lance Dafadar Mahomed Habib Khan
(30th Lancers, France)

Karauli State [Urdu]
Rajputana 18th March 1916

I have heard with much pleasure about your welfare and about the excellence of your work. If you are worthy you will render good service and secure a name. My father (your grandfather) was a soldier. I have reached the rank of Kot Dafadar – now let us see to what rank you can attain by exertion and bravery. Promotion (it is true) is a matter of fate: nevertheless, practise every earnest endeavour in your work, and let your work always be clean and faithful. Do not let slackness come anywhere near you. Each duty that you have do, do it intelligently [and] with due thought. Rely on God and you will surely get a good result and a good name. When

I hear from others that 'Mahomed Habib is working excellently' I am so pleased that I cannot describe my feelings. Work well and satisfy your officers. Shun evil society and always be present at the time of duty, so that your officers may be pleased with you. Meka Singh is weak; give him a helping hand. [Letter passed]

273

Firoz Khan (Punjabi Muslim) to Rajalal Khan (Shahpur District, Punjab)

Secunderabad Cavalry Brigade [Urdu]
France 20th March 1916

If you have sent Nadir Khan to school let me know. If you have not done so already, you must certainly do so. I have seen in this country that no person is uneducated. Even the women are educated, and there is no woman who is uneducated. All the inmates of a house are educated, and when they see one of our men going about with a letter in his hand [to have it read] they are very surprised. No doubt they think that we are very stupid since we can't read.[1] Truly they are right. What is a man without education? Nothing. God is pleased with a man who is educated. These people are very prosperous and are in want of neither money nor property. Rain and snow fall freqently. Men and women both work so hard and cheerfully that we regard them with wonderment. Women even drive a plough. What more am I to say? You must certainly send Nadir Khan to school. [Letter passed]

1. Further evidence of the men's dependence on scribes.

274

*Sawar Khan (Pathan) to Lance Dafadar Nainu Shah
(17th Cavalry, IEF, France)*

Peshawar [Urdu]
[NWFP] 24th March 1916

I hear that Government have given orders that all soldiers [who are] natives of Afghanistan will have to resign.[1] If it is true, then you should resign and come back. We have lost all the *izzat* that we had with the Government. All those in the 17th Cavalry have struck their names off and have left. [Letter passed]

1. Transfrontier Pathans frequently deserted because of their religious objections to a war against Turkey. Because of this, recruiting among them was stopped at the end of 1915.

275

*Pensioner Jan Mahomed Khan to Fateh Mohamed Khan
(Hindustani Muslim, 6th Cavalry, France)*

Rohtak   [Urdu]
[Punjab]   24th March 1916

I am very glad to hear of your having those sacred readings in France about the birth and career of God's Holy Prophet. What pleases one most is to think that among the various nations and various religions of Europe you have been able to spread abroad the story of our beloved Prophet. I am hopeful that people of other religions, when they hear the story of the Prophet, will become his followers, and I believe that the seeds have been sown in many hearts which will bring forth fruit for Islam. You should all be careful that your prayers and religious observances are carefully carried out. It would not be surprising if this war has been permitted in order to encourage the propaganda of Islam. God seems to have adopted this means of spreading the truth to the furthest corners of the earth. For this reason it is incumbent on every Muslim soldier to fight his best for the King, taking care that he does not lose the support of his religion.[1] Fear God, [and] honour your King and the officers who are set over you. [Letter passed]

1. Contrast No. 276. See No. 1 for a similiar view of Islam and world politics.

276

*Ashraf Ali Khan to Signalling Instructor Dafadar Fateh Mahomed Khan
(Hindustani Muslim, 6th Cavalry, France)*

6th Cavalry
Sialkot   [Urdu]
[Punjab]   24th March 1916

We have got the depot of the 15th Lancers here now; and they were in France from the beginning of the war, and went thence to Basra. The whole regiment united there for the purpose of taking an oath not to fight against Muslims.[1] They all took the oath and laid the Qu'ran on their heads, and swore not to tell anyone of their compact. But a jemadar of that regiment told the CO all about the affair. He at once ordered the 'fall in' to be sounded and everyone had to fall in just as he was, whether dressed or not. When the men had fallen in, the other regiments took possession of their arms. They were then ordered to embark on a ship and all refused.

After that it was decided that the denial of the Indian commissioned officers of all knowledge of the affair should be accepted. They denied it all (in spite of the fact that they too had sworn on the Qu'ran) and they were acquitted. The rest – non-commissioned officers and troopers, 429 in number – were arrested and punished with various terms of imprisonment. Three Kot Dafadars got penal servitude for life, and the rest of the non-commissioned officers [got] fifteen years. The senior privates got seven years' transportation. As to the recruits who came in drafts, they got three years in jail and were despatched to Bombay to serve their sentences. There were sixty of them. The CO has had his sword taken away from him and he has been called upon to answer the charge of not knowing what was going on in the regiment, although the whole regiment were Muslims. He has also to explain how it was that he sent three applications for his regiment to be sent to Mespotamia from France.

The Colonel Sahib of the 15th Lancers arrrived yesterday at Sialkot [Punjab] and told the [Regimental] Depot all about it, saying that it was useless to try and keep the affair secret, although the officer commanding the Depot had done his best to keep the story from the men. The pay of the sowars has been stopped since 23rd March. The Risaldar-Major in charge of the depot, an universally esteemed and straightforward man who has been in the regiment thirty-three years [Muhammad Amin Khan, Sardar Bahadur, 51], lamented what had happened to the Colonel, who said 'don't worry, the deeds of the regiment in France have been written in letters of gold, but it is fate that this should have happened'. The list of men punished, and their punishments, have been published in the regimental orders.

1. This account is remarkably accurate in detail. For another reference to this mutiny see No. 259.

277

Shah Wali Khan (Punjabi Muslim?) to Zaman Ali (Jhelum District, Punjab)

Ambala Cavalry Brigade   [Urdu]
France   26th March 1916

The money that I sent you, may, if you think [it] fit and just, be made into jewellery for my daughter, Rezma Bibi. It is not fair that you should be annoyed with me, for you know the saying:

> A sepoy's life is for some[1]
> And his death is for others[2]
> But all his discomforts and trials are his alone.

[Letter passed]

1. Meaning 'for his family'
2. Meaning 'for his country', or 'for his King'.

278

*Abdur Rahman Khan (Deccani Muslim) to
Malik Mahomed Sultan Nawaz Khan (Hyderabad, India)*

Secunderabad [Brigade?] Field Ambulance   [Urdu]
France   28th March 1916

I swear by God that, since your letter came, I have eaten and drunk but little and
have had no sleep. Know that not a day passed that I do not remember you and
despair. The earth is hard and the sky is distant. If I had wings, I would fly to you.
If there were no sea I would run to you. I am separated from you by the seven seas.
I have eaten the pay of the Sirkar till today, and it is proper that I should serve.
You know how many thousands of God's servants are present here. For the sake
of God, don't be so disturbed. If I live we shall meet again. You should not worry.
I am quite well. Be content. [Letter passed]

279

An anonymous Muslim to the Risaldar-Major of the 6th Cavalry, Troop No. 1

No. 786   [Urdu]
Karachi   [March 1916?]

My dear friend, you are in a sorry plight owing to the treachery of those swindlers
and rogues. I can see no hope of your further existence. Your family is in misery
as your pay has been stopped from November last. You are entangled in a war in
which no victory has been gained nor can any be gained in the future. What you
ought to do is raise your fellow caste-men against the English and join the army
of Islam. If you die in its service it would be better than living as you are doing
now. Act as I have advised you, or you will be sorry for if afterwards. God's orders
have been received to the effect that the destruction of the British Raj is at hand.
They are having to face great losses everywhere. You ought to think over this, for
by sticking to the English you will gain neither this world nor the next. All the
Muslims who have died in this war fighting for the British will spend an eternity
in hell. Kill the English whenever you get a chance and join the enemy. If you do
not win in this world you will at all events gain Paradise. You will certainly be
safe from this King of the traitors. Everything out here is very dear and there is a
regular famine. Be watchful, join the enemy, and you will expel the Kafir from
your native land. The flag of Islam is ready and will shortly be seen waving. You
Indians make ready and we here in two days will rebel and imprison all the English.
Please God we shall do this, for every caste out here complains of them. All are

weeping, for the soldiers are not paid and the people have to pay for the war. Enough – the wrath of God is about to descend on them, and this will be in two or three months, by which time they will have fled from India.[1]

1. This unsigned letter was received by Risaldar Habibullah, who passed it on to his OC. The postmark indicated that it was sent from Agra, and it was therefore relayed to the Government of UP for investigation. The number 786 at the head suggested the Bismullah, or prayer of invocation in the Abjad formula. According to the censor it was 'a specimen of the most virulent type of Islamic fanaticism'. It was quite untypical of the letters sent or received by Muslim soldiers of the Indian Army in this period.

280

Kalwant Singh (third-year Student) to Kot Dafadar Ghamand Singh (Sikh, 3rd Skinner's Horse)

Agra Chank

[Urdu]
2nd April 1916

A terrible affair has taken place here. The Supplementary Lahore conspiracy case has been decided in a way that spells disaster to the Sikh people.[1] One hundred of our beloved Sikhs were sentenced to death, and our brother Nand Nir Singh got transportation for life. Now may the Guru help the Sikh people and rescue the drowning ones! It will be a long time before the Sikh people can raise their heads again! [Letter detained]

1. The Lahore Conspiracy was an attempt by revolutionaries to subvert the discipline of the Indian Army.

281

Dorana Khan (Pathan) to his father Gul Aslam Khan (Jangi, Peshawar District, NWFP)

38th CIH
France

[Urdu]
3rd April 1916

As to what you say about money, it is not money, it is my coffin! I, a wanderer, am very grieved at this, that you, Sir, remember the money, but do not remember me! If you write me such a letter again I shall be exceedingly angry. On a previous occasion I, your servant, asked you not to write to me again about money. But now you have written again. You are concerned about money. I am concerned about my life! For the rest, I understand about Sapas Khan. What am I to do! Once he has enlisted, I have no power. I wrote at the beginning and said 'don't let him enlist'. He did not listen, so what am I to do? Tell me where he is. If his anger was so great, why did he not avenge himself in some other way? Why enlist? ... Don't write to me about Hakim Khan. I have no concern with Hakim Khan. What am I doing to him? Never write me such a letter again. This is not a letter, it is a live coal placed on my flesh. Such a letter I consign to the flames! [Letter passed]

282

To Risaldar Raj Singh (Jat, 3rd Skinner's Horse, France, 33)[1]

Rohtak [Urdu]
[Punjab] 8th April 1916

It is your duty to gain renown for the Jat clan. This is your opportunity. An opportunity is not always present. It is your duty to illumine the name of your ancestors, and of your clan, in the same manner as the 6th Jats[2] have done. It is an obligation on you to serve the Government loyally. A man is born once only, and you now have the opportunity to distinguish yourself. It is desirable that you should impress this on all the men at the time of roll call.

1. Correspondent unnamed.
2. Serving in the Meerut Division, then in the Middle East.

283

Chaudi Lal (Hindustani Hindu?) to
D. Lakini Chand Jaim (Meerut District, UP)

1st Indian Cavalry Division [Urdu]
France 10th April 1916

Ujagar Mal wrote about the marriage of Jivi, our brother. According to Indian standards, his age is sufficient for marriage, but as regards girls I do not think they ought to be married before seventeen or eighteen. At this age they are grown up and physically vigorous. In this country of France the girls do not marry until they are about twenty. I am studying the subject of marriage as it is in other countries. [Letter passed]

284

Bishan Singh to Jemadar Katar Singh (Sikh, 18th Lancers, France, 32)

Quetta   [Urdu]
Baluchistan Agency   10th April 1916

Those subjects of the British Government who have served in this war, will, together with their families, certainly be remembered by the Government as to the fulfilment of their rights. This Government of ours is a very just and humane one. We are indeed fortunate in that we are covered by the shadow of the British Government, and we hope that that shadow will remain over us till the end of time.

Also the late Viceroy, Lord Hardinge, left for England in the beginning of April.[1] In his place the new Viceroy, Lord Chelmsford, assumed office on 4th April.[2] The viceroyalty of Lord Hardinge was very beneficial for the people – let us see what favours the new Viceroy will give to the poor subjects of India. We hear that he also is a very right and highminded person. This inauspicious war started in the late Viceroy's term of office, and may God terminate the war in the new Viceroy's time, and give our Government the victory and confound their enemies.

Write and tell me how far Verdun is from Paris. It appears from the newspapers that the enemy is making heavy attacks there, and, not succeeding, returns crestfallen to his own trenches.[3] Our allies are very brave and strong and it is difficult for the enemy to stand up against them. He hits recklessly right and left, but he has not the strength to establish himself firmly in one spot and fight from there. [Letter passed]

1. Hardinge, Charles (1858–1944). Educated Harrow, and Trinity College Cambridge; entered Foreign Office, 1880; knighted, 1904; Permanent Under-Secretary for Foreign Affairs, 1906–10 and 1916–20; Baron Hardinge of Penhurst, 1910; Viceroy of India, 1910–16; Ambassador to Paris, 1920–22.
2. Chelmsford, Lord Frederic John Napier Thesiger (1868–1933). Educated Winchester, and Magdalen College Oxford; succeeded father as 3rd Baron, 1905; Viceroy of India, 1916–21; a moving spirit behind the Montagu–Chelmsford ('Montford') reforms, 1918–19; Viscount, 1921; Labour First Lord of the Admiralty, 1924.
3. The German assault on the French fortress of Verdun, one of the major battles of the war, began on 21st February 1916. By the time the Germans broke off the attack, in July, both sides had suffered around 300,000 casualties.

285

Lance Dafadar Faizullah Khan to Mir Abdullah
(Punjabi Muslim, 36th Jacob's Horse, France)

30th Lancers
Risalpur
[Peshawar District]   [Urdu]
[NWFP]   10th April 1916

There is no complaint of any sickness in the country, but the want of rain is depressing everyone, and the whole country is suffering from the pain of separation from those near and dear to them. God, if he sends calamity upon us, also sets us free. Work hard and have confidence. God will soon bring round that blessed day when you will all see your hearths and homes again.

286

Risaldar Muhammad Akram Khan (Pathan, 39) to Ahmad Khan (Peshawar, NWFP)

9th Hodson's Horse   [Urdu]
France   11th April 1916

You have no doubt heard of my good services from other people. I am not given to self-praise, and you know the proverb 'it is not the perfumer who gives the perfume to his wares'. On the 26th March I went to London to have an interview with His Majesty the King. The King spoke to me with his own auspicious tongue. I am profoundly grateful to His Majesty for his kind treatment, and am always praying that God in justice will grant him the victory. [Letter passed]

287

Dafadar Bhagat Singh (Sikh) to Ishar Singh (Amritsar District, Punjab)

9th Hodson's Horse   [Gurmukhi]
France   11th April 1916

With regard to what you wrote about Kharak Singh coming to worry you, you must make some arrangement for him. This is my advice, and do you listen to it! When you see him, give him a good shoe beating so that he may be thoroughly dishonoured. Mind you, beat him so as to leave no marks, and take care that there are no witnesses. Tell him also that if he comes again you will take his life. There are four of you brothers and he is all alone. If this does not succeed, then get up a case against him and get hold of a couple of witnesses. You must make such a charge against him that he cannot possibly get off without some punishment. Tell the magistrate that Bhagat Singh has gone to the war and that Kharak Singh wants to murder his small son. If you do this I am confident that he will be either imprisoned or bound over. [Letter detained][1]

1. This letter was detained by the Boulogne censor because it was 'full of bad advice and incitement to crime'. He suspected that the regimental censor, who had passed the letter, had probably not read it.

288

Lance Dafadar Ghulam Mohamed Khan to Mirza Mahomed Hayal (Gujrat District, Punjab)

19th Lancers   [Urdu]
[France]   11th April 1916

What is the reason that the pay I allotted you for the family has never reached you? I have sent in two petitions already and am sending off a third. I hope you will get the pay with arrears. The same is the case with all the men who have come from one cavalry regiment to another in reinforcements. They are all having difficulties with their pay and family allotments. It is a strange thing that some of the men who came with me to join this regiment got their allowances paid to their families ten months after they joined, and, after that, one month their families would get it and another month not. The state of things about the pay is extremely bad and the families are writing and complaining. We are all utterly disgusted. [Letter passed]

289

Nadir Ali (Punjabi Muslim) to Lumberdar Sultan Mahomed (Jhelum District, Punjab)

34th Poona Horse   [Urdu]
France   11th April 1916

Do not be anxious. We shall meet again. To be anxious is wearing to the spirit, and the enemy ridicules such anxiety. The work we are doing is a man's work. I read in some of your letters 'I am weeping day by day on account of this separation.'

Do not under any circumstances write like that. If you write like that again I will not answer the letter. When you write, write like a man and ask God to bring me back victorious to my native land.[1] [Letter passed]

1. For a similar request to write such a letter see No. 134, but contrast No. 174.

290

Jemadar Ganda Singh (Jat, 38) to Gurandate (Jhelum District, Punjab)

6th Cavalry [Urdu]
France 12th April 1916

You know how men go to College in England and return with an excellent degree after three or four years. Just in the same way I am studying and hope to get a good degree. What will that degree be? The privilege of bearing back unfurled to India the Royal Standard fluttering in the gentle breeze. It is that Royal Standard under which we risaldars and sirdars march joyfully forward. It is we and we alone who will have the privilege of unfurling that flag in India because we are, in a way, near relations of King George V. The people will meet us shouting applause and singing songs of victory. [Letter passed]

291

Sirfaraz Khan to Dafadar Alam Khan (Baluchi Muslim, 18th Lancers, France)

61st Camel Corps
Lahore [Urdu]
Punjab 16th April 1916

Remember this, that you must always do the Sirkar's work faithfully. It is very difficult to get such a King [as we have got]. The Turks are not our paternal uncle's children! I firmly rely on you, that you remain the well-wisher of the Sirkar. Still, it is proper that I should advise you. The Turks made war against our Sirkar without any cause. Our Sirkar repeatedly told the Turks before the war to remain neutral, and that their security would be arranged for in every way. But the Turks would not be advised, and now they are giving away their country with their own hands.

292

Mahendra Lal Varna to Lali Kalivati (Hindu Girls' School, Lucknow, UP)

FPO.40   [Hindi]
France   17th April 1916

With this letter I am enclosing a picture card showing the death of an English girl.
You will notice the German in the picture and the young woman lying senseless
on the ground in front of him. She was a nurse in Belgium and used to attend to
the wounded. Nowadays, Belgium is in the hands of the Germans. The name of
the young girl is Miss Cavell. She was charged with the crime of helping English
soldiers to escape to England [via the Netherlands], and was sentenced to death.
She fainted, and the soldiers refused to fire on her body, and then the German officer
blew her brains out with his revolver. This is the horrible act of the Germans.[1]

1. The execution of Nurse Edith Cavell by the Germans in 1915 caused public outrage in
    Britain during the war. Subsequent evidence suggests, however, that she was indeed
    guilty as charged.

293

*Ressaidar Isa Khan (Punjabi Muslim, 42) to Pay Dafadar Niaz Mahomed Khan
(34th Poona Horse, Ambala, Punjab)*

[34th Poona Horse]   [Urdu]
France   17th April 1916

I went to England on the 5th May. On the 10th May I was presented to His Majesty,
the King. I was shown all the famous places in the city. We went over the whole
city in motor cars. Very excellent arrangements were made for us in the matter of
food and accommodation. We met many officers of position who treated us very
kindly. We were shown theatres and many very wonderful sights. I cannot write
more, because the paper is small and the subject very large. [Letter passed]

294

Lance Dafadar Chandan Singh (Sikh) to Urudoh Singh (Lahore District, Punjab)

38th CIH   [Urdu]
France   18th April 1916

I am very fit indeed and the only thing I have to complain of is the separation from
you. The people here show us more affection if possible than our own mothers.

When we are transferred, they weep and embrace us repeatedly. Every now and then we can't help thinking that they must have been our mothers in a former incarnation. You may lose your temper, but they – never. If any one of us gets angry they soothe us and appeal to us, and if we do not respond they weep. [Letter passed]

295

Dafadar Nathan Singh (Sikh) to Sowar Paran [?] Singh (State Cavalry, Jind State, Punjab)

2nd Lancers   [Gurmukhi verse]
France   18th April 1916

        The Sikh roars like a lion on the field of battle
                And yields up his life as a sacrifice;
        Whoever is fortunate enough to be born a Rajput
                Never fears the foe in battle;
        He gives up all thought of worldly pleasure
                And dreams only of the battle field;
        He who dies on the field of battle,
                His name never dies, but lives in history;
        He who fronts the foe boldly in battle
                Has God for his protection;
        Once a Sikh takes the sword in hand
                He has only one aim – victory.

[Letter passed]

296

Indar Singh (Sikh) to Sirdar Dasounda Singh (Ambala District, Punjab)

18th Lancers   [Urdu]
France   19th April 1916

There is a big *maidan* close by us where we exercise. It was covered with crops but Government took it up for a training ground. We are all in houses but the horses are outside. The horses are not in good condition at all owing to their being outside in all this cold and wet ... What you say is true, but the only person who can form an opinion about military service is the man who has done it. It sounds very fine to be in the Army, but there are drawbacks. First of all, you have to be ready at any moment; secondly, you have to take orders from men whom you would not think of employing as labourers in your own village; and thirdly, you have much more inconvenience to put up with than in your own home. There may be honour [*izzat*] to be won in the Army, but, after all, it is nothing when compared to one's family pride. [Letter passed]

297

Dafadar Ali Mardan to Risaldar [Mirza Khalilulla] Khan (Pathan, 10th Hodson's Horse, attached 9th Hodson's Horse, France, 40)

10th Hodson's Horse
FPO.29   [Urdu]
Egypt   20th April 1916

I will tell you of the affair that Sher Zaman Khan was enquiring about, when a Gurkha went mad and wounded three Indian officers. He than ran into the trenches and began firing indiscriminately. The Colonel came to me and I went with him and two other sowars into the trench. He fired at us three or four times but missed and wounded other men at a distance. About 7pm I spotted him again close at hand and he fired and the bullet passed through my *pagri*, just missing my head. Great is God's grace! I fired again and dropped him wounded. We then jumped in and seized him and he died almost at once.

298

Gunga Singh (Sikh) to Dafadar Jaswant Singh (attached 6th Cavalry, France)

16th Cavalry Depot
Lucknow   [Gurmukhi]
[UP]   21st April 1916

The 7th Brigade is surrounded in Mesopotamia.[1] Attempts have been made to rescue them, but without success. There was a fight on 6th March and heavy losses to us in the attempt to relieve them. Some men of ours are in the besieged force, twenty in number. They have eaten their horses and mules. They have a quarter of a pound of flour each per diem. We are hopeful of being sent to join the relieving force. [Letter passed]

1. After being checked at Ctesiphon in November 1915, General Townshend's British-Indian force fell back to Kut-al-Amara, where they were invested by the Turks early in December. After enduring a five-month siege, Townshend surrendered on 29th April 1916. See Nos. 304 and 329.

299

Dafadar Charan Singh to Ressaidar Harphul Singh
(Jat, 29th Lancers, France, 31)

Depot 29th Lancers
Saugor [Urdu]
Central Provinces 21st April 1916

We have got orders to send sixty sowars to France on 15th May, of whom fifty-five are Jats. We are getting only Jat recruits in the depot now. After this party has left, we shall start recruiting again. We have lost twenty-one recruits by desertion ... All the Jats in the depot are utterly disgusted by an incident which has taken place. We all got four days' leave for the Holi, and on the night of the Holi itself we had the Holi celebration going on in the lines, and a dance by dancing girls at the quarter guard. At 11pm, the CO ordered me to bring the men who were celebrating the Holi in the line up to the quarter guard. I remonstrated and said it could not be done, and the CO accepted it. But my enemies stirred up [Captain C.G.] Bacon Sahib, and he called on us for an explanation as to why we had disobeyed the regulations by making a noise in the lines at 2am; and he punished me, and took away my Kot Dafadarship, and stopped all leave to Hindus for a month. All the Hindus complained bitterly and said that such a thing had never been done in holiday time before. All the Jats feel it deeply and I cannot write all that is happening. I am writing this because I should like you to know what has been done, and should like your advice because all the recruits are bitter about it.

300

Risaldar Mir Jafar Khan[1] (Pathan, 50) to Nawab Sahib, Khan Bahadur Abdul
Qayum Khan (Assistant Political Agent, Khaibar, Peshawar, NWFP)

9th Hodson's Horse [Urdu]
France 25th April 1916

This is my thirty-third year of service, and I am the oldest soldier in the Army in Europe.[2] My youth and old age are given in the service of the Government; and if the Government can be served with the dust of my bones, it is theirs. Although I am old, I do not desire to ask for my pension at such a crisis. It is likely, however, that my CO, considering my age and service, and the solitude of my family, will himself give me permission to apply for pension. [Letter passed]

1. The same man writes again on 23rd May 1916. See No. 317.
2. He entered the Army on 12th February 1884. Many other Indian officers had upwards of twenty years' service.

301

Yalait Khan (Punjabi Muslim) to Mohakam-ud-Din
(Chakwal, Jhelum District, Punjab)

Sialkot Cavalry Brigade [Urdu]
France 26th April 1916

We are forbidden to write particulars about the war. Moreover, what is one to write?
If the fighting were confined to one spot, one could give some details, but this war
is spread over the whole world. No part of the world is free from it. In the sea,
warships have heated the market of death, and on land soldiers are constantly fighting.
In the air, airships are fighting vigorously. The guns have overturned the surface
of the earth. What more am I to tell you? If God, the All Merciful, wishes to preserve
anyone, he alone can escape from such a whirlwind.

302

Mir Ahmad Khan to Lance Dafadar Ghulam Hasain Khan
(Pathan, 9th Hodson's Horse, France)

Urtarzai
Kohat District [Urdu]
[NWFP] 28th April 1916

You do not trust my letters about home affairs apparently, but what can I tell you.
Everything is quiet in our village and there have been no births or deaths. All the
men are away in [the] infantry or cavalry, and therefore there can be no births. All
the women are rampant, and ... the only thing to [do] is to send them out to join
their husbands.

303

Veterinary Assistant Kesar Shah (Punjabi Muslim) to his wife,
c/o Sayid Valait Shah (Gujrat District, Punjab)

Rouen [Urdu]
France 3rd May 1916

Dear one, what you say is quite true, that you have never before experienced so long
a separation. Indeed, in our whole lifetime we have never been separated for more

than six months altogether. Remember, however, that if in this world a man has honour, he has everything. Pray that God may keep me well and bring me back so that we may again enjoy those happy times. Things do not always remain the same. God will show kindness, so do not be anxious. You write and say that you are distracted by this long separation. God will give you patience. You must have read my name in the newspapers, and how pleased you must have been! This was the reward of short service rendered faithfully. If God wills, then I shall return quickly [and] with honour. I am in comfort and am getting honour. Five times a day I say my prayers, and beg that God will soon send me back safely with honour. Do not think that, because I am far away, I may forget you, or that my affection for you may grow less. That could never be. If I have any other thought than my work it is for my dear ones. And God will surely give me the fruit of my desire. Do not then be wanting in faith, for He can do everything – even that which may seem to be impossible.

304

*Risaldar-Major Kalander Khan Bahadur to Risaldar Khurshed Ali Khan
(Hindustani Muslim, 20th Deccan Horse, France)*

7th Lancers
Poona   [Urdu]
Bombay   5th May 1916

It is with great regret that I tell you that our besieged force in Kut-al-Amara (of which our squadron formed a part) surrendered on 28th April after a five months' siege, owing to want of provisions.[1] They fought to the last with the greatest gallantry. There were 9,000 of them. It was a great grief to all that relief could not reach them and that all our efforts were in vain. The greatest regret of all is that our squadron with all the Sirdars are prisoners. Risaldar [Ressaidar?] Ajaib Singh and Jemadar Manna Singh were with them, as they were in hospital with wounds and the hospital was taken. [Letter passed]

1. See Nos. 298 and 329 for other references to the siege.

305

Jemadar Ganda Singh (Sikh, 38) to Bhagwan Das (Jhelum District, Punjab)

6th Cavalry   [Urdu]
France   5th May 1916

This is the time when he who desires to do so may illuminate his name and [that of] his clan and country by sacrificing himself. Do you pray in the temple at the beginning of the month and at full moon time, that the enemy may never see my back, but may always be faced by me as by a lion. We soldiers have been fed with money which we have now to earn, with our lives if necessary. Therefore may none of us die of disease. We must all die some day. It is best that we should die in this great war.

306

Mahomed Usuf Khan (Punjabi Muslim) to
Mahomed Ismail (Hissar District, Punjab)

Meerut Cavalry Brigade [Urdu]
France 8th May 1916

The arrangements of our benign Government are deserving of all praise. We receive everything in plenty – clothes and food, and all things that are necessary. We want for nothing – do not be anxious. While I have life, I have everything. Death comes everywhere. Do not be concerned, but pray to God for us.

We expect to get victory quickly, and comfort yourself with the thought that ... our victorious army will utterly destroy the Germans, and will bind the fillet of victory on the brow of our beneficent and just King, George V. Comfort yourselves with the belief that we will return to India having completed our work, and [having] illuminated your name. We look anxiously to that time when our opportunity will come, so that we may then place those Germans (who have spread the horrors of war throughout the world) under our swords, and destroy them utterly, and make them taste a little of that which they themselves have done.

I trust that, on reading this letter, you will put anxiety away from you ... We have now been separated for nearly two years, and except for my welfare you have received no news about me. Your hearts must be longing for our meeting, and our hearts are in the same state. But God has given us such confidence that we can put aside all those troubles. This is the only opportunity we have had for coming to this European war, and our brothers have shown such bravery in the war that the world rings with praise for them. What we have done is impressed not only on our King and country, but also on our Allies. For this reason, both you and we should have no concern for ourselves, and should help all we can in this war. For this reason, we take no thought of having left our country, our parents, and our brothers – nor do you. We pray God that some opportunity be given us that we may be able to use our sharp and glittering swords for the destruction of the Germans, and place our names on the tongues of the entire world.

307

Zamindar Nehal Singh to Dafadar Sri Ram (Jat, Meerut Cavalry Brigade, France)

Gurgaon District   [Urdu]
Punjab   8th May 1916

You continually say 'I don't receive any letters.' What is this you say? The very day on which I receive your letter I send a reply. There is no scarcity of paper or of scribes.[1] I am not concerned with anything beyond the writing of the letter and the posting of it. Either your address must be wrong, or unstamped letters are detained. Write your letters with full information in them. Write them on a large sheet of paper, then one will understand all about you. If you write about the events that are taking place write in signs and symbols. You don't say what the climate is like or what degree of cold is experienced, and in what condition you and our friends are. All you say is 'Ram, Ram, we are quite well and happy!' My friend, what can be gathered from such words? Write and say what the people there are like, and what is bought and sold, what arrangements there are about food. Things that are worth seeing about you studiously avoid. You scribble a couple of words and dispatch the letter. There is no pleasure in hearing what you say, or in having your letter read. Write also and say how far you are from your beloved country. The purpose for which you went; see to it that you do your part well. Serve the Sirkar faithfully and make a name for yourself. At least you might write and say that so and so has done such and such, and so and so has received such and such a reward. Take care! Unless in future you write full details, I in turn will merely write you two words and dispatch the letter.

1.   A rare explicit reference to the way in which the letters were produced. See No. 273.

308

Lehna Ram to Heta Ram (Supply and Transport Corps, Marseilles, France)

Jhang District   [Urdu]
Punjab   9th May 1916

Night and day I pray for you and for our King. Our family have always been servants of the State from the commencement. Death comes to us one day, wherever we may be. Live in confidence and serenity; God will give victory to our King. I served the State for twenty-one years and now receive a pension of Rs.40 from the Sirkar. I live in peace and comfort. I have been to wars in various directions, and always saw victory secured. Your grandfather was formerly in Maharaja Ranjit Singh's army, but after the British conquest, the loyal service which he had given to Maharaja Ranjit Singh he transferred with great pleasure to the Sirkar.[1] For this service of your grandfather, I received a Sub-Inspectorship, and rank of honour, and I have hopes of higher honour still in the future. Do your work well and faithfully, and by the blessing of God you will return home with honour after victory has been secured.

1. Ranjit Singh was ruler of the Sikh state in Punjab until his death in 1839. After the British conquest in 1849, many of his former soldiers then enlisted to serve the British, especially from 1857. He is also referred to in No. 253.

309

Dafadar Ramji Lal (Jat) to Lekh Ram (6th Cavalry, Sialkot, Punjab)

Sialkot Cavalry Brigade					[Urdu]
France							10th May 1916

I asked you to send me a parcel of cigarettes. You reply that parcels get lost. I know well that you were too avaricious to spend Rs.2. Hundreds of parcels are received here daily, none of them get lost, but all your parcels get lost, or they are knocking about from place to place! No doubt you have spent much on me. I will refund the whole amount with interest. Keep a good account of all that you spend. I am very hurt that you should say 'the distance is great and parcels get lost'. The arrangements of Government are so good, that even if a needle is sent by post it is duly delivered. [Letter passed]

310

Ahmad Khan (Pathan) to Mahomed Azim Khan (36th Jacob's Horse, France)

Esa Khel							[Urdu]
NWFP							13th May 1916

On the 10th there was a raid by the Waziris on Mauza Kalwanwala. They carried off a Hindu, and a lot of jewels and money. In the Mali Khel dacoity each man received a sentence of twenty-eight years' imprisonment. Thirteen men were captured and all thirteen were sentenced. The fortification of Esa Khel has been postponed. Two men of the Shazi Khel who went to Bannu [NWFP] to sell two cows, and were returning on foot with the money – Rs.160 – were captured by the Waziris, and their money confiscated. For two days they were bound and locked up in a house. Then some other people came and let them free. In Mauza Lackhi Marwat a Fakir used to live. He collected 150 men and proclaimed them Ghazis. The [British] Deputy Commissioner of Bannu came on the scene with a party of cavalry and infantry. All the Ghazis ran away, with the exception of four who were captured. These four together with the Fakir have been sentenced to fourteen years' imprisonment. The Waziris made a raid on Lian Khani near Tank. Many Hindus were assaulted at the time in a caste-fellow's house. The Waziris fell on them, and captured and took away ten men alive, and left two dead and three wounded. At the Tank Railway Station were some men of Paikhel, who worked for the railway. The Waziris raided the place and cut off the ears of the Paikhel women. The wife of Ahmed Khan Paikhel (who is a railway jemadar) had both her ears cut off and also the flesh from her cheeks.

311

Mir Jaffar (Punjabi Muslim) to his niece (Amritsar District, Punjab)

Ambala Cavalry Brigade [Urdu]
France 16th May 1916

[He encloses a postcard depicting a French girl in military uniform with full accoutrements.] I send you the picture of a girl equipped for battle. Certainly nowadays honourable young girls are making themselves fit for battle, and for this reason – that they may, if required, fight for their King and country ... I went to London for ten days and returned today. I was very pleased with the trip. I had the honour of saluting His Majesty, the King, and I met many of the nobility of England, and saw famous sights and pleasant entertainments. In one place I saw wax figures the size of a man, which are so wonderfully made that it is impossible to say whether they are real live people or not.[1] These figures are of Kings and Queens, Princes and Princesses, and famous generals and nobles. [Letter passed]

1. Presumably Madame Tussaud's.

312

Jemadar Shamsher Ali Khan (Punjabi Muslim, 33) to Raja Rustam Ali Khan
(Gujranwala District, Punjab)

34th Poona Horse [Urdu]
France 17th May 1916

I hope Nasir is leaving, and I trust that you will have him instructed in such a way that he may acquire a thirst for knowledge. Wise parents adopt very effective methods for making their children acquire knowledge – methods which make the children eager for knowledge. For instance, the mother of Sheikh Farid-ud-Din Sahib [a famous religious mendicant] surnamed Ganj-i-Shakar [the treasury or storehouse of sugar] induced in the Sheikh, in his childhood, a great desire for prayer – although at that time of life it is difficult to make a child eager for prayer. She taught him so tactfully that the desire for prayer was created in him. Children are very fond of eating sugar and sweets, and the Sheikh's mother told him that whoever says his prayers wisely receives from God, by the hand of an angel, a reward of sweets, which the angel places under the corner of the prayer carpet. When the Sheikh used to go to perform his ablutions prior to saying his prayers, his mother used to place a little packet of sweets under the prayer carpet. And as soon as the Sheikh had finished his prayer, he used to turn up the edge of the carpet, take the sweets and eat them. Day by day his desire for prayer increased, till in the end his soul longed only for prayer. I hope that you will adopt some such measures to create in Nasir a desire for knowledge. [Letter passed]

313

Rahimdad Khan (Pathan) to Sher Khan (Mirpur, Kashmir?)

19th Lancers   [Urdu]
France   21st May 1916

I learn from Karamdad's letter that Fateh Khan has been sent to transportation [for mutiny]. A thousand pities! It is a subject for great thankfulness that Alladad Khan escaped as he was in hospital at Bushire [Persia]. 439 cavalrymen [of the 15th Lancers] were transported for refusing to fight against the Turks.[1] This was a great mistake to behave to our King in this way. The enemy no doubt are Turks, but in spite of this our men ought not to have been untrue to their salt. It is a thousand pities that I, poor creature as I am, can do nothing in the matter. Well, we must have patience and trust that in time they will be released.[2] I hope so, for there is a great talk about the matter.

1. See Nos. 259, 276 and 315.
2. They were, on the King's birthday in 1917. See No. 550.

314

Dilbar (Pathan) to Abdul Hakin Khan (19th Lancers, France)

Veterinary College
Lahore [Pashtu]
Punjab 21st May 1916

I neither see your face nor does any letter come to me from you; how then am I to beguile my heart which is full of grief? This is not the way a friend should act. I am crying out to you in supplication and you take no notice. Go, my letter, and tell him that when you [the letter] were leaving me I was weeping and overwhelmed with grief. Tell him that when the rain of his presence falls on me again, the dust of separation which is settled on my heart will be swept away. Tell him that your friend was so overcome with weeping that he lay prostrate on the ground. He was as a little child, who at the very thought of sorrow commences weeping, and longs for some loved face to console him. Where is now that happy time when each mail used to bring two or three letters from you? However much he tries to appease his sorrow, it grows. At the expectation of a single letter from you he is, as it were, prostrated by sickness. If you did not know it before, know it now that he remembers you day and night in his affliction. He conjures you by the earth, [not?] to make any friendship with white clay.[1]

Censor Officer, for God's sake let my paper [letter] go free, so that it may reach my friend! I adure you, Censor, by the pure God, not to detain my letter! High officers of the postal service, for God's sake do not destroy my letter. Tears fall from my eyes; my pen weeps. I write this paper with drops of my blood, and so send it to my brother.[2]

1. 'White clay' perhaps means 'white people'.
2. For another attempt to address the censor directly see No. 117.

315

Veterinary Assistant Kesu Shah (Punjabi Muslim) to
Ressaidar Abdul Rahim Khan (15th Lancers, Mesopotamia, 28)

Rouen [Urdu]
[France] 22nd May 1916

When I read about the behaviour of the regiment I was overwhelmed with grief.[1] It was indeed a great pity that they should have acted thus at such a time. This is the time to show loyalty and give help to the Government and not to be false to one's salt. It was to work for Government and not for disobedience that they girded their loins and left their nearest and dearest. I read about it in the paper and then saw it in your letter in detail. What God has written in a man's fate will come to pass. I feel sure that you will remember your hereditary services and show yourself worthy of your family traditions ... Our duty is loyalty and bravery. I again say I am deeply grieved and hurt by the behaviour of our people.

1. He is referring to their mutiny. See Nos. 259, 276 and 313.

316

Gholam Mustafa (Punjabi Muslim) to Mahomed Akbar Khan
(c/o Mehr Baksh, Shopkeeper, Bombay, India)

Machine Gun Squadron
Sialkot Cavalry Brigade   [Urdu]
France   22nd May 1916

You write and say that you too are desirous of enlisting. I am very glad of it, but let it not happen that dishonour should come of it. Do not say after two or three months that you are unable to serve [as a soldier] or unable to ride. Stiffen your heart first, then enlist. For unless one's heart is in one's work one cannot perform it properly. We here, at the present time, are required to do things of which we had never dreamed in our whole lives, but we meet trials and misfortunes with so much tact and perseverance that fame is secured thereby to the whole of Hindustan and to our illustrious Government. I feel sure that you can act with tact and determination, therefore by all means enlist and be at goodwill with all. For the rest, do as you please.

317

Risaldar-Major Mir Jafar Khan (Pathan, 50) to Abdul Wahid Khan
(Swabi, Peshawar District, NWFP)

9th Hodson's Horse   [Urdu]
France   23rd May 1916

My service extends to thirty-three years, but I tell you truly that if in this war I were to lose my life for my King ... I would count it as [a] gain.[1] I have been in Hodson's Horse for the whole thirty-three years. During a railway journey when two people sit side by side for a couple of hours, one of them feels the absence of the other when he alights: how great then must be the anguish which I feel at the thought of having to sever myself from the regiment! I have heard it rumoured that the CO Sahib Bahadur contemplates sending me back to India. Although, no doubt, I should be pleased to see again my country and my people, that pleasure would be as nothing compared with the sorrow I should feel at having to part from the regiment.

1. See No. 300 for a letter from the same man.

318

Gholam Rasul Khan (Hindustani Muslim) to his father
Mahomed Nawas Khan (Aurangabad, Gaya District?, Bihar?)

Secunderabad Cavalry Brigade [Urdu]
France 24th May 1916

The photo you sent is near me. When my thoughts turn towards you and look at it and see all three of you, I become happy and my grief disappears. You say it [the photo] is a useless thing, but for me it is worth all the money I possess. I don't see you in my dreams and, for this reason, it is a comfort to me to gaze on your picture.

Night and day I pray to God that He will quickly take me back to my country, that I may remove your grief. I constantly regret that I did not see you, as much as I wished, before coming here. My eyes throb with longing desire to see you again. Here one sees many wonderful and beautiful things, but I do not see your forms! It is my bad fortune that has made me thus helpless. But one day of gladness will certainly come. In the desire to see that day, hundreds and thousands of men are daily sacrificing their lives. That day will most certainly come. At present there is pain and grief, but in the end there will be joy. I myself do not know what joy is: in solitude joy is useless to me. Life holds only sorrow and grief for me at present.

I realize what this war is when I think of my separation from my brother. God alone knows how I eke out the days. I have sworn to be faithful and true to the Sirkar. I must, therefore, give them my best service, even if it costs me my life, what matter! I must die one day. As regards this, I do not feel the same sorrow as I experience from the loss of Mustapha Khan. I live in hope that some day I will again see my brother Mustapha Khan. At the present time he is 'missing'. If my fortune is good and God has heard your entreaties, and if he is alive in the hands of the enemy, then, sooner or later, we shall meet again.

319

*Dafadar Habib Ulla to his father Mahomed Atta Ulla Khan
(Karnal District, Punjab)*

36th Jacob's Horse   [Urdu]
France   26th May 1916

Show me favour and enlist fifteen or twenty men from the Mianwali [District, Punjab] and Bannu District [NWFP], and hand them over to Captain Nixon at the regimental depot at Ambala [Punjab]. After you have done so, get a letter of recommendation from him, and send it to the CO here. Get recommendations too from the Deputy Commissioner and others, to the effect that you and your family have rendered services to the Government, and that you and I have attained such and such a rank in Government service, and that you have now helped to raise recruits, and asking that your son may be promoted to jemadar. If I become an officer it will increase your *izzat*, and I also will benefit. There was another dafadar in my regiment, who became a jemadar in this very way. His father raised recruits for my regiment in India, and obtained and forwarded a recommendation. Do you try also.

320

*Acting Lance Dafadar Amir Dog to Risaldar Jafir Hasain
(Viceroy's Bodyguard, Dehra Dun, UP)*

Machine Gun Section
Viceroy's Bodyguard   [Urdu]
Meerut Cavalry Brigade   29th May 1916

Our pay is lower than that of any other cavalry in France. For instance, twenty-six men of the Governor's Bodyguards who are serving here are drawing twice the pay they did in India, and even the recruits in the cavalry are drawing Rs.6 a month more than I am, and even the reservists and Imperial Service Troops get more than we do. If I speak about this grievance to the Colonel Sahib he says 'you should get an exchange into another cavalry regiment and you will get their pay'. It would pay me financially to get an exchange, but then there would not be the *izzat* that attaches to the Viceroy's Bodyguard. Give me your advice on the subject, and tell the Commanding Officer of the Bodyguard and the Military Secretary about this grievance. As long as my name remains on the Bodyguard list I cannot get proper pay.

321

Shah Pasand (Punjabi Muslim) to Jemadar Raja Mustafa Khan
(17th Cavalry, Allahabad, UP, 48)

18th Lancers [Urdu]
[France?] 30th May 1916

You tell me to do my work faithfully. That we shall certainly do; for the rest, it is the will of God. I have experienced this 'benefit' here that the CO has deprived me of my rank as Acting Lance Dafadar. He has issued a regimental order, that when a man with acting rank comes as reinforcement from another regiment, he will be treated as a sowar. God grant a proper settlement of this matter. Do you tell both the Woordi-Major and the Colonel Sahib how I have been treated. For how am I to give good service, when my hopes are blasted in this way? Moreover, in my regiment in India my juniors will get acting rank before me, while here in France, I get no promotion. Ask the Woordi-Major, therefore, to get the Colonel Sahib to write to the people here to give me my promotion or get me returned to the regiment, in the same way as Sher Ali Khan was sent for by the Colonel Sahib.

322

Pensioner Gholam Khan to Bugle Major Haq Nawaz Khan
(Punjabi Muslim, 18th Lancers, France)

Miani
Shahpur District [Urdu]
Punjab 31st May 1916

Keep firm to your promise and never seek to depart from it. Look! Amir Khan of our house, the son of Alam Khan Biloch and resident of Jamali, who was in the 15th Lancers, being afraid of death, deserted in the direction of Iran. When he was returning from Iran, he became sick on the way and died. In this way the house of Alam Khan became extinct. What God, the Almighty, has said in the Qu'ran is true; that death, which you shun, will not leave you, however much you seek to avoid it. The next incident is that concerning Nawab Khan of Didhal. He was ordered to the front but refused promotion to stay behind. In two months' time he died of plague in Peshawar. If he had gone to the front, his family would have received a pension. It were better to die, than to fail in one's duty like the men of the 15th Lancers.[1] God is all powerful. He alone can protect one from death. The atheist never achieves *izzat*, and his mind is always unsettled. He never has any consolation. [Letter passed]

1. See No. 259 for an account of their mutiny.

323

Mir Shamshad Ali to Syed Karamat Ali Sahib (Delhi)

Meerut Cavalry Brigade   [Urdu?]
France   [May 1916?]

Here everyone is well and happy. I swear to you by God, that I am much better
and stronger than when I was in India. I tell you this so that you may not think,
when you read my letters, that I say I am well and happy simply to prevent you
from being anxious. I send you a photo that was taken in April of 1916. Compare
it with the photo that was taken in April of last year, and judge for yourself whether
what I write is true or false. I swear again by God, that I am extremely well and
comfortable. Since the day I left Hindustan I have not had as much as a headache.
Except for the pain of separation from you all at home, I have nothing whatever
to complain about. We ought to be truly grateful to God for this.

324

Lance Dafadar Mastan Singh to Harnam Singh (Sikh, 19th Lancers, France)

13th Lancers
Risalpur   [Gurmukhi]
[NWFP]   1st June 1916

In a troop of Dogras a young girl served for four years and then went away. The
handsome young man in the troop was not a man at all, but a young woman. In the
Malakand detachment an infantry havildar detected her by her appearance. He said
'this is surely a woman!' This saying gradually extended, but Bhuri Singh, for whom
she was acting as groom, knew all about the matter, and he had her sent home secretly.
Then he himself went home on ten days' leave and married her. [Letter passed]

325

*Risaldar-Major [Risaldar?] Ahmad Yar Khan (43) to Malik Sher Bahadur Khan
(ADC to the Governor of Madras)*

18th Lancers   [Urdu]
France   6th June 1916

The tribe of [the] Tiwanas[1] is not as famous in this war as it used to be before. The
reason is that many Sirdars and men have become 'sick' without being wounded.

The same thing has happened in almost all the regiments in this campaign, and in this matter the Tiwanas are most to blame.

1. The major Muslim military clan of Western Punjab, and important allies of the British. They provided eighteen commissioned officers in the war, and many men. They enlisted and equipped some of their own troops, and also helped to alleviate Muslim disquiet over the campaign against the Turks. See Talbot, *Punjab and the Raj*, p. 44.

326

Bishan Singh (Sikh) to Arjan Singh (Jullundur District, Punjab)

Sialkot Cavalry Brigade [Urdu]
France 6th June 1916

Nowadays the fighting is very violent everywhere. There has been a great naval battle, in which fourteen British and fifteen German ships were sunk.[1] Among the German losses were two very big ships. The fighting took place in the sea between Germany and Norway. One or two German ships in addition to the above number are missing. One ship costs a crore of rupees to build. In size it is equal to a village. The loss of life will be known later. Nowadays the Germans are making very violent attacks in the direction of Verdun.[2] In two days they expended as much ammunition as has been consumed previously in the entire war. Notwithstanding this intense bombardment, and all the other efforts made by them, the Germans were entirely unsuccessful. It seems likely that the war will end this year.

1. This is a roughly accurate sketch of the battle of Jutland, fought between the British and German battlefleets on 31st May 1916.
2. After a week-long assault, they succeeded in capturing Fort Vaux on 7th June.

327

*Kohar Singh (Jat) to Daya Singh (Sub-Inspector, Abbottabad,
Hazara District, NWFP)*

Attached 3rd Skinner's Horse
Cavalry Railhead [Urdu]
France 7th June 1916

I am more comfortable here, I swear it, than any high officer could be in India. Of course there is always the risk of death, but who is free from that risk, or can avoid it? This, however, I know, that this period of my life is extremely happy and enjoyable. It is now one and a quarter years since I came here, but the time has passed as happily as if it had been a holiday.

328

Dafadar Shah Madar Khan (Pathan) to his brother Shah Rindan Khan
(Swabi, Peshawar District, NWFP)

36th Jacob's Horse [Urdu]
France 7th June 1916

Nawab Khan writes and tells me to return home by hook or by crook. My brother, consider, I am not to blame in this matter. There is no clear reason that I could give for returning home. There are many men here whose pension is due but who are not allowed to go. Night and day these people urge 'our pension is due, let us go'; but they will not set them free. How then will they set me free? Unless, or until, I can give some substantial reason, it is extremely difficult for me to come. Otherwise – well I know my condition, and I know the conditions at home. But what remedy have I against the will of God? I do not think of money, I think only of you; but I am helpless. Do you all keep on praying. If life is vouchsafed to me, we shall soon meet again. Do not be concerned; by the grace of God, I am quite well and strong, and have nothing to complain of, except separation from you. It is extremely difficult for me to return. My brother, at all times keep my children happy: they are in your keeping, and if they suffer in any way, you are responsible.

329

Karm Singh (Sikh) to Kalyan Singh (Jhelum District, Punjab)

Machine Gun Section
Sialkot Cavalry Brigade [Urdu]
France 8th June 1916

It is a matter of very great regret that our brother Chet Singh has been taken prisoner at Kut-al-Amara.[1] Other men from Dhudial [Jhelum District, Punjab] who were with him have also been captured. Well, we should not grieve; nothing is to be gained by grieving. At the end of the war, they will return home alive.[2] All those brave fellows did their duty faithfully to the very end. They deserve the highest praise. This event was written in their fate, and no one could have prevented it.

1. For an account of the surrender, see No. 304.
2. In fact, many of them did not.

330

Ghirdari Lal (Hindu) to Ward Orderly Permanand [?]
(Indian General Hospital, Rouen, France)

Saugor [Urdu]
Central Provinces 9th June 1916

We are greatly grieved to hear that our Lord Kitchener has been killed.[1] See how a great man, who has done so much good work for the country, has had to meet death! It is not we only who are grieved, but the entire people of Hindustan are grieved. Still, God will certainly avenge him. Nowadays, many Indian troops are being got ready, and many are being despatched. Our Hindustani braves will now slay the Germans with all their might, and will again raise the fame of this fallen country. Remember, it is the same country which produced Rama, Lachman, Krishna Arjun and Pandwa. Are we not of the same people as they? They also were mortals who slew the Rakahash, but in these days men regard them has having been immortals. Man can do everything. Man himself is God. [Letter passed]

1. This is the earliest securely dated reference in the collection to the death of the Secretary of State for War, Lord Kitchener of Khartoum. He drowned on 5th June 1916 when HMS *Hampshire* sank after striking a mine during a voyage to Russia. Britain's most famous soldier in 1914, Kitchener was a former Commander-in-Chief of the Indian Army (1902–9), and many sepoys expressed grief at his death. The bad news clearly travelled very fast.

331

Daya Ram (Jat) to Rohlu Ram (Teacher, Ambala, Punjab)

2nd Lancers [Urdu]
France 14th June 1916

The fighting is very severe.[1] The moves are like those of a game of chess. When an attack is made in one direction a countermove is made in another, and attention is drawn off the first attack. The war is on entirely new lines and is full of surprises. It is impossible to understand it. At present we are in trenches near Arras [word deleted by censor] waiting for orders. We do not know what will happen. A new kind of smoke [gas?] has been invented which is let loose in the trenches and if you get a sniff of it you lose consciousness at once. It does not matter whether you are armed or not, as you lose all your senses. Such inventions have been made that one's mind is utterly confused. There is a new kind of gas that catches fire directly it is let out of the cylinder. It is liquid fire and burns anyone who is in front of it. It is real magic. [Letter passed]

1. Presumably referring to the Verdun battles.

332

Alla Nakha Khan (Punjabi Muslim) to M. Nazar Ali
(6th Cavalry Depot, Sialkot, Punjab)

6th Cavalry   [Urdu]
France   16th June 1916

There is no good news here but, on the contrary, depression reigns for the great
leader has been transferred to the next world.[1] You have heard about this, I have
no doubt. There are rumours of a peace this year. [Letter passed]

1. Another of the many laments for Lord Kitchener.

333

Bishan Singh (Sikh) to Risaldar Peshawra Singh
(19th Lancers, Sialkot, Punjab, 46)

Sialkot Cavalry Brigade   [Urdu]
France   20th June 1916

Russia has made a great impression on Austria. Austria had brought great pressure
to bear on Italy; but now, through the effort made by the Russians, the one who
was in the act of despoiling the other has in his turn been despoiled. Russia has
entered Austria to a depth of eighteen miles. One and a half *lakhs* of Austrian prisoners
have been made, and we hear that the Austrian killed and wounded number five
lakhs.[1] If one or two more victories of this kind were obtained, complete victory
would certainly be secured at an early date. [Letter passed]

1. This well-informed writer is describing the Russian offensive launched by General Brusilov
    in Galicia on 4th June 1916. The fighting continued for three months, with some
    300,000 Austrians eventually being taken prisoner. See No. 365.

334

Lance Dafadar Teja Singh (Sikh) to Sub-Inspector of Police
Sirdar Sadu Singh (Peshawar, NWFP)

9th Hodson's Horse   [Urdu]
France   26th June 1916

In this place the country is hilly. If India were like it, the people would die of hunger.
But, by the grace of God, it rains frequently. It is only occasionally that the sun is

seen in summer. Otherwise it is cloudy and showery. There is never any fear here of theft or of any other crime. As regards marriage, there is affection first between the two parties, who are never less than eighteen years of age. After marriage there is never any discord between husband and wife. No man has the authority here to beat his wife. Such an injustice occurs in India only. Husband and wife dwell together here in unity.[1] [Letter passed]

1. Several men make this observation.

335

Mal Singh (Sikh) to Nihal Singh (Head Clerk, 29th Lancers, France)

Adjutant-General's Office   [Gurmukhi]
Rouen   26th June 1916

Two letters have come from home to say that the letters received in their homes from the men who are on active service with the Expeditionary Force have the addresses written in English. The local postmasters know little English, and the letters go astray and few reach the addressees.[1] If you will be good enough to speak to your CO he may be able to arrange that the addresses are written in vernacular. This is most urgent. [Letter passed]

1. The censor commented, 'there is probably exaggeration in the complaint, but it is not unlikely that there is some foundation for it. A considerable number of letters pass through the censors' hands which bear addresses only in English, and though I am informed that it is the duty of the local postmasters in India to add the addresses in vernacular it is probable that many of the postmasters have not sufficient knowledge of English to make a proper translation. The matter may therefore be worth taking up and I intend to mention it to the staffs of the local Divisions.'

336

Niaz Hussein (Punjabi Muslim) to Altaf Hussein (Hansi, Hissar District, Punjab)

Mhow Cavalry Brigade   [Urdu]
France   27th June 1916

For God's sake, control your pen, and write only after due consideration. Our letters are read ten times before they reach us. Either do not write at all, or, if you write, simply say how you are.[1] [Letter passed]

1. The censor commented, 'this letter is for his wife, who had been airing her family grievances rather too freely'.

337

Jewan Singh (Sikh) to Gurdial Singh (Rawalpindi District, Punjab)

Sialkot Cavalry Brigade   [Urdu]
France   27th June 1916

The fight here is very intense; no doubt you hear something about it through the
newspapers. There is no indication of the end of the war; but whatever God does
in this matter will be for the best. Up to the present the cavalry have had a good
time, but we expect that their turn will come soon, and that the end of the war will
follow. In reality the war is one of artillery; the firing is continuous.[1] [Letter passed]

1. The writer probably refers to the massive Allied bombardment which preceded the Somme
   offensive. In the week before the infantry attacks of 1st July 1916, 460 British and 850
   French guns fired 1.7 million shells into the German lines.

338

*Kot Dafadar Imdad Ali (Deccani Muslim) to Dafadar Khariat Ali (Depot, 29th
Lancers, Saugor, Central Provinces)*

Probably 29th Lancers   [Urdu]
France   28th June 1916

From the time we left Poona, Ghulam Bache never ceased to behave towards me
with *badmash*. His friends and relatives have turned things topsy-turvy over a little
matter of promotion. Well, great is the power of God! The night before last, a Jat
shot him dead at 8pm. The bullet struck him in the forehead and he never moved
again. [Letter passed]

339

*Abdul Alim (Hindustani Muslim) to Dafadar Majat Ali Khan
(6th Cavalry, Rohtak, Punjab)*

Signalling Troop
6th Cavalry   [Urdu?]
France   30th June 1916

Steel helmets like those of the French have arrived for all regiments. The Sikhs
decline to wear them but the [Hindu] Jats and [the] Muslims are thinking over the
matter.[1] Some say they ought to be worn as they protect life. Others say that

religious considerations prevent them wearing them. Two men of the 6th Cavalry, a Sikh and a Jat were wounded while digging trenches and one man in the 19th Lancers was killed and two wounded. We are all sitting waiting for the grand attack to begin.[2] We are close to the firing line. God is our protector. [Letter passed]

1. Sikhs were enjoined by their religion to keep their hair uncut; they wore turbans to contain it, and were very reluctant to remove these. See No. 495 for another reference to helmets.
2. On the Somme. The infantry offensive began on 1st July.

340

Fateh Ullah (Punjabi Muslim) to Fateh Ahmed
(Supply and Transport No. 5 Base Supply Depot, France)

Lyallpur   [Urdu]
Punjab   30th June 1916

We have learnt from Nasir Khan's letter that his brother Raja Khan has been sentenced by court martial to fourteen years' imprisonment. This has caused us much grief. The details which he gives are that when the 15th Lancers reached Basra [Mesopotamia] they were ordered to fight against the Turks. They, however, declined to take up arms against their brother Muslims and asked to be sent to some other theatre of war.[1] A court martial was convened and 400 men were sentenced to various terms of imprisonment. Since then, it has been reported in the newspapers that the new Viceroy has ordered that these men should be sent to some other theatre of war, since they did not in reality decline to fight for the Sirkar, and should not have been called upon to fight against the Turks against their wish. I do not know why action has not been taken on this order. It is very sad that fate should have dealt thus cruelly with this regiment in the end, after they had done such good service and gained so much renown elsewhere. Now they are all imprisoned in the fort Rangoon in Burma, and are not allowed to receive or send letters. My idea is that the Government have acted in this way simply to vindicate their authority, and that after the war all these unfortunates will be released.[2] [Letter passed]

1. See Nos. 259, 276, 313 and 315.
2. In fact they were released in the summer of 1917, on the King's birthday, after agreeing to serve in the depot of the regiment. See No. 550.

341

Abdul Majid Khan (Hindustani Muslim) to
Sowar Mahomed Salim Khan (Bikaner State, Rajputana)

6th Cavalry   [Urdu]
France   3rd July 1916

Our First [Cavalry] Division[1] went for ten days to the trenches and has just come
back. We suffered a little and lost two men killed and six wounded. I don't know
what the other regiments lost. As to the losses of the British regiments ... Alas!
Alas! What can I say![2] You will see the losses of ours and other regiments in the
papers. Sowar Sadal was killed, and one Hindu. We were relieved by a kilted
regiment. We are ten miles behind and in marching order. We are told to be ready
at half an hour's notice to ride. May God grant that the order may not come, as it
means we shall be wiped out. May God in his mercy preserve us. My brother, there
seems no prospect of the war coming to an end. [Letter passed]

1. Of which the 6th Cavalry were part.
2. He refers to the British attack on the Somme sector, in which there were 57,000
   casualties on 1st July 1916, the first day of the offensive. The despondent tone of this
   letter is not typical of those written by Indian troops at this time.

342

Dafadar Gholam Mahomed Khan (Punjabi Muslim) to
Malik Nawab Khan (Jhelum District, Punjab)

34th Poona Horse   [Urdu]
France   5th July 1916

By the grace of God and through your intercessions my heart is as strong as a lion's.[1]
In the field of battle I became doubled[2] by the help of God and your prayers. Do
not be alarmed; the battle is very severe, but by the help of God we shall win it.
May God give victory to our King so that we may pass under his flag with joy.
Remember that my pay for one year – Rs.403,10 – is accumulated in the treasury,
and I don't know how much more is due for the current year. If I die it will be of
service to you. If I live, it will still be your possession. [Letter passed]

1. This letter is typical of those written during the first week of July 1916, when many
   Indian soldiers believed they were about to join the fiercest fighting on the Somme. Most
   of the usual grumbles about separation from home and friends ceased, and the men began
   to steel themselves for action.
2. He means 'became like two men'.

343

Amar Singh (Dogra) to Thakur Puran Singh (Jammu, Kashmir State)

9th Hodson's Horse [Urdu]
France 5th July 1916

You enquire about the wedding. Why do you enquire about leave? A wedding is about to take place here, and many men have already been married.[1] The altar [*bedi*] for my marriage has been fixed and it only remains to perform the final rites [*lawan*].[2] In the next letter perhaps you will hear the result. Don't be anxious. It is all very beautiful.

1. He implies 'there is about to be an offensive, and many men have already been killed'.
2. He believes he is fated to die.

344

*Daya Ram (Jat) to Subedar Mahomed Khan
(Depot, 24th Punjabis, Hyderabad, Sind)*

2nd Lancers [Urdu]
France 5th July 1916

On the 18th June I went into the trenches and came back all safe on the 29th. The fight is very severe. The fire of bombs descends all night long, and the rain of machine guns never stops. I live in a dug-out. They are splendidly built and have wire beds, and in some places these underground rooms are large enough to contain many men at once. I saw one such place at the bottom of a hill in which three full regiments could have lived. Everybody sleeps, eats and drinks underground. These trenches used to belong to the French, but now belong to us. I am alive up to date through your kindness, but God knows what will happen. There is great discomfort in the trenches, and the lice swarm on the men. The cavalry can't move about much in the winter and so get an easy time, but in the warm weather they are always moving about from one front to another. [Letter passed]

345

Dafadar Niaz Mahomed (Hindustani Muslim) to Muzafar Hussein (Bijnor, UP)

Sialkot Cavalry Brigade   [Urdu]
France   [early July 1916?]

Cannot you find a scribe who will write all details instead of the few meagre lines you send?[1] Well, it is something to be thankful for, that since Ibrahim came here you have commenced to write at all. Before he came it was like the story of the oil-presser's ox. It wandered away one day and entered into a mosque, and ate up all the flowers that had been placed in the mosque. The oil-presser, having searched fruitlessly elsewhere for his ox, at length reached the mosque. Seeing him, the *moulvi* said, 'You worthless one, your ox has entered the mosque and despoiled it of its flowers!' The oil-presser replied, 'Sir, it is an ox and a stupid animal to enter the mosque. For, say truly, have you ever before seen *me* in this mosque!' So it is with you. Since Ibrahim came, you have condescended to write to me; before that, you utterly ignored me. [Letter passed]

1. A rare reference to the means by which letters were produced. See Nos. 273 and 307.

346

*Rustam to Zabur Shah (Hindustani Muslim,
5th Cavalry, attached 38th CIH, France)*

Raipur
Fatehgarh
[Farrukhabad District]   [Urdu]
UP   6th July 1916

The Sharif of Mecca has revolted and news is being received daily of his continued success. In Lucknow at a public meeting of the Muslim League[1] the conduct of the Sharif of Mecca was compared to that of Sir Roger Casement.[2] On the other hand, the Haji Sait Sahib of Madras has commented very favourably on the Sharif's action. [Letter passed]

1. The main Muslim political party in India, founded at Dacca in December 1906. See Nos. 453 and 619.
2. Casement, Sir Roger David (1864–1916). Critic of Belgian atrocities in the Congo; Irish patriot; arrested for running German guns to Ireland; executed August 1916.

347

Lance Dafadar Budha Khan (Hindustani Muslim) to Kallu Khan
(Bulandshahr District, UP)

Machine Gun Section
36th Jacob's Horse   [Urdu]
France   8th July 1916

You write and say that my wife is sick unto death. I can do nothing as I am very far away. I have no choice. My trust is in God and His Prophet. You say further that there is no one to minister to my children. God nourishes all his creatures. I am very far away: except for God I have no help. You say that all my goods in my house are perishing. Well, let them perish. If you can assist in looking after them, well and good; otherwise let them go. My fortune is bad. Since I came here there has been a succession of misfortunes; there has never been any benefit. Well, it is my fate, and no one is to blame. [Letter passed]

348

Niamat Ullah (Pathan) to Farrier Ali Mahomed Khan
(10th Lancers, Loralai District, Baluchistan)

9th Hodson's Horse   [Urdu]
France   9th July 1916

I shall be much obliged if you will send me as soon as possible some almonds and raisins *together with an ounce of bhalwa which the dhobis use to mark clothes.*[1] I impress this on you most earnestly. Pack the things securely, but see that the parcel is not above weight. As soon as I receive the parcel I will remit the cost.

1. The words in italics were deleted, because malingerers used *bhalwa* to produce swellings on the portion of the body to which it was applied – thought to be a sure passport to hospital. There had been no allusions to it in the letters for some months.

349

*Mahomed Nawaz Khan to Trumpet-Major Haq Nawaz Khan
(Punjabi Muslim, 18th Lancers, France)*

Shahpur   [Urdu]
[Punjab]   9th July 1916

Only by trusting in the Almighty can one's heart remain undisturbed. Then ease
and trouble are all the same to the man who follows this advice. Impatience and
anxiety upset the heart altogether and Fate is inexorable. Those whose hearts are
confident and who rely on God are always at peace. We ought to accept the
ordinance of God just as did His Highness the Imam Hasain.[1] Those who do not
put their hearts into the work of fighting the King's enemies are clearly worthy of
the greatest blame. Who does not know that soldiers are kept to fight, and get their
pay for this. Can there be any greater faithlessness than this to draw your pay in
peace and then to cry out when war comes on? Such people die a death of disgrace
from which may God deliver everyone!

Your own actions show your bravery and rightmindedness. Do not brood over
the fact that you have not been appreciated and have not got promotion. You
remain a private soldier although you are accomplished in all the details of a
soldier's life. You are not to blame for this. If blame attaches to anyone it is to those
who have failed to recognize your merit.

There is another saying I want to quote to you. In the Gospel it is written that
God has selected the unworthy and poor to put to shame the distinguished and worthy,
so that no one may boast except in Him. In the history of His Highness the Caliph
Hazrat Umar, it is written that Muslim soldiers went from country to country
fighting, and, owing to continuous war, could not come back to their homes for
years. His Highness on his rounds one night was accosted by a woman who laid
before him her grievances and said 'it is you that have kept my husband away from
me all this time and tempted me to evil ways'. Hazrat Umar recognized the mistake
he had made and had a law passed that in future every married soldier should be
allowed to return to his home on leave once every six months.

I have been astonished to think that when we have such a King, renowned
throughout the world for his kindness and justice, he has never considered this
problem and passed a rule enabling the sepoy to visit his wife and family from
time to time and render to his wife 'due benevolence'. I wonder whether no
distinguished officer has ever brought this question to the notice of His Majesty.
Unless a law like that of Hazrat Umar is passed I believe that the wives and
families will never believe that the men are alive at all.[2]

You may remember that I sent you a little poem of my own in which I said that
Turkey had made a mistake in joining Germany and that no good result could possibly
follow. It may be that this poem did not please everyone. Now we hear that the

Sharif and the leaders at Mecca and Medina, resenting the subservience of the Turks to Germany, have revolted, and the wise men of India are disgusted with the Turks. Hazrat Ali the Imam laid down a rule that in times of disturbance it was well to be a two-year-old camel able neither to give milk nor to carry a burden. It is a thousand pities that Turkey did not take the advice given her by the Kings who are now fighting against her, to remain neutral. If she remained neutral and anyone attacked her, he would have been considered a tyrant. [Letter passed]

1. Presumably Husayn ibn Ali, regarded by Shi'ites as the third Imam, killed at the Battle of Karbala in 680 AD.
2. The same story, with variations, appears in No. 219. Compare No. 302. I have been unable to securely identify the Caliph.

350

Unsigned (Punjabi Muslim) to Malik Secundar Khan [?]
(Shahpur District, Punjab)

18th Lancers   [Urdu]
France   11th July 1916

The fighting [on the Somme] has increased in intensity since the 25th June. It has never been so intense as it is now. The enemy has been forced to retreat, in some places as much as five miles, in others from one to three miles, leaving much material and many dead behind.

I will now give you an account of the underground places [dug-outs] constructed by the enemy behind his trenches. They were dug down to a depth of some 50 feet and the floors and roofs were timbered. They were furnished with chairs, tables, and gas [electric light]. From this it would appear that the enemy has become weak, for he would never have left so strong and permanent a place, except under very real pressure. But he was compelled to leave it, because our bombardment was so strong and effective that it overturned the timbers in the floors.

Two or three towns which were behind the enemy trenches are now completely obliterated. We saw heaps and heaps of dead, which would be impossible to describe. We were ready and expectant for some days, but our opportunity did not come. What I have described above, I saw with my own eyes. We (the British and Indian Cavalry officers) were permitted to go and see everything. The fighting continues to be intense. Both sides are suffering losses, but daily the enemy is being forced to retreat. Today he retreated further. Now it is expected that the end of the war will soon come.[1] [Letter passed]

1. Several men expressed similar hopes at this time.

351

Natha Singh (Sikh) to his mother (Ludhiana District, Punjab)

Secunderabad Cavalry Brigade [Urdu]
France 11th July 1916

I am very happy. In the end I have to die, and to die is best.[1] Except for resignation, there is no remedy. I have met you and have eaten and drunk of India – all that was decreed. Now I am ready to die, and it is best that I should die in the service of the Sirkar. [Letter passed]

1. Many letters from mid-July 1916 express similar sentiments of resignation. The Secunderabad Brigade had just taken a share in the Somme offensive.

352

Engine Driver Ghulam Dastgir to Lance Dafadar Wazir Khan (29th Lancers, France)

Hyderabad
Deccan 13th July 1916

You write that we shall meet in a few days. But what we have heard here is that you have purposely shot yourself and have been imprisoned for this. If this news is false, you have escaped a great calamity. I can't believe that a clever man like you would do such a thing. [Letter passed]

353

Driver Lal Din (Punjabi Muslim) to Manlair Karim Bakhsh (Sialkot District, India)

U Battery RHA
1st Indian Cavalry Division [Urdu]
France 14th July 1916

If I have offended you in any way, forgive me, for I am wandering about in a confused condition. Above all things let me know what are the orders about keeping fasts over here. This is Europe and the people are Christians, and you know that they are utterly destitute of religion. Yet they are very kind to our people, and are very lucky, and God has given them the pleasures of the Universe. May God give us all such enjoyments! If we want to keep the fast then what arrangements shall we make? The nights are very short and if we do not get our snack before 2am the day is on us, and we can get nothing more till 9.30pm the following evening.[1] We have to sleep booted and spurred and get no time for prayers. We don't even know what are our sacred days and festivals. Therefore I want you to say clearly what are the orders about keeping the Ramazan when on a journey.

If anyone reads this letter and tears it up, whoever he be, he will responsible in eternity. This is a matter of religion.[2] [Letter passed]

1. During Ramazan, Muslims were enjoined to fast during the hours of daylight. This was more difficult if Ramazan fell in the summer, especially in the more northerly latitudes of France.
2. The last two sentences suggest that the soldier believes that the censors will treat a 'matter of religion' with respect. For another letter directly addressing the censor see No. 314.

354

Fakir Mahomed to his son Mahsud (Pathan, 38th CIH, France)

Shankagarh
Peshawar District   [Urdu]
NWFP   14th July 1916

Abdul Hamid has given your wife to someone else in the Chikar Village. When I heard of this and asked Abdul Hamid for an explanation as to why he had given my son's wife to another, he said 'take back your Rs.160. I won't give my sister in marriage to Masaud because he has gone to the war in France, and no one has yet returned alive from that war.' I remonstrated with him, but without effect. Consequently, I have instituted proceedings against him in court. I tell you this in order that you may make your CO acquainted with facts, telling him that it is a great shame that men who have gone to the war should be treated in this way – their wives being given to others. If this sort of thing is to happen, who will care to go to the war! It is for you to get pressure put on through your officers. I have no influence, and am poor. All the money I had – Rs.160 – was paid to Hamid for your marriage. Today, under the British Government, an act of tyranny has been committed against you, such as no other person has experienced. [Letter passed]

355

Tara Singh (Sikh) to Sirdar Karbar Singh
(Teacher, Rawalpindi District, Punjab)

6th [?] Cavalry   [Gurmukhi]
France   17th July 1916

You ask me if you should send combs and iron bracelets.[1] We have no need for them here. When we return to India we shall see about it.

The state of affairs here is that when I returned from Marseilles to the firing line, we had to change trains en route, and we wandered about Paris for eight hours. On that day, we all ate at the same table. Our company was composed of five sepoys (of whom three were Sikhs and two Muslims) two sweepers and three cooks; but we all ate together at the same table. Moreover, we have often eaten food and drunk tea prepared by Muslims.

If you look at the condition of things in this country you cannot but see that all men here are considered equal in the sight of God. Mothers have no modesty towards their children. There is nothing hidden between brother and sister. If the brother's [lady] friend comes in, the mother and sister make merry. If the mother's or sister's [male] friend comes in, the brother makes merry. It is a case of doing just what the heart dictates – there are no hindrances. They eat everything – donkey, dog, horse, pig, cow – they abstain from nothing. They do all kinds of work themselves, even to the cleaning of the WC.[2] They are fixed in their manners and customs, but they worship idols. [Letter passed]

1. Two of the 'five Ks': objects of religious importance to Sikhs.
2. In India, a task normally reserved for Untouchables.

356

Shah Mirza (Deccani Muslim) to Mohirud Dhula
(Saifabad, Hyderabad, Deccan)

20th Deccan Horse   [Urdu]
France   18th July 1916

You must have learned from the newspapers how well our Brigade did its work on the 14th July.[1] We have now broken the German second line, where the fighting is taking place, on a front of about 3,000 yards. That morning at 3.30[am] a very heavy bombardment was made on the enemy's trenches. Every kind of cannon was used, and the bombardment lasted for an hour. The terrible noise of that hurricane of shot and shell was such that I am unable to describe it. When the enemy's trenches were sufficiently demolished, the infantry attacked and took them. We were ready waiting close by.[2]

When we learnt that there were not many enemy trenches in the rear, we were ordered to advance. The trenches that were taken had to be filled in places or bridged to enable us to cross [on horseback]. At certain places we were unable to cross at all. After a while, another way was found for us to cross, but we crossed with difficulty. What I saw in the course of the advance I shall never forget. We had to pass amongst the dead bodies of the men who had fallen during the morning's attack, and the trenches were full of German dead. The ground was torn and rent to pieces by the shell-fire and there were holes five and six feet deep. On that day, 1,700 prisoners were taken.

When the Dragoon Guards and Deccan horse reached one end of the line, they had an engagement with a party of Germans.[3] One troop of each regiment charged, killing sixteen Germans and taking forty prisoners. All the prisoners taken on that day were from seventeen to nineteen years of age, and appeared to be dazed. Our losses among the Cavalry were not heavy. [Letter passed]

1. At dawn on 14th July, after a three-day bombardment, the British Fourth Army under General Rawlinson launched a major attack in the Somme sector, near Mametz Wood. The Secunderabad Brigade of the 2nd Indian Cavalry Division supported the 7th Division of XV Corps, in the centre of the attack.
2. The 2nd Indian Cavalry Division was waiting around Morlancourt, four miles south of Albert. At 7.40am they were ordered forward, starting to move at 8.20am. The ground was pitted with shell-holes, and cut with trenches, and it was not until noon that the Secunderabad Brigade arrived in Carnoy Valley. See Plates 8 and 9.
3. At about 7pm, the 7th Dragoon Guards and 20th Deccan Horse joined the advance against High Wood. They saw some mounted action before it became dark. The other brigades of their division were not engaged. This man's account is very accurate. For other references to the action, see Nos. 362, 367, 393 and 400.

357

Mukhtar Ahmed to Abdul Jabbar Khan (Hindustani Muslim, Sialkot Cavalry Brigade HQ, France)

Sialkot [Urdu]
Punjab 19th July 1916

My friend, I have done well in that I came away to India. I hear that, since I left, you have been knocked about without any rest. In short, I enjoyed the pulp and left you the stone to suck. [Letter passed]

358

Ressaidar [Jemadar?] Harnam Singh (Sikh, 39) to Gurdial Singh
(Ludhiana District, Punjab)

6th Cavalry
France   21st July 1916

The Khalsa nowadays join in the *Gurubani Prem*,[1] and the Granth is carried in procession through the entire village, and is shown to all the Sikhs in the Cavalry ... One man is so efficient in reciting the Granth, that he is employed on that duty alone. Prayer meetings are constantly held, and our Sirkar gives us every opportunity for holding them. At the present time, the fortunes of the Sirkar in the fighting are very high.

It is impossible to praise this country sufficiently, because the people are so high-minded and truthful. There is never any fraud or dissention, or untruthfulness amongst them. They are very kind and helpful towards each other. And what is the root of it all? Knowledge and learning. And why are our people defective? Because of our ignorance. My friends, exert yourselves. Learning and knowledge are essential things. [Letter passed]

1.   Literally 'words of love from the writings of the Guru', a Sikh ceremony.

359

Jemadar Bostan Khan (Muslim Rajput, 39) to
Lumberdar Mahomed Zaman Khan (Lyallpur, Punjab)

38th CIH   [Urdu]
France   21st July 1916

The 14th July was the birthday of the President, and all the Royal forces which are in France were invited to be represented.[1] Fifty men from the Indian Cavalry were invited – seven from each regiment – and I was one of them. We saw Paris. It is a splendid city and there is none finer in Europe. The people are very handsome and kindly and were very nice to our people. We joined in the march past the President, and we saw many lovely places which I will tell you about when I come home. [Letter passed]

1.   He has mistaken the *Quatorze Juillet*, the anniversary of the storming of the Bastille in 1789, for a Presidential birthday celebration. For another account of the day see No. 374.

360

Jemadar Rala Singh (Sikh) to Indar Singh (Jagraon, Ludhiana District, Punjab)

Sialkot Cavalry Brigade [Urdu]
France 22nd July 1916

I have received dear Nand Kor's letter full of love. On reading it, my heart troubled. I know very well that he who loves truly, ardently returns love; but we, nowadays, are absorbed in such a work that we have lost all capacity for love. Alas that we should have become so stony-hearted! [Letter passed]

361

Gajan Singh (Sikh) to Sirdar Harbans Singh (Ludhiana District, Punjab)

18th Lancers [Urdu]
France 25th July 1916

At the present time the war has reached a degree of violence which it is impossible to conceive. The number of thousands of shots per second fired by the artillery cannot be counted, and as regards rifle fire it would be quite impossible to estimate the intensity of it. When it rains there are a few spots here and there, perhaps, which the moisture fails to touch, but not even the smallest portion of the surface of the ground has escaped damage by rifle, bomb and shell-fire. If you were to estimate five shots on every square inch of ground you would not be far off the mark. The enemy is now giving ground. His losses have been enormous. The fire of the machine guns and artillery is so rapid that one cannot keep time with it even by chattering one's teeth.

The work of our brave men is worthy to be seen. One forgets the achievements of Bonaparte when one sees what our men have done. How our heroes have gone forward, quite regardless of life, and crushed the head of the enemy on the ground! Battalion after battalion follow their music, filled with enthusiasm, just as a snake dances to the pipe of the charmer and darts forward to strike. Such intoxicating music has never been played before. Battalions go forward with even step, steadily and firmly, just as an elephant moves along the road swaying slightly from side to side, to show the worth of their valour. Truly even from the enemy's lips they must have wrung applause. Thousands of heroes have arisen in this war as brave and illustrious as was Bonaparte. Even the heavens do not cease from shedding tears on our warriors, so great is their valour. Hail Europe! From time immemorial the fame of your valour has been spread over the whole world!

What in truth can I write and tell you about this war. Things are being done here which stagger the onlooking world. Alas the regulations prevent me from writing more fully, otherwise I would write you a volume of details, the perusal of which would inflame your soul.[1] [Letter passed]

1. It is unclear whether the writer of this letter is celebrating the valour of Indian or of British troops. The references to 'our brave men', 'our heroes' and 'our warriors' suggest the former; the mention of 'battalions' (not a cavalry formation) and the exclamation 'Hail Europe!' suggest the latter. Perhaps he means both.

362

Jemadar Shaikh Mohi-ud-din (Deccani Muslim, 33) to
Pensioned Risaldar-Major Karimdad Khan (Hyderabad, Deccan)

20th Deccan Horse [Urdu]
France 27th July 1916

C Squadron is now made up of Troops 5, 6 and 7. Owing to the few Deccani Muslims available, perhaps we shall have only one troop of them, and if this goes on we shall eventually have none at all and the tribe will be disgraced. No one seems to take any trouble to recruit Deccani Muslims. The OC told me that HH the Nizam [of Hyderabad] had written to him that they would not enlist as they were afraid of the war. My answer was that if anyone took the trouble in the matter plenty of recruits might be obtained. I am over here and can do nothing. I am writing to you because you and Ressaidar Hayat Mir Khan [45] and Risaldar-Major Amir Muhammad Khan [51] and Jemadar Fyazuddin [Shaikh Faiz-ud-din, 33] and Jemadar Nabiyar Khan [47] are all there, and I want you to do your best to recruit our people. If you do not, the regiment's reputation will be gone for ever.

On the 14th July there was a cavalry attack in which the 20th greatly distinguished themselves.[1] No other Indian cavalry regiment has done anything yet, but we have made two attacks and made a great name for ourselves. The Corps Commander and the Divisional Commander wired to HH the Nizam telling him how well the regiment had done. [Letter passed]

1. See No. 356 for an account of the action, near Mametz Wood.

363

Sham Singh (Sikh) to Kehar Singh (Ludhiana District, Punjab)

6th Cavalry [Urdu]
France 30th July 1916

We are now in the trenches and are fighting with great courage. We have now come to understand what this war is. We do not wish the war to stop yet; we want it to continue. In our village [in India] the fair is held once a year only; here there is a continuous fair. There are many beautiful things to see and fruits to eat. You will have to use much persuasion if you wish us to return. At the present time the war is about a quarter finished. We still have three quarters to accomplish. We are not fated to die; we have come through some very trying times safely. When we return we will tell you everything. We see men of all nations here, and we have seen all the countries. Formerly, those people who had been to China used to come and boast of what they had seen and done. Now we have seen all the countries and we shall never again let the China people come and sit on our doorstep [and boast]. You will understand [our worth] when we return with rows of medals on our breasts. Heretofore a 'one medal man' has been accustomed to swagger amongst us, even though his medal was pinned onto a shirt of coarse home-spun cloth. We shall experience very many and grave difficulties here, but we shall surmount them all and return victorious, even if it takes us one hundred years to succeed. [Letter passed]

364

The mother of Sher Mahomed Khan (originally of 34th Poona Horse) to Risaldar-Major Raja Gul Mawaz Khan (Muslim Rajput, 18th Lancers, France, 41)

[no address given]

[Urdu]
1st August 1916

Except for you and God, I have no helper. If anything can be done for my son, I beseech you to do it. It appears to me, however, that you do nothing. If you were to go to the CO of the 34th Poona Horse and say to him that, since the war began, news has always been received of all missing men except those belonging to the 34th Poona Horse, it would be well. If the CO were to interest himself he could get information from the German side, in the same way as all other COs who interest themselves get information in regard to their men. It appears that no one in the 34th Poona Horse takes any trouble. What is the reason for this?

Be so kind as to go to the CO yourself and ask him to obtain news of the missing men of his regiment. I weep so [much] that I am becoming insane. Except for God, I had no one in this world but Sher Mahomed Khan. [Letter passed]

365

Dafadar Wazir Khan (Punjabi Muslim) to Gholam Hussein (Army Remount Depot, Shahpur District, Punjab, India)

18th Lancers
France

[Urdu?]
1st August 1916

I wish to represent that I cannot write you the details of the subject you desire. Moreover it is not desirable that I should do so. If I were to do so, you would become alarmed, as you would realize that it would be impossible for my distress to be greater than it is; but be reassured – I am not in the least despondent or afraid. The splendour of spring reigns and the scenery is grand. It is a case of hunting from morning till night and from night till morning. The time that I am taking up in writing this letter is, as it were, snatched from necessity, for we never get any leisure whatever. Today we have again been victorious. On the other side, the Russians have made a big advance, capturing 651 officers and 32,000 men by encircling the Austrians.[1] Pray God that our King may obtain victory. The fighting is now all in our favour. The charge of the cavalry was worthy of praise. [Letter passed]

1. Another reference to the Brusilov offensive in Galicia. See No. 333.

366

*Zafaryab Khan (Hindustani Muslim) to Risaldar Wajid Ali Khan
(32nd Lancers, New Cantonment, Delhi, 32)*

34th Poona Horse   [Urdu?]
France   1st August 1916

Eighteen men of my regiment and Jemadar Zafaryab Khan have been transferred to the 20th Deccan Horse, and I am still with the 34th. Major [G.M.] Molloy and [Reserve] Lieut. [W.S.C.] Hamley[1] are in the 20th, and we know them, and I [would] have [had] no grievance against our men's transfer if only it had taken place at an earlier or later date. But, as it is, we in the Poona Horse feel the transfer because we have no officer or NCO left in the regiment who cares about us and can appreciate us. I hope Zafaryab will be made a ressaidar.

1. This is one of the very rare occasions on which a letter-writer mentions British officers by name. As usual, particular names crop up when there has been a problem.

367

*Mirza Ahmed Baig (Deccani Muslim) to Pensioned Sowar Kasim Ali Baig
(1st Lancers, Imperial Service Troops, Deccan, India)*

Secunderabad Cavalry Brigade
France   2nd August 1916

It appears to me that God has at last been moved on our behalf by the increasing supplication of the people. Before going into the 'attack' the other day I had a dream.

I dreamed that a great snake appeared in the trenches in France, and at the same time my Pir Murshid [spiritual advisor] Lala Bahadur appeared with a heavy stick in his hand and forthwith destroyed the snake.

Well, our lot went into the attack and returned from it safely.[1] Those others who were fated to be the victims of DEATH were taken, and those who were fated to be wounded, were wounded; while all of our party returned in safety. At the same time, our Government obtained a victory over the enemy and the regiment secured much renown. Perhaps you have read in India in the newspapers how gallantly the Deccan Horse swept over the trenches and how the Germans, being alarmed at the sight, turned and fled? The leaders did not consider that the occasion was suitable for a cavalry charge and stopped the pursuit. In the future, when the opportunity occurs, we shall without fail wreak vengeance on the Germans for the blood of our brothers, and utterly crush and crumple them up.

Subsequently, I had another dream. I dreamed that the assembly of people was being held and that songs were being sung. I was also present in the assembly and I went up to the Pir Murshid and said to him 'two years have passed, what is going to happen now?' The Pir Murshid regarded me with a sorrowful look, but gave no reply. Tell the Lala Bahadur of these two dreams, and ask him for a complete and precise interpretation.

Two months only remain before the appearance of winter. May God bring the end of the war before that trying time is on us again. [Letter passed]

1. He is referring to the attack of 14th July 1916, described in No. 356.

368

Yakub Khan (Hindustani Muslim) to Lance Dafadar Ali Ahmed Khan
(5th Cavalry, Rawalpindi, Punjab)

2nd Cavalry   [Urdu]
France   2nd August 1916

When the Indian cavalrymen are transferred from one place to another, all the French girls from twelve to eighteen are very distressed and weep. I can remember a French verse: 'Que malheur! Indiens soldats partis, Mademoiselles France pleurer' [sic].[1]
[Letter passed]

1. 'What sadness! Indian soldiers leave, French maidens cry'.

369

Feroz Khan (Hindustani Muslim) to Karam Ali Khan (Hissar District, Punjab)

6th Cavalry   [Urdu]
France   2nd August 1916

Abdul Ghami Lumberdar and you should try hard to get recruits. If anyone wants service there is a promising vacancy. Tell Yakub Khan and Azim Alla that there is no need to give a deposit to enter the cavalry.[1] I think that the cavalry service is good. Whether good or evil comes out of it, belongs to Fate. It is better to join the cavalry than the infantry, and the pay is good, and there is *aram* [rest or ease]. Ask Bhura, Abdulla, etc. about this, and whoever wants service can be enlisted now. It would be a good thing for them all to enlist. In the Punjab the number of recruits they are getting is astonishing – Sikhs, Jats and Punjabis are enlisting freely. The pity of it is that our caste is not coming forward freely to help Government as they should. The caste that helps Government in this war will have a great reputation and will always be looked up to. Tell everyone to try, for now's the time. There are many of our people in the depot of the 6th Cavalry. Go and see them and they will help in recruiting. [Letter passed]

1. The *silladar* system, by which new cavalry recruits paid a deposit against the cost of their horse, arms and equipment, was now virtually defunct.

370

*Sawai Singh (Jat) to Ganesh Singh (Administrative HQ,
Police Office, Hyderabad, India)*

20th Deccan Horse   [Urdu]
France   4th August 1916

Although Colonel [G.E.D.] Elsmie [Commandant, 25th Cavalry] and Major [F.] Adams [20th Deccan Horse] wrote about me, the reply was that I had too much service to secure a commission. Here, apparently, responsible posts are given only to young men of short service. Then, for the same reasons, from general officers down to commanders – all should be sent back. I am getting nothing whatever in the way of promotion and for this reason I applied to return. Sirdar Singh has been made jemadar: to whom am I to complain? This is all due to my bad luck, and there is nothing left but to endure it. I applied to return, but my CO said that he would not allow me to return as long as he is in command; and that if anyone else came in his place he might either promote me or send me back as he pleased. Now

I am helpless and don't know what to do. I can neither get what I claim, nor can I obtain leave to go. What is to be done? This is wartime and if I fight for my rights, goodness knows what will happen to me. For this reason I keep silent, but I mean to have another try to get my pension and return. Whatever you read in the newspapers about our trials in the fighting line is correct; we are not allowed to write about it in our letters. [Letter passed]

371

Pailad (Jat) to Naik Udmi Ram (10th Jat Infantry, Bannu, NWFP)

20th Deccan Horse [Hindi]
France 4th August 1916

My friend, my condition is that there is no one here of my own village, and no one even whom I can converse with. I am, as it were, solitary and alone, belonging to no one. The people here take thought only for their own lot. Jhajri entangled me in this place and himself went away. If I had remained in my own regiment I should have been a dafadar by now. Here there is nothing to be had and no patronage to be secured. It makes me quite despondent when I think of it. [Letter passed]

372

Lance Dafadar Laherasab Khan to Jemadar Shah Nawaz Khan
(Punjabi Muslim, 11th Lancers attached 19th Lancers, France, 27)

11th Lancers
Dera Ismail Khan [Urdu]
NWFP 4th August 1916

Sarwar Khan is quite well, and treats us with greater kindness than I am able to express! I pray continually that God may send a party from Troop No. 7 to the front, and that either Sarwar Khan or I may go with it, so that I may escape from him with my life. There is no need for me to write in greater detail. You are wise and will understand. If I were to detail all the troubles which we experience at his hand, an envelope would not contain the letter I should have to write. This is my one prayer, that God will remove me from under his command. [Letter passed]

373

Ghulam Khan (Deccani Muslim) to Rahman Khan
(Depot, 20th Deccan Horse, Neemuch, Gwalior, Central India)

20th Deccan Horse   [Urdu]
France   5th August 1916

You have heard about us, no doubt. God has been very gracious to us, and we have won reputation.[1] If He had not been with us it would have been very difficult. You will have seen in the newspapers the name we have got. I was well again by the 1st, and fit for duty. God alone knows what my condition is. When I consider the state of things here I have no hope of life. I get through each day by taking the name of God. I have made over my Ramazan and Id to God's care. If I get home again I will tell you all about it; and if I am not spared I leave my children in your care. If I get back all right I will devote three months' pay to God in the cause of charity. [Letter passed]

1. In the attack on High Wood on 14th July 1916. See Nos. 356 and 362. For a more sceptical view from a writer in another regiment, see No. 400.

374

Sirdar Ali Khan (Punjabi Muslim) to Malik Dost Mahomed Khan
(Sargodha, Shahpur District, Punjab)

Sialkot Cavalry Brigade   [Urdu]
France   6th August 1916

We left for Paris on the 12th July and arrived there on the 13th at 5pm. Along the route from the station to the camp, vast crowds of people were collected whose welcome to us was beyond description. They cheered us, and shed flowers over us, and were very enthusiastic. We were lodged in a beautiful house, the front of which you see in the accompanying picture which I had taken. The furniture was of the very best, being upholstered in velvet with cushions ... All these arrangements were made by the French Government whose guests we were. There were arrangements for daily baths and shaving; and food of the best quality (suitable to our taste and caste) was supplied in plenty. Paris is fairyland. In fact, if there is any place on earth with approaches Heaven, it is Paris. The roads and gardens are so beautiful that [in] contemplating them a mortal man becomes overwhelmed with wonder.

We arrived, as I said, on the 13th July, and the 14th was the French Great Day.[1] On that day we 'fell-in' on parade at 8pm at the appointed place. We were conducted there from the camp with much applause. We numbered fifty, and other troops were there also – namely 150 British troops, 200 Russian troops, some horse and foot Belgian troops, and the French troops, comprising infantry, cavalry and artillery, together with the Algerian troops (who are Muslims and are subjects of France).

The review ground was in front of the French Palace. It was all paved, and a road thirty-five yards broad, paved with rubber [sic], ran through it. On one side of the road were the French troops, and on the other the Russians, the British and the Belgians. At 9am the French President, together with the staff officers of the various countries, inspected all the troops on foot and then left the place. We were then given an hour's leave and told to fall in again at eleven o'clock. The troops of the several nations at once mingled with each other, being anxious to become acquainted. We did not know each other's language, but we shook hands and smiled at each other. This was the only way in which we could greet each other.

When the hour had elapsed, we resumed our places for the review, and presently the 'march past' commenced. The French President stood in front of the Palace, and the troops marched before him and saluted in turn. The review lasted from 10am till 3pm and we were marching all that time through dense crowds of people whose numbers were beyond conception and who cheered us enthusiastically; men, women and children – they were all frantic. We reached camp at 3pm and we were told that we were free to do as we liked for three days and to see as much as we chose of Paris, provided only that we were back in camp each night before ten o'clock.

The arrangements for sightseeing were excellent. From morning till evening thousands of people were assembled in front of our camp to see us. As soon as we set foot outside the billet we were asked by some people whether we spoke French or English. I know very little English, but I have acquired a lot of French and can speak and understand it well. All the others with me also knew French, more or less. We therefore told the people that we understood French, at which they were much delighted. They begged that, if we desired to go sightseeing, we would accompany them, and said that we would be conferring a great honour on them. We went with them gladly and they conveyed us in their own motor car, because as Paris covers an area of fifty-five square miles it would be impossible to see much of it on foot. We were taken to all the famous places, and were treated more graciously than it is possible for me to describe; but you will understand how well we were treated when I tell you that, although the motor car was a private one and no hire had to be paid, 150 francs were spent on our entertainment and refreshment. There were only three of us Indians, and we were sightseeing for five hours daily, and yet this large sum of money was spent on us! One franc is equal to ten annas, so that Rs.84 [sic] was spent on us!

It was with the greatest of difficulty that we were able to induce the people to let us go home after five hours' sightseeing. They took us to dances and bioscopes and musical entertainments and museums and zoological gardens and to various old historic buildings. We saw the palaces of former Kings of France built 800 years ago but which are kept in perfect repair. There is one palace built 300 years ago, which contains one hundred thousand rooms and has its own gardens and lakes. The Palace and grounds cover an area of four miles. The palace is in such perfect state of repair that one might think it had been completed only yesterday. In the city one house vies with another in beauty, and God knows what sum of money must have been spent in building each. The roads are generally 32 yards wide, of which 16 yards in the centre are paved with rubber and eight yards in each side with stone, one and a half feet above the level of the central road, and polished to such a degree that one's foot slips as one walks on it. The main roads which run in the vicinity of the principal public buildings are 45 yards wide, of which 22 and a half yards in the centre are paved with rubber, with stone pavements on either side. There are amusements everywhere.

This city is greater than the great city of the world of which we used to be told, but whose existence we did not credit. Its beauty is beyond description. I have seen many places and countries including Hindustan, Punjab, Kabul, and many towns in France, and I am quite certain that in the whole world there cannot be any town the equal of Paris. The buildings [and] the bazars are most magnificent, and as regards the people they are noted for their beauty. Out of every 100 people, 80 are beautiful, and the remaining 20 are more beautiful than the most beautiful of any other nationality. Moreover, their intelligence and affection and sympathy and politeness are beyond description. There is much more that I could write; indeed there would be no end to all that I could write. [Letter passed]

1. *Le Quatorze Juillet.*

375

Hemayat Ullah Khan (Hindustani Muslim) to The Moulvi Sahib,
Imam of the Mosque, Mahomed Alim Ullah Khan (Daulatpura Village,
Bulandshahr District, UP)

6th Cavalry   [Urdu]
France   6th August 1916

Leaving Hindustan, to take a part in the work of helping the Government, I arrived in France, and today this honour has been conferred on me that I find myself in the field of battle, facing the enemy's trenches fifty paces distant, ready to do my loyal duty towards the Sirkar with my naked sword in my hand. I hope that my presence here will find favour for me in the eyes of the Government ...

The billets that we occupy behind the firing line are worth seeing. Often I have climbed to the top of a seven-storied house and watched the battle, and have seen the perfect arrangements of our Government. Shells from the enemy's batteries fall now and then among the buildings, and one feels sad to see such fine buildings destroyed in this ruthless way. Still, the big guns of our Government, whose fire shakes the earth, very quickly silence the guns of the enemy.

If I had not come to this war, I could never have conceived what war really means. The man in this world who has not seen the war with his own eyes, or has not participated in it, and who has had to content himself with what he hears or reads in the newspapers, is like a child who listens to tales from the lips of its mother and is entertained by them, whether the tales are true or false. This war is such that mountains and cities are battered by it, till they become no better than decaying grave yards.

Nevertheless I tell the truth, that not one vestige of fear or anxiety is to be seen in the faces of the men who form our Army. God Almighty first of all makes each man in this war dead to sorrow, and then he implants in each man's heart the belief that he will come through all right, whatever may happen to others. I too, having consigned myself to the keeping of God, am now so free from anxiety that neither in the sea voyage did I fear the German submarines, nor on land, whether on foot or horseback, or engaged in hand to hand fighting, do I feel any fear.

At the present time our Government is gaining successes everywhere. Whenever we watch fights in the air over our heads, we see two or three at least of the enemy's machines brought down to land. When an artillery engagement starts, the guns of our great Government thunder so loudly that the drums of our ears are in danger of being shattered. Our fellows are now so inured to danger, that unless and until the enemy shells begin to fall in our immediate vicinity, we cannot resist the temptation to rise and observe all that is happening. So also in the trenches, however many shells and bullets whizz over us, we are not disturbed. In the matter of mines, we are in no way inferior to the enemy. In fact the bravery and resource of the entire British Army is worthy of the very greatest praise.

And indeed how could it be otherwise, for I have seen, with my own eyes, hot meats, bread and tea and necessaries of every kind taken to the British soldiers in the very firing line. In the same way, however heavy may be the firing, whether of shells or bullets or both, fresh goat's flesh, and *dal* and cakes of various kinds with *gur* [a half-refined sugar] and tea reach the trenches of the Indians without fail. The entire force is very pleased with these arrangements. If we have to make a journey by road of fifty miles, we find, when we reach our destination, that our rations are already there, having been sent on by motor cars.

If anyone should become suddenly ill, or be wounded, he is straight away conveyed on a stretcher to the motor ambulance and in a few minutes he finds himself in a hospital. The hospital is a place of greatest comfort, and there so much attention is shown to him, as he has never in his life experienced before, even in his own home. Government has secured the services of extremely kind and sympathetic men and women for this work.

If one regards the condition of that portion of France which is in the possession of the Germans, one's eyes are filled with tears. Nevertheless, it is perfectly clear that neither our Government nor France will allow themselves to be daunted in the slightest degree by this state of affairs.

Although I am desirous of writing fully about all that our Government is doing in this war, in the first place the bombardment around me prevents me from collecting my ideas (thousands of shells are being fired from a spot not more than 100 yards behind our trenches and a much smaller number from the enemy's side are falling and exploding not very far away in front of us) and in the second place there are restrictions to writing fully about matters relating to the war under the cover of a green envelope. I have tried to look at what I have already written with the enemy's eyes, and I beg the Sahib who reads this letter to be just and consider whether I have written anything in it which is likely to be of use to the enemy. If he should find anything in it which he considers objectionable, I very willingly give him permission to erase it, and even to destroy the letter if he thinks fit.[1]

We have become such tea drinkers, that until we get our tea we do not converse. Our principal expenditure of money is in tea, since milk and sugar are very expensive. We get various kinds of vegetables on payment. [Letter passed]

1.   For other examples of soldiers directly addressing the censor see Nos. 117, 314 and 355.

376

Khadim Khan to Sowar Ghiba Khan (Pathan, 9th Hodson's Horse, France)

24th Hazara Mountain Battery	
Nowshera	[Urdu]
NWFP	8th August 1916

All the men of long service have gone away to the war, and I have become disgusted with the service, since I secured no benefit from it. I am anxious to leave, but the Sirkar will not let me go. What am I to do? Nothing. If the issue were left to me I would not serve another day. I hear that the cavalry now at the front will return to India shortly, and that regiments now in the Punjab will be sent to replace them at the front. [Letter passed]

377

Lance Dafadar Chaudra Singh (Sikh) to Harchand Singh (Hissar District, Punjab)

2nd [?] Lancers	[Urdu]
France	9th August 1916

Just look at the English! They spend their lives in far-off countries and they appreciate knowledge. As for us, we are like spiders which do not leave their web, and just like them we are unwilling to leave our village boundaries. A man gets experience by travelling in other countries and cities and you can't get that by sitting in your house. I am more comfortable here than I ever was in cantonments, and therefore you should not talk nonsense. [Letter passed]

378

Jemadar Nur Mahomed (Pathan) to Maulavi Absan-ud-din Khan
(Turangazai, Peshawar District, NWFP)

38th CIH [Urdu]
France 9th August 1916

I can tell you nothing except that we have kept the fast [of Ramazan]. We had the Id prayers in the trenches. What sort of Id was it? We broke our fast and that is all you can say for it. About thirty of us said our prayers out in the open with nothing over our heads and no strength to do anything. It was a bad time. May God have mercy. We have no other resource. 'If I tell you with my tongue all that I am suffering, my tongue burns. If I refrain from telling you, then my brain and liver are burnt.'[1] [Letter passed]

1. A Persian prayer.

379

Signaller Feroz Khan (Hindustani Muslim) to Ali Baksh Khan
(Karnal District, Punjab)

20th Deccan Horse or 34th Poona Horse [Urdu]
France 13th August 1916

I was glad to get your letter. No doubt you rejoice while we are being offered up as a sacrifice for Great Britain. By the grace of God we shall return victorious and famous, and then you will be sorry and will be green with envy at having lost such an opportunity. It is a cursed thing that you should rejoice! It is a man's work to be in the fight, not to eat the bread of peace. There is a proverb: 'It is the gallant man-at-arms that falls in battle; what can the babe which plays round his mother's knees do?' This is the answer that I give to your harsh and sulky letter. [Letter passed]

380

*Abdul Wahab Khan (Hindustani Muslim) to Dafadar Nawab Inayat Ali Khan
(Rohtak District, Punjab)*

Sialkot Cavalry Field Ambulance   [Urdu]
France   14th August 1916

I am telling you what the common talk is. There is a rumour that all the Indian
Cavalry will return to India in the winter.[1] This is a very strong rumour and even
the officers mention it. May God grant that it may be true! [Letter passed]

1. Many letters from this period contain similar rumours.

381

*Maula Dad Khan to his son Mahomed Usuf Khan
(Hindustani Muslim, 2nd Lancers, France)*

Aligarh   [Urdu?]
[UP]   17th August 1916

Formerly I had experienced but one sorrow, and that was the death of your mother.
My childhood and manhood were spent very happily. Now in my old age I have
had to endure the sorrow of long separation from you, and as a consequence my
eyesight is failing rapidly. It is not fitting that I should dilate on my infirmities,
and up to the present time your brave words of comfort and hope have sustained
me; but many people like me have, through grief for the loss of their offspring,
departed this life. I live in the belief that by the mercy of the Pure God that day
will come quickly, when my sightless eyes will again look upon your face, and
looking will regain their lustre. Regarding what you say about the money, namely
that I shall receive it shortly, I have no concern whatever for money; my concern
is for you alone. The Government may pay me what and when they please; it makes
no difference to me. [Letter passed]

382

Lance Dafadar Jawani Singh to Har Narain Singh (Hindustani Hindu,
22nd Cavalry attached 2nd Lancers, France)

22nd Cavalry
Bolarum [Urdu]
Deccan 17th August 1916

Our regiment, numbering 505 men, is going to Iran [Persia] shortly to relieve the
17th Lancers. We will take their horses, and they will take ours. Practically all the
men in the regiment are recruits; there are only one or two old men in each troop.
This matter causes us great concern, for these men can neither ride nor shoot. Men
of only two months' service are being sent to the front. [Letter passed]

383

Anwar Shah to Aurangzeb Shah (Punjabi Muslim, Signal Troop,
Lucknow Cavalry Brigade, France)

Camel Corps [Urdu]
Suez 18th August 1916

The holy festival of Id was celebrated here by the Egyptians in a very strange way.
We had a holiday to celebrate the auspicious day, and about ten o'clock we
assembled in a body at the place on the canal specially set up by the Egyptians.
The place was adorned and decorated as if for the reception of a bride at a wedding.
Roundabouts were erected everywhere on which 'nightingales' and 'cuckoos'
[women] of Egypt, each with an admirer, sang songs to allure the listening
foreigners. Each place of entertainment one went to contained some novelty.

The festival lasted from the 1st to 3rd August. On each day, twenty-one guns
were fired by the Egyptian Government after each five hours' period of prayer.
During these three days, we did not meet a single Egyptian who was not the reverse
of virtuous and well conducted. Each man encountered was more or less the worse
for drink, and, having at least one 'nightingale' sitting beside him in his carriage,
indulged in all kinds of lewd and obscure songs. It was all very wrong, but at the
same time there is no fault attaching to us for showing our fellow countrymen how
the people of this country (which is our present abiding place) act.

The part of town occupied by courtesans was worth seeing. On one side a
'nightingale' in the possession of an Arab sang loudly. On the other, a 'nightingale'
embraced an Egyptian, while some poor Hindustani looked on and wondered
when his turn would come. But the 'nightingales' had not leisure even to scratch

their heads! Great *kazis* [judges] and *muftis* [law givers] and devotees [who had rigorously kept the fast for a month] merely waited their opportunity at the approach of evening to carry away their 'nightingales' and despoil them in the dark. It was a strange sight watching the flittings in and out, here and there, of the 'rose-faced' ones. Shame! Shame! The very ground cried out for protection, and praying to God, said 'for a day like this make a new earth, because I am no longer able to endure the suggestive gait, and the thrust of the pointed heels of these creatures'.

Each place was illuminated and crowded with gaily-dressed and beautiful ones. They had no shyness or fear of evil glances. When their glances and those of the Hindustanis encountered [each other] what can I say? It is beyond description! There was no trace of the Hindustani custom of friends meeting and partaking of the Id banquets. Each one went about 'empty-handed' after his own pleasure – no one knew whence he came or whither he went. Nothing that we have seen in Hindustan, even during the Holi festivals of the Hindus, approaches the things we have seen here during the Id. Thank God, for this, Our Country! [Letter passed]

384

Jemadar Wali Mahomed Khan (Hindustani Muslim) to
Ahmad Ali Khan (Rohtak District, Punjab)

6th Cavalry   [Urdu]
France   18th August 1916

I am not at all pleased at being made a jemadar, and when the order of promotion reached me I wept to a degree that I can hardly express. Those who saw me then said 'you ought to be delighted, and you are crying'. I replied 'my feelings are just now absolutely upset. If my father and mother had been alive, I should have been happy.' [Letter passed]

385

Roghan Shah to Dafadar Gulbar Khan (Pathan, 19th Lancers, France)

Peshawar   [Urdu]
NWFP   22nd August 1916

Do not send discouraging messages to the people of the village. It is the duty of youth to bear and surmount all difficulties. Difficulties themselves do not kill a man. [Letter passed]

386

Shah Dauran to Sowar Shah Jehan (Pathan, 36th Jacob's Horse, France)

Jangal Khel
Kohat District [Urdu]
NWFP 22nd August 1916

People say that there, in France, Shah Jehan wastes his money in riotous living: that he takes advances and squanders them. If this is true, all the members of your family will be very annoyed with you. Others have sent money to their homes – some Rs.200, others Rs.300 – but from you not a single *pie* has been received. What advantage is there for us in such service? You have not yet made good the advance we provided for your horse and equipment.[1] I congratulate you on your excess of intelligence! [Letter passed]

1. Cavalry recruits normally paid a deposit of Rs.50 upon enlistment. This was a vestige of the *silladar* system, now virtually defunct, by which a trooper paid for his own horse, weapons and equipment. See No. 369; and Omissi, *The Sepoy and the Raj*, pp. 71–4.

387

Bakhlawar Singh (Sikh) to Gugar Singh (Lyallpur, Punjab)

6th Cavalry [Urdu]
France 23rd August 1916

We are always in the trenches and the fighting is very scarce [sic]. We are very keen on the fighting, and do not be anxious about us. We hope the war will soon be over as day by day the enemy is being crushed. The guns fire all day like the thunder in [the month of] Sawan [July–August]. The heaven and earth are undistinguishable and at night there is a regular Diwali festival. There are thousands of men and thousands of different kinds of fighting – on the earth, in the nether regions, on the sea, and under the sea and in the air. This fight is being waged with the greatest ability. It is a very difficult war, but the arrangements are marvellous. The shells are passing over our heads as we sit in the trenches, but there is no danger. After ten days we get relieved, and then after ten days' rest we come back again. We are full of fight and ready to do our bit as long as the war lasts. We are fortunate men to have been able to join in this great war. We will do our best to uphold the family traditions and the reputation of our tribe. [Letter passed]

388

Mahomed Hasan to Sowar Raja Khan Zaman Khan
(Muslim Rajput, 38th CIH, France)

Rawalpindi   [Urdu]
[Punjab]   26th August 1916

I am very glad you went to fight for our King in Europe, the great map of which
I am accustomed to study so carefully. It is a very useful thing to visit foreign countries
and I hope you will keep these advantages in mind. Especially in France you, as
a soldier, have a chance of studying the habits and natures of the inhabitants, which
have given them superiority to us. Don't be afraid of the stories you hear that the
Germans have adopted Islam and that it is wrong to fight against Muslims.[1]
William II, King of Prussia, is not a Muslim at all but a Roman Catholic [sic]
Christian.[2] Another thing is that this vast war is not a religious war at all, but a
political one. I have read all the histories of the European wars, including those
of Napoleon, and the lesson I have learnt is that any sepoy who works hard and
obeys orders has the chance of becoming a general. I am telling you now the lesson
which we ought to learn, and that is, if we Indians bring back to India the flag of
victory which we have helped win for our King George, we shall have proved our
fitness and will be entitled to self-government.[3] I am giving you good news when
I tell you that the Hindu and Muslim universities, the Benares University and those
of Dacca and Mysore, and hundreds of colleges and schools have been created.
We Indians are acquiring educational fitness. The teaching in Aligarh College is
superior to that of Oxford, and the Punjab University is flourishing, while the Islamic
College at Lahore has greatly improved. [Letter passed]

1. In efforts to demoralize the Indian troops, the Germans fabricated rumours that the Kaiser
   had converted to Islam.
2. In fact the Hohenzollerns were Protestant.
3. These sentiments are quite untypical of the collection. The writer seems better educated
   than most of the other correspondents.

389

Fazal Khan (Hindustani Muslim) to Mahomed Abdulla
(Government Cattle Farm, Hissar District, Punjab)

Lahore Indian General Hospital   [Urdu]
Rouen   30th August 1916

From the newspapers it is evident that our condition is very much better than it
was before; but God alone knows the real truth. We are eagerly hoping for victory,

since Romania has now joined our side, and obviously our forces have increased very largely.[1] Now all that remains for us to get is the help of God. Let us see when He will turn to our help. On the surface there is no clear indication of the end of the war, but if God wishes he can bring the end into view in a moment. There are only a few states left who are not engaged in this war; practically the whole of Europe is involved in it. This is a case in which the outcries of the poor and afflicted will have effect; but it is not known how long our enemies will continue to wage war, although they are now in a bad way. They were the originators of the war, and they separated us from our country and entangled us in all these troubles. In India there is famine and we have been separated from our dear ones for two years, and our hearts yearn to see their faces again. Except for God we have no hope ... Recollect that every letter is censored before it reaches us, and every letter that we send passes through the censor's hand before it is forwarded. [Letter passed]

1. Romania declared war on Austria-Hungary on 27th August; but the writer's hopes were misplaced. Romania was overrun by the Central Powers between September and December 1916.

390

Karam Singh (Jat) to Shankar Singh (Saidpur, Bulandshahr District, UP)

29th Lancers [Urdu]
France August 1916

My mother asks me to sent Rs.100. Is she in earnest? I have already allotted Rs.18 per mensem in your name – why then this importunity? What hidden store have I, from which I could send additional remittances. Don't you yet realize my position? Nothing in it is obscure. Alas, all I have left is the skin on my body, and if you want that also, say the word and I'll have it taken off and sent to you by parcel post. [Letter passed]

391

Sayed Abdul Wahib to Lance Dafadar Sayed Abbas (Madrasi Muslim,
27th Light Cavalry, attached 20th Deccan Horse, France)

Assistant Commissioner's Office
Velore [Urdu]
Madras 1st September 1916

People say that, if, when you go into action, you take with you a piece of raw onion, bullets will not touch you. [Letter passed]

392

Kasim Ali Khan (Deccani Muslim) to Pensioned Dafadar Hayat Khan (Neemuch, Gwalior, Central India)

20th Deccan Horse   [Urdu]
France   3rd September 1916

You think what I tell you about Mahbub is untrue. You must never think to yourself 'why does no letter come from Mahbub?' or 'why does not his name appear in the list of prisoners?' You must recollect that he was so badly wounded that he could not rise, and he must therefore have remained in hospital for a long time. I have heard that he is not allowed to write letters. I swear to you by God that he is alive. In a few days I will inform you of the fact by telegram. I have now made arrangements to get news of his condition. [Letter passed]

393

Mirza Mahomed Ali (Deccani Muslim) to Mirza Kazam Ali Beg (Hyderabad, Deccan)

20th Deccan Horse   [Urdu]
France   3rd September 1916

The end of this world-wide war will come in a short time. We expect that God will give complete victory to the British Government – otherwise peace will be made on the terms proposed by our Government.[1] Our Government has plenty of troops, and the rations we receive are so plentiful that we cannot eat all we receive. From this it is inferred that all the arrangements of our Government are good. Moreover, we saw with our own eyes on the field of battle, that the Germans who were made prisoners in the fighting of the 14th July were in a bewildered state and very tattered and emaciated, as if by famine.[2] In fact they appeared to be half dead through starvation. From all this, and also from the severity of our bombardment, it is evident that the enemy is in a very shattered state. It is probable that in a few days he will leave his present front by night. Nowadays the Germans don't achieve any successes, but in the end God knows what will happen. [Letter passed]

1. Rumours of this nature appear in several letters around this time.
2. On 14th July, a British attack overran the second line of German trenches in the Bazentin sector of the Somme battlefield, although much of the ground was soon recaptured. The Deccan Horse supported the attack, with the 7th Dragoon Guards. See Nos. 356 and 400, and Plates 8 and 9.

394

Daya Ram (Jat) to Kalu Ram (Ambala City, Punjab)

2nd Lancers [Urdu]
France 5th September 1916

I went into the trenches on 7th August and returned on 28th August. Some of our men were wounded. I am not permitted to give any fuller details. The battle is raging violently, and various new ways of fighting have been introduced. The ground is honeycombed, as a field with rat holes. No one can advance beyond the trenches. If he does so, he is blown away. Mines are ready charged with explosives. Shells and machine guns and bombs are mostly employed. No one considers rifles nowadays, and serviceable rifle ammunition is lying about as plentifully as pebbles. At the trenches, thousands of *maunds* of iron, representing exploded shells, lie on the ground. At some places corpses are found of men killed in 1914, with uniform and accoutrements still on. Large flies, which have become poisonous through feasting on dead bodies, infest the trenches, and huge fat rats run about there. By the blessing of God the climate of this country is cold, and for that reason corpses do not decompose quickly. It rains frequently and that causes much inconvenience. At the present time we are suffering, as the horses are tethered outside and the rain has converted the ground into slush. Sometimes we have to march in the rain and then the cold is intense. However, after two years' experience, we have grown used to all these troubles and think lightly of them. I have lots to write about, but I have no leisure, nor have I permission to do so. Even this I have had to write very prudently, otherwise it would be withheld. [Letter passed]

395

Nadir Khan (Pathan) to Nur Mahomed Khan (Jhelum District, Punjab)

38th CIH [Urdu]
France 6th September 1916

The rumours that you narrate about the return of the Regiment to India are all without foundation.[1] No orders have been issued, nor can anyone tell what is to happen. Perhaps it may come to pass after a lapse of time, but I have no hope. What you say about taking pension is in the hands of God, but I hear of nothing to my advantage. The times are very unsettled and for this reason I cannot get retired on pension. However, do not be anxious. If I am destined to live we shall meet again. [Letter passed]

1. Many rumours of this kind were circulating at this time. Several writers suggested that all regiments which had served more than two years would return to India, to be replaced by fresh units; others mentioned particular regiments by name. All the rumours were false. No leave was granted until November. See Nos. 439, 443 and 446.

396

Abdul Jabbar Khan (Hindustani Muslim) to
Munshi Dost Mahomed Khan (Calcutta, Bengal)

6th Cavalry   [Urdu]
France   6th September 1916

Why do you ask about our condition here? Our five fingers are in the butter and our heads in the cauldron.[1] But, thanks be to God, I think it is probable that we shall meet before the winter sets in. The war will not be finished till the day of Judgement. It increases in intensity daily. We are like bubbles that rise to the surface of the water, and the place is like a pigeon house.[2]

1. 'We experience both comfort and adversity'.
2. 'Life is very precarious here, and people are continually coming and going'.

397

Sher Dil Khan (Punjabi Muslim) to
Jemadar Sultan Khan (18th Lancers, France, 33)

Sargodha
[Shahpur District]   [Urdu]
Punjab   9th September 1916

What you have written about the affair of the 15th Lancers is quite correct.[1] But it is clear that they were not to blame. Our Government is just. They only made a respectful representation, but some evil person deceived the regiment. Their letters have reached me and they show that the 15th Lancers never refused to serve but only made a respectful protest and said they were ready to go wherever the fight was hottest in France, and to give their lives for the King. They also said their bravery was well known in Europe and they were ready to risk their lives again. Their only prayer is that God may give victory to our King. [Letter passed]

1. He is referring to their mutiny in February. See Nos. 259, 276, 313 and 315.

398

Abizar (Baluchi) to Jemadar Malik Khuda Bakhsh Khan
(39th CIH, Lucknow, UP, 33)

36th Jacob's Horse [Urdu]
France 9th September 1916

I have no hope of promotion. The reason is that your friends, the two sirdars, do not wish me to be made dafadar. Thousands of opportunities [for my promotion] have been fruitless, and all the while I possessed my soul in patience. They show no preference to the man of your party, although they know each man of the party to be of good antecedents and quite capable. I do not know the reason – perhaps there may be some hidden reason which they do not disclose.

I have achieved something which reflects credit on our family. It happened two months ago, but I had no opportunity to write and tell you, because all my letters are read by the two sirdars, and they would have thought that I was publishing my good fortune. They were not pleased at my success, but all the British officers were greatly pleased, since what I did brought credit to the regiment. I won a medal which was made in England, and on which all the particulars are inscribed. I, with my patrol, secured first place amongst all the Indian cavalry for scouting work in a foreign country, and for this, which was considered a great achievement, I secured the medal. In many other competitions, too, I have brought lustre on the family name. [Letter passed]

399

Malik Sher Khan (Punjabi Muslim) to
Alam Sher Khan (Lyallpur District, Punjab)

18th Lancers [Urdu]
France 11th September 1916

I am acting faithfully on your advice; be easy in mind. I pray five times a day. I and Maulvi Alam Khan live together. We milk the cows with our own hands and use the milk. Up to the present time we have abstained from eating with, or from the hands of, these people [the French]. [Letter passed]

400

Dilawar Khan (Punjabi Muslim) to
Pensioned Risaldar-Major Safaraz Ali Khan (Gujrat District, Punjab)

18th Lancers   [Urdu]
France   11th September 1916

On the 1st July the Cavalry Division remained behind the [Somme] firing line all day in expectation of making an attack. In the evening they returned. Then on the 14th July the entire Indian cavalry joined in the assault.[1] The 20th Deccan Horse alone got an opportunity to attack, but they suffered loss and failed to obtain success. The remainder of the cavalry remained in support, and in the evening all returned to camp. On the 14th July a very severe attack was made by the British infantry; and the enemy was forced to evacuate three lines of trenches and retire.

On the 15th July the 18th Lancers went alone to the attack. They reached the foremost line in the early morning at five o'clock, but did not get an opportunity to attack, and had to go into action dismounted. Then the regiment retired two or three hundred yards and rested in a sheltered position while patrols were sent forward to reconnoitre. The patrols lost a few in killed and wounded; the rest returned in safety.

The battles fought on these days were very violent indeed. Altogether the British and French are very much more powerful than the enemy, who is forced to retreat constantly. They are gaining in strength daily, and it is expected that in a short time the enemy will be forced to retire to a distance. The British front in the battle extends over nineteen miles and they have massed 14,000 cannon there. This is the measure of the British might. Some of the guns are so powerful as to carry [shells] from twenty-two to twenty-four miles. On all sides the British ascendancy is on the increase. Very few enemy aeroplanes are seen nowadays, for the simple reason that if one ventures to approach our lines it never returns. The British gunfire is very accurate and cripples the aeroplanes and brings them to earth. [Letter passed]

1. In fact only the Secunderabad Brigade saw any action. See No. 356 for a glowing account.

401

Jemadar Indar Singh (Sikh) to Chattar Singh (Ludhiana District, Punjab)

FPO.42[1]   [Urdu]
France   15th September 1916

I am off for a cavalry attack on the 15th September.[2] It is quite impossible that I should return alive because a cavalry charge is a very terrible affair, and therefore

I want to clear up several things which are weighing on my heart at present. Firstly, the sharp things you have written to me have not annoyed me. Don't be grieved at my death because I shall die arms in hand, wearing the warrior's clothes. This is the most happy death that anyone can die. I am very sorry that I have not been able to discharge my obligations towards my family because God has called me already. Well, never mind; you must forgive me. I have abandoned to you all my worldly possessions which you must make use of without hesitation. Don't worry your grandparents after I am gone. Give my love to my parents and tell them not to grieve as we must all die some day. Indeed, this day of death is an occasion for rejoicing. [Letter passed]

1. The censor commented 'no regiment is given, and, as the cavalry are moving about very much just now, the number of the FPO is no guide'.
2. On 15th September the British attacked in strength on the Somme, supported by tanks – the first time the latter were used in battle. See also No. 447.

402

Lance Dafadar Mahabat Ali Khan to Irshad Ali (Punjabi Muslim, 5th Cavalry attached 6th Cavalry, France)

5th Cavalry
Risalpur   [Urdu]
NWFP   15th September 1916

We hear that the 6th Cavalry, 2nd Lancers and 20th Deccan Horse are returning to India. On hearing this, our hearts were filled with rejoicing, but on the 8th September a draft left Sialkot [Punjab] as reinforcement for the 6th Cavalry. We don't understand why. Tell us truly how the matter stands. Many men have returned on a month's leave. My friend, work in a cavalry regiment nowadays is not anything of a catch. The work has become hard and exacting, and the treatment too is harsh, especially that meted out by the black monkeys [Indian Officers?]. If you return, perhaps things may become a little better for us. I am anxious about Mahomed Ali. He has been beyond the frontier in Seistan [Persia] for two and a half years, and has not had a day's leave. We have had no letter from him for about sixteen or seventeen days. [Letter passed]

403

Sultan Mahomed Khan to Jemadar Nur Mahomed Khan (Pathan, 38th CIH)

Turangazai   [Urdu]
NWFP   16th September 1916

There are two points about the case of Kasim Shah. The first is our pleasure that he has escaped and come back home without punishment, having only been dismissed. This is his good fortune. The second point is that we are sorry that after all he has undergone in his service in France he has had to come back and sit at home without anything to show for his trouble. In my opinion he is a very fortunate individual to get off scot-free like this ... What I am afraid of is that his escape may in some way tend to lower your reputation. I wish you would let me know (if you are allowed) whether you take this view or not. Here everyone says that Kamaluddin Khan has made up the case and wounded himself to escape from the war. If in reality two shots had been fired at him how could he have escaped? It is his own invention. If anyone had enmity with him and wanted to kill him, why did his enemy not do it in the trenches? This clearly proves that he shot himself in the flesh of his thigh. It is common knowledge that every sowar is a trained shot. How then could two shots have missed their mark? [Letter passed]

404

Fazullah Khan (Punjabi Muslim) to Chandhir Ghulam Sarwar Khan
(Gujrat District, Punjab)

AG's Office   [Urdu]
Rouen   17th September 1916

I was removed from the regiment and sent to hospital suffering from piles, and I was then stationed in the Adjutant-General's office. While I was in the regiment I did good work, and was in the trenches. I gave up Rs.40 allowance to go and fight for Government, and I am ready if necessary to lay down my life for Government. Now is the time to show one's loyalty. I wrote to you about getting up a cavalry regiment of Gujars, and you must try and do it. I am convinced that only in the Army is any *izzat* to be acquired. It is nothing for you to get up a regiment of 300 men, and if we do not succeed I tell you plainly that our caste will be despised. If we get up this regiment, from our house we shall be able to recruit four jemadars, eight dafadars and twelve lance dafadars. You must talk to the Deputy Commissioner about it, and I am quite ready to come back and help if necessary. If you don't do this, our caste will be disgraced and our connection with the cavalry will be gone for ever. Now the time of the Allies has really come and I have seen it with my eyes the diminishing power of the Germans. Their return fire is only one-tenth of what it was. [Letter passed]

405

Jemadar Hasan Shah (Punjabi Muslim, 33) to a lady addressed as 'Dearer than Life' (c/o shopkeeper Ram Bheja Mul, Adowal, Jhelum District, Punjab)

9th Hodson's Horse   [Urdu]
France   19th September 1916

You reproach me with having sent you a card [instead of a letter]? My life! What can you know of the vicissitudes of my existence here. Perhaps I wrote the card on horseback during a wild charge! Or perhaps I wrote it under a shower of bursting shells! Or perhaps I wrote it at the last gasp of life! My unjust Beloved, you reproach me when you should praise. Still, I am that lover whose lips at the moment of death will utter one word – victory. You reproach me for having not written a letter? Happy indeed am I, in that I received a letter from you, even though it contained a reproach! I kissed it till my lips were like to wear away, and now it lies over against my heart! You blame me? I love to be blamed by you!

Listen. I will tell you of an incident which occurred to me, the day before yesterday. I was on the battlefield accompanied by a sowar, and came upon a wounded British soldier. 'Well friend', I said to him, 'how are things going with you?' 'Quite all right', he replied. 'I am proud I was of service in the fight, but I am thirsty.' I gave him water to drink, and asked if he wanted anything else. 'I regret nothing', he said, 'except that I shall not meet my sweetheart. She would have nothing to say to me at first, but four months ago she wrote and said that in the whole world she loved only me and begged me to come to her soon.' 'My friend', I said to him, 'may the All-Merciful God satisfy the desires of your heart, and unite you with your beloved!' 'I am finished' he said. 'And when my end comes, my one regret will be that when my love called to me I was unable to go to her.' 'My friend', I said, weeping with pity, 'my own condition is the same as yours'. I told the sowar to remove him to a safer place, as shells were falling near. He lifted him and was carrying him away, but he had not gone a hundred paces when the soldier cried out 'my beloved' and expired. [Letter passed]

406

*Risaldar-Major Amar Singh (Sikh, 44) to Head Clerk Yakub Khan
(Depot 38th CIH, Agar-Malwa, Gwalior, Central India)*

38th CIH   [Urdu]
France   19th September 1916

I am very hopeful that the opportunity for which we have been looking out for a
year and a half is now at hand and that we shall have a chance of crushing the proud
and tyrannical enemy, and be soon back in India to greet you.[1] [Letter passed]

1.   This is a rare example of correspondence between men of different religions.

407

*Prisoner Alam Sher (15th Lancers) to
Lance Dafadar Alla Dad Khan (19th Lancers, France)*

Central Jail
Madras   19th September 1916

I do not experience any trials. I am merely kept in custody.[1] They are not very strict.
The final result of our imprisonment will only be known when the war is finished.
Write to me about your welfare. I can write only under great difficulties. The order
is that I am to write only once in three months. After all, the sentence is not a heavy
one. What are three years? And of these, seven months are passed already and [only]
two years and five months remain. Do not be anxious. All is well with me, but it
is a matter of great regret that I am unable to learn how things are at home. What
is the reason? Be so kind as to write home, and tell the people there to let me know
in what kind of state they are. Which country are you serving in now? If you are
not allowed to name the country, inform me according to the following numbers:
– (1) France, (2) Mesopotamia, (3) Suez, (4) Persia, (5) Africa, (6) Somaliland,
(7) East Africa, (8) China. Is your regiment in comfort, or is it experiencing trials?
[Letter passed]

1.   Because of his involvement in the February mutiny of the regiment. See Nos. 259, 276,
     313 and 315.

408

Farrier Major Khan to Wali Mahomed Khan
(Punjab Muslim, 18th Lancers, France)

Jhelum   [Urdu]
Punjab   19th September 1916

I have heard all about your amours with the French women and how the officers forbid it. I can quite imagine how, if you know enough of the language, you have a great time and try to make yourself out a trustworthy person. I have no doubt you are always meeting the French people. It is a great pity that you never write any real account of the war in France. No doubt your officers read the letters. But cannot you devise any way of dodging them? I will tell you what to do. When you write a letter, on one page write in invisible ink made out of lemon juice and I will read everything. If you cannot get this, take some lime which has not been wetted and grind it up and mix it with water and write and I shall be able to read it all. Mind you, take my advice and write all about the fights with the Germans. With God's help the Germans will be crushed and our King victorious. I make long prayers every day for this. You must make an effort to see Paris and London too. [Letter passed]

409

Risaldar-Major Hira Singh (Dogra, 38) to Kuar Bhagwant Singh
(Nandpur, Kangra District, Punjab)

19th Lancers   [Urdu]
France   22nd September 1916

I understand from your letter that you are about to enlist in the 11th Lancers, with a view to learning the work. In my opinion you have done well, as Ressaidar Ram Singh [34] of the 11th Lancers is my great friend. I have written to him about you and he doubtless will assist you. Although at the present time there is a surplus of Dogra officers in the 11th Lancers, and there is thus no prospect of your early advancement, you should not let that fact disturb you. You should do your work well and earn the approbation of your British officers.

You should never consider any part of the work as being beneath the dignity of a man of birth, such as you are. You should regard yourself as nothing more than a common soldier, and should cheerfully support all the difficulties of your position. In this way only can you hope to become efficient. As a rule, the sons of well-born people are unable to advance themselves in the ranks of the Army, because of their easy and comfortable upbringing, and thus they gain discredit. You should become expert in all the duties of a common soldier and confine yourself to the society of respectable men.

You should also be careful not to incur the displeasure of any of the sirdars. If you do this, I will effect your transfer as soon as I return. You should be very particular to let the sirdars know that you do not intend to remain permanently in the 11th Lancers and that you have joined merely to learn the work, otherwise someone or other of them will certainly seek to discredit or suppress you as they have no friendly feeling for outsiders. [Letter passed]

410

Jemadar Khwaja Muhammed Khan (Pathan, 41) to
Dost Mahomed Khan (Peshawar District, NWFP)

19th Lancers   [Urdu]
France   24th September 1916

You write a second time about my returning home. Well, I have already told you in a previous letter that nothing is settled about our return. But, be of good cheer, for when the Sirkar gets a suitable opportunity, assuredly some arrangement will be made. The Sirkar is not unmindful of the fact that the sepoys have been separated from their families for a long time, and the Sirkar always does everything that is reasonable to mitigate the hardships of the sepoys' lot. Moreover, the Sirkar now has an abundance of troops and its seapower is greater than that of all the other Kings, and, for this reason, there is no difficulty in the transfer of troops. [Letter passed]

411

Pahlwan Khan (Punjabi Muslim) to
Mauladad Khan (15th Lancers Depot, India)

18th Lancers   [Urdu]
France   25th September 1916

There is great sport going on. The players have assembled in great crowds and the number of the tent peggers has increased threefold and we are trying hard to get one real good burst of tent pegging. If we succeed in getting this opportunity

there ought to be some really fine spearing and we shall soon see each other again.[1]
[Letter passed]

1.   The last phrase suggests that he is trying to disguise his meaning. 'Sport' probably refers to fighting, and 'tent pegging' to the mounted charge that he hopes will bring victory, and hence an honourable return to India.

412

Hafiz Faizullah Khan to Risaldar Mahomed Sadik Khan
(Baluchi, 36th Jacob's Horse, France, 33)

Dehra Ismail Khan   [Urdu]
[NWFP]   26th September 1916

Nowadays on account of the European war, foodstuffs, cloth, gold, silver, meat, butter, vegetables – in fact, all the articles required by man – have become very expensive. Things which cost four annas a *seer* before the war, now cost eight annas a *seer*.

413

Rama Nund (Jat) to Balmokano (Havelian, Hazara District, NWFP)

29th Lancers   [Urdu]
France   3rd October 1916

Do not go anywhere till I return, and certainly do not enlist in the cavalry. If you do all our home affairs will be disarranged and the neighbours will jeer and scoff. If it pleases God, I shall be with you this winter, for that regarding which you wrote is quite true and I shall be with you again in two or three months. Look for something else to do, and do not even mention the word 'cavalry'. If you disregard this advice of mine, I shall never write to you again, and on my return I shall not speak to you. [Letter passed]

414

Dafadar Fazl Khan (Punjabi Muslim) to Pir Sadiq Ali (Sialkot District, Punjab)

19th Lancers   [Urdu]
France   4th October 1916

I want you to be good enough to advise me on a point. I am in France and the holy place of Mecca is between 130 and 180 degrees from here, and we look in that direction when we pray. But when we bury a man, in which direction should be put his head? Should we attend only to the direction of the North Pole, or should we put the head on the right side of the worshipper as he stands with his face to the Ka'aba? [Letter passed]

415

Risaldar Kushal Khan [Punjabi Muslim or Pathan, 40] to Manshah Khan (Peshawar District, NWFP)

19th Lancers   [Urdu]
France   4th October 1916

[We] got the order to go on patrol duty beyond a village which the infantry had taken, and to occupy an emminence there. But when we got into the village itself, we found heaps of the enemy, and bombs and machine guns were very active. In fact, our infantry had not taken the village but were all round it. Our Squadron dashed into the village with great bravery and surrounded a number of Germans, but they managed to break away and get into a trench on the corner of the village. We dismounted and, holding our horses, took up a position in the middle of the village. There were few casualties owing to God's mercy. We held that village for five hours, and then the infantry came up and relieved us.[1] I hope you will read in the *Fauji Akhbar* all about our attack and the way we held the village. [Letter passed]

1. He is probably refering to an action on the afternoon of 26th September, when a squadron of the 19th Lancers left Mametz to take the village of Guedecourt, on the Ancre beyond Flers.

416

*Dafadar Fazl Khan (Punjabi Muslim) to
Zilladar Ghulam Hasain (Sargodha, Shahpur District, Punjab)*

18th Lancers   [Urdu]
France   4th October 1916

When I got your letter there was a red carpet spread before my eyes.[1] That will be the day of rejoicing when we meet again. The war increases in violence day by day. You must have read in the *Fauji Akhbar* that the King recently visited the trenches taken from the Germans. We have just taken a place that the Germans evidently hoped to hold till the end of the war. It is perfectly clear that the battle is going in

our favour, and day by day our hopes of victory increase. The enemy has no longer
any hope of getting back the trenches he loses. The artillery fire of our French friends
is worthy of praise. It is such a fire that the German troops are driven out of their
trenches and go mad. They do not know whether they are in the trenches or out of
them. Just realise this, my friend, that until we reach Berlin there is no returning
to India for us. You will soon hear by telegraph or wireless that the Indian cavalry
have charged the enemy and what a calamity has befallen the latter! We should be
ashamed to go back till after we have won the victory. [Letter passed]

1. 'There were rows of corpses in front of me'.

417

*Ressaidar Kala Singh (33) to Risaldar Shibdeo Singh
(Remount Depot, 22nd Cavalry, France, 32)*

16th Cavalry
Loralai   [Urdu]
Baluchistan Agency   6th October 1916

As you remark in your letter, Rouen cannot compare with Marseilles. I hope you
will return to Marseilles. It is a portion of heaven. How beautiful are the hills about.
La Valentine is a lovely and clean camp ... While I was with D Force [in Mesopotamia]
I saw plenty of fighting; in fact I was present in all the fighting. At the commencement
of operations the cavalry frequently got good opportunities, and my regiment did
excellent work. Alas that we should have returned to India! Goodness knows for
how long we shall remain absent from the war. I cannot describe to you how great
fascination there is in fighting at the front. One experiences a feeling of exhilaration.
He who has never been present in an action at the front has seen very little indeed
– in fact he has seen nothing. Do you think it would be possible for me to join you
in France?

418

Hazara Singh (Sikh) to Dogar Singh (Amritsar District, Punjab)

Mhow Cavalry Brigade   [Urdu]
France   10th October 1916

You are a wise man and you should understand that it is very difficult for anyone
to go to India from here on leave. The sea voyage takes one month. So what is the

good of pressing me to come? I am not my own master. I have to obey orders, whereas you write as if it were open to me to go or to remain at my pleasure. If God will give victory to our King then we will all return to India. Pray therefore that the enemy may soon be overthrown. Otherwise the thing [returning to India] is practically impossible. [Letter passed]

419

Hira Singh (Dogra) to Pensioned Risaldar Albal Singh
(19th Lancers, Hoshiarpur, Punjab)

19th Lancers   [Urdu]
France   11th October 1916

I have done what I can for you, but you know that once an officer has given a decision he does his best to maintain it. All that was possible in your interest was done from here, but the Depot Commander (why I don't know) sticks obstinately to his decision. I am afraid he will make thousands of efforts to avoid his judgement being upset. It is a great pity that you were not aware of what was going on, and let the golden opportunity pass by. What can we do at such a distance? That is the reason why your adversary was successful and you were left out in the cold. You must put your trust in God and, when you get the chance, take your revenge. The Dogra troop is in God's hands. I am powerless. Still, you must think of your caste and do everything to get Dogra recruits. It is the duty of every Rajput to sacrifice his life for his caste.[1] [Letter passed]

1. See Nos. 44, 111, 234 and 256.

420

Dafadar Tara Singh (Sikh) to Sirdar Sikander Singh
(Gujranwala District, Punjab)

6th Cavalry   [Urdu]
France   12th October 1916

Fateh Singh meant to say in his letter that he intended to get the senior men set aside and promotion to dafadarships given to junior men who are his relatives. He has succeeded in doing this. In this war, no one thinks of looking at good work. Promotion depends on recommendation only. If you can do anything now, do it – for it is no use waiting till the end of the war. What, are you a person of no influence in the District? There is no one in the District equal to you. Why do you not send letters to the officers? I must be careful what I say for this letter may fall into an enemy's hand. We hoped that the regiments would be relieved, but this hope has now vanished and we shall have to wait another year. No leave is given. The useless ones are sent back to India and they get leave from there. [Letter passed]

421

Harman Singh to Jemadar Hazura Singh
(Sikh, 39th attached 38th CIH, France)

Dera Ismail Khan [Urdu]
[NWFP] 13th October 1916

I am very sorry to report that your young son is not working satisfactorily. He is very lazy and is getting himself a very bad name. I can't help thinking he is working to get himself dismissed. Service in the Army is like the display of a courtesan's charms. If you do not show yourself worth having, how do you expect that your officers will take any notice of you? It was his duty to make himself useful during the past eighteen months, but he has succeeded in proving the opposite.

422

Jemadar Abu Khan (Pathan, 34) to Kot Dafadar Zori Gul Khan (36th Jacob's
Horse, Ambala, Punjab)

36th Jacob's Horse [Urdu]
France 13th October 1916

You write and say that the recruitment of Afridis has been discontinued, whereas Bahadur Ali Khan writes and says that recruitment is open. Perhaps you are unable to obtain recruits. Without fail enlist Afridis. Don't sit unconcerned. [Letter passed]

423

Asim Ullah (Hindustani Muslim) to
Hassan Khan (Raipur, Farrukhabad District, UP)

19th Lancers [Urdu]
France 16th October 1916

May God keep your eyes from beholding the state of things here. There are heaps and heaps of dead bodies, the sight of which upsets me. The stench is so overwhelming that one can, with difficulty, endure it for ten or fifteen minutes. Fine, stalwart young men are stricken down into the dust, and others are struggling in the combat like fish pulled out of the water and thrown down on the sand, with their handsome faces dimmed by the grime of war. Nevertheless, the warriors, undismayed, continue their onward course, despite the hail of shot and shell, and the numbers that fall on the way wounded or killed. God does not show any pity for them in their awful trial. In fact, the state of affairs is such that, on beholding it, one's power to describe it ebbs away. The fact, however, has been proved that unless one's fate comes, one cannot die. Such a one may march right through shot and shell and even a hair of his head is not disarranged.

In a former letter I wrote and said that my regiment would probably return to India this year, and at that time the rumour was very strong. Now, however, it has weakened considerably, and although there is just a chance left, I have little hope. [Letter passed]

424

Bishan Singh (Sikh) to Ranjit Singh (Ludhiana District, Punjab)

6th Cavalry   [Urdu?]
[France?]   18th October 1916

I understand that some arrangement is being made here about leave. If I can possibly manage it, I will come on leave, and arrange for Kartar Kor to attend school, and you must wait till then. If I fail to get leave, then I will write to you further about the matter. If I get an opportunity, I will also go to England on leave for a few days. Such an opportunity generally happens during the winter. I have written to Narangwal and told him not to bore holes in the nose and ears of any of the girls.[1] About the question of my marriage do not bother. I have stopped the proposals everywhere, because this war is a long one. If I do marry it will be according to my own choice or to your advice. It would not be surprising if I contracted a marriage here. (This I have written as a joke and therefore I strike it out.) [Letter passed]

1. To take jewellery, as a sign of marriage.

425

Dafadar Ramji Lal (Jat) to Mola Mistri (Rohtak District, Punjab)

6th Cavalry   [Hindi]
France   27th October 1916

I am told that anyone who has put in eighteen years' service may go on pension. I have served the full time and my pension is due, but I am hoping for some advancement. If my hope is realized I will remain – otherwise I will return on pension. What do you say? Shall I return or stay? You know well that here we cannot count on the certainty of life for a single day, but at the same time one saves money. There are only two sides to the question: either one saves money and risks one's life, or one preserves one's life and misses the profit. [Letter passed]

426

Karbar Singh (Sikh) to Sirdar Sahib Singh (Nabha State?, Punjab)

18th Lancers [Urdu]
France 28th October 1916

You are right in supposing that the Germans are being trampled under foot. The day is at hand when the tyrant will receive the reward of his villainies, and the ideas he had of world domination will be scattered far and wide, and his dreams of playing the part of Napoleon will be dissipated. The time is near when the echos of victory of dear India will be heard and we, wearing the insignia and medals which are the reward of bravery, will be restored to the bosom of our beloved mother India. I am very proud to think that I have been accorded the privilege of sharing in this great war. [Letter passed]

427

Mohamad Alam to Dafadar Mahomed Din Khan
(Punjabi Muslim, 18th Lancers, France)

[Jhelum District?] [Urdu]
India 29th October 1916

Nowadays the stars of army officers are so in the ascendant that those of other departments have never even dreamt of such distinction. Government looks after the officers day and night. Therefore I want you to write a strong letter of recommendation which I may present somewhere. If you get the chance, put in a word for a grant of land and ask the Deputy Commissioner of Jhelum [District].

428

Sattar Khan (Rajput Muslim) to Rusan Patwani
(Goona Cantonment, Central India)

38th CIH   [Urdu]
France   3rd November 1916

I will petition the Depot Commanding Officer to send you the money, as soon as I
hear how much you require. If I die, all my money will be paid to my children. You
should understand very clearly that it is next to impossible for the British Raj to
pass away. If I return alive, I will withdraw all my money and retire from the service.

429

To Lance Dafadar Nasab Ali Khan (Pathan, 9th Hodson's Horse, France)
from his wife

Hazara   [Urdu]
[NWFP]   3rd November 1916

If you want to keep your *izzat* then come back here at once; but what you are after
is wealth. Have you got anyone except God who can run your house? Then why
do you not return? Your mother has gone out of her mind, and does not sleep at
home, so I am alone all night. The winter and dark nights are ahead and how can
I, a lone woman, stay by myself? If you agree, I will go to Darwaja. If you do not
answer at once I will go to [illegible] and report the affair to the Officer Commanding
at the Depot, and you will be sent back with a flea in your ear. I go round begging
the neighbours for water and wood, yet you never think of all this. You write that
you have been made Lance Dafadar. I don't care a rap whether you are made a
dafadar. If you were a man you would understand, but you are no man.

430

Dafadar Jan Mahomed (Baluchi) to Mahomed Abdullah Khan
(Dehra Ismail Khan, NWFP, India)

36th Jacob's Horse   [Urdu]
France   5th November 1916

The merciful God has delivered Risaldar Sadik Muhammad Khan [33] from the
hands of his enemy and has prolonged the span of his life and blackened the face

of the enemy. These are the facts. About noon on the 31st October, Karim Haidar Shah (Mahomed Shah's youngest son) fired two shots at the Risaldar Sahib.[1] The Pure Cherisher, however, brought both shots to naught. The distance between Karim Haidar Shah and the Risaldar Sahib was about three yards. The first shot passed through the tip of the Risaldar Sahib's waterproof turban cover. The bullet passed within an inch of the Risaldar's eyes and forehead. The Risaldar said to him 'boy, through the grace of God I have escaped death by your hands', and, advancing towards him, knocked up his rifle as he was about to fire the second shot. The bullet passed over the Risaldar's shoulder – thus God disgraced the enemy! – and the Risaldar Sahib bravely grasped the rifle and wrenched it out of the enemy's hands and captured him. At the same moment, all the English Sahibs came to the spot (the General, the Colonel, the Adjutant and all the Sahibs, big and little) and congratulated the Risaldar Sahib, and said that God had indeed been gracious to him. The enemy was placed in [the] charge of a guard, and sent to the military prison. I and Abdul Samad [?] Khan were close to the Risaldar Sahib when this happened. Be not alarmed. God did not allow the bullet to come within an inch of the Risaldar Sahib's head.

1. For other letters about this incident, see Nos. 460 and 464.

431

Kartan Singh (Sikh) to Sirdar Ram Rakha Singh (Jullundur District, Punjab)

6th Cavalry   [Urdu]
France   6th November 1916

You say in your letter that the postmaster of Adampur had taken out some opium. What was the necessity of telling him? You should not have said a word on the subject to him, and should not have mentioned it in your letter. When you send opium you should not mention it, but should say you are sending a preparation for the beard and should send it off secretly. You have made a great mistake. I get everything you send.[1]

1. The censor commented, 'this advice about the dispatch of opium has been deleted from the letter'.

432

Abdul Majid Khan (Punjabi Muslim) to
Haji Allah Dao Khan (Nabha State, Punjab)

6th Cavalry   [Urdu]
France   7th November 1916

I received your letter after an interval of a month and a half. I read it with great joy, and pressed it to my eyes and forehead, because it announced that my dear father was well. In regard to the message he sends to me to return and let him see my face once again, even though I return penniless and beggared, it caused me great grief and many tears. Day and night, standing and sitting, my prayer to God is that my eyes may rest once more on my dear father. Nothing is impossible with God, therefore have patience and petition him.

433

Kot Dafadar Talib Mohamed Khan (Punjabi Muslim) to
Reservist Fazal Karim Khan (1st Lancers, Risalpur, Peshawar District, NWFP)

34th Poona Horse   [Urdu]
France [?]   9th November 1916

I am very glad to hear that you have arrived safely in your native country. May God grant us all to get there soon! I expect you have already gone on leave. [I wish you could be good enough to send me something which will make the doctors declare me unfit for service, and at the same time will not be dangerous to life.[1]]

1. The Boulogne censor deleted the passage in brackets, which had been passed by the regimental censor (who was probably affixing his stamp of approval to letters which he had not read).

434

Ali Haidar to Risaldar [Jemadar?] Dost Mahomed Khan
(Punjabi Muslim, 38th CIH, France, 35)

Jhelum   [Urdu]
[Punjab]   9th November 1916

You must always be pulling Shah Parsad's ear and tell [illegible] not to neglect a scrap of his work. Letters are often examined on the way to you and opened, in order that nothing improper may be written. Often the stamps bear the legend 'Opened by Censor'. This arrangement is a good one in some respects, but, although our lives and property are at the disposal of Government, yet they cannot trust us! Well, in any case, our duty is to serve Government faithfully whatever they may think of us.

435

Kehar Singh (Sikh) to Sirdar Sahil Singh (Amritsar District, Punjab)

19th Lancers	[Urdu]
France	9th November 1916

The orders about leave have come and it is open now, but the conditions are very hard.[1] Necessities at home and personal health are two things which are chiefly taken into account. The men who had urgent private affairs at home, or who are soft and useless owing to ill health, have been sent off for three months. They will spend three months in the company of their dear ones, and therefore my prayer is that you will write such a letter that I can produce before my Sahib and get leave in this way. I am very down on my luck. The first thing to do is to get the Deputy Commissioner [of Amritsar District?] to send a letter to my Officer Commanding, or, if you cannot do that, get the witness of at least four *lumberdars* and send the letter on to the Colonel. You must also write me an urgent demand to return at once.

1. Leave was opened by an order of 8th November. See Nos. 439, 443 and 446.

436

Zabru Shah (Hindustani Muslim) to
Jemadar Shirin Khan (Remount Depot, Rouen)

6th Cavalry	[Urdu]
France	11th November 1916

After thousands of troubles and toils I have escaped from the jail of the 38th Central India Horse. I had hoped to pass the remaining days of my stay with comfort, but crooked fate has decreed that we Indians should still suffer. The Muslims of the Squadron who are at headquarters gave a feast to celebrate the *Fatiha*[1] of the Imam Mahomed Hasain. When I joined the feast, there was an extraordinary spectacle which I should like to have photographed. It was an astounding *Fatiha*. It was held in a coffee shop, and there was a big table in the middle covered with vases of flowers. Lamps and candles were burning. There were French pictures on the walls, and chairs, and little tables all round the room, and everyone was wearing his boots. There was the *Maulud-i-Nabi*[2] on the table. The first thing was the prayer *Bismallah* and then everyone sang. There was a crowd of French women and children at the doors looking in, and the scene lasted for an hour and a half, and then we all took tea. During the tea there was a loud conversation going on, such irregularities and unlawful practices that are beyond belief. From first to last there was not a word to remind one of the solemn Karbala and not a word of the story of the Prophet and the holy Imam. If any part of the *Maulud-i-Nabi* was read, it was that part which cannot be substantiated.

1. Literally 'The Opener', or first *sura* of the Qu'ran: 'In the name of God, the Merciful, the Compassionate ....'
2. History of the Prophet.

437

Clerk Mohamed Abdul Karim to Atta Mahomed Khan
(Punjabi Muslim, 34th Poona Horse, France)

Government High School
Shahpur District   [Urdu]
Punjab   11th November 1916

Do your work cheerfully and carefully. Doubtless you feel the separation, but it is a well-known saying that a soldier and his horse have no country. Wherever their master takes them, that place is their country for the time being. Do not be overanxious about your home and keep on doing your work well. God, the most Merciful, will bring you back with victory, and will so steep your five fingers in melted butter[1] that avaricious ones will burn and die of envy.

1. 'Give you the full reward of your labours'.

438

Mozafar Ahmed Khan (Pathan) to Ashuraf Khan (Hazara District, NWFP)

9th Hodson's Horse   [Urdu]
France   13th November 1916

All the pleasure I had in life was bound up with Ali Akbar. Be patient. This calamity has fallen not only on us but on the whole world. Fine young men, dearly beloved of their parents, of astonishing beauty, I have seen so often naked on the field of battle. Thank God our dear brother got a proper burial. There was a coffin, and a proper grave, and a tombstone which will be a memorial to him in the world. Whoever sees it will say 'that is the kind of tomb they build in this great war for the gallant dead'.

439

Jemadar Shamsher Ali Khan (Punjabi Muslim, 33) to Pensioned Risaldar-Major Hazin Ali Khan (Farrukhabad District, UP)

34th Poona Horse [Urdu]
France 13th November 1916

Now the rain and the cold are daily on the increase. The duration of the war is being extended in an appalling manner and there is no end in sight. The hearts of the people have become depressed owing to the indefinite state of affairs. The war, coupled with the long distance from home, the separation for years, and the unsuitable climate – cold, wind and rain – have tired everyone out, and crushed them.

A few days ago, an order was issued to the effect that the British Government had, as a favour to the Indian troops in France, opened leave for them to India.[1] Five per cent of those who have put in two years' service in France are to be granted leave for three months, and on their return another five per cent will be granted leave, and so on. Thus every man granted leave will spend about a month at home. On this calculation, if thirty men from each regiment are granted leave at intervals of three months, 120 men per regiment will have leave per annum. Thus very few men will reap the benefit of the orders, since there are very many men who have been here since the commencement of the war. It is probable that the Government, when they come to realize the effect of their order, will increase the percentage. Anyhow, the orders as they stand must be accepted as a great concession. It is a matter of astonishment that the 3rd Skinner's Horse and 30th Lancers have reached India, while the 20th Deccan Horse and 34th Poona Horse are still in France, although the latter were the first units to enter the war!

1. See Nos. 435, 443 and 446 for other references to the opening of leave.

440

*Kahn Singh to Risaldar Hazura Singh (Sikh, 7th Lancers,
attached 20th Deccan Horse, France, 41)*

7th Hariana Lancers
Bolarum   [Gurmukhi]
Deccan   14th November 1916

Our regiment reached Bolarum on the 2nd November, and on the 7th all the men from the field were given leave. The recruitment of Sikhs for No. 5 Troop has been stopped. They have filled up half a troop with Jats. The sixth Troop was filled up with Sikhs by Risaldar Bishan Singh [46] with much trouble. At the commencement of the war he enlisted 79 men for this purpose. The Jats, taking counsel with Kalandar Khan, Risaldar-Major, decided to make up another troops of Jats. Carrying Major [G.F.] Grettan Sahib with them, they obliged Bishan Singh to go on pension. Now there is great difficulty about recruitment. The *izzat* of Sikhs in the regiment is not equal to that even of a *syce*. Major [G.P.] Carnegy Sahib Bahadur, becoming angry, has gone to make recruits. All this misfortune is due to dissension amongst the sirdars.[1]

1. One of the rare letters in which British officers are mentioned by name. As usual, they are named only because their actions have created a problem.

441

Bhagirath (Jat) to Pensioner Habib Khan (Rohtak District, Punjab)

2nd Lancers   [Urdu]
France   14th November 1916

My brother, I have come to the conclusion that we are Government donkeys who always get a full load. I only want life and health, and that is all I think of. If God grants these I am happy; but if not, well ... The only news is that leave is open. Only those are going who have done two years. I am not in the running at all, as I have only been out a year and a half. I have not the slightest hope of returning before the end of the war. If God takes the case up, that is another matter.

442

Dafadar Chanda Singh (Sikh) to Arur [?] Singh (Lahore District, Punjab)

38th CIH   [Urdu]
France   15th November 1916

You say that you are always worried about me. I am so comfortable here that I can hardly express my feelings. These good people take more care of us than ever our parents did. Parents sometimes get angry with their children and stop their dinner. Not so with these parents. They give us milk to drink every evening, dry our clothes and continually ask after our health. I cannot sufficiently praise their affection, and I must say that no mother or wife or brother or sister has ever shown us such kindness. There is no anxiety and no discomfort; only one thing is lacking – your presence.

443

Indar Singh (Sikh) to Masa Singh (Amritsar District, Punjab)

38th CIH   [Urdu]
France [?]   15th November 1916

An order has been issued as follows, dated 8th November:– 'Some of the Indian cavalry will be allowed on leave. Six men will be allowed to go per squadron [twenty-four per regiment] and these men are to be selected at once, and they get forty-eight hours' notice to leave. In selecting them the following considerations are to be kept in mind:–

(i)   length of service
(ii)   good character
(iii)   men who came from India with the Expeditionary Force
(iv)   special reasons for their going
(v)   Indian officers who are not urgently required in France.'

This regimental order was read out on parade.

444

Jemadar Hayat Bakhsh Khan to Jemadar Shaikh Mohi-ud-din
(Deccani Muslim, 20th Deccan Horse, France, 47)

20th Deccan Horse
Neemuch   [Urdu]
Central India   18th November 1916

Jemadar Nabiyar Khan has gone to Berar. He writes to say that all the people there
are stricken with terror. The reason is that there are recruiting parties from several
regiments here, who at first dealt very harshly with the people and molested them.[1]
This treatment quite upset the people, and they object to becoming recruits.
Moreover, the present is harvest time and the majority of men are engaged in cutting
the crops. Please God, in fifteen or twenty days we shall certainly begin to get recruits,
as 'lectures' are being given, and some few men are joining up.

1. Enlistment in the Indian Army was nominally voluntary; but wartime demand for
    recruits was so heavy that, from the autumn of 1916, various forms of coercion were
    also employed. For further discussion of this point see Omissi, *The Sepoy and the Raj*,
    pp. 123–5; Brief, 'The Punjab and Recruitment to the Indian Army', especially pp. 125–80.

445

Bhagirathi (Rajput) to Jhandu Singh (39th CIH, Goona, Central India)

39th CIH (attached 38th CIH)   [Hindi]
France   20th November 1916

I will tell you stories of the leave people. Listen to me attentively, and do not laugh.
The leave men are ready, but when they go we do not yet know. What can I do,
for I am not in the running for leave at all, and I am afraid you will be sore about
this. Better than coming on leave is for me to write [to] you regularly every week.
We are very comfortable apart from the cold, which is excessive and keeps saying
'I will not leave you now'. My dear fellow, my liver is split when I think of this
cold, and my life is drying up. The cold says 'how are you going to avoid me?'
and I reply 'by putting on four blankets and a coat'. Even then the cold is ever
there. This is how we pass the time – our lives imprisoned in this far country. You
say 'when are you coming back?', and my reply is 'when God shall deliver me
from this country'. I see no hope of it at present. Do not be anxious. I will return
one day, if I live.

446

Sher Ali (Punjabi Muslim) to Raja Shajiat Ali Khan (Jhelum District, Punjab)

18th Lancers [Urdu]
France 21st November 1916

I have just come back from digging in the trenches. We are very comfortable. God save the King! Leave is open and twenty-five men will go from each regiment.[1] In other regiments lots have been drawn and the fortunate men in whose fate it is written that they will see India again will go; but in our squadron only those men have been recommended for leave who are the favourites and associates of the Indian officers.

1. See Nos. 435 and 443.

447

Mahomed Wazir (Pathan) to Mahomed Anwar Khan
(Hangu, Kohat District, NWFP)

36th Jacob's Horse [Urdu]
France 25th November 1916

We had a great attack on 15th September, and won a great victory.[1] Several thousand prisoners were made and every day thousands more are taken. There are hundreds of thousands of men on the battle front. Our guns, machine guns and troops increase in numbers day by day, and our aeroplanes are countless. Every one is working his best. The Germans are becoming enfeebled day by day, and we are strengthening.[2] There is nothing like seeing with one's own eyes.

1. See No. 401.
2. Several letters from this period express the (misplaced) hope that the Germans would soon be defeated.

448

Dafadar Ranji Lal (Jat) to Prem [illegible] (Rohtak District, Punjab)

20th Deccan Horse [Urdu]
France 26th November 1916

Grandfather dear, I understand these things perfectly well, though they are still hidden from my revered elders. I know well that a woman in our country is of no more value than a pair of shoes and this is the reason why the people of India are low in the scale. You educated Ramjas, and got him a situation, but you never thought of educating any of the girls. You said to yourself 'Ramjas will be able to help me in my old age, but the girls will get married and leave the house and will not be able to do anything for me.' I should like to write to my wife, but she would have to get the letters read by somebody else and all the home secrets would come out. When I look at Europe, I bewail the lot of India. In Europe everyone – man and woman, boy and girl – is educated. The men are at the war and the women are doing the work. They write to their husbands and get their answers. You ought to educate your girls as well as your boys and our posterity will be the better for it.[1]

1.   These sentiments became widely shared by the troops. See Nos. 572 and 654.

449

Mahomed Zabu Shah (Hindustani Muslim) to Abdul Salaam Shah (Farrukhabad District, UP)

6th Cavalry	[Urdu]
France	28th November 1916

We are spending our days most comfortably here. We have every convenience for living and the best of food. In fact, we are better off than we were at Rawalpindi. I do not suppose you will believe this, however strongly I assure you that it is true. I have dropped the Qu'ran two or three times accidentally and the hair of my head stood on end in fright. Pray for me that God may forgive my sin! The old people in the house are full of kindness. They wash my clothes and take even better care of me than you when I am on leave. One day they cooked a hare for supper, and they were much excited when I would not eat it. They asked the reason and I told them. The next day I found a fowl hung up with its throat cut and they said 'now you will have to eat this fowl'.[1]

1.   He would not eat the hare because it was not *halal*, and hence not suitable for Muslims. Having heard his explanation, his hosts killed the fowl in the appropriate way.

450

Hazur Singh (Sikh) to his mother (Ludhiana District, Punjab)

6th Cavalry	[Urdu]
France	30th November 1916

The regiment is not returning at all, and what Risaldar Harain Singh said about the matter is entirely false. Leave will probably be given to a very few men – those who have urgent affairs at home. I am not likely to get leave, nor do I wish to go (even if I could succeed in obtaining permission) till the war is finished. Because, if I were to go on leave, it would be very hard to return. When I used to go on leave before, I used to be very disinclined to return to the cantonment. How much more disinclined then would I be to return to the war! When I return, I will tell you all about the war. It is impossible to write about it. The war will not be finished for a very long time. It will certainly not be finished before 1918. My regiment will certainly not return. The Guru Maharaj has kept me alive for two and a half years; is it likely then that he will not keep me alive for another two years? I have pledged myself not to return [on leave or ill] until I return with the entire regiment.

451

Fateh Mohamed (Punjabi Muslim) to Dafadar Jan Mohamed Khan (Rohtak District, Punjab)

19th Cavalry   [Urdu]
France   3rd December 1916

The cold for the last five or six days has been more intense than we have experienced during the two former winters. If one puts water into a vessel it is frozen in ten minutes. At the same time, there is a strong wind. If France had not been such a sympathetic country, existence under such conditions would have been impossible. Through the kindness of these people [the French] we pay no regard to the cold. They themselves refrain from sitting near the fire-place and insist on our sitting there. Moreover, instead of water they give us *petit cidre*, which is the juice of apples, to drink. Personally, except in the trenches, I have never drunk water. In short, however much one praises these people, one's praise falls short of the mark. Apart from the thanks due by us to our Government, it is incumbent on us to praise these people.

452

Ressaidar [Jemadar?] Jawand Singh (Sikh, 37) to Sirdar Dur Singh (Amritsar District, Punjab)

38th CIH   [Urdu]
France   3rd December 1916

What you say about there being no letter-writer handy is no doubt correct. It is a well-known saying that 'the water-carrier is always thirsty and the cobbler, ill-shod'.

The point is that the school is not more than ten paces distant from you, and yet you say you cannot find anyone to write a letter!

453

Hussein Shah (Punjabi Muslim) to Veterinary Inspector Mahomed Abdullah (Quetta, Baluchistan Agency)

Indian General Hospital   [Urdu]
Rouen   5th December 1916

There is no indication as to when we shall return. It would be very difficult to return unless victory is secured. God give us victory, so that I may be free and see my dear ones and friends again. Two and a half years is sufficient separation and, moreover, the field service is such that it does not contain a single day's leave, and is otherwise of so hard a nature as to be beyond any previous experience. My heart yearns to unburden itself, but:

> Oh *bulbul*, hide your voice in your throat.
> Kings have very sensitive temperaments,
> And cannot endure words![1]

If you can send me a report of the 'League and Congress' in Urdu, I shall be obliged.[2]

1. Probably an oblique reference to the censorship. A *bulbul* is an Indian songthrush. The attractive song of the Persian *bulbul*, a nightingale-like bird, is often mentioned by poets in that language.
2. This is one of the very few references to the major Indian nationalist parties, who had just negotiated a pact at Lucknow. It is significant that he is writing to a veterinary inspector. Presumably both men were rather better educated, and politically informed, than the Indian rank-and-file. For other references to the Muslim League see Nos. 346 and 619.

454

Nadar Khan (Punjabi Muslim) to
Raja Zaman Ali Khan (Khanpur, Hazara District, NWFP)

19th Lancers   [Urdu]
France   10th December 1916

This is no ordinary war. It is a world-wide war. We have no certainty of life, and do not look beyond today or tomorrow. In this infidel country I cannot secure any [religious] benefit for myself.[1] Whatever prayers I say, night and morning, I consecrate the advantage gained thereby to my deceased parents and ancestors.

My string of [prayer] beads dropped one night and was lost in the mud of the trenches, and I am much inconvenienced thereby. The cold is intense; but the climate of this country is so salubrious that I have not had a single day's illness since I came here. Thanks to God, as health is itself a priceless treasure.

1. Meaning he cannot conform to religious rules, because of contact with unbelievers in Islam.

455

Lance Dafadar Teja Singh (Sikh) to
Sirdar Balwant Singh (Gujranwala District, Punjab, India)

9th Hodson's Horse   [Urdu]
France   12th December 1916

Veterinary Assistant Chattar Singh was deprived of his Kot Dafadar's rank, because he wrote to a Frenchman and posted the letter in the French post office. He went away ill for a time, and when he returned he wrote another letter in the same way and was caught. The result is that he has lost his dafadar's rank also.[1]

1. For several months, Chattar Singh received one or two letters a day from Frenchwomen. The Boulogne censor never saw any of his replies, so concluded (probably rightly) that Chattar Singh was evading the censorship by sending his own letters through the French civilian postal service. This was against regulations, hence his reduction to the ranks.

456

Sowar Ajab Gul (Pathan) to Bhai Ahmad Bul (Peshawar District, NWFP)

38th CIH   [Urdu]
France   22nd December 1916

I have had a dream and must tell you about [it]. My father appeared in the shape of a dried up insect, and [my] brother [illegible] Gul drove him away, and he fell on the ground. My mother said 'you tyrant, that was your father and you have killed him'. When I awoke, I thought over the dream and came to the conclusion that it had an evil meaning. I then prayed that God would give me a glimpse of my father; and I went to sleep again, and had another dream, and saw my father washing his teeth, seated on a *charpoy*. I then woke up and prayed to God that, if he were dead, I might see him as he was, and then fell asleep and saw my father in his grave in our own house. Then his head and his feet appeared, and then he came out of his tomb. I was delighted, and said 'father, you are all right?' He replied 'no I am not'. Then I saw a mullah appear, and my father and he began to read the Qu'ran together. Then I put my father back in his tomb, and directly afterwards the grave was illuminated and I woke up. I am disturbed in mind. What does it all mean? Write and let me know at once.

457

Wali Mahomed Khan (Punjabi Muslim) to
Dafadar Nawaz Khan (18th Lancers, Marseilles)

18th Lancers   [Urdu]
France   25th December 1916

The only news I have to give you is that, until further notice, all leave to India is stopped. They say that the Germans are bent on peace, and are always asking for it nowadays.

458

Kot Dafadar Kasim Ali Khan (Hindustani Muslim) to
Abdul Haq Khan (Farrukhabad District, UP)

2nd Lancers   [Urdu]
France   27th December 1916

We think of you with every breath we breathe. Otherwise we are dead, and should not be thought of as living. Death stands before us at all times, even in the shape of shells, bullets and bombs, and by whichever of these means I am destined to die, my life will be extinguished forthwith.

1917

Abdul Ghafur (Pathan) to his brother Abdul Hakim Khan (38th CIH, France)

Nowshera
[Peshawar District]   [Urdu]
[NWFP]   2nd January 1917

You must be loyal to the Sirkar, whose pay you draw, and fight with bravery against the foe. It would be a dreadful thing to be faithless during a war, when our Government is so just and kind. I am always thinking of serving Government, but what can I do – a schoolboy of six years old? If only I were twenty what would I not give to be a soldier of the King! But, alas, I am only a boy of six. Our King is now the chief King in the world, and it is our duty to help him. I am always thinking how I can kill the King's enemies or give my life for him. I swear this, that when I am big enough I will enter the King's army.

Risaldar Sadik Muhammad Khan (Pathan, 33) to
Mahomed Abdullah Khan (Dehra Ismail Khan, NWFP)

36th Jacob's Horse   [Urdu]
France   3rd January 1917

Of course Karim Haidar Shah had intended to murder me; but my days were not numbered, and so he failed to achieve his object. His first bullet went between my turban and my head, and I still bear the mark. I caught his rifle when he was about to give the second shot, and the bullet passed over my shoulder.[1] Thus the Preserver is always stronger than the Destroyer. He has been sentenced to ten years' imprisonment. At the court-martial I did not speak in his favour, nor did I wish him to be hanged. It is well for him that his sentence is for ten years' imprisonment. He is a young man, and when his sentence is completed he will still be only thirty years of age and not too old to work. Don't you be anxious on my account, for it has happened time after time in the past that sirdars have been killed by young men. At the same time, I do not wish to be killed by a sowar. I wish to be killed by the Germans. One day I must deliver up my life to God, and the person that is to slay me has been preordained for that deed. Leave the matter to God. He alone is the Giver, the Preserver and the Taker of life. Each one that is born into this world must drink the cup of death, and all that I ask of God is such a death as will bring honour to my name in the world.

1. For another account of this incident, see No. 430; and for a reaction to it, see No. 464.

461

Sucho Khan (Pathan) to Dafadar Yakub Khan (38th CIH, France)

Peshawar   [Urdu]
[NWFP]   4th January 1917

As to your writing to me to buy land, there is the greatest difficulty in getting any. I have just managed by stratagem to get hold of a bit, but when anyone wants to sell or to mortgage there are at once twenty purchasers ready. The war has filled the pockets of the people in the village, and everyone wants to buy.[1]

1. The censor remarked that this letter 'shows the prosperity of the village people in the Punjab, due partly no doubt to remittances from their relatives serving in France'. He was probably right.

462

Ressaidar Raj Singh (Jat, 34) to Ressaidar Cogan Singh
(20th Deccan Horse, France)

3rd Skinner's Horse
Rawalpindi   [Urdu]
Punjab   5th January 1917

Regarding what you say to me, namely that my heart is not brave like the heart of a flesh eater, this country is not civilized like Europe. It is very difficult to get the uneducated people of this country to see reason, and for this one has to be careful. You should never regret that you did not get an opportunity to return to India. The saying is well-known that he who eats sweetmeat made of sawdust regrets it as well as he who does not eat.[1]

Listen to the news of the regiments that have returned to India. From my regiment, 261 men have been taken and sent to other regiments, and now one sees no one but recruits in the regiment. I consider you as very fortunate indeed that you are in such a beautiful country. Death in that country is preferable to life in this country.

1. 'The one suffers for what he has eaten, while the other, eager to taste, grieves because he does not get the chance.'

463

Woordi-Major Kala Khan (Punjabi Muslim) to
Nadir Khan (Rawalpindi District, Punjab)

Ordnance Base Depot
Rouen [Urdu]
France 7th January 1917

I am about to give you evidence of the generosity of the Sirkar towards our Indian troops at the present time. The Sirkar has increased the rates of both pay and pension, and at the same time has granted free rations. On hearing this, all the Indian troops gave rousing cheers on the 1st of January, and prayed for victory for the Sirkar.

464

Ahmad Khan (Pathan) to Risaldar Sadik Muhammad Khan
(Pathan, 36th Jacob's Horse, France, 33)

Dera Ismail Khan [Urdu]
India 7th January 1917

It is extraordinary that Karim Haidar Khan, who fired at you with intent to murder you, only got three months! He intended to murder you, and why was he not punished according to law? According to Indian law he should have got penal servitude for life under section 302. Are the laws of Europe different, or the Parliaments different? It is contrary to justice that he should get three months for a crime which merited death or transportation for life. If he escaped these, then at least he might have got ten years, but alas! he only got three months. When the regiment comes back, take care he does not get into the regiment again, for he will try [to murder] you again and will not spare you.[1]

1. Ahmad Khan's concern was misplaced. Karim Haidar Khan in fact received a sentence of ten years and three months' imprisonment. See No. 460. See No. 466 for another letter to the Risaldar.

465

Hazura Singh (Sikh) to his father, Pensioned Risaldar Indar Singh
(Lahore District, Punjab)

38th CIH   [Urdu]
France   8th January 1917

I hear that Sirdar Chattarpal Singh wants very much to join. You must try to get
him into some good regiment. You must try and remove any doubts he may have,
just as you did with Teja Singh. As regards the latter, you must go and see his Sahibs
and see what you can do about his promotion. Do not think at all of the fact that
if Chattarpal joins you will have three sons serving. If it is the Guru's will, we shall
escape even from blazing fire. If we help the Government on such an occasion as
this we shall reap our rewards. Take him to the Deputy Commissioner and make
him join, and don't listen to what people say.

466

Ahmad Khan to Risaldar Sadik Muhammad Khan
(Pathan, 36th Jacob's Horse, 33)

Dera Ismail Khan   [Urdu]
[NWFP]   9th January 1917

You are a lucky man to be in the 36th. It is a very old and gallant *risala*. By God's
grace it will remain famous and successful. It went to France in the beginning of
the war and is still there fighting the tyrannous German. Never once has it retreated,
but has faced the enemy boldly. As long as its flag waves it will remain loyal and
gallant. I am sure that you will always be the same distinguished and faithful soldier
that you have always been, and will follow in the footsteps of your brave ancestor,
Captain Mahomed Khan, and serve the Government as he did.

467

Sultan Khan (Baluchi) to Jemadar Malik Yar Muhammad Khan
(36th Jacob's Horse, Ambala, Punjab, 32)

36th Jacob's Horse   [Urdu]
France   10th January 1917

Dafadar Haji Ahmed Khan has been awarded the IOM of the 1st Class, and
promoted to jemadar from 6th November 1916. This has brought great credit to

the clan, and the whole regiment is filled with pride. May God give long life and prosperity to our King.

468

Sub-Assistant Surgeon Second Class Daya Ram (Punjabi Hindu, 31) to teacher Kalu Ram (Ambala District, Punjab)

2nd Lancers [Urdu]
France 11th January 1917

I will go into the trenches on the 11th or 12th January, and will write to you later. At the present time, rain and snow-storms are frequent and the cold is intense. The fighting is heavy and great preparations are being made for the summer. There is no indication of the end. God knows when the business will be finished. Leave is in abeyance, because ships are not available for the purpose, all shipping being urgently needed for other more necessary purposes. When ships become available, leave will be reopened. At the present time, moreover, the sea voyage is very dangerous.

469

Amlok Ram (Rajput) to Sita Ram (Head Constable of Police, Rawalpindi, Punjab)

2nd Lancers [Urdu]
France 17th January 1917

I hear from the depot that there are twenty-three places vacant and that no recruits are forthcoming. There is only one troop of our clan in this regiment, and other clans are about to be recruited. If at this time a troop comprised of men of another clan is raised, it will be a great disgrace for us. This third troop was raised by a single man, and recruitment of another clan was closed by a single man. I impress it on you that you should assist recruiting as much as you can; you should enlist into the regiment all men who are released from the police. There is no need for any *chanda* deposit. If any is required, it is limited to Rs.50.[1] Advise everyone to enlist without fail. Death is everywhere, and one should not fear the field of battle. This is now our third year in the field, and a hair of the head of a single man has not been injured. Look at our country; how many men in it have died of plague and other diseases?

---

1. Originally, under the *silladar* system, new recruits to the Indian cavalry were expected to purchase their own horse, arms and accoutrements from the regiment. If a trooper

returned these items intact when he was discharged, he had the cash refunded. By the later nineteenth century, recruits normally paid only a deposit on enlistment, and made up the balance through monthly deductions from their pay. This system survived only vestigially during the First World War, when recruits handed over their Rs.50 bounty money to the regiment for safekeeping until they were discharged or killed. See Omissi, *The Sepoy and the Raj*, pp. 71–4.

470

Sher Bahadur (Punjabi Muslim) to Raja Khan Alim Khan (Shahdara, Delhi)

34th Poona Horse [Urdu]
France 17th January 1917

I have seen such examples of fortitude and bravery among the French that I can hardly express myself. I saw one day a peasant ploughing, and a bicycle orderly came up to him and gave him a telegram and went off. I asked the orderly what he had given him, and he said it was a telegram telling him his son had been killed. The old man read the telegram and waited two or three minutes and then went on ploughing. I have seen many cases in which the old people have lost three or four sons, and yet have remained unshaken by the blow. There is no wild lamentation as with us in the Punjab, nor do they get into the same state as we do in our ignorance.

471

Dhan Singh (Sikh) to Lahore Singh (Patiala State, Punjab)

6th Cavalry [Gurmukhi]
France 20th January 1917

I cannot get leave, nor is there any other method by which I could come, until the war is over. There is absolutely no indication as to when I am likely to return, as there is no indication when the war will be over. By the kindness of the Guru my life has been preserved up to the present, and as long as I live I will continue to write, for you are to me as a father and a mother. I cannot write to you about my difficulties and trials, because it is forbidden to write about anything but our welfare. The orders are to the effect that, however much one may be suffering, only may only write and say that one is quite well and very happy; one is forbidden to write about one's trials and about the war.[1]

1. These may have been the orders, but they were clearly disregarded, at least in some units.

472

Balwant Singh (Sikh) to Sundar Singh (Amritsar District, Punjab)

19th Lancers [Urdu]
France 21st January 1917

As a New Year's greeting, the King has sent his picture to each [and] every man serving in the Army here.[1] May God grant long life to the generous-hearted sovereign who has deigned to think of his humblest soldiers!

1. Several men remarked on the distribution of this card, which was evidently appreciated. See No. 483.

473

Ressaidar Natha Singh (Sikh, 36) to Jemadar Mal Singh
(38th CIH, Agar-Malwa, Rajputana, India, 36)

38th CIH [Urdu]
France 22nd January 1917

I hear that nine recruits have absconded from D Squadron. Write and tell me why they absconded. Who incited them to abscond, or is there any other reason. Either someone perverted them, or some harshness was inflicted on them. Some credit is obtained when recruits are raised, but much discredit results when recruits abscond. The British officers ask how it happens that recruits abscond only from D Squadron. I cannot presume to cast any reflections on you, and I mention the matter so that you may not be accused of making insufficient arrangements or of allowing recruits to be harassed. You are responsible for the Squadron. You two are [Majha] Sikhs, and it is strange that only [Majha] Sikhs abscond. Exert yourself fully in the matter of recruiting and do not let discredit come to the Majha sirdars through slackness in this matter. Pension, pay and rations have been considerably improved everywhere.

474

Bhagail Singh (Sikh) to Chain Singh (Lahore District, Punjab)

38th CIH [Gurmukhi]
France 22nd January 1917

I did not write the truth to you before. Now I write the truth. Do whatever you think fit, and do not expect anything from me. Consider us as having died today or tomorrow. There is absolutely no hope of our ever returning. Only those who are predestined to long life will return. This war is terrible and of those who have come to take part in it, none will survive. I pass both day and night in lamentation.

475

Sowar Mir Safir Ali (Hindustani Muslim) to Mir Qaim Ali (Fyzabad, India)

2nd Lancers   [Urdu]
[France?]   24th January 1917

As for the letters that came from home, I have not the heart to read them, but I tear them up and throw them away. Every one of them asks for money, and there are many things in them which I have never told you of. You ought to know, for I have told you over and over again that they are always read by the censors. Tell them when they write never to mention things that happen behind the purdah. If the censor sees them, what must he think?

476

Jemadar Mahomed Yasin Khan (Punjabi Muslim) to
Pensioned Dafadar Taj Mahomed Khan (Rohtak District, Punjab)

34th Poona Horse   [Urdu]
France   25th January 1917

I went to England on leave, and have now returned to the Regiment. Our generous Government made most excellent arrangements for us while on leave. One could not have secured the same results privately by the expenditure of thousands of rupees. May God speedily give victory to our gracious King, and may he blacken the face of the enemy and humiliate him, both in this world and in the world to come. Amen.

477

Ressaidar Mokand Singh to Ressaidar Gugan Singh
(Sikh, 20th Deccan Horse, France, 31)

Rawalpindi   [English]
Punjab   30th January 1917

I am always unhappy here in this hilly station. The trouble is that there is no society. The people are b****y rogues, and they are all business-like people. I have not come across any gentleman here up to now. I generally hear from Paulette; but I cannot make out why Louise is so quiet – and you are a Devil. I am really jealous that you, lucky dog, are having such a ripping time, while I pass such dull days.

478

Gurmukh Singh to Bishan Singh (Sikh, 20th Deccan Horse, France)

Rawalpindi [Urdu]
Punjab 30th January 1917

So, you do not desire to return? True, although India is your native land, what of it? Certainly Europe is not our native land; but it is the native land of our King, George the V; and you should therefore esteem it better than your native land and fight with your whole heart. God will Himself bring that day when we shall meet you again in India. That day is about to come, for God will destroy our enemy and give victory to our King.

479

Risaldar-Major Ganga Dut (Jat, 49) to Contractor Gajju Singh (Punjab, India)

2nd Lancers [Urdu]
France 31st January 1917

At the present time the cold is more intense than can be described. If you pour hot water on the ground it immediately becomes solid like *ghi*. This is my third winter in this country; but it has never before been as cold as it is now. Flowing water is frozen hard like stone. Still, all the men are well and happy. We get good rations, and sufficient. All the arrangements of the Sirkar for food and clothing are most excellent. The climate here is such that no one gets ill. Although the cold is so severe, there is no sickness, except discomfort of the feet. Many men get their feet swollen through the cold.[1]

1. This letter is typical of those written during these weeks. Many soldiers complained about the cold, but added that their plentiful rations and winter clothing made it bearable.

480

Khushal Singh to Woordi-Major Sher Singh
(Sikh, 20th Deccan Horse, France, 33)

Khairatabad   [Urdu]
Deccan   1st February 1917

You asked me to place before the Depot CO any man who wished to enlist, and
you said I would be rewarded. My dear brother, in Hyderabad no one will enlist
because of the fear of death. When the war is over, the young men will come forward
to enlist. I took advice from Ganesh Singh and he said he could provide men for
enlistment after the war is over, and that at present no one would enlist.

481

Station Master Kehar Singh to Sher Singh (Sikh, 29th Lancers, France)

Ludhiana District   [Urdu]
Punjab   2nd February 1917

Is there any prospect of you having to go to the front, or will they let you remain
where you are? As to your returning [to India] what am I to say? You are an intelligent
person. You should get clear from this calamity by every possible means. If you
are in comfort and run no risk, then remain there quietly, because the sea voyage
is very risky. But do not go to the front on any account. Send in your application
for pension.

482

Kot Dafadar Abdul Jabar Khan (Hindustani Muslim) to
Fateh Mahomed Khan (6th Cavalry, Digging Party, France)

6th Cavalry   [Urdu]
France   4th February 1917]

The General Sahib commended the regiment for its signalling, and the Colonel
then proceeded to punish me by making me a kot dafadar. The Colonel meant to
reward me, but it seems to me a very heavy punishment. To me it is to give [up]
my authority and liberty, and to enter prison. Two dafadars who were passed over
were very angry about it, and one of them, Faijab Khan, tore off his stripes and

threw them away and went round all his French friends weeping. Then he went and wept in the Commanding Officer's office, and everyone laughed at him. The pith of my letter is simply this: that my promotion has offended others and is a punishment. I go wandering about all day like a dog prowling round the outskirts of the village.

483

Jemadar Khisan Singh (Sikh) to his wife (Nabha State, Punjab)

36th Jacob's Horse [Gurmukhi]
[France?] 6th February 1917

[He encloses the New Year's card for Indian troops, depicting the King-Emperor.] I have sent you thrice before pictures of His Majesty. As you framed those and put them up on the wall opposite the door, so do the same with this portrait after framing it. Worship it every morning when you get up. This is an act of religious merit, and the portrait will be a memorial. Every morning, pray to the Guru that He will give victory to the King. Do not be anxious about me. I am quite happy.

484

*Jemadar Abdul Rahim Khan (Deccani Muslim) to
Mir Hassan Khan (Hyderabad, Deccan)*

36th Jacob's Horse [Urdu]
France 7th February 1917

Don't be anxious about us. We are like goats tied to the butcher's stake. We have no idea when he will come, and there is no one who will release us. We have given up all hope of life. It would be a good thing if my soul were to quit my body. How long, how long, can we stand all this? If I were to tell you all we have to face, it would make a book; but there is no road of escape for this helpless one. Oh God! turn thine eyes upon us sinners and forgive us![1]

1. The censor commented that this was 'a letter which might possibly have been detained, but which, after consideration, I allowed to proceed. It shows a miserable and cowardly spirit, and it is hard to believe that the writer is in his proper place as a jemadar.'

485

Woordi-Major Jivan Singh (Sikh, 35) to his wife (Gurdaspur District, Punjab)

2nd Lancers   [Urdu]
[France?]   7th February 1917

It is very wrong of you to work yourself up into a state of illness through anxiety
for me. Just look at the people here. The women have their husbands killed, and
yet they go on working just as hard as ever. It does one's heart good to see them.
May God teach our women to behave like them! You must let these words sink
into your heart, and must be as brave as a man.

486

Risaldar [-Major?] Hira Singh (Dogra, 40) to
Babu Rohlu Ram (Hoshiarpur District, Punjab)

19th Lancers   [Urdu]
[France]   8th February 1917

You wrote about Sadhu Singh's leave. It is a great pity that you are so worried about
his marriage, but we are compelled to stay here. Not a man has got leave to India.
Only those who are very senior and who have earned their pensions have gone
back – or those invalided home. Through God's grace neither condition applies to
Sadhu Singh. Lots were drawn for men to go on leave, and Sadhu won a place,
but now that idea is knocked on the head. But, if God wills, the war will be over
soon, and we shall all return together, and then you can bring off the wedding.
Everybody understands the necessity of our presence here, and I need not enlarge
on the subject.[1]

1. The sentiments of the last sentence are in striking contrast to those typical of British
   troops at this stage of the war, as shown by their famous marching song – 'We're here
   because, we're here because, we're here because, we're here.'

487

To Dafadar Prayag Singh (2nd Lancers, France) from his wife[1]

[Moradabad?]   [Hindi]
UP   20th February 1917

My heart feels that it could not sustain separation from you for a single minute;
but it is now three years since I was last blessed with your presence – what then

must my heart suffer! I am wandering alone in the wilderness of this world. I cannot realize when it was that I last looked on your face, and I would thankfully give my life as an offering to anyone who would bring me into your presence once more. What words of yours, my dear, need I recall to mind, when my very veins are full of love for you! And how can I enjoy any degree of happiness in separation from you! Therefore I make this one request, that you should send for me, or write and tell me to come to you. But tell me precisely the place you are in, so that I may not fail to find it. You write to me about money, but what care I for money. I need you alone! I am in need of nothing else, and I do not hanker after riches. I am my lord's handmaid, and would count it happiness even to starve in my lord's presence. May God speedily bring the day when I, the grief-laden one, gazing in the glory of your countenance, will renew my life.

1. For a similar letter from the same woman, see No. 206.

488

Sowar Yakub Khan (Pathan) to
Abdul Jabbar Khan (21st Cavalry Depot, Jhelum, Punjab)

36th Jacob's Horse   [Urdu]
France   12th February 1917

For the last two years I have abstained from everything unlawful. It is a great pity that everything that is most useful in this country is absolutely barred by our religion, but we have to put up with it. If we have to abstain we can only get along with great difficulty. I have not touched meat for two years, even though it be *halal*. I have not touched meat for this reason – that it all comes together, both that intended for Sikhs and for us; and I have not eaten any baker's bread nor have I drunk any milk. Send this letter to the Moulvi Sahib, and ask what is laid down in the law.[1]

1. The censor commented that the writer was 'evidently very ill informed as to his religion, but there may be something in what he says as regards the meat ration. I am informed that the slaughtering used to be done at Railhead, but, since the departure of the Corps, the meat is sent up from Rouen. It is possible, under the circumstances, that the meat for Muslims killed by the *halal* process might get mixed up with that killed for the Hindus by a stroke at the back of the neck. But I think that if there had been any general complaint we should have heard of it in the letters.' Compare No. 490; and see Plate 10.

489

Rozi Khan to Malik Dilasa Khan (Punjabi Muslim, 19th Lancers, France)

Lahore   [Urdu]
Punjab   14th February 1917

It is said that from wherever in the Punjab troops have been taken away, Japanese troops will be sent there. That is to say, Japan is furnishing the British with a kind of assistance. God knows whether this rumour is true or not.[1]

1. The rumour was not true, but it appears in several letters from North India during this period.

490

Jemadar Abdul Khan (Punjabi Muslim) to
Hazrat Sahib Khanka Mujidali (Delhi, India)

18th Lancers   [Urdu]
[France?]   20th February 1917

I hope you will regard this petition of your humble servant who used to be a disciple of yours. I am now on the very edge of fear I shall be drowned, and I ask your help for God's sake, as I am without any resource. I have scrupulously performed all the necessary rites, prayer, charity and abstention from what is unlawful; but, through weakness, the flesh is now beginning to assert itself. I have used nothing of this country up to date, except water and fruit, and have not touched even any tea, coffee, biscuits or jam, but now my inner man begins to prompt me and I am afraid of falling. Many distinguished people here have given up making any distinction between clean and unclean things, and I suppose there is not one per cent of them who refuse to eat with the French. They do not drink wine or eat pork, but they use all their places and table napkins. Pardon my presumption in addressing you and let me have your advice.

491

Balwant Singh (Sikh) to Janmeja Sinth (Lyallpur District, Punjab)

6th Cavalry   [Urdu]
France   25th February 1917

Your letter shows that you are very anxious about Sujan Singh and Dyal Singh, and that your eyes are suffering from your anxiety, and your teeth too. I am very worried about this. You are a wise man and trust in the Guru, then why be humbled in mind? You are always exhorting me to be brave, then do not be downhearted yourself. We are all together and very happy and comfortable. Instead of being anxious, you should always be thanking the Guru for giving your family a chance of serving the King in Europe. We believe that the Guru will soon give victory to our King, and that you will receive great *izzat*.

492

Abdul Ali (Hindustani Muslim) to
Risaldar Farzand Ali Khan Bahadur (6th Cavalry, Sialkot, Punjab, 51)

6th Cavalry   [Urdu]
France   28th February 1917

There was an extraordinary affair in the regiment yesterday, although there have been similar incidents before in other regiments. Mahomed Khan, the lance dafadar, is engaged to a Frenchwoman on the understanding that he becomes a Christian. The marriage ceremony is to take place in two or three days. We have done our best to prevent it, but all has been in vain. You can judge the state of affairs when it has got to the length of our marrying Frenchwomen.[1]

1.   This marriage elicited much comment, and led to friction between Mahomed Khan and his family. See Nos. 535, 568, 588.

493

Dafadar Mastan Singh (Sikh) to Daya Singh (Ludhiana District, Punjab)

38th [?] CIH   [Gurmukhi]
France   28th February 1917

On account of the snow, my back pains [me] more than ever, and if I were to go to hospital people would say that I am afraid. If I had wished to return [to India], I could have come long ago, through this disease. But my belief is that it is honourable for one to die on the field of battle, and brings great credit to the mother who bore him. If a man returns to his home and death finds him there, can he escape it? He comes home ill and dies there, and that brings him no honour. Now, after a long time, our Government is plunged in an affair, and it is my duty to help with all my soul and strength.

494

Jewan Singh (Sikh) to Nur Din (Sialkot District, Punjab)

19th Lancers   [Urdu]
France   4th March 1917

We are serving the Sirkar well, and have no anxiety about the war. *Lakhs* of other mothers' sons are also present at the war. We are not tobacco consumers. We are Sikhs, and the duty of Sikhs is to exalt in battle and show their prowess. When we were in India, except for God, we feared no one, and enlisted of our own free will. Now people say we enlisted from fear of the police; but we have no regard for *lumberdars* or police or anyone else. If we had had anything to fear from the police, we should have soon settled accounts with them. Our object [in enlisting] was to obtain some benefit from the Sirkar, and now people say we enlisted from fear of the police! Let it be well known that if anyone oppresses our families or injures our crops, we will, if our lives are spared, return and deal out to them just what they have dealt out to us.

495

Alam Sher Khan (Pathan) to Jemadar Malik Sarfaraz Khan
(125th Napier's Rifles, Shahpur District, Punjab, 25)

36th Jacob's Horse   [Urdu]
France   13th March 1917

For some time past, we have been wearing steel helmets when we go into the trenches. These helmets furnish protection for the head against bullets and bits of shells, and are very effective. The helmet suits robust-looking men very well, and is not unbecoming in the case of men with long hair. It certainly effects a great saving of life. Uncle Jahan Khan, who is both fair and robust, looks splendid in a helmet, and cannot be distinguished from a European at a distance.[1]

1. There was initially some resistance among Indian troops, especially Sikhs, to the wearing of steel helmets. See No. 339.

496

Alam Khan (Punjabi Muslim) to Jemadar Malik Sarfaraz Khan
(125th Napier's Rifles, Shahpur District, Punjab, 25)

36th Jacob's Horse   [Urdu]
France   31st March 1917

The special work for the performance of which we left our beloved native land is
now going strongly. Various people amongst us whose destiny allots them a grave
in France are fulfilling their destiny, after having done their duty honourably in
the field. It is a matter for congratulation that our regiment was amongst the
foremost to grasp this opportunity, and they have gained for themselves higher credit
than any other regiment. Our losses were quite ordinary, and we pursued the
enemy far, and are still engaged in pursuing them.

497

Katar Singh (Sikh) to Sahib Singh (Nabha State, Punjab)

9th Hodson's Horse   [Urdu]
France   1st April 1917

Nowadays we get but little leisure, as work is heavy. The wicked and impotent
enemy who are in the British front have been so pressed by the British this year
that they have been forced to evacuate their positions and to retire about twenty
miles. In this affair, we got our chance to do our share. There is every prospect of
victory this year, and of our meeting in the winter.[1]

1. The German retreat to which he refers was in fact the deliberate withdrawal of March
    1917 to the prepared positions of the Hindenburg Line. The optimism of his letter is
    typical of those written during these few weeks.

498

Farman Ali to Zabu Shah (Punjabi Muslim, 38th CIH, France)

Karachi   [Urdu]
[Sind]   1st April 1917

The spring is on us, but you and I cannot enjoy it as we are far from our homes.
But you are far better off than I am, for you are in the great war and have the

opportunity of serving your King. May God give our King the victory! Under his aegis we live safely and happily.

499

Samundar Khan (Pathan) to Malik Sher Zaman Khan
(Dehra Ismail Khan District, NWFP)

36th Jacob's Horse   [Urdu]
France   3rd April 1917

We were the first to go into action. We took five villages from the enemy. Doubtless you have read about it in the newspapers. This was the first engagement of the cavalry on horseback, and was secured by the Lucknow Brigade who acquitted themselves right well. Our regiment in particular made a great name for itself. All is well in our squadron. God protected us, each one. The other three squadrons had casualties. For the last three or four days we have been near Albert, and expect to be sent somewhere in a day or two.[1]

1. Soldiers were normally forbidden from naming particular places in their letters, for fear of passing military information to the enemy. But, curiously, both the regimental and the Boulogne censor seem to have let the mention of Albert village (twenty miles behind the lines, on the Somme sector) pass unchallenged.

500

Atma Singh (Sikh) to Narain Singh (Amritsar District, Punjab)

38th CIH   [Urdu]
France   7th April 1917

You write and say that the boy wishes to enlist. If, since the day I enlisted, I have given you cause for satisfaction, then by all means send him to enlist. But if it has been otherwise, do not send him. I beg of you not to let him enlist. There is no profit in soldiering.[1]

1. By 1917, it had become unusual to advise friends and family at home not to enlist.

501

Veterinary Doctor Daya Ram (Jat) to
Schoolmaster Neblu Ram (Ambala District, Punjab)

2nd Lancers   [Urdu]
France   7th April 1917

We are in the open, and it is very cold with continual snow and rain, and we are suffering a good deal. The horses are up to their necks in mud, and it is owing to our having to look after the horses that we are saved from a worse fate. We have put our little tents in the mud. There is no village near us, only ruins which have been caused by shell-fire. We are all very worn out, and our feeding arrangements are unsatisfactory. We have no opportunity of bathing. Sometimes we cannot bath for a month, and we are in a regular hell and tired of life, yet our souls are so shameless they do not leave our bodies. How life can be sustained under such circumstances I cannot understand. At night we wonder whether we shall see another morning, but morning comes all right and with it fresh trials to endure. One day we marched three miles and slept in the open with one blanket only, and it snowed the whole night, and we lay shivering. In the morning we expected to be dead, but we got up all right and shook the snow off our blankets. There are many other things which I cannot write.[1]

1. The despairing tone of this letter is quite untypical of those written at this time. As the censor pointed out, the author was not a fighting man.

502

Ganaishi Lall to Havildar Ganga Ram (Punjabi Hindu,
Indian General Base Depot, France)

Multan   [Urdu]
Punjab   7th April 1917

It is a matter for regret, that you have been away for three years, and have never sent any money for the maintenance of your family. Do you think of your own desires only? It is a well-known saying that 'the Hindustani is [an] evilly-disposed person. He swaggers about and enjoys himself while his children starve and his wife appeals to him in vain.' For two years I had already arranged for the expenses of your family. That cost me Rs.16 per mensem. For the last four months I have again been feeding your family. I am not your debtor that I should do this thing. Moreover, you told your old mother to live at home and that you would send her money; but till today she is living in expectation of receiving your money, saying 'my son the "General Havildar" is earning much money and will send me some shortly so that I may eat'. Shame on all your pretensions to bravery while you leave your children to be fed by charity! Today your wife was about to commit suicide by throwing herself into a well, owing to your neglect of her. If you have any spark of good left in you, you must immediately mend your ways.

503

Majid Ullah Khan (Pathan) to Dafadar Amir Khan (19th Lancers, France)

Peshawar District   [Urdu]
NWFP   7th April 1917

For one year, my brother Ali Khan has attended to your affairs and to the cultivation of your land. But consider – for how long can an outsider be expected to help in this way? You know well that your father is dead, and that you have no near relation here to look after your affairs. Therefore, as soon as you receive this letter, approach your Sirdar and ask him to represent your case to the British officer, so that you may be sent back. I do not urge that you should quit the service of the Sirkar altogether. You have eaten the salt of the Sirkar, and must continue to serve if required. But you might be sent back to the Depot, whence you could arrange for the conduct of your affairs. It is impossible for women to cultivate land, and to move about to transact the ordinary affairs of life.[1]

1. This letter is typical of the many written at this time asking soldiers to come home. For a typical reply see No. 521.

504

Gugan Singh (Jat) to Mular Singh (Editor, Jat Gazette, *Rohtak, Punjab)*

20th Deccan Horse   [Urdu]
France   8th April 1917

Be so good as to publish this letter in the *Jat Gazette*. Today the Lt.-Governor of the Central Provinces did our regiment the honour to visit it. He telephoned, asking particularly to see the Jat officers which I consider a great honour. He arrived with his staff, and, after talking to the Colonel and Adjutant, shook hands with all the Indian Officers, and – laughing and chatting gaily – asked each how his family was, and if he was suffering any discomfort. When my turn came, he asked me where I came from, and when I said 'Rohtak' he said 'is the Jat Squadron complete?' I replied 'yes, and there is another at the base'. After that, I told him about the special recruiting party in Rohtak ... He said that Rohtak had given much help, and that the Jats had won a great name for themselves. Then he spoke to Ressaidar [Jemadar?] Dalip Singh [32], who comes from my village, and asked him with a laugh whether he removed his boots when he took his meals. Dalip Singh said they had given up all that sort of thing in the war, and had no objection to eating and drinking with [the] French and English. His Honour said 'Bravo! that is as it should be.' He told us that he had come from India as a representative to the Imperial Conference, and that he was going back to India. He said he was delighted to get a glimpse of the Indian troops before returning, and that he was pleased to see we all looked fitter and had a better colour than in India, and were evidently ready for anything. He concluded by saying that what we had done would be a source of pride to India for ever.

505

Sayed Habib (Pathan) to Sujab-us-Shah (Swabi, Peshawar District, NWFP)

9th Hodson's Horse   [Urdu]
France   9th April 1917

Shah Sayed Lalla and Kasim Lallh have made a separate house. Well, what concern is it of yours? Let them do what they please. By the grace of God, what harm can they do you? They are evilly disposed, and God will reward them accordingly. All you have to do is practise patience. In these matters, the customs of this country [France] are most excellent, and each man dwells peacefully in his own house, and seeks nothing from others. They are all on the same level, and pass their existence in cheerfulness and good nature. The rain comes in accordance with their need, whereas in Hindustan, by reason of the evil disposition of the people, the rain does not come for years at a time. Whatever these people sow in the fields, whether on the hills or in the plains, it comes to maturity in the same degree. The harvest is nowhere a failure as it is in India. In India the soil itself devours the seed that is sown in it. This is all due to the evil disposition, the ignorance and the stupidity of the people. I swear to you that I am disgusted with life in India, and if God spares me to return I will tell you all I know. I have neither the leisure nor the paper to write fully, otherwise I could produce a volume. If I had my way, I would put every man and woman in India on board ship and, after bringing them here, showing them over this country, would return them to India, so that they might learn how to use their lives to best advantage.

506

Ghaib Shah (Pathan) to Abdul Ghafar Khan (19th Lancers, France)

Peshawar District   [Urdu]
NWFP   10th April 1917

It is the practice of brave men to engage in warfare. Be a brave man, therefore, and a loyal one, since you have eaten the salt of the Sirkar. Do not be alarmed or disturbed, and when you go into battle, call on the name of God. Your mother, your two grandmothers, and your grandfather pray for you every day. Be not afraid, therefore – God will sustain you. Brave men pass long periods in warfare away from home.

507

*Ressaidar Malik Mahomed Latif Khan (Punjabi Muslim, 35) to
Jemadar Usuf Ali Khan (19th Lancers, France)*

28th Light Cavalry
Seistan   [Urdu]
Persia   15th April 1917

You must have heard that the Indian forces of our King of Kings, George V, have achieved a splendid victory and taken Baghdad the Holy.[1] It is a matter of the greatest joy to us Muslims that this sacred place has escaped out of the hands of the evil Germans, and has come into the possession of our just King and Cherisher of his subjects; and it is sincerely hoped that it will remain under his protection till the end of time. May God the All Merciful speedily give victory to our gracious King over the entire world.

1. The city was captured by a mixed British and Indian force on 11th March 1917.

508

*Risaldar [Jemadar?] Zabta Khan (Pathan, 40) to Risaldar-Major Munshi [?]
Akram Khan (1st Lancers, Risalpur, Peshawar District, NWFP, 49)*

1st Lancers, attached 19th Lancers   [Urdu]
France   17th April 1917

I got your letter on the 15th in a storm of rain and wind. May God destroy them! Snow, rain and wind are the daily portion of those unfortunate ones. No one gets a moment to breathe. It is so hard that, seeing it, one's heart comes into one's mouth. Well, I must not say too much what is happening to me: [that] is known only to me and to God. I thank God a thousand times! I am sorry about Talimand Khan, but it is the will of God. God is gracious and you are praying. We will see what [will] happen. He has staked his head and his body, but life is the thing most precious to every one, and at present he is sitting down and biding his time. Victory and defeat are in the hands of God, but this war is a boundless ocean.

509

Clerk Bhagat Ram (Punjabi Hindu) to Khan Shirin Khan
(Remount Depot, Rouen, France)

Commissariat Department
Jullundur   [Urdu]
Punjab   19th April 1917

Do not set your heart on those scentless and artificially lovely flowers [women] and do not become infatuated with their seemingly innocent appearance. Where, in God's name, can you get in any temperate climate that delightful, beautiful thing which grows in the tropics? There [in France] the outward appearance is cold; but within there rages a fiery furnace. If you should be scorched in that flame, it would be difficult for you to escape.[1] But, if you should be unfortunate, do not be like that wretched sowar who used to sit near your tent and bewail his condition. Rather, stand in the open, sword in hand, and call everyone to witness what the enemy [venereal disease] has done. Do this, and then there will be no delay in your getting the Victoria Cross [a cure].

1. 'The French women look attractive, but have venereal diseases. If you catch one, it will be hard to find a cure.'

510

Jemadar Shamsher Ali Khan (Punjabi Muslim, 33) to
Raja Rustam Ali Khan (Gujranwala District, Punjab)

34th Poona Horse   [Urdu]
France   20th April 1917

I regard our existing customs and rules as useless, as it is quite true that the only result which comes from their observance is expense. For instance, when the Raja Sahib died, you had his corpse brought home and buried it there. Now this was done simply because it is in accord with custom, and the only practical result to you was expense. You must see that in Hindustan it is a matter of daily occurence that officers, from lieutenant to general, die and are buried in the station where they die. Besides, there is no command either of God or of His Prophet [that a man should be buried at home]; further, it will be seen that Prophets and Saints have been buried in the place where they died. What then is to be gained by following this practice [of interment in one's home]? Nothing, and it is quite time that poor people should recognize this, and adopt more reasonable customs.

The same applies to the case of circumcision. You write and say that you will delay carrying out the ceremony on Mahomed Nazir till I return, and the whole family can be present at the ceremony, which would then be performed with much *éclat*. In my opinion, not more than Rs.10 should even be spent on this ceremony. It amuses me when I think that so much ceremony is observed, and so great expense incurred, in the cutting off of an inch of skin which is of no value whatever! I regret that I did not learn anything of 'Doctoring', otherwise I should have promptly circumcised him myself when I was last at home. Well, I trust that now you will have the ceremony performed promptly and with as little expense as possible.

This war has been prolonged in an amazing manner; but there is every indication that it will be followed by an era of peace and plenty, and the signs point to the early termination of the war. Who is there whom this war has not saddened and depressed; but one is bound to discharge the obligation laid on him. It was for this, that for generations our family has been eating the salt of the Sirkar and receiving salary and pension, and, therefore, this is no time to be disturbed in mind and for turning one's face away from duty. Rather it is the time for showing valour; and, please God, but a few days remain for the end to come.

511

Jemadar Alam Sher Khan (Punjabi Muslim) to
Malik Samand Khan (Sargodha, Shahpur District, Punjab)

18th Lancers   [Urdu]
France   22nd April

Congratulate your servant on having won the 2nd Class of the Indian Order of Merit! This means that I shall get an extra Rs.15 a month above my pay or pension. We got altogether four medals, of which three were gained by our own C Squadron. They were awarded for the fight on the 18th, 19th and 20th March. The regiment got a great honour in the fight, and C Squadron was the most distinguished in the regiment. Of the two troops in our Squadron, mine had the most opportunities and did the best work. By the grace of God, we had not a single casualty in our Troop. I got the medal for my work on that occasion, and the officers were all very pleased, and the General himself thrice congratulated us.

512

Sowar Singh to Khushial Singh (Sikh, 19th Lancers, France)

Shrine of Dehra Baba Jai Mall Singh
Amritsar [Urdu]
Punjab 24th April 1917

Regarding your enquiry about leavened [French-baked] bread. You need not hesitate at all to consume it. But you should strictly abstain from eating flesh and drinking wine, which are both forbidden and noxious; and also antagonistic to that state of mind and body which is necessary for the proper contemplation of God. You must also abstain from having any liaison with another man's wife. If you have a book of extracts from the Guru Granth, read a portion whenever you have time. This will keep your mind pure. Recite your prayers daily. God is everywhere the Protector of those who serve Him.

513

Ali Ahmed Khan to Sher Ahmed (Pathan, 36th Jacob's Horse, France)

Khushab
[Jhelum District] [Urdu]
[Punjab] 25th April 1917

I have heard that your regiment has suffered very heavy casualties. Is this true or not? You have never written a single line to your home. It is a great shame! You are literate and yet you never write. Why is this?

514

*Retired Dafadar Iman Khan to Wali Mohamed Khan (Punjabi Muslim, 18th
Lancers, France)*

Sargodha [Urdu]
Punjab 25th April 1917

The family of Gulab Shah have received a letter from His Majesty himself, sent by the Viceroy, expressing the King's regret at the death of Gulab Shah. Just look at the kindness of our Government which joins in the mourning for an ordinary sowar. May God give victory to such a government!

515

Bhugwan Singh to Lance Dafadar Santa Singh
(Sikh, 21st Cavalry, Frontier Force)

Gujrat   [Gurmukhi]
Punjab   27th April 1917

Be loyal and hardworking. This incarnation will never come again, so be useful
to your King. I am ready to do anything I can to help you, and am willing if necessary
to give my life. I am prepared to give three quarters of all I possess to the
Government and live on what is left. Write and tell me what you think; shall I be
right in doing so or not? In your first letter you said 'now is the time for you to
help'. I am ready, for I am very happy and comfortable under the British Raj. For
this reason my family and I pray every morning, when we rise, that the British Raj
may endure for ever.

516

Chattar Singh (Sikh) to Sirdar Bishan Singh (Multan District, Punjab)

6th Cavalry   [Gurmukhi]
France   1st May 1917

There is no information that I could give you, and you must pardon me for not
sending you any. The result of writing anything that is outside the area of our family
concerns is that trouble comes to me in the first place, and, in the second, the service
of our King might suffer through the diffusion of information.[1]

1. This writer is clearly treating the censorship rules very scrupulously. In fact, many soldiers
    were far from reticent about matters that were not of direct concern to their families.

517

Jemadar Bagga [Bhagwan?, Bhan?] Singh (Sikh) to Dasvanda Singh
(Ludhiana District, Punjab)

19th Cavalry [?]   [Gurmukhi]
France   1st May 1917

The war of today is a strange and wonderful thing. When the day is fine, combats
in the air are very numerous; if not, balloons, in which the observers sit, mount up

for observation to a height of two or three miles. Thus any movement of troops that takes place by the enemy is immediately known. The contending troops on either side were sheltered in trenches and dug-outs – some of the latter being fifty feet underground. But the German dug-outs, which were made strong with cement and were very deep, have been completely destroyed by our guns and the enemy had to evacuate them and to retire in some places to a distance of fifteen miles.[1] Some of the positions evacuated by the enemy were strongly defended by line upon line of barbed wire to a depth of thirty yards and a height of four feet.

1. He is presumably referring to the German withdrawal to the Hindenburg Line in March 1917.

518

Lance Dafadar Mahomed Khan (Pathan) to
Arsalla Khan (Rawalpindi District, Punjab)

38th CIH [Urdu]
France 5th May 1917

A matter which I am desirous to urge on you is this – that in the mosque you should establish a teacher to give instruction to the little boys and girls. Whatever money is required to carry out this plan, I will provide. You should apply yourself earnestly to this work, because, through learning, the conditions of the various parts of the world and the characteristics of the varous peoples become known. The people in other countries [than India] live in a happy and prosperous fashion. In my young days I did not learn anything, and to this day I am regretting my mistake.

519

Risaldar Lakha Singh Bahadur (Sikh, 39) to Ressaidar Sirdar Sajjan Singh
(4th Bullock Corps, Supply and Transport, Bombay)

18th Lancers [Urdu]
France 5th May 1917

More than ever before, the cavalry has had opportunities for engaging and defeating the enemy and driving him back. It is a matter for congratulation that, though a few of our men have been wounded, we have inflicted very heavy losses on the enemy. At the present time, the enemy's line has been driven back many miles, and we expect that our King will soon secure victory, and that we shall return with joy to meet you. In every way the Indian troops are doing good and cheerful work for the King and the Government.

520

Jemadar Man Singh (Sikh, 23?) to Shyam Singh (Sargodha, Shahpur District, Punjab)

6th Cavalry   [Urdu]
France   8th May 1917

Today is lovely, with a bright sun. The strongest sun here is about equal to our weakest sun, but it is an astounding thing that after being so long in a cold climate we feel even this little amount of sun. Just imagine how we shall feel the sun when we get back to India. Today we are perspiring and thirsty. I have come out with a party to graze horses, and [we] are camped in a very fine abandoned grove. No one knows where the driver is, or who he is.

We feel miserable to see the shattered houses all round. There is a fine house here which has been spared, apparently by both parties; and when I go upon the roof I can see no one but a few Indians, nor is there any sign of cattle or of cultivation, only a waste of trenches and wire, overgrown with grass, over which our poor horses have to walk. Here and there are the graves of gallant youths who have died for their country, and God has covered their graves with wild flowers. These are the heroes who gave their lives to drive out the tyrant German.

521

Dafadar Abdur Rahman Khan (Deccani Muslim) to his mother
(Parbhani, Hyderabad, Deccan)

29th Deccan Horse   [Urdu]
France   9th May 1917

You write that everyone is getting leave to India [and] why do I not come? My dearest mother, the people who get leave are those who are in Bombay or Poona. We are on the battlefield. This is the place where, if you are spared till the evening, you go to the field of Karbala in the night. Many are killed and wounded, but the greater number return safe and sound and enjoy themselves. How do you think a man can get a single day's leave from such a place! Leave was granted, but the journey was too dangerous. Keep good heart. I shall soon, please God, be back with you victorious, bringing the [Indian] Order of Merit.[1]

1. This patient letter is typical of the many replies to pleas, such as No. 503.

522

Risaldar Prem Singh (Sikh, 43) to Honorary Captain Risaldar-Major Mir Jaffar Khan Sardar Bahadur (Zaida, Peshawar District, NWFP, Late 9th Hodson's Horse)

9th Hodson's Horse   [Urdu]
France   13th May 1917

Our Sirkar Bahadur is progressing daily. The country which our cavalry now occupies has been brutally devastated by the tyrant Germans. All the fruit trees have been cut down (you must have read of it in the papers). We can get nothing, [not] even milk, in the villages, for the Germans have carried off the cattle and the women.[1]

1. When the Germans withdrew to the Hindenburg Line in March 1917, they scorched the earth in their wake. Several Indian letter-writers lamented the destruction, especially of fruit trees, and raged at the Germans for causing it.

523

Ressaidar Jai Singh (Sikh, 37) to Shiv Singh (Hoshiarpur District, Punjab)

6th Cavalry   [Gurmukhi]
France   14th May 1917

You write about my taking leave. If I could do as I please I would be with you without a moment's delay. I have been here nearly three years, and I feel sure that we shall meet again very soon.

Because I came here at the war, you suppose I am enduring great hardship. But it is not so, because in Europe, wherever there is a single house you can get, on payment, whatever you require in the matter of food and drink. Further, in the winter when we live in billets, we are in reality more comfortable than we would be at home, because we are provided with fire-places. In fact I have nothing to complain of here. Of course, when we have to go into the trench we do suffer some inconvenience, but when you consider that we are soldiers and that a great war is on, the inconvenience is nothing much, nor novel.

As regards life and death, that is all in the hands of God. If one's destiny is a long life, one remains untouched under a deluge of shot and shell. Such indeed has happened to me on various occasions. In truth, when I compare your trials with my own, yours seem many times heavier. I cannot help you because I am a soldier and the present is the time for me to serve my country.[1] I trust in God.

1. This generally upbeat letter is typical of those written during these few weeks, with the exception of his unusual reference to serving his country. Indian soldiers almost always talked in terms of their duty to the King and to the Sirkar, not to India itself.

524

Dafadar Tok Chand (Jat) to Lance Dafadar Kishan Singh
(5th Cavalry, attached 6th Cavalry, Rouen)

6th Cavalry   [Urdu]
France   19th May 1917

I am here in the place where the French formerly had their front lines. It is a beautifully green place, and there is every kind of comfort. The stretch of verdant fields cheer one's heart. I am sure the Rouen people will soon be here, and you must come with them. Do not be anxious. We are ready for the trenches. We hope that we shall get another opportunity, and shall not be found wanting when it comes. It is now clear that there is no use for cavalry at present, and we shall now work as infantry in the trenches. You must come at once. I have much to tell you, but I cannot do so till I see you.

525

Sahib Nabha to Woordi-Major Sirdar Kartar Singh
(Sikh, 18th Lancers, France, 32)

Nabha   [Urdu]
[Punjab]   21st May 1917

Why does God not hear our prayer? He is good to all the world; why then does he not listen to us? We pray day and night for your victorious return. May He soon crush the vile German Kingdom, and his heart too, and give our King the victory. I know how brave and loyal is your heart, but yet I cannot help saying that you are bound to serve such a King and Government heart and soul. Even if we suffer by it, what does it matter? We have promised [the] Government loyal service.

526

Sarup Singh to Hira Singh (Hindu Rajput, 29th Lancers, France)

Hapur
[Meerut District]   [Urdu?]
UP   [late May 1917?]

You said in a previous letter that, God willing, we should soon meet. Subsequently, however, you ceased to mention anything about returning. This does not worry me. Neither should it worry you. Still, whenever you write, say that you are well and happy and expect to return shortly. I ask this on behalf of these ignorant women folk, as whenever they hear such messages they are consoled. I know well that you cannot return till orders to that effect are issued, and this issue of such orders is a matter of destiny. It is unprofitable to be concerned about one's perishable body, since it will not abide in this world for ever. Therefore, all should have no regard for one's earthly life when discharging one's duty towards one's King and country. To go away from home and return there is a matter of destiny; but the Rajput's offspring who does not desire to engage in this war and to help his King and country, is no true son of a Rajput.[1]

1. See Nos. 111, 198, 234, 256, 419 and 533 for similar statements.

527

Chaman Singh (Sikh) to Mangal Singh (Montgomery District, Punjab)

19th Lancers   [Urdu]
France   5th June 1917

We get everything here that we are accustomed to get in India – plenty of milk, sugar, *ghi*, oranges and grapes. Every day the forces of our King continue to advance, and we expect that our King will soon secure complete victory and that we shall return victorious to our native land. The Germans are so much exhausted and can do no harm whatever to our King's army, whereas our King's army inflicts heavy losses on them daily. What I tell you is the literal truth, and if anyone says anything to the contrary he is a liar. I know what I am writing, as I have seen it with my own eyes. The Germans are reduced to misery. They have nothing to eat, whereas our King gives each soldier even more rations of every kind than before. He also uses much ammunition and consequently the loss of life amongst the troops is very small.

528

Jemadar Sultan Khan (Punjabi Muslim, 34) to
Malik Fateh Mahomed Khan (Shahpur District, Punjab)

18th Lancers   [Urdu]
France   5th June 1917

I want to tell you one thing. Our caste is very low down in the scale, just because we do not serve in the Army. Every one knows I am an officer, but no one knows who the Buranas are. Officers ask 'who are the Buranas?' The reason for this, [is] that though we are a caste superior in many ways to others, we are inferior just because we are not soldiers. Now, it rests with God and with you to raise the name of the Buranas. You must make a great effort and you can do it in this way – by getting the *lumberdars* to enlist men of Burana village as Buranas. You must emphasize this – that our caste has got to win a name by serving Government. I will quote some instances which are apposite. Just look at the Biloch caste. Who used to know anything about them, and now, how do they stand? Look also at the Mahals; and there are many other instances. With us it is the case that if any effort is made we refuse to have anything to do with it. We get our livelihood here all right, but what about our *izzat*? The whole object of military service is to raise the reputation of one's caste, and that is what we have to do.

529

Shankar (Jat) to Sona Lal (Peshawar District, NWFP)

FPO No. 18[1]   [Urdu]
[France]   7th June 1917

I have no hope of seeing you again and getting safe and sound out of France. I am always thinking of the possibility of seeing India and my friends again. Pray God night and day about this. There seems no prospect of peace. Give my *salaams* to Chintaman, and tell them not to be angry for we are about to die.

1. Regiment not stated.

530

Kartar Singh (Sikh) to Jhaman [?] Singh (Lyallpur District, Punjab)

38th CIH   [Gurmukhi]
France   8th June 1917

The bullets fall here in the same profusion as fireworks at the marriage of a rich man's son. We will not return till we have penetrated into Germany and exploded our fireworks there. Our lust for battle is not yet satisfied. For three years we have experienced many trials and fought in various ways; but the real fighting will commence when we begin to burn their houses and break open their doors and despoil their goods. Then the end will be in sight. It will come, about the completion of the third year – not before. Never mind, even if the war lasts ten years, we shall have our mark here. If we die, no matter. If we survive, no matter; but to die in battle is a glorious end. It is not well to die in one's bed wrapped up in a blanket. Better a bullet, and then oblivion in ten minutes.

531

Sant Singh (Sikh) to [illegible] Singh (Bareilly District, UP)

2nd Lancers [Urdu]
France 8th June 1917

I have been in the trenches since the 22nd May. The Germans are now losing strength and are giving ground daily. The British, Indian and French forces are advancing, and countless German prisoners have been made and are being made. The sight here is a truly wonderful one. Night and day the big guns, machine guns and rifles are fired. Some are wounded, some killed; though in my regiment the casualties have been few. The end of all this is not in sight at present, because all the Kings are engaged in the war. We expect that the Germans will be defeated; but one cannot say when that will happen as it appears certain that this war will last a very long time. There is no prospect whatever of peace till one side or the other has been completely defeated. If we are alive then, the Indian cavalry regiments will probably be returned to India, after they have completed three years' service here, or they will be relieved by other regiments coming from India. Time after time you reproach me about not coming on leave. Do you think that I delight in undergoing hardships and risking my life? If you think that I purposely avoid coming on leave, you are quite mistaken.

532

Man Singh (Sikh) to Risaldar-Major Sirdar Bahadur Gurdit Singh
(Depot, 6th Cavalry, Sialkot, Punjab, 50)

6th Cavalry [Urdu]
France 9th June 1917

There is a matter which I am very loath to write about, which has inflicted a great stain on us, but I feel obliged to tell you about it, because official notice is sure to reach the depot. Sowar Sham Singh and Ram Singh on the 30th were tried by court martial for not relieving each other on sentry duty and leaving the place without any sentry. They were sentenced to be shot, but this punishment is generally commuted to one of a year's imprisonment. These two men have disgraced the caste and the squadron.

533

Dafadar Bahrisalls [?] Singh (Rajput) to Panch Singh
(Ajmer District, Rajputana)

34th Poona Horse   [Hindi]
France   9th June 1917

Sivari Singh was wounded on the 27th May. All the other men of our village are
well. We are Rajputs and it is our privilege to fight bravely in battle, and if we are
wounded or die, we gain renown and honour. For this reason do not be concerned
about us.

534

Sant Singh (Sikh) to Madho Singh (Bareilly District, UP)

2nd Lancers   [Urdu]
France   14th June 1917

My regiment is doing duty in the trenches like infantry. Up to the present we have
not had many casualties, and the other regiments have fared in the same way. Our
British and Indian forces are getting the upper hand, and the enemy gives ground
daily. The French, too, are driving the enemy back. The German is so great a tyrant
that whenever he has to retire from a town, he sets it on fire and carries the
inhabitants away with him. This is great tyranny; but we hope soon to give the
German his just reward. His country will be destroyed in the same way. Neither
the British nor the French will be content till they have entered Berlin.

535

Mahomed Khan (Hindustani Muslim) to [illegible]
Mahomed Khan (Rohtak District, Punjab)

6th Cavalry   [Urdu]
France   18th June 1917

I want to tell you of my misfortunes. I was stationed in a village and was in a house
where they were very kind to me. There was a young woman in the house and the
parents were very pleased with me. She wrote to the King in London and asked
permission for me to marry her and the petition came back with the King's signature

on it, granting leave. But she did all this without my knowledge. The Colonel sent for me and asked whether it was true. I said it was, and asked his leave to marry, but said I must make the girl a Muslim. The Colonel then got very angry and took away my rank of Lance Dafadar, and said he would not give me leave to get married. When this came to the girl's ears, she sent another petition to the King and he gave leave, and said that directly the marriage was celebrated he should be informed. According to His Majesty's order, the wedding came off on the 2nd April. There was a General Sahib and a Muslim jemadar as witnesses. But I swear to God that I did not want to marry, but after the King's order I should have got into grave trouble if I had refused.[1]

1. Muslim, but not Hindu, troopers had recently received permission to marry Frenchwomen. Mahomed Khan's tale about the King's intervention was almost certainly fabricated to avert the wrath of his family and the scorn of his comrades. See Nos. 492, 568 and 588.

536

Bilaza Khan (Pathan) to his father Abbas Khan (Attock District, Punjab)

19th Lancers [Urdu]
France 19th June 1917

I know you are longing to see me and [are] praying for the day to come when we return. I cannot predict the future, which is in God's hand; but I feel, all the same, that the time is at hand. If you can understand the secret implied in this, you will bear up with God's help.[1]

1. The secret is, perhaps, that he intends to desert.

537

Fakir Mahomed (Pathan) to Hazrat Habib
(Depot, 19th Lancers, Sialkot, Punjab)

19th Lancers [Urdu]
France 20th June 1917

Do not believe what you hear in anyone's letters, because people write such lies. We are very fit and well, thanks to God's mercy, and have no troubles of any kind. You are an intelligent man.[1]

1. He implies, of course, that all is far from well.

538

Sahib Ali (Hindustani Muslim) to Talukdar Mahabir Prasad
(Amropur, Gurhapur PO, Sultanpur, UP?)

6th Cavalry [Urdu]
France 29th June 1917

My father writes that a war contribution is being levied. I read the letter to my CO, and he said I should write to you, and say that subscriptions should not be taken from the families of those who were fighting in France. Please act on this or else a petition will be sent to the District Commissioner. I live in the midst of a storm of shells and am fortunate to be alive. What greater service can I render to my King than this? Please write at once and I will show your letter to the OC.

539

Kilullah (Hindustani Muslim) to Head Clerk Dilawar Ali
(Forest Office, Dharamsala, Punjab)

8th Cavalry, attached 2nd Lancers [Urdu]
France 4th July 1917

I am sick to death of this military life, and I wish to ask your advice. If I return alive from this war, I shall certainly take my discharge and I want your advice as to what kind of work I should then take up. My wish is to enter the Forest Department. Do not speak of the matter to my father or to any one amongst my relatives. My father is not conversant with the times. He thinks service in the Army to be the best and most honourable; but those times are gone when honour was shown to the Army. Nowadays, the Army is without honour. Perhaps in forty or fifty years such a time will return when the Army will enjoy honour; now it has none. Certainly during the three years I have served in the Army I have gained in bodily vigour and mental capacity, and these will now serve me well in civil life.

540

Dafadar Tal Singh to Risaldar-Major Hira Singh
(Rajput, 19th Lancers, France, 40)

Depot 19th Lancers
Sialkot [Urdu]
[Punjab] 7th July 1917

In regard to Bhura Singh I wish to say that he sent a letter by the hand of Baj Singh in which it was stated that he was experiencing very great hardships in France, and that he did not expect to survive them. And he asked that as far as possible the men of his village should be prevented from enlisting. Accordingly, I urge on you that he should be told never to write such a letter again.

541

Risaldar Samand Khan to Jemadar Muhammad Hayat Khan
(Punjabi Muslim, 18th Lancers, France)

[Punjab?]

[Urdu]
11th July 1917

May God give you victory and defeat the Germans. Serve the King well and illuminate your name:–

> Whose salt you eat,
> Sing his praises.
> Never forget him;
> Satisfy his needs.

The Government has given us great honour, and you must not take things lightly as though they were of little account like the grass that springs up suddenly in the month of July. You must take them seriously like a game of chess. I will recognize your claim to bravery when you have justified it by deeds. Now is your opportunity to make a name for yourself. If you miss it, you will regret it, just as a false move at chess is followed by many difficulties.

542

Shah Pasand Khan (Muslim Rajput) to his brother
Ali Khan (Jhelum District, Punjab)

38th CIH [?]
France

[Urdu]
11th July 1917

It has been ascertained from Mahomed Ghazan Khan's letter what Madat Khan's daughter has done. Now write and tell me whether she has been found or not. If she has been found, taunt Madat Khan loudly and say to him 'now live on the earnings of your daughter. We told you she was a bad lot, and you fought with us in consequence, saying that we were idle talkers. Now do you realize the truth of what we said or not?' When she is found, then, if it can be done, make an end of her and kill her, because she has made it impossible for us to show our faces anywhere [through shame]. Somehow or other free us from this calamity; make an end of her; kill her. Otherwise, as long as she lives, she will not quit her evil ways. [Letter detained[1]]

1. The letter was detained because it contained an incitement to murder.

543

Malik Mahomed Khan to Tikka Khan (Punjabi Muslim, 38th CIH, France)

Punjab Canal Colonies

[Urdu]
13th July 1917

You wrote about taking vengeance when you come back. That opportunity, my brother, is far distant. First of all, do your duty towards your Emperor of India, whose salt you eat, and then you will be a loyal subject when you return to your country; after that you can get your own back. What is the use of firing blank cartridges from France? Do you think your enemy will be awed by a letter? When you show your valour on the field of battle, then he will be afraid of you.

544

Gul Khan (Muslim Rajput) to Hafiz Mehruddin (Gujrat District, Punjab)

38th CIH
France

[Urdu]
13th July 1917

Tell me all about the present occupant of the *Pir*'s seat of office; give him my compliments and tell him that one of his humble servants is fighting in Europe; and ask him to pray for me, and also to send me some prayers to say, so that I may be preserved from any violation of my faith, and that everyone may have me in regard, and also that I may not be harmed by the enemy; also that God may from His treasury give me the means of livelihood.

545

Risaldar Dayal Singh (Sikh, 42) to Chuni [?] Lal
(Campbellpur, Attock District, Punjab)

6th Cavalry
France

[Urdu]
14th July 1917

I am not afraid either to live or die. This is all in God's hands. I have escaped hitherto from a rain of shells and bombs, and I believe it will be the same in the future. If

He has laid down that my work shall lie in the midst of such a blazing fire I shall go on doing it with His help. There are two points to note in this. The first is that God has ordained my career; and the second is that loyalty to the King compels me to serve him and to be true to my salt.

I am sure victory is at hand, and we shall soon return to our native land. The enemy's condition is very bad and it is difficult for him to preserve his life. He is surrounded on every side, and you will soon hear of a glorious victory being won. He will soon be crushed under foot, for the condition of our Army and those of our allies is improving day by day. No one fears death. If a demand is made for a volunteer to go ahead, a thousand offer.

The evil deeds of the German have excited universal indignation. He utterly destroyed all the towns and villages, and blew up the roads, and cut down the fruit trees, and has burnt everything. He has seized and taken away the civilian inhabitants. This is not a royal way of waging war.[1] Our Government's behaviour is of a very different kind. It is that of a real King.

1. He is referring to the 'scorched earth' policy carried out before the retreat to the Hindenburg Line in March 1917. Many German soldiers were themselves distressed by the policy.

546

Dayal Singh (Sikh) to his wife (Rawalpindi District, Punjab)

6th Cavalry   [Gurmukhi]
France   14th July 1917

You say you are ill; but what you do not say is the nature of your sickness. In a former letter the same thing happened. I don't know what has happened to your understanding. The present times are such that, leaving all other matters aside, women are doing all the work of their houses; and they are even engaged in war and in ploughing the land. In short, women are doing work which men find it impossible to do. I can't understand how you who are sitting at home can do no work.

547

Zabu Shah (Hindustani Muslim) to his mother (Farrukhabad District, UP)

6th Cavalry   [Urdu]
France   17th July 1917

Today we are keeping the fast. We had to give it up for a fortnight, but today we have begun again. We do not feel hungry or thirsty, but should very much like to have a pull at a *hookah*. We are in the trenches. A Muslim named Amir has sent about fifty excellent *hookahs* for each regiment. Just think of where we are and what luxuries we have! Life and death are in the hands of God, but there is no real discomfort in this war. Here in the midst of the battlefield, in [the] most dangerous places, we get not only necessities but every sort of luxury.

548

Botan Khan (Punjabi Muslim) to Abdul Aziz Khan (Lyallpur District, Punjab)

39th, attached 38th CIH   [Urdu]
France   17th July 1917

You say that I am burning a heart that has already been consumed [in writing to you as I did]. From this it would seem that you had bestowed a kingship on me. But I would remind you that in these days even Kings are involved in anxieties, and my own anxieties will be disclosed to you partly by what the newspapers say, and partly by the photographs which I sent you recently. Between the 5th June and the 9th July, the following events have occured. Take the photographs which have a round mark at the back, and then regard the face of the photograph. All the men who have a dot placed over them have been killed. Those who are indicated by a dot in the middle of a circle are either prisoners or missing, and those who are marked with a cross have been wounded. If you look at these photographs you will doubtless realize how matters are with me. I gave the same information to Abdul Majid Khan, and he congratulated me on my skill.

549

Risaldar-Major Amar Singh Bahadur (Sikh, 45) to
Dafadar Lal Singh (Amritsar District, Punjab)

38th CIH   [Gurmukhi verse]
France   17th July 1917

What news can I give you but the following:

Many bridegrooms whose thoughts were with their brides have passed away.
Many other men have struggled with death like fluttering pigeons.
Their widows are weeping, since nothing but sorrow remains for them on earth.
Many who were met by the canon's blast have passed silently beyond,
            as one sails away in a ship.

550

Safdar Ali Khan to Signaller Jalib Hussain Khan
(Punjabi Muslim of Baluchi origin, 18th Lancers, France)

15th Lancers, attached 27th Lancers
Saugor [Urdu]
UP 17th July 1917

We have arrived safely in India, having been released. The King has been very gracious to us. We have been released. We were blameless. Now we are in the Remount Depot, and each man has three horses to train. We first came to Calcutta. From there we went to Madras where we received equipment and recruits. The Regiment was then sub-divided, one portion going to Bangalore [Mysore], another to Sehore [Central India], and the third to Saugor. After having seen the face of Hell, and after having in fact lived there for one year and three months, we have returned in safety. God has been merciful to us.[1]

1. On the King's birthday in the summer of 1917, the mutineers of the 15th Lancers (other than 'ringleaders') obtained their freedom in return for work in the Remount Depot of the regiment. For an account of the mutiny see Nos. 259 and 276.

551

Jagat Singh (Sikh) to Kot Dafadar Jai Singh (19th Lancers, Sialkot, Punjab)

19th Lancers [Urdu]
France 18th July 1917

This long separation has unsettled my mind. God knows when this calamity [the war] will be removed from us, and a new spirit enter our half-dead bodies. Why has our Government ceased to think of us who have been exiled from our native country for three years, while at the same time diverse calamities are devastating our homes? Why cannot something be done to release us from this servitude? There must be hundreds of fresh men in India who are only too ready to come in our place.

552

Dafadar Tak Chand (Jat) to Jhanda Singh (Rohtak District, Punjab)

6th Cavalry [Urdu]
France 18th July 1917

In the beginning of July we had a good chance of fighting, and though the regiments lost in different proportions we all did good work. We had only six casualties in our regiment. In the 20th [Deccan Horse] Jug Lal when scouting was struck on the head by a bomb and killed instantly. Jemadar Gaya [Ganga] Bishan took some men and brought in the body, and he was buried in the customary way as becomes a brave soldier. One man of your village was killed, and I went at once and saw the grave and put some earth on it. Such a death is a glorious one, and if God gives such deaths ten times a day, praised be He!

553

Bhaga Singh (Sikh) to Mihan Singh (Raewind, Lahore District, Punjab)

[38th CIH or 2nd Lancers] [Gurmukhi]
France 21st July 1917

Be it known to you that [Sowar] Darbara Singh [38th CIH] has been awarded the [Indian Distinguished Service] Medal for bravery. He did very good work in the trenches. We made an attack on foot, and took three trenches from the enemy. We suffered heavy losses. We took thirty of the enemy prisoners, and four machine guns. Many of our men were killed. Seven men were taken prisoners, forty-six wounded, and thirty-three were killed. Darbara Singh killed three men with the bayonet, and brought away a machine gun. For this reason he received the medal for bravery. I was struck by two bullets. One passed through my breeches, and the other through my turban. Two or three signallers who were with me were killed. The enemy attacked and retook the trenches, which we had taken from him, and the Sikhs fled like deer. Our condition is very bad. There is no remedy. We are in great straits. Reply to this letter quickly. I impress it on you. Read this letter carefully. If it is all right, write and tell me so. I impress it on you. What I have told you is the happening of one day. Write and tell me whether the letter is all right or not. I am quite well. Do not be anxious. [Letter detained[1]]

1. The censor remarked that this was 'an unpleasant letter and moreover was written in cipher. It was sent to GHQ and forwarded thence to Army Headquarters'. It is hard to see why it was considered so objectionable.

554

Abdul Ali Khan (Hindustani Muslim) to Fazl Ali Khan (33rd Cavalry, Multan, Punjab)

6th Cavalry   [Urdu]
France   22nd July 1917

We had the Id on the 21st. My congratulations! Owing to your good fortune it was a very happy day.[1] Thanks be to God, such joy was shown as I have not yet seen out here. All the Muslims of the Division had their prayers together and the assembly was close to our regiment. We as far as possible gave them food and tea also. About 1,500 men assembled and prayers were offered for the victory of our King. After that we had sports and such a display of joy that I cannot describe it. All the Sahibs thanked us for what we had done, and now at midnight full of happiness I am sitting down to write this letter.[2]

1. We do not learn what the good fortune was.
2. The collection contains several accounts, mostly joyous, of this Id. For many of the troops it was their third in France.

555

Munshi Ram to Risaldar Man Chand (Jat, 6th Cavalry, France)

Rohtak District   [Urdu]
Punjab   24th July 1917

It would seem that you do nothing but eat rations there [in France]. When you have the opportunity you should fight with all your might and make the Germans suffer; in fact you should destroy them utterly. It grieves me that, owing to my hand being useless, I am unable to do anything. If it had not been for that, I should endeavour to return to France for the second time. Recruiting is going very strongly in my district. The Government thinks much of our clan, and in fact all are now recognizing our merits, and it is likely therefore that in the future better civil appointments will be given to men of our clan.

556

Jan Mahomed Khan (Hindustani Muslim) to
Abdullah Khan (Rohtak District, Punjab)

2nd Lancers   [Urdu]
France   25th July 1917

I have received your letter, the reading of which gave much pleasure to one of my
hearts, but caused sorrow to the other heart which Government have presented to
this exile. I understood from it that they [the girl's family] are pressing for the marriage
to take place. In this there must certainly be some object, because on the one hand,
at [the] present time, all Hindustan is aware that the loyal soldiers of India are fighting
for their King and country in France, and are ready to sacrifice their lives if
necessary; whereas on the other hand those people who are pressing for the
marriage act as though they were blind and deaf. It would be better if, instead of
pressing for the marriage, they would send up prayers to God that Jan Mahomed
[himself] be speedily come back to India. I am here in a strange land, surrounded
by anxieties and trials, and they chose this time for pressing for the marriage to
take place! Tell me, how do you think I could, at the present time, leave all my
fellows in the Regiment here, and present myself in India? Jan Mahomed is here
at the present time after having traversed the seven seas, and instead of praying
for his return they grieve him by their persistent requests for him to return for the
marriage! Now, I have no fear of death; but the wound caused by these letters will
remain in my heart. As long as I live, I shall not forget the hurt they have caused
me. You yourself could have told them, that at a time when the whole nation is
preparing to sacrifice itself for King and country, it was not proper for them to act
in this way.[1]

1. This is one of many similar responses to relatives urging soldiers to return to India on
    leave or for marriage.

557

Udel Singh (Sikh) to Dil Singh (Ludhiana District, Punjab)

38th CIH   [Gurmukhi]
France   31st July 1917

Our condition is like this. Some days it is very bad – so bad that hanging would
be preferable. Some days it is enjoyable, as though one were at a fair watching the
sports. Some days it is such that we are enabled to pass weeks and even months

in ease. Some days it is such that shells fly about grazing one's body, and we lie sleeping but by the grace of the Guru. We have passed through such days even in safety. There is no news yet about our return. I myself have no hope that I shall live to return; but if the Guru wills otherwise we shall meet.

558

Samandar Khan (Pathan) to
Khan Zaman Khan (Jangal Khel, Kohat District, NWFP)

36th Jacob's Horse   [Urdu]
France   [early August 1917?]

I have been tried by court martial just like Pir Badshah and I have been deprived of my dafadarship. This is all due to the kindness of Makbul Shah of Mian Khel; also of Altaf Shah and Wazir Khan. The English officers have found out all the truths of the affair, and they contemplate restoring my rank, but those three men are doing their best to prevent this. I can settle this business here in France but still it might have a deadly effect on our caste, and for this reason I have decided to put up with the affair for the present. If the Sahibs decide to act on the advice of these three men then you will hear that life is dearer than property, but that *izzat* is dearer even than life itself. I have made my complaint. It is quite possible that I shall see none of you again. I have no debts, and it is quite on the cards that I shall not get your next letter.[1]

1. The censor noted that 'a copy of [this letter] was sent to the OC Jacob's Horse, and the writer was tried by court martial and dismissed the Army'. He gives no reason for this punishment; but it seems probable that the second half of the letter refers to the writer's intention to kill his three enemies, named earlier.

559

Risaldar-Major Ganga Dat (Jat, 49) to
Risaldar Mukh Ram (Depot, 2nd Lancers, Allahabad, UP, 47)

2nd Lancers   [Urdu]
France   1st August 1917

We had our Divisional sports on the 25th and 26th, and our regiment was highly praised by all the officers for its proficiency in trick riding. There were also many French officers present. Dafadar Raj Singh got a medal and thirty francs – the first prize for jumping. For section jumping, his section won the fifty francs prize. D Squadron won the prize for wrestling on horseback, and eight men got forty francs each. Forty men were in for the gymnastic competition and got 550 francs amongst them. There were fourteen men of our D Squadron in this competition.[1]

1. At this time, the Fifth Division (of which the 2nd Lancers were part) was quartered some distance behind the lines. The regimental, brigade and divisional sports were apparently a great success. Letters written by British officers and men of the division express great admiration for the trick riding of the Indian cavalry, especially that of the 2nd Lancers. According to the censor, this letter revealed that 'the money prizes given at the sports were highly appreciated'.

560

Risaldar Samand Khan (retired) to
Jemadar Muhammad Hayat Khan (18th Lancers, France, 35)

India

[Urdu]
1st August 1917

Serve the Government with all your mind and strength, and do not grow weary and impatient. When God has brought the Germans low to destruction you will receive your just rewards in fame and honours. The Germans are now regretting that they ever started this war, since it still remains unfinished. Their success was short-lived, but now our King has the upper hand, and India is giving him great assistance. Now please God, he will soon obtain victory. There was also great activity on the frontier here, but now the Pathans have been completely beaten – as badly beaten as they were in the Tirah campaign [of 1897] when, as you know, we wrought such havoc amongst them that they prayed for mercy with clasped hands. Now the Pathans are again beseeching Government to show mercy on them. The Government, however, will not pardon them, and it is expected that the Sirkar will take all their country as far as Kabul. Do your work well and secure a medal.

561

Gokul Singh (Jat) to Ressaidar Siri Lal
(5th Cavalry, Risalpur, Peshawar District, NWFP, 47)

6th Cavalry
France

[Urdu]
5th August 1917

This letter is for my mother, but I am addressing it to you. We have no discomfort of any kind. We are all strong and fit and loyal to our kind Government. Our loins are girt and we are ready and have made up our minds to discharge our obligations to the King whose salt we have eaten. Our kind Government gives us everything that is possible – food, clothes and amusements.[1]

1. There are many letters in this vein, written to reassure anxious relatives.

562

Dafadar Ghulam Mahomed Khan (Punjabi Muslim) to
Munshi Ghulam Mahomed (Gujrat District, Punjab)

19th Lancers [Urdu]
France 8th August 1917

I will send you money in two months or so. At the present time we do not know whether we are returning to India or not.[1] In six weeks or two months the affair will certainly be settled. Either the Indian troops will go back to India or else we shall be detained for another year. But I am full of hope that we shall return at the beginning of winter because the forces have been here a long time, and our three years will be up in November.[2] I am therefore not sending you money now, because if we do go back we shall want the money on the voyage. Another thing is that the commission on money orders is as much as Rs.3 for Rs.15 – so you see what a loss it would be to send money in this way. If I send you Rs.18 you will only get Rs.15.[3]

1. Rumours that the troops were about to return to India had begun to circulate once more. This letter is one of several examples.
2. Several men expressed the belief that they would obtain a discharge after three years. What they do not seem to have understood was that enlistment was for three years, or for the duration of the war, if that were longer.
3. This was probably an excuse to avoid remitting money. An Indian soldier was allowed to send home a sum equal to his pay without the levy of any money-order commission, as the writer was likely to have known.

563

Harji Singh (Dogra) to Ressaidar [Jemadar?] Bhagwan Singh
(19th Lancers, France, 39)

Dhariwal [Urdu]
Punjab 10th August 1917

The letters which come from you have been opened and closed again. Is it in accordance with orders, that letters should be checked in transit? For this reason do not write anything in your letters beyond your welfare ... Cannot you get leave even after three years? You should come back, if only for a few days. Thousands of sirdars and sepoys come home on leave; have you then taken a vow not to return? Does the Sirkar propose to give you a gratuity in place of leave? Whether they have or not, still there is nothing wrong in your coming for a few days just to see your family and friends. You could return again after a few days. Would it be preferable if a petition were sent from here? You need not reply to this question, because the purport of your reply might be distressing to the Sirkar, and if I were to send a petition without your consent you might be displeased.

564

Jemadar Abdul Rahim Khan (Deccani Muslim, 34) to
Havildar Mahomed Ibrahim (Hyderabad, Deccan)

29th Lancers   [Urdu]
France   10th August 1917

This war is one of brave men. If any faltering is shown it is an act of treachery to one's salt. It was for a day like this that the Sirkar trained us up like its own children, and asked holy men to pray for us just as we do for our children. Do you think that it would be fair to ignore these things? Never! Be comforted and go on praying that the men now fighting may return victorious.

565

Arjan Singh (Sikh) to Bachittar Sing (Khalsa School, Sialkot, Punjab)

6th Cavalry   [Urdu]
France   16th August 1917

The Colonel today wrote to Sialkot about your being enlisted. So go at once to the Major Sahib and, when you are accepted, write to me. I have thought the whole thing out, and it is for your profit. Mind you enlist, and do nothing else. Do not follow any other counsel. I shall be very angry with any one who advises you to the contrary. Once you are enlisted, eat well and dress well, and in your leisure moments play football. You will be seventeen in September, so you must enlist.

566

Chattan Singh (Sikh) to Harman [?] Singh (Gurdaspur District, Punjab)

19th Lancers or 6th Cavalry   [Urdu]
[France]   17th August 1917

Do not be anxious because we are very comfortable here, and the Government treats us with the greatest consideration. Even the King and the Queen (who is a real Princess) came here *four* times to see us. They asked all the men if they had any complaint to make about anything at their homes and they all said 'no'. The Colonel asks us all every month whether we have any trouble at home, and, if anyone says he has, the Colonel sends on his petition to the Deputy Commissioner who decides satisfactorily.

567

Nadir Khan (Punjabi Muslim) to Raja Khudadad Khan (Abadan, Persia)

19th Lancers   [Urdu]
France   20th August 1917

The people at home have made up their minds that I shall not come back, but they do not know the power of the Almighty. This no doubt is not an ordinary war, but a very great one. If you listen to what men say who have shared in the war and gone back, no doubt not much comfort is to be got; but those who trust in God come to a different conclusion. You know that when corn is being ground between millstones, some grains get into the centre hole of the millstone and escape being pulverized. In the same way your servant, by His Grace, will escape and will see you again. Amen. The German is retreating precipitately from his Hindenburg Line, and our friends are pursuing him vigorously.[1]

1. His remark is overoptimistic. In fact the Hindenburg Line was not breached until the late summer of 1918.

568

Mahomed Khan (Hindustani Muslim) to Dafadar Manuch Khan
(5th Cavalry, Risalpur, Peshawar District, NWFP)

6th Cavalry   [Urdu]
France   20th August 1917

I have received a letter today, the perusal of which has made me much ashamed. Well, whatever I have done, it was my fate. When I came here to the field, nothing was further from my mind [than] that I should contract a marriage here. My sole desire was to make a name for myself. However, whatever God wishes will happen. Things do not happen according to the wishes of men. This net was drawn very tightly round me, and if I had not married I should have been separated from you for the rest of my life. Regarding your enquiry as to whether my mother will be expected to perform the service of maid to my wife, my reply is no. My wife has no need of the services of a maid, nor will she go to Hindustan. Why do you think evil? You are welcome to my home [in India] and to my village. When were you pleased with me formerly, that today you are displeased? From the commencement you were at enmity with me.[1]

1.　For other references to this marriage, see Nos. 492, 535 and 588.

569

Ramdial Singh (Rajput) to Kalyan Singh (Alwar State, Rajputana)

Jodhpur Lancers　　　　　　　　　　　　　　　　　　[Hindi]
France　　　　　　　　　　　　　　　　　　21st August 1917

You wrote about exhanging and getting into one of our regiments. You are so far right, in that this is the time for earning your livelihood. But you ought also to consider whether it is wise to put your hand into a blazing fire. But just as you please. You are alone, and that is why you are going. Then for whose sake are you going to encounter such troubles? God has given you a livelihood there, and I think it would be wise to stay at home. I will send you money if you want it.

570

Dafadar Sher Bahadur (Punjabi Muslim) to Raja Khan Alim Khan (Delhi)

34th Poona Horse　　　　　　　　　　　　　　　　　　[Urdu]
[France]　　　　　　　　　　　　　　　　　　23rd August 1917

Major Grimshaw[1] who commands the [Regimental] Depot has written to our OC complaining of the bad behaviour of the Punjabi Muslim recruits in the Depot. It is a great pity that the Major Sahib should be worried in this way. He has actually complained that when there is a likelihood of the recruits being called up to fight they do their best to go sick using unlawful means. Such a complaint is a cause not merely of regret, but of deep shame to all [of] us. The OC is preparing to send Risaldar-Major Husain Baksh [Bahadur, 42] out to India to set the Depot in order, but I feel doubtful as to his capacity for getting things right. The reason for my opinion is that the Risaldar-Major belongs to Shahpur [District] and the majority of the recruits to Jhelum [District]; and also he has qualified for pension and may not be very energetic.

1. R. W. W. 'Roly' Grimshaw, in command of the regimental depot after being severely wounded at the end of 1914. See No. 220.

571

Kartar Singh (Sikh) to Risaldar Moti Singh (Sangrur, Jind State, Punjab)

6th Cavalry   [Urdu]
France   25th August 1917

Ever since March we have been visiting the trenches. The war is at its height and every day four or five attacks take place. We are working on foot day and night, and you know what we suffer – there is no need for me to write. We get plenty of rations; the trouble is that we are always in uniform and get no time to sleep, and as for bathing, we can never think of it. The lice are crawling over us. Our hearts are failing us because of the length of the war. All the rest of our force has been transferred and we have no hope of leave. We are weak and the war is long because it is only this year that our Government has advanced. It is a great fight and we advance every day and we shall conquer, but it will take five or six years.[1]

1. War-weary letters like this one were becoming more common in late summer 1917.

572

Ressaidar [Woordi-Major?] Bishan Singh (Jat, 39) to
Choudhuri Dobi Dyal (Jullundur District, Punjab)

6th Cavalry   [Urdu]
France   28th August 1917

My prayer to you is that you will give up your foolish customs and extravagant expenses, and if you love your country will get others to follow your example. All our eyes have been opened since we came to this country. There are no beggars and no poor here. The country produces less than ours. Why then are they so much richer? Because they do not waste money on marriages, funeral and birth ceremonies, and do not put jewellery on their children. The children [in India] go about in ragged, torn clothes, and eat bread made of *gram* [chick peas], and yet when they are married we spend thousands of rupees on the ceremony. Then comes the moneylender with his decree, and attaches the property, and we go out and wander about in search of employment to keep us alive. What we have to do is to educate our children, and if we do not we are fools, and our children will be fools also. Give up bad customs and value your girls as much as your boys.[1]

1. For similar sentiments see Nos. 448 and 654.

573

Risaldar Samand Khan (retired) to Mahomed Hayat Khan (Punjabi Muslim, 18th Lancers, France)

Lyallpur District   [Urdu]
Punjab   29th August 1917

Night and day I pray to God to give our King victory, and satisfy the desires of my heart: to bring the tyrant German to the dust and destroy him. Give your best service to the Government. To serve the Government is an excellent thing, and for generations our ancestors have benefited by such service, and endured no hardships. The Muslims should understand this, and join together to render good service. The rains have never been so plentiful as during this season, and the crops are splendid. Those who are not engaged in playing this game of chess [the war] are happy, while the players have thought only for the game, and have no thought for the crops.

574

Mahomed Hasan Khan to Risaldar Dilawar Khan (Punjabi Muslim, 38th CIH, France, 49)

Jhelum   [Urdu]
Punjab   1st September 1917

The Deputy Commissioner and other high officials are always sending for the *lumberdars* and *ilakadars* and telling them about recruiting. The general public is being recruited, and an order for a census has been given. You can understand what this means, and it might be a fault if I said more. Great highhandedness is being shown nowadays, and I am afraid that our people's *izzat* will suffer greatly. If all the men are taken, then what will become of the women's purdah? You are a wise man. In my opinion the situation is a critical one. If it be possible, you or some other of our caste should return to India.

575

Sabir Ali (Hindustani Muslim) to Haidar Khan (Sultanpur District, UP)

6th Cavalry   [Urdu]
France   3rd September 1917

I hope Mahbot Khan will remember my exile. It is three years since I was separated from you, and I am like a fish out of water struggling convulsively on the bank. May God have mercy on me and grant my wishes and give me a sight of you. My heart is longing for a sight of you all.[1]

1. Many men wrote similarly homesick letters at this time.

576

To Dafadar Prag [Prayag?] Singh (Rajput, 2nd Lancers, France) from his wife

Moradabad   [Hindi]
UP   4th September 1917

Send for me. I will go with you and fight against the enemy and will never give way a foot, but will meet the Hun and keep my faith. I will show them what Rajput women are. I will behave like the heroes of old, and on the field of battle you shall see my bravery. The enemy will taste the edge of my *talwar*. I am with you for weal or woe, which is my religion. Let me keep my vow and fight along with you and smite down the foe. I am a Rajput woman. My bravery is second to none. I am so strong that if I be cut in pieces I shall not give way, and the enemy will be obliged to praise me. What, am I but your wife? My heart is like yours.[1]

1. See Nos. 206 and 487 for other, similar, letters from this woman. Two others (not reproduced in this collection) are quoted in Omissi, *The Sepoy and the Raj*, p. 76.

577

Dafadar Gokal Singh (Jat) to Lumberdar Hazari (Rohtak District, Punjab)

6th Cavalry   [Urdu]
France   9th September 1917

Do not be in the least concerned about us. It is three years since we left you, and if we are destined to live we shall see you again. But if not – well, we have already been separated for three years. If God is kind to us, then no one can do anything to us. No one thinks anything of the war by now. One and all enjoy the fighting and are quite content.[1]

1. The following day, in a letter to a different correspondent, the same man writes, 'all are well and happy ... There is nothing to complain of. Ears [censors] are always listening, you must understand', which perhaps implies that he means the opposite of what he says.

578

Dafadar Sher Bahadur (Punjabi Muslim) to
Raja Gul Nawaz Khan (Gujrat District, Punjab)

34th Poona Horse   [Urdu]
France   11th September 1917

No doubt you feel greatly this separation of three years, but you should not have any regrets. I am present in the war, and I take pride in serving our just Government, and in the fact that I am one of the number who are working to crush the head of the tyrant. That tyrant has not only disturbed the peace of the world, but aims at the destruction of all civilization. It needs no explanation to make evident that our Government has taken part in this war solely to uphold right and justice; and for this reason we have the confident belief that our efforts to overcome and destroy the enemy will soon be crowned with success, and that the haughty German will be made to repent of his evil deeds.

There is no doubt that we shall have to practise patience and endurance in order to prevail against these trials and difficulties which stand in our way to victory. The greatest difficulties have already been removed, and we now look expectantly for the end. No one, whatever his nationality, should, at such a juncture as this, leave the field of battle in order to satisfy a craving to return to his home. It would be shameful for anyone who enjoys sound health to seek to return, for this is the time when each and every one should join to give their best service to their country.

579

Nawal Singh (Jat) to the Hon. Chaudhuri Lal Chand (Rohtak District, Punjab)

20th Deccan Horse   [Urdu]
France   14th September 1917

Our country is just the same as ever. If a man gets a little of any kind, he begins to think himself a great swell. Is it not incumbent on you gentlemen to keep on writing letters of encouragement to your fellow caste-men wherever their squadrons are, and to say to them 'onward you lions, you will gather the fruit of your labours'. But I am afraid that those gentlemen who are so very highly educated look on the soldier as a fool, and it is certain that Indian gentlemen do not honour the profession of arms as it is honoured in the country of France. Pleaders say to you 'he is only a soldier; why do you weary your brains trying to instil anything into him?'

580

Dafadar Jeswant Singh (Sikh) to Dr Prem Singh (Rawalpindi District, Punjab)

19th Lancers   [Urdu]
France   14th September 1917

'British' rank has now been sanctioned for Indians. It is a matter for much congratulation that our Government has conceded this right to us.[1]

1.   From 1917, ten places a year were reserved at Sandhurst for 'suitable Indians' – defined as 'selected representatives of families of fighting classes which have rendered valuable services to the State during the War'. These men obtained the King's Commission (previously closed to Indians) if they passed out successfully.

581

Balwant Singh (Rajput) to Doti Singh (Jaipur State, Rajputana)

Jodhpur Lancers   [Hindi]
France   14th September 1917

I am very happy here, and am doing my master's work continually with heart and soul just as my ancestors have always done. We hope that our Government will be victorious, and for this we are praying. Besides, it is the special duty of a Kshatriya to give his life for his King on the battlefield, just as his forefathers did.

582

Azad Khan (Pathan) to Jemadar [?] Khan (Peshawar District, NWFP)

19th Lancers   [Urdu]
France   17th September 1917

Alas for our condition! It is a great pity that we cannot write you an account of the fighting, for if we did, you would weep over our fate ... All of you must pray to God to deliver us from the vicinity of unbelievers, for we are no longer Muslims

– our faith is gone. It is really the Last Day! No one here can help his neighbour, and death would be preferable to such a life.

583

Azad Khan (Pathan) to Dafadar Zaidullah Khan
(Depot, 19th Lancers, Sialkot, Punjab)

19th Lancers   [Urdu]
France   18th September 1917

For God's sake, do not enlist any more Swatis, for we have no *izzat* here, but are in a bad way. We have no sirdars, and are spread all over the regiment. We are chaffed everywhere, and told we are shameless and false persons because we have been enlisted in the middle of the war. But we have not earned these reproaches and have fought well, and it is a great pity that we have been treated thus. I therefore abjure you to recruit no more Swatis.

584

Abdul Jabar Khan to Kot Dafadar Mohamed Yar Khan
(Hindustani Muslim, 6th Cavalry, France)

Jais
[Rae Bareli District]
UP   [Urdu]
                                                    24th September 1917

When I got out of the station [at] Jais, it was filled with people, and rockets were sent up and a band accompanied me home. On the road there was a scene just as if a general had arrived. When I got near my home, copper coins were thrown all over the place to the crowd. Yet it was only I! I could hardly contain myself, and when I came out of my house I found a crowd waiting. Every day for the past week there has been a crowd round the house. I can hardly find time to write as the house is crowded with people wanting to hear about everything.[1]

1. The censor commented, 'it is pleasing to hear ... of the rousing welcome given to a returning soldier by the good people of Rae Bareli in the UP'.

585

Lance Dafadar Dip Chand (Jat) to Sri Kishen (Delhi)

29th Lancers [Urdu]
France 26th September 1917

I am like a soap bubble, and have no hope of life! How many days is it since I was separated from you, star of my eyes. But you must realize that this is the time for brave men. I have Government work to do, and I must do it heartily. I consider it an honour that I am called to do this work, and am looked upon as a loyal subject. Do not be anxious. If I do not see you again, my name will be written in letters of gold and inscribed in the list of the brave. Then you will be proud of your friend who has given his life for the Sirkar. Our Government has done everything possible to make things easy for us and has provided us with every comfort, but up to date I have not been able to make any recompense. Now is the time.

586

Ghulam Mahomed Khan (Punjabi Muslim) to
Lumberdar Mahomed Hyat (Gujrat District, Punjab)

19th Lancers [Urdu]
France 2nd October 1917

Go on praying to God that He may have mercy on us. Up till now I am very well and not at all disturbed in mind. We have heard nothing about our return to India, and in fact I have no wish to return until our great King gains a full victory. We believe that such a victory is near at hand.

587

Risaldar-Major Muhammad Akram Khan (49) to Risaldar Zabte Khan
(Hindustani Muslim [?], 1st Lancers attached 9th Lancers, France, 41)

1st Lancers
Risalpur [Urdu]
[NWFP] 6th October 1917

Recruits are plentiful. The common people are desirous to secure victory in the near future. My regiment is indeed unfortunate in that it has not yet seen active service. You are fortunate and have set a fine example. May you get the Victoria Cross. This is the opportunity for the Punjabis to distinguish themselves.

588

Zabur Shah (Hindustani Muslim) to Risaldar Sayid Muhammad Amir Shah (5th Cavalry, Risalpur, Peshawar District, NWFP, 49)

6th Cavalry   [Urdu]
France   6th October 1917

Our Indian Government deserves to be congratulated. Notwithstanding the very great difficulties of distance, they arrange to perfection everything connected with the clothing and rationing of their Indian troops. Certainly their arrangements are superior to those of any other Government. I tell you truly (and don't think that I have any ulterior object in saying this) that the food supplied to us is not only sufficient, but abundant. As regards clothing, no troops are so lavishly supplied with good clothing as the Indian troops. If we fail to make the most of it, that is our fault entirely. The people of this country treat us with the greatest consideration and respect. One of our men has, with the consent of the French and British Governments, married into these people and a daughter has been born to him.[1] He gets leave frequently to see his family.

1. A reference to Mahomed Khan, whose marriage to a French girl caused such friction with his family. The wedding was in April, so the girl must have already been pregnant. See Nos. 492, 535 and 568.

589

Dafadar Ram Prasad (Rajput) to Ram Singh (Jampur, UP)

2nd Lancers   [Urdu]
France   8th October 1917

The same old rain and cold which mark the winter have now begun and will last till March. We hope, as I wrote before, that some arrangements for relief or leave will be made, and I am confident I shall see you. The state of the war is excellent, and the enemy is being beaten everywhere. With God's help we shall soon be victorious. All is well in the regiment.

590

*Safdar Ali Khan (Punjabi Muslim) to
Signaller Talib Hussain (18th Lancers, France)*

Remount Depot 15th Lancers
Saugor   [Urdu]
[UP]   8th October 1917

You asked me to write full details of my circumstances. You must by now have heard everything; and Gholam Sowar has also written, and you must have received his letter. There [in the Andaman Islands] we lived in comfort. It was only a case of our being under arrest. We received good rations and good food. We were blameless, and so Government showed us mercy. May God give our noble King and our illustrious Government victory for having treated us with such clemency. In the future we shall be careful not to be caught in the same kind of snare. What has happened, has happened. Without a shadow of doubt, this misfortune came on us through the treachery of our sirdars. Well, they are reaping their reward. Originally we were reported to be evilly-disposed people; but afterwards when our work was inspected by successive officials, and our conduct observed, they said with one accord 'these capable and well-behaved men are blameless'. We hear that we are now to received dismounted pay for the entire period of our arrest, and that our other rights and claims are to be admitted. Our non-commissioned officers have not yet been reinstated; but that will be remedied in due course.[1]

1. He is writing after having been released from imprisonment in the Andaman Islands, where he was sent for his part in the mutiny of February 1916. See Nos. 259, 276, 313, 315 and 550.

591

Jai Singh (Sikh) to Sundar Singh (Jhelum District, Punjab)

[19th Lancers or 6th Cavalry]   [Urdu]
France   9th October 1917

I forgot to write last week because I was so busy building a house to live in. It is a beautiful little shanty built of wood and scrap iron. There are twenty-five beams in it which would have cost Rs.15 each to buy in India. My house is the best in the Brigade, and I have a stove inside. I have made full arrangements against the cold, as we expect to spend the winter out here and not in billets. My uncle came to see it, and he said 'you have had great practise in building huts and barracks'.

I said, 'when we go back to India, if you and I don't hit it off with the others at home we can leave them and build a little house for ourselves'. We have been here three months, and I have spent all the time building, and I have now made a palatial residence with a kitchen. The materials would have cost Rs.200 to buy. If we march, all these things will have to be thrown away and at our next station we shall collect everything just as before. This is how we do it. I go out into the ruined villages and collect tables and chairs and everything that we need. Through God's goodness I am able to build a house in which I can really take pleasure, and to build it for nothing!

592

Khan Mahomed Khan (Baluchi Muslim) to his father
Mahomed Abdulla Khan (Dera Ismail Khan, NWFP)

36th Jacob's Horse   [Urdu]
France   11th October 1917

Get Gul Sabab, Mahomed Zaman and Allah Nawaz as much teaching as you can, because that age is coming – in fact it has already come – in which the educated will be highly esteemed. This war has caused an upheaval of the times, and has opened the eyes of the careless. The people of Europe live in ease and comfort simply through education. Both men and women are sufficiently educated to know wherein lies their profit and loss, and to plan and secure their advantage. My own eyes have been opened since I came to Europe, and I have entirely altered the views which I held before. I wring my hands with regrets that I did not set myself to acquire learning, but regrets are of no avail now. I missed my chance and I am now well in years. If I live to return, and if God gives me children, I will fashion their lives according to my new ideas. Please God, I will give them a good education, whether they be sons or daughters. When I was in Hindustan and used to hear of anyone going to England for education, or even of anyone setting himself to acquire complete education in Hindustani, I used myself to say 'these people lose their religion and return as Christians'. Now that I have come here, I realize how wrong I was in my ideas. There is no question at all of religion – it is education alone which makes them wise, and teaches them to hate and abandon those habits and customs in our country which are improper, and to live according to their new ideas. Such people, however, are only one in a thousand, and have to contend with great difficulties at the hands of the majority who treat them as if they had lost their senses, whereas in reality it is the majority who are blinded by ignorance.

593

Lance Dafadar Chattar Singh (Sikh) to Hira Singh (Jullundur District, Punjab)

2nd Lancers	[Urdu]
France	15th October 1917

The winter has commenced here; and the snow, which causes much discomfort, is about to arrive. Bravo the sentry, who in the service of his King stands at his post, unmoved in spite of wind and cold, until he is relieved in due course! If, at such a time, his mother should see her son standing there, in spite of heart-rending shell and machine gun fire, she would instantly press her hands over her heart. Fortunate indeed are those parents whose sons have come to this war and are taking part in it. It is fitting that such sons should be born to their parents, otherwise they are useless. I daily call on the name of my brother, Arjan Singh, who testified to his loyalty with his life.

594

Azad Khan (Pathan) to Dafadar Zaidullah Khan
(Depot, 19th Lancers, Sialkot, Punjab)

19th Lancers	[Urdu]
France	15th October 1917

My brethren, for the sake of God and His Prophet do not come over here, for our people have no *izzat*, and nowadays we have two sirdars, Naslim Khan and Sarbaland Khan, who are such bad men as I have never come across before. If you can preserve your lives, stay in India. [Letter detained]

595

Kartar Singh (Sikh) to Risaldar Indra Singh (1st Lancers, Sagar)

6th Cavalry	[Urdu]
France	16th October 1917

Do not be anxious about [me]. I am not in any distress. I have no hope of leave. If I live, I will see you again, and if not – well. The fighting is so severe that we have no hope of leave. But do not be worried. It will come to an end someday.

596

To Dafadar Gurjit Singh (Rajput, 2nd Lancers, France) from his sister-in-law

[Karnal?]   [Urdu]
[Punjab]   17th October 1917

Send letters quickly every mail in order that our hearts may be comforted. You ought to tell us something about the war. Is it a very great war just now? There are all sorts of reports floating about, and men are being asked for from every household, and many recruits are being fetched. What is the cause of it all? I am much disturbed in mind hearing of it all. You ought to write something about it.

597

Raja Khan (Punjabi Muslim) to Mahomed Fazl (Rawalpindi District, Punjab)

38th CIH   [Urdu]
France   17th October 1917

Be good enough to tell my father to write every week. If it is too much trouble to write at length it will do if he simply makes his thumb impression on a sheet of paper and sends it. That will satisfy me, for I do not want long letters. What I feel now is that, if I get no letter from India I have no appetite at all and feel useless for my work. How can I help this? It is not in my power to feel otherwise. It is such a long time since I saw you that my heart has gone very soft.[1]

1. Many soldiers were writing similar homesick letters as winter approached. For many men, it was to be their fourth winter in France.

598

Abdul Alim (Hindustani Muslim) to Ibrahim Khan
(Remount Depot, Aurangabad, Gaya District?, Bihar?)

6th Cavalry   [Urdu]
France   19th October 1917

If you can get this book, send it to me: *Germany and the Present War* by General von Bernhardi.

[He encloses the following extract from an Urdu newspaper of unknown title.] '*Germany and the Present War*, by General von Bernhardi. In this book the General has described the full naval and military and the air forces of all the nations, and has compared them. He has discussed the political, financial and military conditions of the countries with a keen brain and with the greatest ability and with the most valuable knowledge. He has entered into the detail of every species of power included in the world, and the extent of force which each country can provide, and the various measures which each can undertake. He has shown with extraordinary skill the forces against which Germany has to contend, and he has shown how in this war she will fight on earth, sea and in the air, and what will be the result of the war. Lakhs of this book have been printed, and it is in the 27th edition. To be had at the office of the "Albayan" Asi Press, Lucknow.'[1]

1. The censor commented that this letter 'was sent to GHQ for orders, and has been sent from there to the War Office. The enclosure was a cutting from an Urdu paper which it is impossible to identify. One of my Indian assistants who has just joined from India tells me that ... the translation of von Bernhardi's book into Urdu has had a very large circulation in India ... This translation and its popularity are no doubt known to the authorities in India, but, although the publisher has no doubt no object beyond selling his book, it seems open to question whether an "appreciation" like this of an enemy book, or the book itself, should be allowed to circulate freely in India, especially among the soldiers.'

599

Mahomed Jalaluddin to Colour-Dafadar Mahmud Ali Khan
(Deccani Muslim, 29th Lancers, France)

Hyderabad [Urdu]
Deccan 19th October 1917

A petition is about to be sent on the part of your mother to the Commander-in-Chief and the Viceroy about your return. In it is stated that you have been on field service for three years, that your mother is ill, and there is no one to manage your home. For this reason, it is urged that you should be sent back for a short time. It is said further that your mother is suffering great loss owing to your being absent from home, and it is urged that her helplessness may be taken into consideration and that you be sent back. We are hopeful that on reading this petition the heart of the Sirkar will be moved with pity. A petition was sent in the [first] instance to your Commanding Officer, and the answer received to it was to the effect that leave cannot be given at present, but that when leave is sanctioned your case will be borne in mind. In view of this reply, a petition is now being sent to the Commander-in-Chief and the Viceroy.

600

Mahomed Mazafar Khan (Punjabi Muslim) to Sahib Khan (Gujrat District, Punjab)

19th Lancers   [Urdu]
France   21st October 1917

Comfort your heart, because this war is not going on for ever. Wherever one is, there is a chance of death. Everyone except God has got to go one day. Pray to God that He will spare us. I am suffering for one end only – *izzat*. My duty is to help Government and increase the reputation of our family.

601

To Ali Mahomed (Hindustani Muslim, Lucknow Casualty Clearing Station) from his mother

Lucknow   [Urdu]
UP   23rd October 1917

My son, my soul craves to see you again, and my eyes search for you. You have been away three years, and so you can now get leave of absence. Why do you not come on leave? I spoke to Mirza Ahmed Beg about the matter, and he said that after three years' service you can get three months' leave. Write me the name of your Commanding Officer, and also the name of the officer under whom you enlisted, and I will get the Mirza to write a petition on your behalf. The one thing is that you should show me your face again, as I have an intense longing to see [you]. After that, you can return to your duty. I pray for your life and welfare at all times, and ask that I may quickly see you again. My son, show me your face again before I die, for you know well that you are all I have in this world.

602

Lance Dafadar Jug Lal (Jat) to Ram Sarup Sarma (Rohtak District, Punjab)

6th Cavalry   [Urdu]
France   25th October 1917

I am always thinking about home now, but otherwise have no anxiety often. I comfort my heart by remembering that God is Lord of all. What I think is that, since our Government has spent large sums in bringing us over here, we are bound to accomplish the purpose for which we were sent. I am zealous for the glory of our King-Emperor, and am praying continually for his speedy victory, and [for] our return to India with our kind officers.

603

Lance Dafadar Sher Mahomed (Punjabi Muslim or Pathan) to the editor of the Khabit *[?] (Delhi)*

38th CIH [Urdu]
France 26th October 1917

I hear a story from Africa that a big fish was caught in a river there which had on its head, written in good Arabic characters, the *Kalima* [confession of faith]. The professors were very doubtful about this, but they made further enquiries and came to the conclusion that it was true, and that it was a demonstration of the power of God. Shortly after that, another fish was caught with the *Kalima* written on its head, and now all doubt is at an end. I have never seen Maulana Abul Kalam Azad, but I know his writings and as I am a devout Muslim I have great affection for him.[1] When I read the tyrannical declaration of the Court which has forbidden the Maulana the exercise of his religion I was full of sorrow. I never expected such a thing of Government, and do not expect it now. What I do complain of is the decision of the *Hakim* [judge or magistrate] interfering with our religion, for there can be nothing which would hurt the feelings of the Muslims here [more] than this. May God have mercy on us, and may He forbid that such things should ever be done to us.

1. Maulana Abul Kalam Azad (1888–1958) was a nationalist Muslim and political thinker, president of the Indian National Congress from 1939 to 1946. His Urdu religious weekly *al-Hilal*, first published in July 1912, was forced to close by the British in November 1914. Its successor, *al-Balagh*, closed in March 1916, when the Government of Bengal expelled Azad from the province. Azad himself was interned in July 1916, for three and a half years, at Ranchi in Bihar. This letter is the only one in the collection in which he is mentioned.

604

Jemadar Sultan Ahmed [Mahmud?] Khan (Punjabi Muslim) to Lumberdar Ghulam Mahomed Khan (Shahpur District, Punjab)

18th Lancers [Urdu]
France 1st November 1917

I urge you to get all the recruits you can for the 18th in my name. This is the time to help Government. Do your best, especially in Burhana, as I wrote to you before.

You have hitherto paid no attention to my request. If you don't get recruits you will suffer for it. The war is not going to last for ever, and not everybody is going to be killed. Put forth your best efforts.

605

Kishan Singh to Veterinary Assistant Gajan Singh (Sikh, 18th Lancers, France)

Nabha State   [Urdu]
Punjab   2nd November 1917

My son, you are indeed fortunate in that you have had the opportunity to discharge your debt of loyalty towards the Sirkar. You are not far from us; you are the son of your country, and a ready sacrifice in her welfare. My hopes are fixed on you, and our King takes pride in being served by such as you. You are a hero of this great age. May the Guru keep you well and happy. You are under the protection of God. You are a hero, and the security of my life. Our Government relies on you. When Aurangzeb[1] ruled over the land, he desired to root out our race [the Sikhs] root and branch. Today our King, ruler over the seven Kingdoms, is the protection of our race. His armies have subjugated Baghdad.[2] To you and to your fellows is due the honour of this achievement, and of the fact that the heart's blood of the Germans is being consumed ... We should send up unlimited thanks to Almighty God who has bestowed on us such honour and glory. Now I pray that God will speedily bring the day when your voice will be raised in the 'Hurrah' of victory, when you will feel the kisses of your mother, and be clasped in the arms of your wife, and when all of us, being filled with happiness, will raise our voices in praise to our Government.

1. Mughal Emperor (1659–1707) and oppressor of the Sikhs.
2. Captured by British and Indian forces in March 1917.

606

Dafadar Ram Nath (Jat) to Headmaster Baldev Singh
(Jat School, Rohtak, Punjab)

20th Deccan Horse   [Urdu]
France   4th November 1917

My idea is that, since it is now four years since I went to my home, my wife should, if she wishes it, be allowed to have connection according to Vedic rites with some other man, in order that children may be born to my house. If this is not done, then the family dignity will suffer. Indeed, this practice should now be followed in the case of all wives whose husbands have been absent for four years or more. It is permitted by Vedic rites, if the wives are willing. Everyone knows that that article, the consumption of which is increased while the production is stopped, will in time cease to exist. If any article is allowed to decrease through ignorance, no one is to blame; but when every one knows that an article is being consumed to extinction, while at the same time they are aware of the steps available to supplement production, they are greatly to blame if they hesitate to take those steps.

607

Jai Singh (Jat) to Sirdar Singh (Lahore District, Punjab)

6th Cavalry or 19th Lancers [Urdu]
France 6th November 1917

I am off to Paris, which has hitherto been 'out of bounds' to everyone but officers. Now we [dafadars?] can go. Paris is a city of fairyland, and God will now give us an opportunity of seeing it. I will write you all about it. I am taking Rs.250 to spend. Whatever happens do not let anyone know about this. I intend to enjoy whatever pleasures there are. Do not let anyone know that Jai Singh is spending Rs.250 in four days. If father heard of it he would be very angry.[1] I should like to marry in France, but I am afraid the family would be ashamed. You can marry very fine girls if you like.

1. Unsurprisingly, given that Rs.250 represented several months' pay.

608

Mohamed Muzarar [?] Khan (Punjabi Muslim) to
Sahib Khan (Gujrat District, Punjab)

19th Lancers [Urdu]
France 6th November 1917

When I read your letter, I began to weep. You are distressed; what, am I not in distress too, who have been enduring calamities for three years, and facing death every day? But you ought to remember that war was the profession of our ancestors, and it is mine too; and it is a subject of pride that so and so's son or grandson is in the war. It is the time to help the Government and to face death. The brave man has no home or country. They are for women only. You ought to be ... strengthening their hearts, and yet you write in such a way that your letters take away my appetite altogether.

609

Nur Zaman Khan (Baluchi Muslim) to
Syed Mahmud Khan (Mianwali District, Punjab)

36th Jacob's Horse　　　　　　　　　　　　　　　　[Urdu]
France　　　　　　　　　　　　　　　　　8th November 1917

Regarding what you say about increasing my family allotment, I desire to observe that at the present time the Government is in great need of recruits, and gives a bonus of Rs.50 to each recruit.[1] You, five brothers, are all lusty and strong, and it would be a grand idea if one or more of you were to enlist and thus secure the handsome Government reward. The Government would benefit, and you would get credit, and at the same time you would save much money.

1.　The bonus, payable on enlistment, was introduced from June 1917 in order to attract recruits.

610

Raja Khan (Punjabi Muslim) to
Mir Alam Khan (Khanpur, Hazara District, NWFP)

19th Lancers　　　　　　　　　　　　　　　　　[Urdu]
France　　　　　　　　　　　　　　　　　11th November 1917

Tell me whether the Court of Wards still exercises control of the property or not. You had written on a previous occasion to the effect that the Chief of Ghakkar had been given control over his property, and it now appears that the facts are otherwise. It is a disgrace that the men of our clan live in discord and wrangling, each one till his dying day, and thus heap up trouble for the clan. Well, the displeasure of God is on the clan because of their deeds.

If anybody doubts this, let him come here and see for himself the proof of what I say in this country of France. These lands and towns formerly owned by France, which were overrun by the enemy, have been so scourged by God that they are now in ruins, so much so that the owners of property cannot now say where their house stood originally. If the full details of all that has happened here were to be disclosed, the narration of them would break the hearts of the listeners.

Therefore all the dwellers in Hindustan should raise their voices in thanksgiving to Almighty God, day and night, that he has placed them under the shadow of a strong and just King, so that they live in peace and contentment. No tyrant King of another country dare raise his eyes in their direction. Open your eyes and see how the subjects of other countries are entangled in the snare of misfortune and are unable to extricate themselves – then you will be able fully to appreciate the worth of our great and just King. Day and night I pray Almighty God to lengthen his days, to elevate the star of his greatness, and to give him victory over the tyrant enemy. Amen.

611

Jemadar Man Singh (Sikh, 23?) to Sirdar Jeinal Singh
(Director of Agriculture, Jhalawar State, Rajputana)

6th Cavalry   [Urdu]
[France]   17th November 1917

This is the fourth Diwali festival since I left India. The state of things in India and France is very different. The chief difference is that in India tonight everyone will assemble in his house with his wife and children and father and mother and other relatives, and will have an excellent meal and be full of rejoicing. Here we see the very opposite. Everyone is separated from his kith and kin, and is thousands of miles away in a foreign country. Yet, thanks to God, I am fit and well and have everything I want, and there is only one worry – separation from you.

612

Lance Dafadar Zabur Shah (Hindustani Muslim) to
Mahomed Manawar Zaman Khan (Farrukhabad District, UP)

6th Cavalry   [Urdu]
France   19th November 1917

A petition came from India regarding leave to Mazar Ali Khan. I do not think it has the least chance of meeting with success. The Colonel Sahib and the Squadron Commander Sahib expressed their sympathy. It may perhaps be that some arrangement will be made for leave to men of three years' service. We hope so. For the rest, the matter rests in the hands of God. Here it is rumoured that orders have been issued that four thousand recruits must be raised in the Farrukhabad District. God knows how far the rumour is correct. At the same time that Mazar

Ali Shah's petition was sent, a communication was also sent by my foolish old mother in regard to leave for me, urging as an excuse the condition of her eyesight. This is the first occasion on which such a petition has been received in the Regiment. Shame! Impress it on my mother, for God's sake, not to trouble me in this manner. If God wishes it, and I remain alive, I shall come soon. Nothing is to be gained by sending profitless petitions of this kind.[1]

1.   Contrast the tone of this letter with that of Nos. 613 and 622, which are both from the same man to his mother (of whom he speaks so dismissively here).

613

Lance Dafadar Zabur Shah (Hindustani Muslim) to his mother
(Farrukhabad District, UP)

6th Cavalry   [Urdu]
France   19th November 1917

In what strain am I to write, so that you many understand that here, notwithstanding the war, I have not, up to this very day, endured any hardships comparable to those which I used to experience in Rawalpindi during camps of exercise.

As for life and death, I swear to you by God, that it is unthinkable that Muslims should cease to have faith in God in this matter, while unbelievers here have perfect faith. One day here when I was feeling uneasy in my mind, I opened at random the sacred Qu'ran and commenced reading just where the book opened. The very first text on which my eyes fell said 'Muslims think that in a battle they will perhaps die, whereas if they remain at home they will surely live. They do not remember that life and death are in my hands.'

Of course, during the winter we feel the cold somewhat. Mother, think, is this the kind of war that your fears for me make you imagine, when not a single day has passed during three years that I have not eaten my dinner at the appointed time nor a single night when I have not slept? I remember well that on ten occasions at least, during camps of exercise at Rawalpindi, I did not sleep for two nights running and had no food for even longer periods. During the winter here we get such an abundance of warm clothing that I swear to you that last year I did not have occasion even to wear the padded jacket which you sent me. God has been so gracious to me that I cannot be sufficiently thankful to Him for all His mercies.

614

Sowar Abdul Latif Khan (Punjabi Muslim) to
Abu Zar Khan (Jhelum District, Punjab)

38th CIH   [Urdu]
France   20th November 1917

I want you to get the *Pir* Sahib to pray for me and use all his influence to prevent
the sirdars and the sowars from viewing me unkindly and to make them select me
for any important duty. Get this done at once with 'his holiness', as these men are
bent on destroying my reputation and say I am a thief and a *badmash* of No. 10.[1]
Do not say a word about this except to the *Pir* Sahib.[2]

1. The allusion is to the Register No. 10 of 'bad characters' maintained under the Criminal
   Penal Code.
2. The censor commented that this and similar letters showed 'the way in which Muslims
   on active service cling to their *Pirs*, or spiritual guides, and the exaggerated ideas they
   have of the *Pirs*' powers'.

615

Lieutenant Narain Singh Bhai, IMS (Sikh) to
Ikbal Mahomed (Jullundur City, Punjab)

Mhow Field Ambulance   [Urdu]
France   26th November 1917

We have signally defeated the enemy and made him run. The cavalry had some
opportunity for fighting. We progressed to a distance of seven miles and captured
ten thousand prisoners.[1] We were in the vicinity of the fighting for three days and
nights, during which we neither ate nor slept. Still, we are very pleased as our work
was good, and we have [had] a suitable opportunity for showing our work. May
God speedily give us another such opportunity so that we may crush the enemy
and secure victory for our King, obtain peace for the world, and reunite those who
have been separated for so long.

1. On 20th November 1917, British Imperial forces, including 381 tanks, attacked the German
   positions in front of Cambrai. Over the next nine days, the allies advanced up to five
   miles. Some Indian cavalry units were involved in the fighting. Success was short-lived,
   however, as German counter-attacks regained most of the lost ground by 7th December.

616

Mahomed Usuf Ali Khan to Acting Lance Dafadar Ali Khan
(Hindustani Muslim, 2nd Lancers, France)

Amethi
[Sultanpur or Lucknow District]   [Urdu]
UP   28th November 1917

The Secretary of State for India, Montagu Sahib, has come to India and is staying
at Delhi.[1] Formerly he had declared his intention of visiting the principal towns
in India, so as to meet the people; but when the Hindus started rioting he said he
would not leave Delhi. He gave a whole day to the Muslims, conversing with them,
and made a favourable impression. They feel honoured. The Hindus are agitating
for Home Rule, but the Muslims are against it and wish the Government to remain
as at present they do not wish for Home Rule. This is the reason for the trouble
between the Hindus and Muslims. The Hindus have rebelled in various places, and
in Bengal seditious letters have been found in which it is urged that the unclean
races [the Muslims and Christians] should be driven out of the country or slain.
This is what they did in Arrah. Many disturbances are taking place.

1. Edwin Montagu (1879–1924) was Secretary of State for India from 1917 to 1922. In
   August 1917, he declared in the House of Commons that Britain's Indian policy would
   henceforth involve 'the gradual development of self-governing institutions, with a view
   to the progressive realization of responsible government in India as an integral part of
   the British Empire'. He toured India from November 1917 to April 1918. His discussions
   with the Viceroy, Lord Chelmsford, resulted in the Montagu–Chelmsford Report of 1918,
   which in turn laid the foundations for the limited devolution of power under the 1919
   Government of India Act.

617

Supply and Transport Agent Behari Lal (Punjabi Hindu) to
Babu Anandi Pershad (Agra, UP)

Supply and Transport Corps   [English]
Secunderabad Cavalry Brigade   28th November 1917

There is no likelihood of our getting rest during the winter. I am sure German prisoners
would not be worse off in any way than we are. I had to go three nights without
sleep, as I was on a motor lorry, and the lorry fellows, being Europeans, did not
like to sleep with me, being an Indian. [The] cold was terrible, and it was raining
hard; not being able to sleep on the ground in the open, I had to pass the whole

night sitting on the outward lorry seats. I am sorry the hatred between Europeans and Indians is increasing instead of decreasing, and I am sure the fault is not with the Indians. I am sorry to write this, which is not a hundredth part of what is in my mind, but this increasing hatred and continued ill-treatment has compelled me to give you a hint. [Letter detained[1]]

1. The censor described this – and two similar letters from the same man – as 'evil' and commented that they were 'detained as likely to do harm in India'. They were quite untypical of the majority of letters.

618

Azizuzzaman (Hindustani Muslim) to Lalla Ram Lal
(Farrukhabad District, UP)

6th Cavalry [Urdu]
France 28th November 1917

If I am taken by Death, then you must practise resignation. Consider how many dear sons of mothers engaged in this war have fallen wounded and dying in the mud and dirt. We see them lying there as we pass, and express our sorrow. How comely they were, those young men, who have been thus stricken down in this war, and how many such are dying every day! Yet their bereaved parents will think of their loss with resignation, even when their life is cut off by the death of their sons. When I go on leave to some big town here, I see scores of cripples whose parents have to practice resignation. Therefore you must recognize that patience comes from God, and you must receive what He gives you with thankfulness.

619

Clerk Mohamed Yusuf (Punjabi Muslim) to
the Manager Paisa Akhbar *(Lahore, Punjab)*

DAG's Office
3rd Echelon [Urdu]
France 3rd December 1917

Please send me the weekly edition of your paper. I want to see all the proceedings of the All-India Muslim League, which no doubt will be recorded in your paper. I am particularly interested in this matter.[1]

1. The censor commented that 'the writer, though a clerk ... is presumably a soldier, and shows the interest taken in the propaganda of the All-India Muslim League'. That said,

the reference to the League (or indeed to any political party) was very unusual. For other references see Nos. 346 and 453.

620

Khalil Ullah (Hindustani Muslim) to Salim Ullah (Muttra Cantonment, UP)

9th Cavalry attached 2nd Lancers   [Urdu]
France   6th December 1917

My friend, the black cloud came over the Regiment. We had escaped for three years; but unfortunately the 1st of December was an ill-omened day for us. Our hero, the lion-hearted one whom we all loved, and to whom the Regiment had given [the] title of 'The Lion' – that is to say our brave Colonel, who was named Colonel Turner – was killed. He was a great and good and clever man. Such men are rare in this world. He made a name for this Regiment amongst the whole Army, and has earned for himself a great reputation. We attacked the enemy and we took the position we were sent out to take, but unfortunately we suffered heavy losses. We don't know what the future holds for us, but while there is life there is hope. If death is one's fate, one cannot avert it.[1]

1. For another reference to Colonel Turner's death, see No. 623. There are several similar letters from men of the 18th Lancers, lamenting the death of their commander, Colonel Corbyn, who was also killed in the Cambrai fighting. See No. 630.

621

Tara Singh (Sikh) to his wife (Lyallpur District, Punjab)

6th Cavalry   [Gurmukhi]
France   7th December 1917

If you desire to come here, there is no reason why you should not do so. What you have to do is to write a petition to the Viceroy, saying that your husband has been in France for four years, and that you desire to be enlisted in some hospital corps and sent to your husband in France. Add whatever else you please. You will get a proper hearing.

622

Lance Dafadar Zabur Shah (Hindustani Muslim) to
his mother (Farrukhabad District, UP)

6th Cavalry [Urdu]
France 9th December 1917

Mother, have faith in God and I shall quickly return if He wills. Do not write any more petitions for my return. In fact, do not speak of the matter to anyone, for such things result in shame and nothing else. I suffered greatly for two or three weeks in consequence of the petition which you sent. It has achieved nothing, nor can it achieve anything. You should have consulted me before sending it. God knows who advised you to send it. Do not suppose, mother, that anyone has questioned me as to why the petition was sent. Nothing of the kind has happened, but I dread being ridiculed by others on account of your having petitioned for my return.

623

Ressaidar [Jemadar?] Jiwan Singh (Sikh, 36) to
Pensioned Subedar-Major Bhagat Singh (Amritsar District, Punjab)

2nd Lancers [Gurmukhi]
France 10th December 1917

This is the first time we have been called upon to fight as cavalry in our three years' field service.[1] Our regiment was in the forefront of the attack, and [so was] my squadron. Thanks be to God, the attack was made with the utmost bravery and it achieved splendid results. The fury of our charge and the ardour of our war cries so alarmed the enemy that he left his trenches and fled. At first we were assailed by machine gun fire like a rain storm from left and right, and afterwards from the front, but how could the cowardly Germans stand before the onslaught of the braves of the Khalsa! This credit is not due to us, but to the Guru, through whose favour we speared many of the routed enemy on our lances, and brought back many prisoners. On our return, celebrated generals came and congratulated our Regiment.[2] Our losses were light – two British officers and two Rajput sirdars were killed, and some sowers. Our brave Colonel Turner was also killed. Alas![3]

1. The Indian troopers were normally sent into action dismounted.
2. There were several letters in this vein. The censor commented: 'If the tone of their letters home is any indication of the morale of the troops, the Indian Cavalry, as might be expected, are in excellent fettle. This weather must be extremely trying, but there is hardly a grumble.

Whatever may have been the value of the recent operations in front of Cambrai, there is no doubt that the Indian Cavalryman realizes that he did his part of the work satisfactorily, and he is content.'

3. Lt.-Col. H.H.F. Turner, 49, Commandant of the Regiment. See No. 620 for another reference to his death.

624

Ressaidar Jowan Singh (Sikh) to [illegible] Singh (Gurdaspur District, Punjab)

2nd Lancers [Urdu]
France 10th December 1917

The Guru has forcibly taken Kartar Singh from me. I could do nothing for him, though I kept him constantly under my eye. It happened in this way. We were under very heavy shell fire, but had almost galloped through it when one fatal shell fell on us, killing Kartar Singh and another outright, and wounding several men. Do not be dismayed. Your son is a hero who has given his life for his King. He is not dead; he lives for ever. He has gone straight to Paradise, because that is the reward of death in the field of battle in the service of the King.[1] He has in fact achieved in an instant that which saints can only hope to secure after many years of trial. Earthly love is a small thing compared with the joys of Paradise.

1. See Nos. 12, 17, 62, 118 and 198 for other references to the end of the cycle of death and rebirth.

625

Zaildar Jawala Singh (Sikh) to Dafadar Kartar Singh
(9th Hodson's Horse, France)

Lyallpur [Urdu]
Punjab 11th December 1917

May God grant speedy victory to King George, that the anxiety of our hearts may be removed! I am in great trouble. My child of eight months is dead, and your sister-in-law is dead, and thirdly I am threatened with dismissal from my position both of *zaildar* and *lumberdar.* If my life would depart, that would be the best solution of the difficulty! On the 29th November, the Deputy Commissioner sent for me and gave [me] a month to finish my recruiting, saying that if I did not supply the men in that time I should be dismissed from both my zaildarship and lumberdarship.[1]

1. From 1916, to increase the flow of recruits, Indian officials were told to provide a given quota of men from their districts, on pain of losing their posts if they failed.

626

Sowar Abdul Wahab (Hindustani Muslim) to
Bahadur Singh (Rae Bareli District, UP)

Sialkot Field Ambulance [Urdu]
France 18th December 1917

When I think of your dear faces I can do nothing but weep, and for hours I sit gulping down my tears, and am in [an] extraordinary condition. I am really, just now, mad. How long shall we have to stay in this condition? I have no strength left to fight against misfortune, and the least thing affects my health. How long can I sustain the burden of separation, and yet there is no hope of release! It is bitterly cold and snow has fallen in abundance. As we are not as strong as we were last year, we feel the cold more.[1]

1. The censor remarked that this letter was 'a hysterical production; but the writer, though a sowar, is on ambulance work for which he is presumably more fitted. It is certainly not typical of the spirit of the men, and is the only letter of the kind which I have come across during the [past] fortnight.'

627

Abdul Majid Khan (Punjabi Muslim) to Mahomed Salim Khan
(Bikaner State, Rajputana)

19th Lancers [Urdu]
France 27th December 1917

You must write three or four petitions in English every week, as [if] coming from your sister. In them, you should say that I have been absent for about four years, and that she is in great difficulties as her father and mother have died. Say also that, owing to excessive rainfall, her house fell down two or three months ago, and that she is now obliged to live with other people. Ask then that I may kindly be given leave for two or three months, in order to rebuild the house as she is put to extreme inconvenience owing to her having no house of her own; and add that there are numberless other matters which require my personal attention. Write similar petitions on behalf of Sidik of the 20th Deccan Horse to the Colonel Sahib. For God's sake have mercy on us, and do as I say. True God is our helper, and His will must be done, but much can be secured by the energy of men.[1]

1. It was rumoured that men who had been in France for three years or more would get leave, if they received urgent petitions from relatives in India requesting their presence

(in connection with marriages, the rebuilding of homes or the death of close family members). This letter is one example of several attempts to 'work' what was thought to be the system.

628

Kala Khan (Punjabi Muslim) to
Iltaf Hussain (Bhatinda, Patiala, Punjab States)

Indian Labour Corps   [Urdu]
France   27th December 1917

You enquire about the cold? I will tell you plainly that the cold in France is like when I meet you. At present I can only say that the earth is white, the sky is white, the trees are white, the stones are white, the mud is white, the water is white, one's spittle freezes into a solid white lump, the water is as hard as stones or bricks, [and] the water in the rivers and canals and on the roads is like thick plate glass. What more am I to say? Our kind-hearted Sirkar has done everything possible for us to protect us from the cold. We are each provided with two pairs of strong, expensive boots. We have whale oil to rub in our feet, and for food we are provided with live Spanish sheep. In short, the Sirkar has accumulated many good and wonderful things for our use.

629

Mahomed Latif Khan (Punjabi Muslim) to
Sayed Abdullah Shah (Jhelum District, Punjab)

38th CIH   [Urdu]
France   28th December 1917

If you cast your glance with favour on your servant and keep in your kind remembrance, much benefit will accrue to him, and he will serve you even more faithfully, and will even bend his head in submission before you. You did not favour your servant with any reply to the request which he made, and you did not say anything in regard to those men who practise enmity against him, nor did you send him a talisman such as he desired for the fulfilment of his desires. Your prayers are of great efficacy; but what your servant wanted were such incantations, as he might use by reciting and then exhaling his breath in the direction of his enemies so that their thoughts towards him might become kindly – such incantations, moreover, as would give him prospects of promotion. If, at the present time, your servant were, through your help, to obtain promotion he would be prepared to serve you in whatever manner you might mention. Your servant also desires to make his sirdars favourably disposed towards him. At present, they regard him with disfavour, and whenever there is any duty to be done they excuse [each] other and place it on him. They say that your servant is inefficient, and make complaints to the British officers about him.[1]

1. The censor commented that 'this letter has psychological interest, and shows how superstitious some of the men are'.

630

Dilawar Chand (Punjabi Muslim) to Ressaidar Wali Muhammad Khan (18th Lancers, Shahpur District, Punjab, 35)

18th Lancers [Urdu]
France 28th December 1917

On the 30th November at noon the Germans made a sudden attack.[1] They did what they would. The cavalry were ordered to the front to attack the enemy. The Ambala Brigade was the first to arrive, and the 8th Hussars[2] attacked on horseback. Great God, what do you expect one to say! The enemy opened up with such an intense fire that men and horses were thrown on to each other. Then the 9th Hodson's Horse took up the attack. Major [A.I.] Fraser [D.S.O.] of C Squadron [Hodson's Horse] with sundry men were killed at the very opening of the attack. Later the attack on horseback was stopped and our Regiment took up a position in the front line facing the enemy. The 8th Hussars and 9th Hodson's Horse supported us; but they had suffered more casualties than we had. At eleven o'clock at night we were warned that we would have to counter-attack in the morning and to take the small wood in front.

At 6.30am we attacked on foot. The enemy saw us coming. Great God, what am I to say? You have been here, and you know. The enemy met us with so intense and rapid a fire that we were unable to advance. Consequently we were ordered to retire to our trenches. Later we were ordered to advance again, which we did. The enemy this time left his trenches and fled; but about fifty Germans came running towards [us] shouting 'India! Kamerad! Kamerad!' The regiment continued to advance in a dashing manner, although heavily shelled by the enemy's artillery; but by the grace of God there were no casualties except Dafadar Sher Mahomed Khan. The enemy's aeroplanes, flying low, fired on us, and Dafadar Falk Sher Khan was slightly wounded. A German prisoner lifted Dafadar Falk Sher Khan in his arms, and carried him to hospital, which was a fine deed. The Colonel Sahib[3] was also killed, but the Regiment did its duty thoroughly.

1. A successful counter-attack (supported by low-flying aircraft) at Cambrai, which regained much of the ground lost to the Allied tank assault of 20th November.
2. A British cavalry regiment of the Ambala Brigade. See Appendix I.
3. Colonel Corbyn. Compare Nos. 620 and 623.

1918

Budda Shah to Riaz Hussain Shah (Punjabi Muslim, 18th Lancers, France)

Sialkot   [Urdu]
Punjab   4th January 1918

The news is that compulsory recruiting is in progress. In addition, the following taxes are being levied – two *seers* of *atta* per house, and one anna on each tree. May God give victory to our King. By the favour of the sirkar, the one rupee note has been supplied to the treasury; but has not yet been put into circulation. 'Our Day' labels have also been issued, and the proceeds of their sale go to benefit the wounded. I have put one of them on this envelope for you to see. Each *lumberdar* has to produce ten recruits.[1] He has also to enlist a son, a brother, or other relative of his own. Thousands of men have been passed as fit and enlisted in Sargodha and sent into the Army. Our own *lumberdar* gets off fairly easily as he has already recruited more than the fixed number of men.

1. For other examples of forced recruiting, see Nos. 444 and 574.

632

Dafadar Khadam Hussain (Pathan) to
Chiragh Hussain (Kohat District, NWFP)

36th Jacob's Horse   [Urdu]
France   10th January 1918

Your letter of light has been received and has illuminated body and spirit, and removed the rust from my heart. The relief and refreshment which it brought to my eyes could only have been equalled by that which came to the eyes of Jacob when someone brought good news to him of his son Joseph. Joy then opened his eyes. Your news filled me with delight, so much so that if the entire ocean were to be converted into ink, the earth into paper, and all the trees of the world into pens, I could not express my feelings sufficiently.

633

Mohamed Muzzaffer Khan (Punjabi Muslim) to
Mohamed Sahib Khan (Gujrat District, Punjab)

19th Lancers   [Urdu]
France   14th January 1918

May God grant we may meet soon! We shall meet if my life is spared, but death
would be preferable to the kind of life I am living. I am heartbroken with this service
in the Army. There is no justice, for if there were I should not have been passed
over for promotion. I am utterly dispirited at having been passed over.

634

Dafadar Abdul Razak Khan (Pathan) to
Dafadar Abdul Halim Khan (11th Lancers, Jullundur, Punjab)

9th Hodson's Horse   [Urdu]
France   15th January 1918

This was my fond hope – that you would join in the war, and thus fulfil your duty
towards our King. Still, this is in itself a help, that you are looking after the Depot.
Nevertheless, I hope the thought will be always uppermost in your mind as to the
manner and time in which you can best serve your King, and that when the
opportunity comes you will certainly grasp it. Such an opportunity [as] at the present
will never come again, either to you or to Akhbar Khan. You are both anxious for
advancement, and neither of you has long service, therefore seize the present
opportunity to obtain your desires.

635

Risaldar Tek Singh (Dogra, 41) to Jemadar [illegible] Singh
(9th Hodson's Horse, France)

9th Hodson's Horse   [Urdu]
Marseilles   15th January 1918

I had not time to say much to you before going away, nor was I able to say what
I wanted to the men as they arrived late at night and tired out. But I have no anxiety
at leaving the troop as I am sure that you will gain reputation for your caste. I thank

God that my twenty-four years' service has been passed with a caste so noble and loyal, to whom I shall be for ever grateful. I feel confident that all you gentlemen will, in days to come, continue to please your officers and gain merit for your caste. I am waiting here for a ship, but do not know when we shall get one. There are no proper arrangments for our comfort here, but we are delighted to get back to India.

636

Jemadar Shamsher Ali Khan (Punjabi Muslim, 34) to
Raja Rustam Ali Khan (Gujranwala District, Punjab)

34th Poona Horse [Urdu]
France 16th January 1918

I am delighted to get your regular letters, but I am very sorry I cannot give you any detailed reply. The truth is that I am prevented from so doing as the war gets bigger and bigger, and longer and longer, and our work increases accordingly. We cannot improve without working harder, and we cannot work without discomfort; as our work improves day by [day] our discomfort naturally increases. Well, it does not matter; it will all pass away by God's grace. I am so busy that every now and then I am unable to write. You will never understand what we have gone through until I tell you all our troubles by word of mouth. It is bitterly cold, and there is snow every day, and the biting wind is very bad for us Indians.

637

Ahmed Syed [illegible] (Hindustani Muslim) to Senior Sub-Assistant Surgeon
1st Class Abdur Rahim Khan (Bara Banki District, UP, 49)

34th Indian Labour Corps [Urdu]
France 17th January 1918

I hear that Hassain has asked to go to the war. I am sure that the services of us two brothers will one day be recognized by Government. The war has changed the sentiments [of the British] towards us. Now, seeing the sacrifice and self-devotion of the people of India, they have begun to praise us. Mr Henderson, chief of the Labour Party, who was formerly a minister, is of opinion that India, like Australia and South Africa, should get independent Government, and many other great Sahibs share his opinion.[1] We Indians are ready to give the sacrifice of many more men.

1. A rare expression of interest in high politics, not by a combatant. For other references to politics see Nos. 346, 453, 603, 616 and 619.

638

Sendir Khan (Pathan) to Dafadar Yakub Khan (38th CIH, France)

Peshawar [Urdu]
[NWFP] 19th January 1918

You have written that the cavalry may be transferred, but we have heard nothing more about this. Write at once and tell us about your movements, that we may be comforted. There is a prevalent rumour here that peace is being negotiated. We have no idea which is true – whether we ought to expect you on transfer or whether peace is coming. I had better say nothing, for my heart is disturbed by all these rumours. Your letters used to be a great source of comfort, but now they are very late in arriving and we do not know the reason. Above all, give us full particulars of the fight of December 1st, because there is great distress and anxiety in the country [the NWFP] in consequence of that fight.

639

Hospital Storekeeper Shiv Ram (Punjabi Hindu) to
Sarab Narain Shah (Jhelum District, Punjab)

Field Ambulance
Mhow Cavalry [Brigade] [Urdu]
France 22nd January 1918

Represent to the Tehsildar Sahib of Chakwal that I have been serving the Sirkar since the commencement, and have put in three and a half years at the front, and that he should not worry my old father on any account. Say further, that he should not do anything that would distract me from my duty in serving the Sirkar: that I am quite willing that my father should subscribe to the war loan to such an extent as he can afford; but if he has nothing to give, and if the Tehsildar's own advancement depends on his extracting something, let him write to me and I will send him something, even though it be at great personal inconvenience. Let him also understand clearly that if he continues to worry my father, he will have no greater enemy than me.

640

Ragonath Singh (Dogra) to Mul Raj
(Canal Department, Jammu State, Kashmir, India)

Signal Squadron
4th Cavalry Division [?]   [Urdu]
France   23rd January 1918

My father writes to say that you intend to leave your appointment and come to the war. Come, by all means, and bring my father with you too, as well as all our relatives. Can't you see that I have been at the war for three and a half years, and that I can neither get leave, nor will they discharge me? If I had been in India, I could have gone home for six months a year had I pleased. But here I am tied down – not for one year, but for an indefinite number of years. Be gracious therefore, and come to the war quickly, for in your absence it will never be brought to a finish, nor will the Germans be slain, nor will our King secure victory!

641

Lance Dafadar Faizullah Khan (Punjabi Muslim) to
Nawab Khan (Jhelum District, Punjab)

19th Lancers   [Urdu]
France   23rd January 1918

When I read about Mahomed Akbar Khan's behaviour, I was very displeased. He should use all his efforts to carry on the work at home effectively, and he should give up all thoughts of enlisting, otherwise he will rue it. It is [only] now that I have come to understand what service in the Army is, and the estimation in which a sepoy is held. Still, whatever is in the will of God will happen. For good service in the trenches I have been made a lance dafadar.

642

Rur Singh (Sikh) to [illegible] Singh (Karnal District, Punjab)

36th Jacob's Horse   [Gurmukhi]
France   24th January 1918

As regards leave, I desire to say that until my King has secured victory, we do not intend to avail ourselves of leave. Don't worry about my marriage. If I live to return, it can be arranged in due course. Rikha Singh is willing to enlist, and you should arrange for him to be enlisted because it is of the highest importance to help the Sirkar in this emergency.

643

Kartar Singh (Sikh) to his father Chanda Singh (Sargodha, Shahpur District, Punjab)

38th CIH   [Urdu]
France   24th January 1918

As regards recruiting, it is our duty to help the Sirkar. But I do not wish to hustle you in the matter, because of our family forty persons are engaged in the war, and a hundred men have enlisted from our village and are now fighting in Arabia. If, therefore, no one remains in the family who is suitable for service, where are recruits to be got from? Moreover, for four years now there have been no births in our family. If you do succeed in getting any recruits, enlist them in our regiment, for we too are in need of men.

644

Kumar Gul (Pathan) to Gholam Haidar Khan (Kohat District, NWFP)

36th Jacob's Horse   [Urdu]
France   25th January 1918

You say that my mother is very displeased both with me and with Miaz Gul, and that she has ceased to pray for us. This [is] because whenever we write letters we make no mention in them of her. I am not displeased with anyone, and if anyone is displeased with me it is without cause. The reason why we don't mention women in our letters is that they read out our letters to our officers, and then they discuss the contents. It is a shameful thing to read out to the Sahibs what may be said about women in our letters.[1] What do you think about the matter? Is it proper or the reverse? Read this to my mother. I impress it on you.

1. Several soldiers make this point.

645

Dafadar Indar Singh (Sikh) to Woordi-Major Badhawa Singh
(31st Lancers, Bannu, NWFP, 37)

[31st Lancers, attached] 36th Jacob's Horse   [Gurmukhi]
France   28th January 1918

You said that you had heard that in the case of those non-commissioned officers who have been detached from their regiments and sent to the war to serve with other regiments, their claim to promotion in their own regiment will be duly considered. You added that this was authentic and that you would certify to its correctness. Now you inform me that Gobind Singh, who is junior to me, has been made dafadar. What have I done that I should be treated in this way? And what is the use of your being Woordi-Major if such things are to happen?

646

Subedar Nabi Bakhsh Khan (Muslim Rajput) to
Nizam Din Khan (Rohtak District, Punjab)

74th UP Labour Company   [Urdu]
France   30th January 1918

You should pray day and night for victory for our King. If I live, I shall get the pension of a subedar. If our King obtains victory, everything is secured; otherwise life itself would be a useless thing. Our constant prayer to Almighty God is that He will give victory to our King George the V, and that he will double the [King's] power by day and quadruple it by night.

647

Lachman Singh (Dogra) to Naik Chattar Singh
(20th Punjabis, Ferozepore, Punjab)

No.2 Ammunition Column   [Urdu]
Marseilles   1st February 1918

You were pressing me to join the infantry, and I am sorry that I did not take your advice and that I joined the artillery instead. It is an easy job, but all classes are mixed up in it, and no one pays any attention to class. For us, therefore, it is not pleasant, as we have to perform work which is derogatory for Rajputs to do. The business of a Rajput is to fight, and I love fighting. I would like to handle a rifle as an infantryman, or to serve in the cavalry. Nevertheless, I am thankful that I am serving the Sirkar, under whose shadow I live free from trouble.

648

Amar Nath (Punjabi Hindu) to Sundar Singh (Indian Base Depot, Marseilles)

Lahore Indian General Hospital   [Urdu]
Rouen   3rd February 1918

You write about our speedy return to India; but I do not understand your reasons for so writing. Perhaps you assume that because the cavalry are going away, they are going back to India; but that is incorrect as they are merely going from this front to Egypt.[1] That is what is being said here. Nothing is being said about returning to India. I was astonished when I read in your letter about returning to India. No order has been issued about sending the cavalry to India.

1. Word deleted by the censor.

649

*Lance Dafadar Mahomed Tahir Khan (Pathan) to
Sher Mahomed (Khushab, Shahpur District?, Punjab?)*

36th Jacob's Horse   [Urdu]
France   5th February 1918

We shall soon be back. If there is anything from France that you want, write at once. Whatever you write for, I will bring it with me. We are all well. Up to date, God the All Merciful has protected us from the flame of fire, and we are looking forward to our home.[1]

1. Many letters from these weeks feature rumours that the Indian cavalry were soon to return home. In fact, they were destined to join Allenby's offensive against the Turks in the Middle East.

650

Lance Dafadar Jag Lal (Jat) to Ram Sarup Sharma (Rohtak District, Punjab)

6th Cavalry [Urdu]
France 17th February 1918

In regard to what you say to me about making a sacrifice of myself, I desire to say that I am always praying to God and saying that I should be filled with joy if by sacrificing my life in the service of the Sirkar I succeeded in furthering the purpose of the Sirkar. Although I say this when my spirit is uplifted, yet I am continually in search of an opportunity for such an act as will draw forth expressions of admiration from my officers, my comrades and my relations.

651

*[Sowar] Dhukal Singh (Rajput) to Suraj Bhan Singh
(Marwar-Jodhpur State, Rajputana)*

Jodhpur Lancers [Hindi]
France 18th February 1918

Through your good fortune your humble servant has been able to show brave deeds. Gobind Singh has won the first prize for bravery, and after this comes your humble servant.[1] Neither he nor I really did anything, but the reputation of our caste for bravery is so great that we win rewards.

1. Lance Dafadar (later Jemadar) Gobind Singh was a Rajput of the 28th Cavalry (attached 2nd Lancers) who won the Victoria Cross. Dhukal Singh won the Indian Order of Merit.

652

*Jemadar Gobind Singh VC (Rajput) to
Amar Singh (28th Light Cavalry, Quetta, Baluchistan)*

[28th Cavalry, attached] 2nd Lancers [Hindi]
France 20th February 1918

We have all been made very happy today, because the Sirkar has shown favour to me, and awarded me the Victoria Cross, and made me a jemadar from 1st December. You too will be very pleased.

653

Kadir Mahomed (Deccani Muslim) to Jemadar Gholam Mohiuddin
(20th Deccan Horse, Bolarum, Hyderabad)

20th Deccan Horse   [Urdu]
France   28th February 1918

So Yatsu has rejoined the service. These people, although they have enough to live
on, yet they will do anything in order to get a salary and save money. These base-
born ones have not produced a single recruit, and for three and a half years have
drawn both pension and salary, flattering themselves that they are helping the
Government. In truth, these thieves have plundered and beggared the Government.
They should be turned out with forfeiture of pension. In one squadron, there
remains only a single troop of Deccani Muslims: the rest of the squadron consists
of other tribes. It would seem that these misbegotten ones had made up their
minds entirely to eject the Deccani Muslims from the squadron, so that there may
no longer remain a single Muslim in the regiment.

654

Khalil Ullah (Hindustani Muslim) to Ganiullah (Muttra District, UP)

2nd Lancers   [Urdu]
France   3rd March 1918

I am sending you a picture of an American lady aviator, and I want you to study
it and see what the women of Europe and America are doing. I want you to contrast
them with our womenfolk, and to think what sort of education they can give to
our children when they themselves are lacking in knowledge and training. I am
hopeful that, if you pay careful attention to what I have written, you will be able
to effect some improvement. The advancement of India lies in the hands of the
women; until they act, India can never awake from her hare's dream. Forgive me
if I have spoken too strongly.

655

Ishar Singh (Sikh) to Jassu Singh (Ludhiana District, Punjab)

2nd Lancers   [Gurmukhi]
France   4th March 1918

Do not worry yourself thinking as to how you are to marry the girls. I ask you,
why are girls brought into the world? Consider, both boys and girls are brought

into the world, and if the girls are neglected or killed off, these families that have boys had better kill them off too! For this reason both boys and girls should be kept, so that they may marry. Both are of the same value in God's eyes, and one should devote the same amount of care to their bringing up, and should treat them in precisely the same way. If you are afraid of the expense which marrying girls may entail, my advice to you is to put away from you those customs of the Brahmins and barbers.

656

Teja Singh (Sikh) to Ganga Singh (Sialkot District, Punjab)

2nd Lancers [Gurmukhi]
France 6th March 1918

If God spares me to return, I intend to start new customs. Look, in our country, people ruin themselves over marriage and law suits. In this country, rich and poor, high and low, go to church together and worship, and there is no distinction between them there. In this country, moreover, people never spend money unnecessarily. In our country, the fools of people spend money for show and they ruin themselves over marriages and law suits. This is all due to ignorance. The very best custom in this country is that a man chooses his own wife, and a woman her own husband, and there are no disagreements and troubles after marriage.[1] The same custom used to obtain in our country formerly; but later it was set aside by the intrigues of the Brahmins.

1. For similar comments see No. 334.

657

Kachahaf [?] (Christian) to Dr Lacchaf [?]
(Mission Hospital, Ranchi District, Bihar)

Ranchi Labour Company [Hindi]
France [9th March 1918]

On March 1st the Military Secretary came from England to see us. He is General Cox,[1] and he knows Hindi very well, and spoke to us in that language. He said we had done excellent work in spite of the cold, and [had] helped the British Raj very much. Now our contract had expired and we wanted to go home, but the war was fiercer than ever and the Government wanted all their ships to carry the troops, so it was impossible to send us all at once, but we should be sent back gradually as occasion offered. We should be obliged to make another contract and should get an increase of pay. For the first new contract there would be an increase of Rs.5 a month, and for the second another Rs.5, and for the third another Rs.5. We should all be sent back gradually within four or five months, and there would be fresh arrangements each month. We are all very depressed indeed and do not want to stay, but what can we do? We are forced to stay.[2]

1. Lieutenant-General Sir H. V. Cox, Military Secretary, India Office. He was also the man to whom the Head Censor, Indian Mails, sent his regular reports, with the appended letters.
2. The Indian Labour Corps remained on the Western Front after the cavalry divisions had been sent to the Middle East.

Appendix I: Order of Battle of The Indian Army Corps in France, 1914–15

Note: This order of battle represents the Indian Corps as it was from the end of 1914 to the end of 1915. From early 1916, the two infantry divisions served in Mesopotamia. In the autumn of 1914, the cavalry were organized as a single division, consisting of the Ambala, Lucknow and Secunderabad Cavalry Brigades. Units of the British Army are indicated with an asterisk.

3rd (LAHORE) INFANTRY DIVISION

7th (Ferozepore) Brigade
    1st and 2nd Connaught Rangers (one unit)*
    4th London (Territorials)*
    9th Bhopal Infantry[1]
    57th Rifles (Frontier Force)
    89th Punjabis[2]
    129th Baluchis

8th (Jullundur) Brigade
    1st Manchesters*
    4th Suffolks (Territorials)*
    40th Pathans[3]
    47th Sikhs
    59th Rifles (Frontier Force)

9th (Sirhind) Brigade
    1st Highland Light Infantry*
    4th Liverpool Regiment (Special Reserve)*
    15th Sikhs[4]
    1/1st Gurkhas
    1/4th Gurkhas

Divisional Troops
 15th Lancers
 34th Sikh Pioneers
 20th and 21st Companies, Sappers and Miners

Artillery
 5th, 11th and 18th Brigades, RFA[*]
 109th Heavy Battery[*]

7th (MEERUT) INFANTRY DIVISION

19th (Dehra Dun) Brigade
 1st Seaforth Highlanders[*]
 1/9th Gurkhas
 1/2nd Gurkhas
 6th Jats

20th (Garhwal) Brigade
 2nd Leicesters[*]
 3rd London (Territorials)[*]
 1/39th Garhwal Rifles
 2/39th Garhwal Rifles[5]
 2/3rd Gurkhas
 2/8th Gurkhas[6]

21st (Bareilly) Brigade
 2nd Black Watch[*]
 4th Black Watch (Territorials)[*]
 41st Dogras[7]
 58th Rifles
 69th Punjabis[8]
 125th Rifles[9]

Divisional Troops
 4th Cavalry
 107th Pioneers
 3rd and 4th Companies, Sappers and Miners

Artillery
 4th, 9th and 13th Brigades, RFA[*]
 110th Heavy Battery[*]

1st INDIAN CAVALRY DIVISION

2nd (Sialkot) Cavalry Brigade
    17th Lancers*
    6th King Edward's Own Cavalry
    19th Lancers (Fane's Horse)
    Q Battery, RHA*

3rd (Ambala) Cavalry Brigade
    8th Hussars*
    9th Hodson's Horse
    30th Lancers (Gordon's Horse)
    A Battery, RHA*

4th (Lucknow) Cavalry Brigade
    1st (King's) Dragoon Guards*
    29th Lancers (Deccan Horse)
    36th Jacob's Horse (Scinde Horse)
    Jodhpur Lancers (Indian States' Forces)
    U Battery, RHA*

2nd INDIAN CAVALRY DIVISION

5th (Mhow) Cavalry Brigade
    6th Inniskilling Dragoons*
    2nd Lancers (Gardner's Horse)
    38th King George's Own Central India Horse
    Y Battery, RHA*

7th (Meerut) Cavalry Brigade
    13th Hussars*
    3rd Skinner's Horse
    18th King George's Own Lancers
    V Battery, RHA*

9th (Secunderabad) Cavalry Brigade
    7th Dragoon Guards*
    20th Deccan Horse
    34th Prince Albert Victor's Own Poona Horse
    N Battery, RHA*

NOTES

1. Left for Egypt, June 1915.
2. From June 1915.
3. Arrived from China, April 1915.
4. Left France, August 1915.
5. The two Garhwali battalions were later combined into a single unit.
6. Originally Bareilly Brigade.
7. Left France, August 1915.
8. From June 1915.
9. Originally Sirhind Brigade; left for Egypt, June 1915.

Appendix II: Composition of Indian Regiments Serving in France, 1914–15

INFANTRY REGIMENTS

Regiment	Regimental Centre	Composition (8 companies)
6th Jat Light Infantry	Meerut	8 Jats
9th Bhopal Infantry	none	2 Sikhs; 2 Rajputs; 2 Brahmans; 2 Muslims
15th Ludhiana Sikhs	Multan	8 Sikhs
34th Sikh Pioneers	Ambala	8 Mazbi and Ramdasia Sikhs
39th Garhwal Rifles	Lansdowne	8 Garhwalis
40th Pathans	Sialkot	2 Orakzais; 1 Afridis; 1 Yusufzais; 2 Dogras; 2 Punjabi Muslims
41st Dogras	Rawalpindi	8 Dogras
47th Sikhs	Rawalpindi	8 Sikhs
57th Wilde's Rifles (Frontier Force)	Dera Ismail Khan	2 Sikhs; 2 Dogras; 2 Punjabi Muslims; 2 Pathans
58th Vaughan's Rifles (Frontier Force)	Dera Ismail Khan	3 Sikhs; 1 Dogras; 3 Pathans; 1 Punjabi Muslims
59th Scinde Rifles (Frontier Force)	Kohat	3 Pathans; 2 Sikhs; 1 Punjabi Muslims; 2 Dogras
89th Punjabis	Meiktila	3 Sikhs; 1 Brahmans; 1 Rajputs; 3 Punjabi Muslims
107th Pioneers	Kirkee	2 Pathans; 2 Sikhs; 2 Deccani Mahrattas; 2 Rajputana Muslims
125th Napier's Rifles	Nasirabad	4 Rajputana Jats; 2 Rajputana Rajputs; 2 Punjabi Muslims

| 129th Duke of Connaught's Own Baluchis | Karachi | 2 Punjabi Muslims; 3 Mahsuds; 3 Other Pathans |

CAVALRY REGIMENTS

Regiment	Composition (4 squadrons)
2nd Lancers (Gardner's Horse)	1 Sikhs; 1 Rajputs; 1 Jats; 1 Hindustani Muslims
3rd Skinner's Horse	1 Sikhs; 1 Jats; 1 Rajputs; 1 Muslim Rajputs
4th Cavalry	1 Rajput Muslims; 1 Sikhs; 1 Hindustani Muslims; 1 Jats
6th King Edward's Own Cavalry	1 Jat Sikhs; 1 Jats; 1 non-Jat Sikhs; 1 Hindustani Muslims
9th Hodson's Horse	½ Sikhs; ½ Dogras; 1½ Punjabi Muslims; 1½ Pathans
15th Lancers (Cureton's Multanis)	4 Multani Pathans and Muslims of the Dejarat and Cis-Indus
17th Cavalry	2 Punjabi Muslims; 2 Pathans
18th King George's Own Lancers	3 Punjabi Muslims; 1 Sikhs
19th Lancers (Fane's Horse)	1½ Sikhs; ½ Dogras; 1 Punjabi Muslims; 1 Pathans
20th Deccan Horse	1 Sikhs; 1 Jats; 2 Deccani Muslims
29th Lancers (Deccan Horse)	2 Jats; 1 Sikhs; 1 Deccani Muslims
30th Lancers (Gordon's Horse)	2 Sikhs; 1 Jats; 1 Hindustani Muslims
34th Prince Albert's Own Poona Horse	2 Rathore Rajputs; 1 Kaimkhanis; 1 Punjabi Muslims

36th Jacob's Horse	2 Derajat Muslims and Baluchis; 1 Pathans; 1 Sikhs
38th King George's Own Central India Horse	2 Sikhs; 1 Pathans; 1 Muslim Rajputs
39th King George's Own Central India Horse	2 Sikhs; 1 Muslim Rajputs; 1 Punjabi Muslims

GURKHA REGIMENTS

Regiment	**Regimental centre**
1st King George's Own Gurkha Rifles (The Malaun Regiment)	Dharmsala
2nd King Edward's Own Gurkha Rifles (The Sirmoor Rifles)	Dehra Dun
4th Gurkha Rifles	Bakloh
8th Gurkha Rifles	Shillong
9th Gurkha Rifles	Dehra Dun

Appendix III: Indian Army Recruitment, 1914–18

RECRUITMENT BY PROVINCE, AUGUST 1914– NOVEMBER 1918

Province[*]	Combatants	Non-combatants	Total
Punjab	349,688	97,288	446,976
UP	163,578	117,565	281,143
Madras	51,223	41,117	92,340
Bombay	41,272	30,211	71,483
Bengal	7,117	51,935	59,052
NWFP	32,181	13,050	45,231
Bihar and Orissa	8,576	32,976	41,552
Burma	14,094	4,579	18,673
Assam	942	14,182	15,124
CP	5,376	9,631	15,007
Ajmer-Merwara	7,341	1,632	8,973
Baluchistan	1,761	327	2,088
Total	683,149	414,493	1,097,642

[*] These figures appear to refer to the provinces of British India only; but they seem to include recruitment to the Imperial Service Troops, as well as to the Indian Army.

Source: *India's Contribution to the Great War* (Calcutta: Government of India, 1923) quoted in VanKoski, 'The Indian Ex-Soldier' p. 90.

RECRUITMENT BY CLASS, AUGUST 1914–NOVEMBER 1918

Class[*]	Number
Punjabi Muslims	136,126
Sikhs	88,925
Gurkhas	55,589
Rajputs	49,086
Jats	40,272
Other Hindus	38,546
Hindustani Muslims	36,353
Pathans	27,857
Dogras	23,491
Brahmans	20,382
Ahirs	19,544
Gujars	18,296
Tamils	16,390
Rajputana Jats	14,967
Rajputana and Central India Muslims	14,224
Rajputana Rajputs	13,104
Dekhani Mahrattas	12,266
Burmans	12,163
Konkhani Mahrattas	12,038
Dekhani Muslims	8,118
Total	657,739

[*] These were the twenty most-recruited classes, who between them supplied nearly 90 per cent of all combatant enlistments. The spellings and the contradictory categories conform to the Government of India original.

Source: VanKoski 'The Indian Ex-Soldier' pp. 89–90.

RECRUITMENT BY YEAR, 1914–18

Year	Recruits
1914 (1 August–31 December)	24,666
1915	84,353
1916	93,388
1917	179,364
1918 (to 30 November)	290,687
Total	672,458[*]
Total Combatants	826,868[**]
Non-Combatants	445,592
Grand Total	1,272,460

[*] Indian Army combatants only.
[**] Including Imperial Service Troops from the Princely States, and Indians enlisted in the British Army.

Source: Leask, 'The Expansion of the Indian Army in the Great War', pp. 27–9.

Appendix IV:
Report on Twelve Months' Working of the Indian Mail Censorship

Towards the end of September 1914, the Lahore and Meerut Divisions of the Indian Army, with the normal complement of British troops included, began to arrive in France. The force was disembarked at Marseilles, and, after a few days' rest there, was conveyed by train to Orleans. The route chosen for the troop trains was a circuitous one leading through Toulouse and other places in south-western France. While the force was in transit, a member of the Indian Revolutionary party, if it may be so called, was arrested in Toulouse, and upon examination his pockets were found to be stuffed with seditious literature intended for dissemination amongst the Indian soldiery.

The authorities, thus set upon their guard, decided that, at least during the stay of the Indian troops in France, their correspondence must be subjected to systematic examination, and cast about for a suitable person to appoint as Indian Mail Censor. It was not easy to find anyone possessing anything like the requisite qualification, but eventually Second Lieutenant E. B. Howell, a member of the Political Department of the Indian Civil Service, who chanced to be serving in France as an interpreter, attached to a regiment of Indian cavalry, was chosen and directed to undertake this duty.

The Indian Mail Censor reached Rouen, where the Indian Base Post Office was then established, on the 3rd November 1914, and forthwith set to work. From the very beginning to the present time the censorship has naturally had to work in close connection with the Indian postal authorities, and it would be impossible to acknowledge too warmly the assistance rendered by those concerned, without exception, from Lieutenant-Colonel Pilkington downwards. On the other hand, the censorship has always worked on the assumption that it was incumbent upon its officers to delay the mails and interfere with postal arrangements as little as possible, and the best relations have been maintained thoroughly.

The original instructions given to the Indian Mail Censor did not require him to do more than examine the 'inward' mails addressed to the Indian troops in France. His first efforts were therefore devoted to causing action to be taken to secure that all communications to this address, from whatever source, would pass through his hands, The Indian public at that time was in large measure not yet quite sure that they really could correspond through the post with their soldiers across the sea,

369

and the troops themselves were too busy to have much time for letter-writing. Even then, however, the volume of inward correspondence alone amounted to not less than 200 letters every week for each regiment of Indian infantry, and very nearly as many for each regiment of cavalry. Moreover, besides infantry and cavalry there was the Indian personnel employed in the artillery, and in the ordnance, supply and transport, accounts, and medical departments, as well as a number of clerks serving in various staff offices. Apart from the very considerable linguistic difficulties involved it was at once clear that the mere bulk of the inward mail alone was more than one man could tackle ... The volume of work has steadily increased, partly because letters have been carried to and fro free of charge, partly through the development of confidence in postal arrangements, partly on account of the addition of more regiments to the original expeditionary force, but chiefly through the enlargement of the censors' duties to include the outward as well as the inward mail. The inward mail is now at least three times as large as it was at the beginning, and the outward mail is as big as the inward. There are also letters from one part of the force to another.

The troops in the field were told at first that they were not to write any news about the war, and a system of local censorship modelled on that in force in British units, and more or less effective in accordance with the personality of the officer by whom it was carried out, was devised to see that they did not do so. It is easy to be contemptuous and to say that the order was unnecessary and its administration inefficient. But, on the whole, it is hard to see what better plan could have been made. If the men had been allowed to write freely, they might conceivably have given information of military value to the enemy, and they certainly would have terrified their relatives and so caused considerable political danger by exaggerated, or even accurate, accounts of the sufferings which they were required to endure. As a deterrent from writing, beyond question the prospect of having the letter examined, however perfunctorily, by the company officer is more effective than anything else. No doubt it is true that in this way India has been starved for tidings of the war. But this need not have resulted and is, in any case, a minor evil.

Besides checking the work of the local and regimental censors and examining letters posted uncensored at the front and at the various bases in France, the Indian Mail Censors were also charged with the scrutiny of letters written by Indian sick and wounded in the hospitals in England, where the men had leisure to write and unlimited notepaper. The task of examining the outward mail had not been carried on for more than a few days before its possibilities were apparent. The Indian Mail Censorship was in a position to supply accurate and unquestionable information on all sorts of matters which could not fail to be of value to those responsible for the bold experiment of employing Indian troops in Europe. The Head Censor therefore began issuing weekly reports supported by budgets of extracts from Indian correspondence, and the same system has remained in force throughout the year, the number of those who desired these reports to be furnished to them having been increased from time to time.

The first budget, compiled in 1914 before any Assistant Censors had been appointed, was necessarily inferior, both in quality and quantity, to those which succeeded it, but it contained satisfactory and welcome news as to the spirit of the force and the tone of Indian sentiment with regard to its despatch and the questions of the hour. It also showed that no systematic attempts were being made to tamper with the troops through the medium of the post.

In December, attention was drawn to the effect upon Indian feeling produced by the return to the trenches of men who had recovered from wounds. This is a serious matter which has engaged ever since the anxious consideration of all authorities from His Majesty the King downwards. In January, what might have easily have developed into a serious danger was averted when, in response to the Indian Mail Censor's warnings, the executive of the Y.M.C.A. was induced to change the very objectionable pattern of notepaper which the Association was distributing broadcast among the Indian troops. In February, it was shown that the breaking strain was near, and correspondence revealing a disposition on the part of certain transborder Pathans to secure safety by deserting to the enemy was brought to notice. The letters, written in very guarded language, from which this inference was deduced, were withheld, and no cases of desertion occurred in the regiment from which they emanated. But a party of men of the same class and tribe (Afridis) in another regiment went over to the Germans, who, it is believed, have since sent them back to their own country. The prominent part which the Indian Corps took in the fight at Neuve Chapelle, and their hopes of a speedy return to India, together with the return of spring, kept the Indians' heart up for some nine months after this, and no very signal discovery was made in their letters. But throughout these months, as well as before and since, the Indian Mail Censorship is believed to have done useful work in bringing to light various minor needs and difficulties over questions of pay, remittances, rations, clothing, suitable gifts from funds, restrictions enforced in hospital and the like, and by stopping occasional seditious letters received from America, as well as by holding up a mirror in which could be seen reflected the current sentiments and opinions both of the troops in the field and of their circle of correspondents in India and elsewhere.

For example, in August, with the advent of autumn, and the prospect of another winter campaign amid the cold, damp, dark, dull and uncomfortable surroundings of Flanders, desertion reappeared amongst the Pathan element of the Indian troops. This time the censorship was able to point beforehand not only to the class and tribe, but also to the regiment, and in one case actually to the individual concerned, though the warnings conveyed in the letters were so nebulous that no action could be taken on them.

Besides its oriental work, the censorship has throughout carried on all work connected with the supervision of the correspondence of the British troops forming part of the Indian Expeditionary Force. As these have been largely increased since the Force landed in France the amount of work entailed has been considerable.

Apart from all present value, the record of extracts taken from Indian correspondence consitutes a document of some historical value and no less psychological interest. If the publication of selections should ever be permitted, a very entertaining book would result ...

(Signed) E. B. Howell, Captain
Head Censor, Indian Mails

7th November 1915

Further Reading

Of the several near-contemporary accounts, the most useful is J. W. B. Merewether and Frederick Smith, *The Indian Corps in France* (second edition, London, 1919). Merewether replaced Smith as Record Officer to the Indian Army Corps in France, when the latter became a member of the Coalition Government in 1915. The book is laudatory in tone, and little concerned with matters of interpretation. It is, however, a very detailed military narrative down to the end of 1915.

The Commander of the Indian Corps, General Sir James Willcocks, published his memoirs, *With the Indians in France* (London: Constable, 1920). These are more personal reminiscences, based on his private papers and diaries. Written in Bermuda, they were primarily intended to record the gallant deeds of the Indian Corps.

We have another British eyewitness account, in the form of J. Wakefield and J. M. Weippert (eds), *Indian Cavalry Officer, 1914–15* (Tunbridge Wells: Costello, 1986). This is the edited diary of R. W. W. 'Roly' Grimshaw, who served in France with the 34th Poona Horse. Badly wounded at Festubert in December 1914, Grimshaw returned to France to take command of an Indian Cavalry War Depot. The diary extends to June 1915.

The more recent literature includes my own *The Sepoy and the Raj: The Indian Army, 1860–1940* (Basingstoke: Macmillan, 1994). It provides some context for the present collection, and uses Indian soldiers' letters, including many that are not reproduced in this book. Philip Mason also refers to soldiers' letters in his stylish general history of the Indian Army, *A Matter of Honour* (London: Jonathan Cape, 1974), as does Jeffery Greenhut in 'The Imperial Reserve: The Indian Corps on the Western Front, 1914–15', *Journal of Imperial and Commonwealth History*, 12 (1983). Susan VanKoski has given them rather more extensive treatment in 'Letters Home, 1915–16: Punjabi Soliders Reflect on War and Life in Europe and their Meanings for Home and Self', *International Journal of Punjab Studies,* 2 (1995). I have borrowed one or two of her points for the Introduction.

We have several unpublished theses on various aspects of the Indian Army during the Great War. These include: David Brief, 'The Punjab and Recruitment to the Indian Army, 1846–1918', Oxford University M.Litt (1979); Jeffrey Greenhut, 'Imperial Reserve: The Indian Infantry on the Western Front, 1914–1918', University of Kansas PhD (1978); I. D. Leask, 'The Expansion of the Indian Army during the Great War', University of London PhD (1989); and S. C. VanKoski, 'The Indian Ex-Soldier from the Eve of the First World War to Independence and Partition', University of Columbia PhD (1996).

Further background material appears in T. A. Heathcote's two books, *The Indian Army: The Garrison of British Imperial India, 1822–1922* (London: David and Charles, 1974) and *The Military in British India* (Manchester: Manchester University Press, 1995). On the 'martial races' discourse, readers should turn first to Lionel

Caplan's *Warrior Gentlemen: 'Gurkhas' in the Western Imagination* (Oxford: Berghahn, 1995). For the Great War context see DeWitt C. Ellinwood and S. D. Pradhan (eds), *India and World War I* (New Delhi: Manohar, 1978).

Two useful books on the Army of the East India Company, which suggest some comparisons and contrasts, are Douglas Peers, *Between Mars and Mammon: Colonial Armies and the Garrison State in Early Nineteenth-century India* (London: Tauris, 1995) and Seema Alavi, *The Sepoys and the Company: Tradition and Transition in North India, 1770–1830* (Delhi: Oxford University Press, 1995).

For the Punjabi background, good places to start include Imran Ali, *The Punjab Under Imperialism, 1885–1947* (New Jersey: Princeton University Press, 1988) and Ian Talbot, *Punjab and the Raj, 1849-1947* (Delhi: Manohar, 1988).

There is now a growing literature on the question, 'Why do men fight?' For a fine synthesis of this work, see Richard Holmes, *Acts of War: The Behaviour of Men in Battle* (New York: The Free Press, 1985). S. L. A. Marshall, in his 1947 classic *Men Against Fire: The Problem of Battle Command in Future War* (Gloucester, MA: Peter Smith, 1974 reprint) argued that the interpersonal dynamics of the 'primary group' were more important than wider ideological concerns to American infantrymen in the Second World War. By way of contrast, Omar Bartov stresses the Nazi ideological penetration of the *Wehrmacht*, especially on the Eastern Front, in his *Hitler's Army: Soldiers, Nazis and War in the Third Reich* (New York: Oxford University Press, 1991). Jean-Paul Bertaud's *The Army of the French Revolution: From Citizen-Soldiers to Instrument of Power* (New Jersey: Princeton University Press, 1988) uses soldiers' letters to assess the extent of ideological motivation during the French Revolutionary Wars; see also Alan Forrest, *The Soldiers of the French Revolution* (Durham: Duke University Press, 1990). Comparisons between the Indian Army and other Great War armies can be made from the relevant chapters of Hugh Cecil and Peter Liddle (eds), *Facing Armageddon: The First World War Experienced* (London: Leo Cooper, 1996), and from Leonard V. Smith, *Between Mutiny and Obedience: The Case of the French Fifth Infantry Division During World War I* (New Jersey: Princeton University Press, 1994).

The methodological problems of approaching history 'from below' are clearly and simply introduced in Frederick Kranz (ed.), *History From Below: Studies in Popular Protest and Popular Ideology* (Oxford: Blackwell, 1985). All historians concerned with Indian history 'from below' owe something to the *Subaltern Studies* project. See in particular Ranajit Guha (ed.), *Subaltern Studies I–V* (Delhi: Oxford University Press, 1982–87) and Ranajit Guha, *Elementary Aspects of Peasant Insurgency in Colonial India* (Delhi: Oxford University Press, 1983). For a thoughtful critique see Rosalind O'Hanlon, 'Recovering the Subject: *Subaltern Studies* and Histories of Resistance in Colonial South Asia', *Modern Asian Studies*, 22 (1988). See Gayatri Spivak's 'Can the Subaltern Speak?', in Patrick Williams and Laura Chrisman, *Colonial Discourse and Post-Colonial Theory: A Reader*

(Brighton: Harvester Wheatsheaf, 1993) for the argument that certain forms of subaltern consciousness are irrecoverable.

Lastly, one should mention John Masters' novel *The Ravi Lancers* (London: Michael Joseph, 1972). Set in France, and by a former Gurkha officer, this concerns a cavalry regiment from a mythical Princely state.

Index

Figures in brackets are page numbers, others are document numbers.